2nd EDITION

India's Economic Reforms

A Companion Volume of INDIAN ECONOMY SINCE INDEPENDENCE

Dedicated to
all those engaged in
the development of India's economy

The Editor :

Dr. (Mrs.) UMA KAPILA is Reader in the Department of Economics, Miranda House, University of Delhi. After her graduation from Miranda House and post-graduation in Economics from Delhi School of Economics, she started her teaching career in January 1960 in Miranda House, University of Delhi where she has been teaching since then. Mrs. Kapila has been a keen student of current Indian economic problems and has been teaching this paper to undergraduate and post-graduate students for the last thirty-six years.

As a teacher fellow at the Centre for Advanced Studies, Delhi School of Economics (1976-79), Mrs. Kapila completed her Ph.D. on "Oilseeds Economy of India." She has also served on the Planning Commission Study Group on "Agricultural Strategies in the Eastern Region of India for the Seventh Five Year Plan" (Perspective Planning Division).

Dr. (Mrs.) Uma Kapila is also the author of the book *Oilseeds Economy of India,* (1982) published by the Institute of Economic Growth under their series "Studies in Economic Development and Planning." She has also edited the widely acclaimed book, "Indian Economy Since Independence." (Academic Foundation, Delhi, Sixth Edition : 1995).

2 nd EDITION

India's Economic Reforms

A Companion Volume of
INDIAN ECONOMY
SINCE INDEPENDENCE

edited by

Uma Kapila

Academic Foundation

2nd Edition : 1996
1st Edition : 1995

Published by
ACADEMIC FOUNDATION
24 - A, Sriram Road, Civil Lines, Delhi - 110 054.
Tel : 232966, 233730.
Fax : 91-11-2911852.

India's Economic Reforms, 2nd Edition
Uma Kapila (ed.)
ISBN 81-7188-111-4

The present volume is a companion volume of
"Indian Economy Since Independence"
Uma Kapila (ed.)

Laser-typeset by AF's D.T.P. Division and
Printed at Taj Press, Mayapuri, New Delhi.

Acknowledgements

I am indeed grateful to all the contributors who responded to my request to contribute their papers for the present volume. I am also grateful to the editors of the journals in which some of the papers were first published. Due acknowledgements have been made in the book.

I must express my thanks to Academic Foundation for taking keen interest in my project and providing me the secretarial assistance. I must also acknowledge my special thanks to Academic Foundation's staff led by Rituraj and Sanu.

— *Uma Kapila*

Contents...

1

Introduction

UMA KAPILA

The economic reforms that were initiated in mid-1991 have now been with us for over four years. It is time for us to make a critical review of the process of reforms, to study its shortcomings and strengths and identify the policy measures that are required in the immediate future for consolidating the positive effects of the reforms.

The present volume is a companian volume to Indian Economy Since Independence. This is an attempt to bring together the well researched papers/studies by distinguished economists and experts who have attempted to analyse the ongoing economic reform measures. In addition to the papers of experts in respective fields, the texts/summaries of relevant policy documents and reports, during the year 1993-94 and 1994-95, have been reproduced. The material has been arranged in fifteen chapters.

Economic Reforms: Rationale and Assessment

An exhaustive and critical assessment of ongoing economic reforms, their effects and future direction, is presented in chapters Two to Five by the Finance Minister, Manmohan Singh, Jagdish Bhagwati, T.N. Srinivasan and Deepak Nayyar.

Profs. Jagdish Bhagwati and T.N. Srinivasan's report on Economic Reforms (Chapter 2) explaining the rationale for the reforms and the principles of reform making as understood by economists from world-wide experience, highlights the need for momentum building on the reforms to date with a number of new steps which would complete the transition to the new policy framework in order t promote greater efficiency, growth and therewith a surer and deeper attack on poverty alleviation. According to them, in the absence of further new steps, the returns from the existing reforms may be meagre in terms of productivity in general and export increases in particular. The report spells out these steps which include actions to consolidate the important and bold reforms already undertaken todate and to correct the mistakes revealed by experience and also to urge for several new measures which would complement and enhance greatly the efficiency of the measures already taken.

According to Prof. P.N. Dhar's assessment of economic reforms (Ch. 3), while many things have been done as part of reforms, what remains to be done is even more important and crucial to its success. To him "if the reforms are allowed to succeed, India will rank among the most dynamic economies around the turn of the century" and the success of the reforms will depend on their political feasibility which, in turn, will depend on the length of the transitional period, the nature of the transitional cost and the manner in which these costs are shared. Most important, it is the understanding of the people about the actual nature and purpose of these reforms which will determine their success.

Dr. Manmohan Singh (Chapter: 5) urges that we have no choice but to persevere with our reform programme because this alone will enable us to achieve our basic goals of growth, self-reliance, modernisation, equity, and raising the living standards of the poor people in our country. "India has the talent and the genius to be the next *economic miracle* but it will not happen by itself. It requires all of us to dedicate ourselves to new ways of thought and action and make a success of new economic policies. India's role in the new world order is going to be decided by our response to the fast changes, particularly to the increasing globalisation of economic processes. We have responded to these changes through a wide ranging programme of economic reforms, we have already undertaken major reforms in our industrial policy, foreign trade and exchange rate policies, taxation policies and the financial sector and the early results have been reassuring." The urgency of reforms is spelt out as below.

"We cannot continue with excessive Government revenue expenditure and high levels of fiscal deficit and still hope to control inflation. We cannot spend more on education, health and rural development if we do not improve the profitability of our public sector and reduce subsidies payable to loss making public sector units. We cannot continue to accord high protection to domestic industry and expect to be sufficiently competitive to secure rapid export growth needed for true self-reliance. We cannot afford to shackle foreign investment without losing the benefits of additional capital, technology, market access and growth that have been so successfully harnessed by our neighbours in East Asia. We cannot continue with detailed, discretionary licensing of imports and still expect to have sustained export growth. We cannot maintain the plethora of unnecessary Government controls, regulations and procedures and still expect the skills and potential dynamism of our entrepreneurs, professionals and workers to be fully exploited. We cannot postpone financial sector reforms without risking a serious banking crisis. We cannot continue to resist flexibility in employment policies in the organised sector and yet expect rapid growth of employment. We cannot deny our farmers access to export markets and yet hope for rapid growth of incomes in agriculture. We cannot eradicate illiteracy without redirecting our priorities within the education sector towards primary education and literacy. We cannot provide high quality infrastructure if the costs are not recovered from beneficiaries. We cannot build social infrastructure in the agricultural sector without reducing existing subsidies which benefit only a handful. It is simply not possible to spend our way to prosperity. Above all, we cannot expect to banish poverty without achieving sustained growth of output and employment."

While P.N. Dhar, Jagdish Bhagwati and T.N. Srinivasan advocate speedy and simultaneous implementation of economic reform measures covering macro-economic stabilisation and structural reforms, Deepak Nayyar (Ch. 5) observes: "In a situation of deep disequilibrium, macro-economic stabilisation and structural reform or adjustment should not be simultaneous events. In my judgement, stabilisation must restore a semblance of equilibrium in the economy before policy reform is used to re-structure the economy. The simultaneous pursuit of stabilisation and adjustment is based on the orthodoxy of multilateral financial institutions. There are two dimensions to the logic underlying this prescription. In terms of economics, stabilisation policies on the demand side have some corollaries on the supply side. In terms of politics, a debt crisis accentuates vulnerability so much that unpalatable reforms can be imposed. Thus, bitter medicine is seen to be best administered in one swallow. However, there are good reasons why stabilisation and adjustment should not be implemented together, for the multiplicity of objectives and of time horizons tends to compound difficulties rather than resolve problems. Such an approach often leads to a situation where the economy achieves neither stabilisation nor adjustment, so that the outcome is stagflation and poverty. For another, if reform is not absorbed by the economy or is not acceptable to the polity, which is not uncommon in crisis situation, disillusionment sets in and even the necessary or desirable components of reform are discredited."

Economic Reforms in the Context of Globalisation

In the paper *Indian Economic Reforms in the context of Emerging Global Economy* (Ch. 6), C.T. Kurien observes that "the nature of restructuring and reforms that the emerging global economy makes necessary, is not as simple as privatisation, liberalisation, marketisation, globalisation or whatever other slogan that is found attractive and marketable for the time being. It calls for a proper understanding of the far-reaching changes taking place in the global economy and intelligent responses to them with a clear perception of social priorities."

Lessons from China

In Chapter 7, Isher Judge Ahluwalia observes that the important lesson to learn from the Chinese experience is that there are no shortcuts, nor clear cuts to economic prosperity. Pragmatism, rather than ideology, pays off. An important ingredient for success is the resolve to handle problems as they surface on the way rather than expect to anticipate all possible roadblocks before you start moving.

Financial Sector Reforms

Financial Sector reforms constitute an important component of the programme of economic policy reforms and is an integral part of the wide-ranging programme of macro-economic stabilisation and structural changes which have been underway since June, 1991. Many significant steps have been taken in the field of financial sector reforms during the last four-and-a-half years with the basic objective of developing a strong, competitive and vibrant financial sector operating on sound commercial principles and within a good, transparent, regulatory framework.

According to the RBI Governor, C. Rangarajan (Ch. 8), the financial sector reforms should help banks and financial institutions to act as autonomous business units fully responsible for their performance. They will have to become efficiency conscious, focussing on balancing profitability with liquidity and servicing the necessary socio-economic objectives of our development efforts. Successful identification and exploitation of the emerging opportunities will help their recovery and performance. If banks and financial institutions become high cost units, they have an impact on the rest of the system. Hence the compulsion to cut costs, improve productivity and show better profitability — and this will have to become the mission of the financial system in the coming years.

The Indian financial system comprises a large number of commercial and cooperative banks, specialised development banks for industry, agriculture, external trade and housing; social security institutions like insurance, pension and provident funds; collective investment institutions like the Unit Trust of India and various mutual funds. During the last few years, several new institutions, such as merchant banks, leasing companies, housing finance companies, venture capital funds, financial advisory services and credit rating agencies, have come into existence. The capital market has really grown phenomenally. There has been considerable diversification of money and capital markets and many new financial instruments have appeared on the scene.

After reviewing the financial system as it exists today, alongwith the major deficiencies in the system, particularly in the banking sector, R.N. Malhotra examines, in chapter 9, the reforms that have been undertaken, the progress that has been made in strengthening the banking system, and the future agenda that needs urgent attention.

Agricultural Strategy and Economic Reforms

Agricultural sector remains critical to the overall health of the economy and both efficiency and equity considerations demand that the reform effort be focussed on it as much as on other important areas such as reforms of the public sector enterprises. Against the backdrop of ongoing economic reforms in India and international trade reforms as a result of GATT, C.H.H. Rao and Ashok Gulati have spelt out an agricultural strategy that can boost agricultural production in a cost effective manner and generate productive employment while protecting the environment (Ch. 10). According to them, the opening up of the economy and correction of over-valued exchange rate will improve the terms of trade for agriculture, leading to a change in the relative incentive structures in the economy, with agriculture likely to attract more resources from the private sector in the years to come. However, for the trade policy reforms to work their way fully through incentive system, domestic marketing reforms will also have to be carried out. This must involve freer movement of agricultural commodities; gradual phasing out of purchase levies; abolition of monopolistic procurement; introduction of future markets; and amendment or abolition of the essential commodities act to the extent that it imposes restriction on the movement, stocking and pricing of goods. These reforms are essential if the pulls of the demand side factors are to be felt, otherwise changes in the incentive environment for investment in agricultural related activities will remain only partial. Agricultural strategy, therefore, must seek to exploit the growth opportunities that will arise, while also providing protective cover to the poor against any threat of unemployment following structural adjustment and inflation. Without the required changes in supply side factors, including research and technology, irrigation, fertilizers and rural infrastructure, critical for raising the aggregate supply response, it will be difficult for the nation to sustain growth in agriculture and without this the overall growth of the nationbal economy may prove disappointing in response to the policy reforms.

Employment Situation

Creating adequate employment opportunities to absorb the existing unemployed and underemployed as well as the increase in labour force, has been among the important and continuing concerns of Indian development policy. According to Vaidyanathan (Ch. 11), the unemployment situation in the country has not worsned in the 70's and 80's whether we take rural areas or urban areas. There has in fact been a remarkably rapid diversification of employment and the structure of labour force has changed leading to a significant rise in the proportion of the workforce depending on wage labour. But the conditions of wage labour have not deteriorated. The picture of overall employment trends contrasts, however, with a significant deterioration in educated employment. The estimated number of persons with matriculate level education or better is estimated to have risen more than eight-fold between 1961 and 1988 and in rural areas it has increased more than ten-fold. There are distinct differences in job preference of educated workers. In rural areas the majority of them are self employed (62 % in the case of males and 58% in the case of females). In urban areas, the large majority of them work for wages.

There are indications that as the opportunities for wage salary employment are becoming scarcer relative to supply of job seekers, more and more of the educated persons tend to go into self-employment. According to Vaidyanathan the only effective and lasting solution, lies in policies designed to stimulate faster overall development; in interventions (by way of training, and credit infrastructure support) to help educated people to take more and more to self employment; and to pay far greater attention for improving the functional content of education both in terms of imparting skills which are needed in the growing economy; and also of equipping people to upgrade the skills or acquire new skills.

The next four chapters are devoted to the texts/summaries of official documents/policies and discussion papers.

Tenth Finance Commission

The Tenth Finance Commission (December 1994) covers the period 1995-2000. The period covered by the recommendation of the Commission will witness the completion of half a century of fiscal federalism. Federal relations, as envisaged in the Constitution, have evolved over the years through political, institutional and functional changes. In this changing scenario, the Finance Commission, as an institution (having an important role to play through resource sharing, based on Constitutional division of functions and finances) is a critical element in the federal system.

While the charter of the Commission flows from the Constitution itself, the terms of reference of each Commission have reflected some of the dominant concerns in the area of Centre State relations and the emerging issues in national public finance. It is, therefore, not surprising that the terms of reference of the 10th Finance Commission mirror the anxiety regarding the finances of the country and have been influenced by the systemic changes in the economic regime that have been initiated since 1991.

The approach of the Commission, their observations, alternative scheme of devolution and the recommendations have been reproduced in chapter twelve of this volume. In stating its approach, the Commission points out "it should be obvious that no policy prescription for the fiscal malaise can be given if a large component of the budget, viz. plan outlay, is left out of reckoning". Even if we leave out that part of the plan outlay which is financed by borrowings and is used for creating new capital assets which would eventually earn a return, there is a revenue plan which ought to be covered by revenue receipts. The clubbing of the revenue and capital components in one category termed as plan outlay has generated a tendency to use borrowings to finance revenue expenditure. It is imperative to match the revenue resources separately with the revenue component of the plan. Failure to appreciate this basic requirement of fiscal discipline is one of the main causes of the endemic fiscal disequilibrium.

In an effort to project larger plan outlays, inadequate provision is made for crucial expenditures like the maintenance of existing assets which are, in current practice, regarded as non-plan expenditure and hence of lower priority. New schemes take priority over maintenance resulting in sub-optimal use of resources. According to the Commission such a bias arises, at least in part, from the artificial classification of expenditures between plan and non-plan and the attitude regarding all non-plan expenditure as of low priority. It needs to be appreciated that a large part of non-plan expenditure is of a developmental nature and should enjoy the same priority, if not higher, as new plan schemes.

The Commission has made general observations with regard to fiscal discipline, reform of the tax system, planning process, institutional reforms and the issue of decentralisation. While making general observations, the Commission, in its report, has pointed out that "fiscal discipline does not stop at bridging the revenue deficit, which in itself would be a very major step forward. Our forecasts do not suggest that this can be achieved by the year 2000, but every effort must be made to do so within the subsequent five years. This will require a careful look at both plan and non-plan expenditures. Equally important is to ensure that resources are not diverted from the purposes for which they are allocated. More generally, expenditure control should involve questioning every item of expenditure every year, rather than giving automatic approvals on the basis of continuity of schemes of projects.

The Commission has recommended an alternative scheme of devolution which may be brought into force with effect from 1st April, 1996 after necessary amendments to the Constitution. A summary of Commission's recommendation is reproduced in section IV of Chapter 12.

Public Sector Commercial Banks and Financial Sector Reform

India's public sector banks have a vital role to play in the new economic environment. They were able to respond to the mandate given to them at the time of nationalisation: the spread of their branches, the expansion of their deposits and diversification of their borrowers all bear testimony to that success. This quantitative success was, however, achieved at the expense of deterioration in qualitative factors such as profitability, efficiency, and the most important, the quality of the loan portfolio, which now need to take the centre stage. The Finance Ministry discussion paper (Ch. 13) presents an assessment of the current problems facing the public sector commercial banks and articulates the broad strategy being followed to overcome them in a phased manner, over the next three to four years. The paper examines the forces which have led to the financial and managerial weakening of banks and quantifies their financial position as revealed by the new accounting norms. The paper outlines the approach to be followed in dealing with the financial weaknesses revealed in the existing portfolio, and discusses measures needed to prevent similar problems from recurring. The paper also deals with the managerial and institutional challenges confronting the banks and the changes in the competitive, legal and regulatory environment within which they will henceforth operate.

Chapter 14 gives the summary of recommendation of Chelliah Committee Final Report (Part II) on tax reforms.

Reforms in the Insurance Sector

Insurance has been a state monopoly for many years during which there has been a large increase in the spread of both life and general insurance business. The Life Insurance Corporation (LIC) and the general insurance companies have an extensive presence throughout the country. Over the years, they have developed financial strength and considerable reservoirs of trained manpower. However, lack of competition has engendered a measure of complacency in the insurance industry which is reflected, among other things, in inadequate responsiveness to customer needs, high costs, instability of marketing networks, excessive lapsation of life policies, growth of restrictive practices and some erosion in work culture, and lags in technology upgradation. Despite overall growth of insurance, many lines of business have not been sufficiently developed and there is a vast untapped potential. Since nationalisation, regulation of insurance industry has atrophied. High levels of directed investment have affected rates of insurance premia, and bonuses on most life policies.

The Malhotra Committee has made far reaching recommendations relating to reforms in the insurance sector. Excerpts from the report, including recommendations, have been reproduced in chapter 15.

2

India's Economic Reforms

T.N. Srinivasan & Jagdish Bhagwati

I. INTRODUCTION

A. India at Crossroads

India is at a crossroads. Intensive economic reforms were launched in June 1991 by the government of Prime Minister Rao and are in mid-course.

The reforms had long been seen to be necessary, though the "political will" to start and sustain these reforms had been lacking until recently. Indeed, steps towards reforms had been taken earlier. But this time, the effort is more sizable, is significant, and has been maintained so far.

The important questions before the government, and the country, now are the following:

(1) Are the reforms, as implemented so far, well-designed in terms of their rationale and relevance to the problems we face; and

(2) what are the next steps that the government must undertake, both in terms of more effective implementation of the reforms already attempted and of the further reforms to be made, in order to bring the reform process to successful, completion?

In answering these questions, we will argue that the Indian reforms have generally avoided mis-steps, perhaps erring on the side of caution but maintaining a prudent but steady course. At the same time, it is important that the government now begin to tackle forthwith a new set of reforms, also discussed in the Report, that constitute logically the next step in the process. These can both cement the reforms already in place and help to earn greater social returns from the reform process. In fact, as we cannot emphasise too strongly, without many of these next steps, some of the key components of the reforms to date could unravel as critics note the limited returns to them and contradictions cause difficulties.[1]

B. Rationale for the Reforms

It is important to understand, and indeed this understanding must obtain at political and bureaucratic levels as well, why the present reforms are necessary. For, only then can the necessary support be adequately mobilised and sustained through the course of the reforms.

As is now well-understood, India faced a macroeconomic crisis that required immediate attention when Prime Minister Rao took office. This crisis had to be attended to forthwith. But, as in many South American countries in the 1980s, the macroeconomic crisis became also the occasion for undertaking substantial microeconomic (or what are sometimes called "structural") reforms that had been long overdue.[2]

In fact, these structural reforms were necessary because we had evidently failed to generate adequate rates of growth of income and of per capita income. Not merely did India's weak performance in this regard fall below her own expectations as defined in the First and Second Five-year Plans.[3] It also put India behind many other developing countries, and way behind the superperformers in the Far East.

Figure 1 underlines this forcefully. Using data for 21 "high income" and 88 developing countries since 1960, this chart shows up India's sorry performance.[4] In turn, it can be persuasively argued that the failure to grow also undercut our efforts to create more jobs and thus to pull up more people into gainful employment, thus undermining the main objective of alleviating our massive poverty.

Since our low growth performance cannot be attributed to failure to raise the necessary savings and investment, for we did pretty well (if not as well as the super-successful countries of the Far East) on that score, it reflected our failure to get adequate returns from these rising investments. In short, our policy framework was inefficient, in fact woefully inefficient. We had to contend with deep-seated "microeconomic" flaws.

The macroeconomic crisis thus provided the opportunity and the necessity finally to address meaningfully the inefficiencies in our policy framework that had hurt our economic performance and to begin seriously the task of undertaking the necessary microeconomic or structural reforms as well. These reforms, necessitating an exhaustive restructuring of our policy framework, had become critically necessary.

Indeed, it is necessary to appreciate that we had become marginalised in the world economy. Not merely were our growth, and hence all else such as poverty

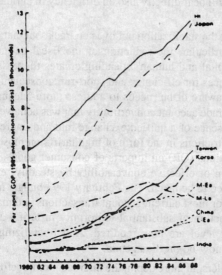

Fig. 1. A comparison of GDP per capita in India and other developing countries, 1960–88

Key:
HI High-income countries
M-EA Middle-income countries in East Asia
M-LA Middle-income countries in Latin America
L-EA Low-income countries in East Asia
Source: The World Bank.

alleviation, unsatisfactory, the multiplying success stories were to be found elsewhere. Increasingly, many of our economic policies were also seen as wittingly foolish, impossible to explain as sensible. Among these were our maze of senseless bureaucratic controls on production and investment. Perhaps the most compelling reason for reforms was then to clean the house and to restore India eventually to the position of respect in the world economy and polity that she enjoyed during the years of Prime Minister Nehru's stewardship.

C. The Report

The rest of this Report is therefore structured as follows.

In section II, in view of the importance of clarity concerning the nature and objectives of the sweeping reforms for a healthy public debate and in order to ensure the successful execution of the ongoing and future reforms, we address the broad principles concerning the design and implementation of policy reforms that the government needs to keep in mind.

Section III then addresses briefly the strictly macroeconomic questions raised by the reforms. These concern naturally the issues of fiscal stabilization, monetary restraint and currency convertibility. [In turn, of course, each of these has microeconomic implications,. For example, the removal of subsidies to reduce the budget deficit will bear directly also on efficiency in agriculture and in public sector enterprises.]

We conclude that the stabilization policy is on track, but that certain correctives are in order. In particular, the reduction of the fiscal deficit through cutting developmental (capital and human) spending creates the possibility of adverse long-run consequences for efficiency and short-run consequences for equity that the government is aware of but needs to address more adequately. In regard to convertibility, the trade account convertibility that was achieved to date had been qualified by the absence of a unified exchange rate and, more important, by the continued trade restrictions in the form of high tariffs on most goods and severe quantitative restrictions (QR) on imports of consumer goods. Steps towards the eventual completion of effective convertibility by steadily removing these two qualifications needed to be taken. The February 1993 budget has already unified the exchange rate for most current account transactions and made modest cuts in tariffs. The introduction of substantial uniformity in tariffs and further phased reductions in their level are now required. And liberalizing consumer goods imports must also now be on the agenda.

Section IV considers, in more depth, the microeconomic reforms that constitute the core of the changed policy framework that will take the economy into a more efficient mode. Since the rationale for many of the reforms (such as the dismantling of the Kafkaesque licensing system) is now widely appreciated, we focus instead on the key issues that now require attending: among them the further liberalization of the import regime, further reform of the direct foreign investment (DFI) policy, the question of privatisation, and reforms in our critical Agricultural sector.

Section V considers broader questions of foreign economic policy on which we must begin to focus immediately if the transition to the New Economic Policy is to be successful. In particular, we consider, in view of India's transition to an outward-oriented economic strategy in regard to trade and foreign investment, the need to consider, among other issues, how India is to fit into the growing trend towards regional blocs in world trade and what we should begin doing about it.

Section VI concludes the Report.

II. DESIGNING AND IMPLEMENTING REFORMS:

Principles

At the outset, some issues concerning the design and implementation of reforms may be discussed. There is now a growing literature in economics on these questions, reflecting both theoretical analysis and empirical examination of the reform efforts in several developing countries. Its insights need to be adapted to the Indian situation and some key lessons learnt and applied.

A. Common Misunderstandings

Since the reforms are both sweeping and often "liberal" in the sense of removing several harmful constraints (on domestic production and investment, on foreign trade and on foreign investment) and permitting a far greater role for market forces in guiding the economy than hitherto, it is natural that they should creat serious misunderstandings, and hence roadblocks to the reforms, unless they are properly understood and, in turn, explained to the populace by the political leadership at every opportunity. There are four specific misunderstandings that are fairly common today and need to be cleared up.

1. "We are turning to laissez-faire"

Occasionally, one hears that the Rao government is turning away from "planning" to "laissez-faire".

It is indeed true that the proposed reforms are, in key respects, aimed at allowing a greater play for markets where bureaucrats and politicians were wholly dominant in decision making. In short, the reforms are intended to remove the government from areas of economic decision-making where our own and more extensive international *experience* (not *ideology*) has shown in the postwar period that governments harm, rather than help, the developmental process.

In short, governments tend to do certain things badly and must be kept away from them. But their role continues to be important in other areas, especially in poor countries. The reforms are thus aimed at taking the government out of some areas and concentrating its energies on others. They aim to refocus policy intervention, not to eliminate it. The reforms are about "appropriate intervention", not about laissez faire.

This is not to say that we are not having to challenge vested interests and defunct ideas on how to manage (or, shall we say, mismanage) the economy. Thus, the extensive framework of detailed licensing and control of production, investment and trade will have to be virtually abandoned. The efficiency of our many public sector enterprises has to become a primary question, necessitating a revision of the earlier hands-off approach to them. We cannot continue treating this sector as a sacred cow, revered and worshipped but often decrepit and destitute. Extensive privatisation and other changes aimed at efficiency will lead eventually to a lower (even terminated) governmental presence and role in those enterprises that survive the reforms as productive units in the economy.

None of this adds upto laissez-faire, i.e. the injunction to let governments do nothing. Even the reform process will require imaginative governmental design and management! And, at the end of the reform process, the government will be heavily involved in the economy: through fiscal and monetary management, in education, in public health, in trade management abroad at the GATT and in bilateral negotiations to assure market access, in science and technology policy, in financial sector regulation, in advancing environmental protection, and indeed in much else that cannot be left entirely to the market place.

Indeed, even if laissez-faire were the objective of some academic reformers, one need not fear that it will arrive. Governments get elected to do things. To expect that they will oblige by self-destructing as per an agenda of laissez-faire is to be utopian, at best, and silly, at worst.

2. "We are abandoning poverty alleviation for growth"

The problem in Indian debate arises from the tendency of many to think that the economic reforms, since they favour efficiency and growth, must be against poverty alleviation. This is however an "anti-growth" misunderstanding, pitting growth against poverty, that reflects in turn three different misconceptions.

(a) *"The removal of poverty requires anti-poverty programs, not growth"*: This view is wrong on two counts. Growth will generally create jobs, pulling people up into gainful employment and hence out of poverty. It is an "indirect" anti-poverty strategy and was, in fact, embraced as such from the beginning of our postwar developmental efforts. The failure to achieve satisfactory growth, *not* the emphasis on it, lies at the heart of our failure to make a more effective dent on poverty.

Next, even our ability to finance governmental support of "direct" antipoverty programs will be crippled if growth yields to stagnation. Low growth means growing inability to raise the revenues without which governmental programmes cannot be financed. This is partly the reason why, around the industrial world, the low growth rates of the 1970s and 1980s have led to growing strains on the budget and to attempts at pruning the welfare state.

(b) *"The planners in India until the 1980s treated growth as their target and neglected poverty in consequence"*: The anti-growth sentiment has also flourished in India because of the ready assumption that, until the 1970s, the Indian leaders and planners were unmindful of poverty alleviation as their objective and enamored instead of growth in itself. Now that efficiency and growth have become an important motive for economic reforms, it is thought that we are regressing back to the old ways.

But there is no basis in reality for these views. From the beginning, growth was regarded as a way of impacting on poverty, rather than as an end in itself.[5]

The pronouncements of Prime Minister Nehru, the contents of the earliest Five-year Plans and the strong stress from the 1960s by our planners on "minimum levels of living" are evidence of our clarity on these questions, and of the obfuscations by those who allege that poverty was not our earliest concern and objective and of their self-serving claims that they somehow redefined our objectives away from growth towards poverty-alleviation in the 1980s.

(c) *"Growth is a conservative 'trickle-down' strategy"*: In turn, these critics have alleged that growth amounts to a passive, conservative "trickle-down" strategy. This too misses the point. In our context of immense poverty, growth represents an activist, radical "pull-up" strategy for removing poverty. And that is exactly how we thought of it when we were planning our assault on poverty from the early 1950s.[6]

The issue before us then is not the artificial one of growth *versus* poverty. Rather, it is one of how, given whatever resources we deviate to growth, we get the maximum payoff in growth and in job creation. In short, how do we redesign the policy framework that has worked so inefficiently and produced such disappointing results? That is precisely where the economic reforms come center stage.

3. "We are yielding to foreign pressure"

The fact that the reforms were part of the conditionality that came with multilateral assistance has also created the impression that they are a result of foreign pressure. In turn, there is the notion that the ideas and policies begin imposed on us are foreign and also that they are ill-designed, in consequence, for us.

Indeed, it is true that, without the crisis being on us, the initial adoption of the reforms may have contined to be postponed. Our earlier efforts at initiating and sustaining them had been hesitant and limited, at best. Conditionality played a role, for sure, in stregthening our will to embark on the reforms. But the seriousness and the sweep of the reforms, and the Rao governments's explicit embrace of them as against the earlier "reforms by stealth", demonstrated that the driving force behind the reforms was equally, even overwhelmingly, our own conviction that we had lost precious time and that the reforms were finally our only option.

The complaint that the ideas being implemented are extraneous does not reflect the reality either. These reforms in our, and indeed in many other developing countries' policies, were being advocated from the early 1960s and the proponents, the pioneers, included Indian economists.[7] It is ironic, in fact, that these ideas, rejected at the time by our authorities and by many of our economists as well, have now been adopted worldwide but have come to be adopted by us only at the end of this revolutionary change. Indeed, these ideas have been recycled back to us, in many cases, by the staff of the multilateral institutions who learnt them from our own pioneering economists. The claim that the ideas are foreign and hence ill-suited to us is therefore incorrect. In any event it is surely odd and indeed counterproductive to accept or reject ideas based on where they are coming from!

4. "We are turning back on all we did earlier"

There is also an understandable feeling that the reforms imply that everything we did earlier, from Prime Minister Nehru's time, was a failure.

In the critical areas where the reforms are concentrated, this is indeed largely true. In some cases, the mistake was not in the original policy but rather in not abandoning it as circumstances changed or became clearer. This is the case with our import-substitution policy which was premised on export pessimism which was widely shared in the 1950s. But as it became evident in the 1960s that this export pessimism was unwarranted, in view of the rapid growth of world trade and the fact that the Far Eastern economies, in particular, had used export opportunities arising from that growth to great advantage, we should have turned more confidently to similar outward-orientation. But we did not, even though these changed circumstances were evident and had been noted by some of our economists at the time.

Then again, the policy of expanding the public sector through increasing investment in successive Plans reflected, at least in part, the early assumptions that the public sector enterprises would be efficient and that they would also generate financial surpluses for the government and help therefore to increase national savings and investment. Already by late 1960s, these assumptions were being seen as unrealistic; and economists began to see that there were serious incentive problems that led to these outcomes almost everywhere, no matter what the political and social situation in a country. But we have been among the last countries to draw this lesson and act on it.

The reforms naturally focus on the areas where we have failed, either from the beginning or because of lethargy in changing course as necessary. But this does not mean that we have failed everywhere. Chief among our achievements is our success at managing democracy – an achievement that has scarcely been rivaled by another developing country in postwar period. Within the economic sphere too, we have some success stories, in agriculture for instance.[8]

When the reforms are taken to the public by the government, it may well be sensible then to present the successes as well as the failures which the reforms address. Then again, the presentation of the reforms as necessary since policies that "made sense earlier" are "inappropriate now" may be politically more prudent than to claim, as is truthful, that many of these policies were simply wrong.

B. The Need for Clear and Repeated Affirmation of Reforms

The government needs therefore to educate the public continually about the foregoing misunderstandings.

The credibility of reforms is necessary because, without it, firms and other decision-makers will not take the decisions that would make the reforms successful. For instance, if it is assumed that the government will revert to licensing and exchange controls on trade, investment in export promotion will be inhibited and a central objective of the delicensing reforms will have been frustrated. To take another example, the continuation of the FERA and COFEPOSA machinery and controls on direct foreign investment (DFI) cannot but fail to make the removal of many restrictions to attract DFI less than credible to foreign investors: this machinery, and the numerous difficulties and roadblocks still in place, mix the signals badly (whereas China, for example, which is attracting dramatic amounts of DFI, sends very clear and credible signals indeed by contrast).[9]

C. The Need for Momentum

It is important also to have the reform process building momentum rather than losing steam. There are several reasons why cascading reforms are likely to be more successful.

(i) A blitzkrieg of reforming measures represents a moving target for opponents, making it more difficult to concentrate criticism than when the target is static.

(ii) Often there will be economic complementarities in the reform process. Thus, industrial delicensing is more effective if the current account has convertibility. But the latter is trickier to implement. So, you begin with the former and pursue the latter in a more measured way, as is indeed the case with our reforms.

(iii) If the momentum builds steadily, the credibility of the reforms also gains in the process and so does their prospect of success.

D. The Need for Comprehensiveness

A broad sweep in the scope of the reforms is also advisable. This is partly because, as we just argued, complementarities increase the efficacy of one reform if another is also undertaken.

But it is also a result of the fact that reforms entail pain because of the adjustments that they impose, forcing at minimum a change in one's way of doing business. If the reforms are extensive, more people are likely to be involved in the pain, thus making it a "shared sacrifice" in the national interest and moderating opposition from any one group in particular.

E. The Speed of Reforms

Perhaps the hardest question to answer relates to the optimal speed of reforms. Opinion seems to divide typically into two camps: those who are impatient to go faster and those who cannot go fast enough.

From the economic point of view, the problem is quite complex. It is also true that the effective speed at which reforms may be implemented is, in any event, beyond the economist's control since some reforms will simply take their own time to get down on the ground. For example, one may want to immediately privatise all public enterprises; but finding buyers may take a long time.

Then again, political factors must be taken into account in implementing reforms. If reforms are undertaken without attempting to build up a reasonable measure of political support, the whole experiment may backfire.

Thus, for instance, the Rao government, already beset by charges of a "sellout", would have been probably unwise to privatise the public enterprises right away: it might have helped cement leftwing opposition to the rest of the reforms. Nor would it likely have made political sense to embank immediately upon an exit policy aimed at relocating the labour force away from inefficient plants and firms: without adequate economic and political preparation to do this, the government may well have precipitated major political opposition of a kind which a fragile government might succumb to.

Thus, it is hard to double guess the government's speed of reforms. It might conceivably have moved faster in some areas. But the fact remains that it did move decisively on many fronts and has not seriously backtracked on any of its major reforms. One *can* say, however, that the time is now ripe for added reforms.

F. The Need for Institutional Change

This is particularly so because the reforms that we have undertaken so far, especially in industrial and foreign-trade delicensing, amount to a radical change in the functioning of the economy that requires substantial, complementary institutional changes if they are to be truly effective. And these institutional changes are the ones that need now to be undertaken with vigour.

An analogy with the former Soviet Union should illustrate well what we have in mind. The Soviet Union was afflicted with even more sweeping controls over production, trade and investment, with an overwhelming role for central planning and virtual absence of private ownership of the means of production when reforms were begun under President Gorbachev. The intention was to shift to a market economy. But the institutions to support such a market economy were often wholly absent. Thus, for instance, when Party control over food procurement disintegrated with *glasnost*, it became increasingly difficult to procure food at low prices for distribution at subsidized prices in the state-owned city shops: the farms simply sold the food at higher prices in the rural areas and the city shops soon had empty shelves. The problem was that fiscal policy instruments had not been put in place when the old "command" system had collapsed[11]. Then again, the response of production and investment to price signals was inhibited in the absence of private ownership of productive capacity in most sectors: this contributed to chaos as the command system collapsed but the institutional requirements of a functioning market system were still not in place.

Our reforms do not pose stark problems of the Soviet variety since we have already had a functioning market economy. But the heavy hand of extensive licensing did mean that we had no significant role earlier for an efficient financial sector (which would help allocate investible resources among alternative claimants) since investments were decided upon by the government, or for an efficient labour market with adequate possibilities for labour reallocation because both firms and labour were, for the most part, effectively protected against the rigours of the marketplace in the shape of competition and possible bankruptcy.

Thus, as we are now effectively entering a delicensed system, it becomes necessary to adapt our institutions forthwith to include financial and labour-market reforms, in particular. The energetic pursuit of these reforms, difficult as they appear, must now be on the government's agenda.

G. Meeting Expectations

Finally, the art of designing and implementing economic reforms must also extend to the task of holding expectations from reforms within manageable bounds while the reforms take root.

What we said so far related to the substance of the reforms and to the task of ensuring that their credibility was maintained for economic decision making to respond so as to make the reforms successful. This would ensure that expectations concerning sustained support for the economic reforms and their momentum would be satisfied.

But expectations about their success, in terms of results, also need to be taken care of. Else, support for them would begin to wear thin. This is, of course, a corollary to the concern of our earlier planners: that the "revolution of rising expectations" would be hard to meet and therefore might lead to a corrosion of the developmental programmes.

The problem has been a difficult one for the Rao government, of course. Partly, this is because the macroeconomic need to stabilise the economy inevitably reins in the economy and dampens the growth of output that the microeconomic reforms would generate. Thus, in an ultimate irony, while the macroeconomic crisis made the microeconomic reforms politically possible, it makes their success slower and hence more difficult.[12]

Partly, the difficulty comes also from the fact that the results often will not be large immediately.[13] There are time lags. Besides, the efficiency of some measures already taken will improve only as others are taken now, as explained earlier. Even in countries like Mexico, where the last decade has witnessed major reforms, the effect on the growth rate has been much less than dramatic, though the high inflation has been brought under control and the economy now seems poised for a major takeoff.

But it is clear that the payoff will be a function of the sweep and depth of the reforms: a proposition that is demonstrated well by China's rapid growth under its substantial economic reforms. The government must therefore proceed, for this reason as well as the others outlined earlier, to build rapidly on the reforms so far.

So much for the general principles of economic reform, many already implicitly underlying the strategic decisions undertaken by the Rao government to date but nonetheless necessary to appreciate if the reform process is to stay on course and if general support for it is to be maintained in the country. We turn now briefly to the macro-economic reforms (Section III) and, at greater length, to the micro-economic reforms that await further action (Section IV).

III. MACROECONOMIC REFORMS

A. The Macroeconomic Crisis

The Indian macroeconomic crisis was precipitated mainly by the growth of the public spending through the 1980s that increased the budget deficit as a proportion of our GNP, although external shocks played a fortuitous contributory role.[14]

The state of our public finances had indeed reached crisis proportions by the end of the 1980s. The public debt-to-GNP ratio increased through the 1980s, going up to almost 60% at the end of the decade, implying a doubling of the ratio at the end of the previous decade (see Figure 2). As is now wellknown, the proximate reasons for this situation were the failure of the public sector to generate investible resources and the explosive growth of governmental current spending that saw the budget deficit as a proportion of GDP rise from 6.4 to 9% during the 1980s. [15]

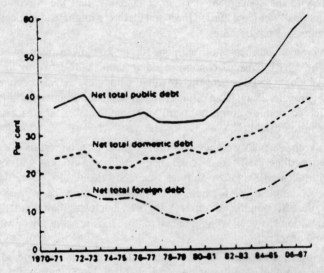

Fig. 2. India's net public debt to GNP ratios, 1970–87
Source: W. Builer and U. Patel, 'Debt, Deficits, and Inflation: An Application to the Public Finances of India', *Journal of Public Economics,* 47 (1992), 171–205.

The question must be addressed:[16] did the microeconomic inefficiencies have anything to do with this, or was "profligacy" the true, final and sole cause of the macroeconomic crisis? Evidently, it was the former.

Of course, the failure of the public sector enterprises to generate profits (and hence their contribution to the macro crisis) is a microeconomic efficiency failure. But, in turn, because these enterprises have dominated the provision of infrastructure and critical intermediates, their inefficiency has led to downstream inefficiencies in a multiplier fashion. Then again, the restrictive trade and industrial licensing framework, for instance, led to serious loss of efficiency by reducing the scale of output, eliminating effective competition, creating bottlenecks, and in myriad other ways. The result was to reduce the returns from our investments and our growth rate. In turn, surely the revenues raised from the economy, for any given tax rates, were adversely affected, the political ability to raise tax rates in a situation of slowly-growing incomes was impaired, and the necessity to undertake budgetary expenditures to support the creation of public-sector jobs and for consumption were also increased-- all factors contributing to the budget deficit crisis.

The two OPEC shocks of 1973 and 1979 hurt, but did not have a sustained impact on the budget deficit. The external shock administered by the loss of remittances and the expenditures incurred to rescue workers in the aftermath of the invasion of Kuwait in August 1990 certainly accentuated the fiscal crisis at the end. But the crisis was certainly "home-made".[17]

The rise in foreign borrowing was a major component of the fiscal crisis, reflecting in turn the excess of domestic expenditure over income.[18] Thus, as evident from Figure 2, the external public-sector debt (and not just the domestic public-sector debt) increased greatly as a proportion of GNP during the 1980s, rising to 21% by 1987-88. This increase in external indebtedness meant that debt service as a proportion of exports increased more than threefold to 32% in 19986-87 from 1980-81.

In fact, reserves plummeted to less than ten days of imports by the beginning of 1991, prompting borrowing from the IMF in January of loans worth $ 1.8 billion and then again, as reserves fell perilously low again and the prospect of NRI-deposit withdrawal and of overnight-borrowing recall a worrisome reality, in October 1991.

The macro imbalance, fuelled by the budget deficit and financed by the external borrowings and the decumulation of reserves, was accompanied by accelerated inflation to double-digit levels. Evidently, a stabilization programme, reversing the growth in the budget deficit and tightening monetary policy, was called for. This, the reforms initiated by the Rao government sought to do.

The Fiscal Deficit And Remedial Action

The key question then is not whether the stabilisation was called for: there was no option. Rather, it is: has the stabilisation been carried out in an appropriate fashion? We answer this question now, concluding that some correctives are in order. In particular, we draw attention to the following areas of concern and remedial action:

*the reductions in developmental expenditure appear to be taking the brunt of the successful effort to cut the budget deficit: this could create difficulties down the road;

*there is scope for further cuts in nondevelopmental expenditure, especially in regard to the emoluments and size of the bureaucracy, and subsidies to public sector enterprises (whose reform we discuss separately below) and to agriculture (also discussed separately in Section IV below);

*there is need to raise more revenue by expanding the tax base, while the reforms recommended by the Chelliah Committee are considered for adoption; and

*a sound management of monetary policy in the interest of financial stability requires that the financial sector reforms (which we discuss separately below) be

implemented at greater speed.

(a) Developmental Expenditure

The reduction of the budget deficit, the principal proximate cause of the macroeconomic crisis, was inevitable. But the difficult problem is to decide whether the government chose the best way of reducing that deficit. In short, two major questions arise: has the government raised revenues or relied entirely on cutting expenditure; and have the cuts in expenditure been too unmindful of the need to take the longer view on developmental expenditure and the need to soften the impact on the poor? We begin by considering the question of developmental expenditure.

That the reduction in the budget deficit has been brought about partly by a reduction in developmental expenditure cannot be denied. For example, while the overall developmental revenue expenditure of the Center is budgeted to remain virtually unchanged in 1992-93 in nominal terms at Rs. 207 billion (compared to the revised estimate of Rs. 214 billion in 1991-92), non-developmental expenditure is budgeted to rise from Rs. 472 billion in 1991-92 to Rs. 538 billion in 1992-93 – an overwhelming part of the increase, roughly Rs. 48 billion, being the rise in interest payments on domestic and external debt.[19] [The consolidated budget data for 1992-93 for state governments were not available to us as of the date of finishing this Report; but it is unlikely that they would show any offset to the above categorisation by revealing that their developmental expenditure had increased substantially.]

At the same time, the Center's developmental expenditure on capital account has also registered only a negligible increase in nominal terms: from the revised estimates of Rs. 57 billion in 1991-92 to Rs. 63 billion in 1992-93. It is highly probable therefore that the overall governmental expenditure in real terms during the course of our stabilisation has been significantly at the expense of developmental expenditure in the revenue and capital accounts. Three comments are in order.

First, the developmental expenditure links directly to the long-term health of the economy. The reduction of developmental expenditure is likely to reduce the growth rate and therefore to come to haunt us in the shape of further pressures to resume excess spending through the budget as in the 1980s.

We are aware that, simply because expenditures are classified as developmental, they are not so, whereas nondevelopmental expenditure may have productivity and growth effects. Also, cuts in developmental expenditure may be offset by improvd efficiency: but this will not happen unless major reforms, especially in the public enterprises, are undertaken with due speed.

Second, therefore, the reliance on (real) cuts in developmental spending holds danger that must be moderated by reforms in the public sector. These reforms will have to include (as we propose below) opening the reserved areas fully to private sector and far more liberally to foreign investment, an energetic demolition of any obstacles in this goal (e.g. price policy restrictions, labour laws that are antagonistic to efficiency and can be altered without sacrificing internationally sanctioned rights), a speedier policy on privatisation of a large number of the existing public enterprises, and a decision to hold back from creating new public sector enterprises in except when security considerations dictate otherwise.

Third, the cuts in (real) developmental expenditures by the government may well affect adversely the private investment expenditures in the economy, creating deflationary impulses in addition to those that the government had intended. Because crucial infrastructure activities are in the public sector, and private investment finds its returns dependent on the availability of these infrastructure inputs (such as power), private investment has traditionally been crowded in, rather than out, by public investment in these infrastructure sectors.[20] Thus, the government must make every effort to ensure that, despite predictable political pressures, the reductions in developmental expenditure are brutally selective, sparing areas where the infrastructure bottlenecks are currently quite severe.[21]

(b) Cutting Non-developmental Expenditure

Cuts in nondevelopmental expenditure are difficult to make. But there are areas where they are necessary, not merely in themselves but also because of their effects in improving productivity in the economy. These desirable cuts relate to subsidies of various kinds, chiefly in two areas: budgetary support to loss-making public sector enterprises and subsidies to agricultural inputs (fertilisers, irrigation and electricity) and to outputs (through the Public Distribution System).[22] We consider these reforms in the wider context of reforms in the Public Sector Enterprises and in Agriculture, in separate sections of the Report below.

The question of Social Expenditures, or "safety nets" to be more precise, especially with a view to protecting the poor from the effects of stabilisation, is also a compelling one. The Finance Minister has been criticised for ignoring this aspect of the stabilisation issue, with talking about it but ignoring it in his actions, and even with complying more with the concerns of the IMF and the World Bank regarding the efficiency aspects of stabilisation rather than their equity exhortations.[23] This criticism is however exaggerated, at best.

The aggregate expenditure on what are generally considered "social sectors" (defined as Agriculture and Cooperation, Food, Health, Education, Women and Child Development, Rural Development etc.) did go up from 15.4% of total government expenditure to 15.7% between 1991-92 and 1992-93, with the nominal expenditures by the central government in Health and on Women and Child Development showing growth rates of as much as roughly 40 and 21% respectively.[24] Admittedly, the total expenditures are small in any event. But then is not the Finance Minister right that it is the lack of efficiency and growth that has driven us into a situation where our capacity to increase such expenditures dramatically has been sapped, and that the stabilisation, once it takes root, and only the completion of the reforms (which must include an expeditious implementation of many of the new steps we recommend in this Report) will put us back into a situation where we can undertake these necessary increases in expenditure. Talk is cheap; and one's social conscience can be readily stroked by such talk. What counts, as the Finance Minister has made amply clear, is the ability to deliver on such talk. Talking about poverty is not to alleviate it.

(c) Raising Revenue

The Indian tax system is in need of reform. The fiscal base is norrow and the structure of taxes is inefficient. The government is well aware of these problems, having commissioned and now secured the Chelliah Committee report on Tax Reforms. We need only to endorse the generally excellent set of proposals made by the Chelliah Committee, except to state that, in the Sections below on Agriculture and on Consumer Goods Import Liberalisation, we make further, somewhat bolder suggestions (which, however, are in consonance with the spirit of what the Chelliah Committee recommends).

(d) Public Sector: Proceeds from Privatisation

We consider public sector enterprise reform below. But we address here the question raised by the use of the sales proceeds from the limited sales of equity so far. These have been treated as revenue receipts to reduce the current budget deficit. Is this a wise decision or, as has been suggested by some economists, should we use these proceeds to retire our considerable debt?[25]

In principle, whether these sales proceeds are used to reduce the current budget deficit or to retire debt would not be a meaningful question if only the overall simultaneous choice of the two objectives were made in the light of the fact that these sales proceeds were available to the government: otherwise, we would be guilty of the fallacy of misplaced concreteness. The issue, however, is a very real one: for, it is being asserted that the government is avoiding such a principled choice and is in fact taking the easy way out of not raising revenues or cutting expenditures or both by pretending that these sales proceeds are revenue. If this is true, and we suspect that this may be true or might become true as sales proceeds continue to accrue from further privatisation, then a rule that allocates these proceeds to debt retirement might be a good idea. Consider then the following.

Thus, the Center's internal rupee debt as a proportion of GDP has increased from 35.6% in 1980-81 to 53.3% in 1990-91. It has declined somewhat as a result of greater control over the fiscal deficit by the Finance Minister, of course, to 52.1% in 1991-92. The large size of the debt has meant that interest payments (net of dividends and profits from public sector enterprises) as a proportion of total central governmental expenditure have increased between 1980-81 and 1991-92 from 5.4% to 14.8%.[26]

A good rule to go by, therefore, would be to follow the Mexican example and to assign to proceeds from equity sales in public enterprises exclusively to retiring the accumulated debt. This would enable us to reduce quickly the burden of interest payments which afflict the budget, while also putting pressure on the government to push ahead with necessary fiscal reforms in regard to both taxation and expenditures .

(e) Financial Sector Reform: Banking

We should also stress here that nearly half of the gross fiscal deficit of the central government in 1990-91 was financed by the banking system (including the Reserve Bank of India). Through instruments such as the mandatory cash reserve ratio and statutory liquidity ratio, the government has traditionally forced the commercial banks to hold a larger share of relatively low-yielding government liabilities in their asset portfolio than they would otherwise hold.

It has also been suggested that the participation of some banks in the recent stock market scandal was a reflection of their urgent need to earn a high return from the free part of their loanable funds since their profitability was seriously affected by having to finance relatively unprofitable government liabilities. This may well be so, though it is hard to imagine that the results would have been much different even otherwise once the chance to make quick if illegal profits, under what was perceived to be inadequate regulatory discipline, was seen by the offending parties.

In any event, the facts that important financial intermediaries such as the major commercial banks and the Life Insurance Corporation (a monopoly) are in the public sector, and that the Reserve Bank of India does not have the autonomy of either the Federal Reserve of the United States or the Bundesbank of Germany, have meant that the central government has faced little external discipline to trim its fiscal sails for fear of being unable to finance its deficits at any inflationary cost.

This means that the reform of the financial sector, including of the Reserve Bank of India, must be treated as an integral part of the fiscal reforms aimed at reducing the likelihood of the 1980s indiscipline resurrecting itself, and hence as central to the general reform of the public sector's working in India.

B. Are We Borrowing Too Much?

We now turn to the question occasionally raised by critics of the reform process: are we borrowing too much?

(1) At the outset, we must dismiss the criticism of borrowing undertaken when we would otherwise have been forced to default in 1991. The decision not to default was clearly wise: a default would have damaged our creditworthiness and forced us into yet more of the policies that had produced the crisis in the first place. For instance, more autarkic policies would have emerged as foreign exchange credits dried up and NRI investments began to drain out with loss of confidence resulting from the default. In the longrun, of course, creditworthiness often returns as memory fades and new opportunities are seen by foreign investors, as in the 19th Century and has happened in Latin America now despite the

widespread defaults in the 1980s. But this too.has required the turn by these Latin American countries to serious reforms. The reforms that were to accompany the lending to us could be then seen as necessary also to maintaining our longrun creditworthiness, to enable us to continue borrowing from the international capital markets for accelerated growth.

(2) Then again, we may think of borrowing in order to smooth consumption over time. This may, for instance, be because of random shocks (such as variations in the monsoon or terms-of-trade fluctuations) leading to fluctuations in income. Such consumption smoothing would then lead to borrowing today, when income has fallen, in anticipation of increased income tomorrow. Such borrowing does occur for us from time to time, as for other countries, often from the IMF.

(3) The critical question for us, however, does not relate to such borrowing. Rather, it concerns whether our overall indebtedness has risen too much altogether, whether we are in the position of the Latin American countries in the mid-1980s, with an intolerable external debt burden that would kill their economic growth for nearly a decade, or whether our borrowing is prudent as was South Korea's in the 1980s.

To consider this question, first examine the facts. According to the *Economic Survey 1992-93*, the total external debt (excluding defence-related debt but including NRI deposits) is estimated currently around $72.67 billion. The ruble debt amounts to about $9 billion.

In terms of absolute size of the debt, India is certainly among the major borrowers. However the debt/GNP ratio is under 30% and the debt-service/exports (of goods and services) ratio is also around 30%. [The corresponding ratios for low-income countries other than India and China were 82.6% and 24.9% respectively in 1990.] The *average* interest rate on India's external public debt was 8%, the proportion of debt with variable interest rates was 17.5%, the *average* maturity was 25 years and the *average* grace period of 8 years in 1990. Thus the average interest rate was not very high and the maturity period was fairly long.

In assessing whether India has borrowed too much, what matters evidently are not the average interest rates and the average maturities but the interest rates and maturities of the loans at the *margin*. One might suggest that borrowing from NRI's represents the marginal loans. And interest on such deposits is substantially higher than the average rate of 8% and the maturities are much shorter. However, one might argue that NRI deposits are essentially short-term loans and the relevant margin is India's longer-term borrowing from the external private capital market. Once again the rates of interest on such loans are higher than the average rate of 8%, and the maturities are much shorter than the average maturity of 25 years.

These represent the cost side of the ledger.[27] As for the benefit side, the return to the borrowing may be viewed, broadly speaking, as the marginal return to the economy. This does not mean, of course, that there is a direct connection between external loan and investment. Indeed such loans could finance activities other than investment. Still, indirectly releasing resources which otherwise would have to be diverted from investment to such activities, loans may be considered to add to investment. Again, the marginal return to investment (in terms of value added) may be equated to the ratio of increment to GDP brought about by the investment.[28]

If so, consider that India has been investing around 25% of GDP, while the rate of growth of GDP sustained by this investment appears, on average through the 1980s, to be roughly 5%. This suggests a return in terms of *gross value added* of 20% to the investment. Using a *net* investment rate of about 16% of NDP and a NDP growth rate of about 5%, the return in terms of *net value added* is about 30%. It is arguable whether the return should be calculated using net or gross concepts of investment and domestic product. Sidestepping this issue, we may use the rates of return derived by using the two concepts as suggesting a range within which the true return lies. Thus, assuming a share of capital in value added of about 40%, the realized *real* rate of return to investment would range between 8 to 12%. If we assume then that the nominal interest rate on marginal loans is of the order of 12%, the real interest rate would be about 7%, assuming a world inflation rate of 5%.

Thus the realized rate of return to investment in the Indian economy is somewhat above (but not very much above) the interest cost. Of course, if the rate of growth could be increased substantially through better policies (or if the share of capital is much higher than 40%), then the realized rates of return would go up substantially. If, in addition, the real interest rate on marginal loans were less than 7%, then the margin of benefits over costs of external loans would be much more comfortable.

Since the real option at our command is not to lower the rates at which loans will be available to us but rather to improve our efficiency and increase the rate of return to our borrowing and investment (though, successful reforms would certainly improve our credit rating and hence indirectly lower the cost of borrowing), we can hardly over-emphasise the need to get on expeditiously with the reform process if we are going to repeat the South Korean experience rather than get into a latin American quandry (though, the borrowing in Latin America was so recklessly large that we cannot properly put our current borrowing into that class even if our reforms go slower than they prudently should).

It is of the utmost importance, therefore, for the next steps in economic reforms to be taken forthwith. Especially, the substantial delicensing of trade and industry and the virtual restoration of current account convertibility have led to the possible creation of appropriate market incentives in the economy. But much needs to be done, as we argue below, to make this an effective reality: State-level restrictions are still in place, and there is much bureaucratic machinery in place with consequent delays and transaction costs that damage the economy despite much delicensing. Then again, with public enterprises still intact, the provision of infrastructure facilities continues to be inefficient: efficient operation still awaits forceful remedies such as privatisation.

These and other reforms still awaiting implementation must be swiftly undertaken or else the supply response to the incentives sought to be provided by the reforms to date, and the returns to the borrowings we have made, will be disappointingly low. This would tend to make the borrowings even counterproductive and would certainly threaten the reform effort with failure and reversal .

Hence, we urge that the microeconomic reforms, where new steps must be taken boldly and in ways that we define in the next section, be implemented as a matter of urgency.

IV. MICROECONOMIC REFORMS

The reforms to date have been mainly aimed at eliminating the chief constituent dimensions of the earlier, unproductive policy framework.

In particular, the licensing system that governed industrial and trade decisions has been largely dismantled. The opening of the economy wider to trade has been ˉompanied by a favourable shift in the attitude and a major shift in the policy towards direct foreign investment (DFI). These reforms are considered below.

At the same time, the reforms have much further to go in other critical areas, chiefly the privatisation of the large public sector, the institution of a flexible labour hire-and-fire policy and the freeing (simultaneously with the necessary social regulation) of the financial sector.

Before we address each of these areas of reform in some depth, we think that two points need renewed emphasis:

First, we are transiting from one *system* to another. The reforms in place and the reforms in prospect dovetail into one another: each without the others produces far less benefits than when all are in place together.

Second, it is important that the reforms in prospect be undertaken now under our own steam rather than having them materialise as part of a *defacto* or *de jure* conditionality package from the IMF as we seek to borrow more money. Conditionality is important when there are powerful anti-reform forces inside the aid-recipient country that need to be and also can be effectively countervailed. When the reform process is broadly accepted, as it seems to be by now in India, reliance on conditionality to usher in the next stage of reforms is both unnecessary and also carries obvious and gratuitous political risk. We would urge therefore that the measures for the next set of reforms, discussed below, are resolved upon *before* we formally borrow afresh from the IMF rather than after (as a set of conditionalities attached to the borrowing).

A. Industrial and Trade Licensing Reforms

The dismantling of industrial and of trade licensing, which crippled efficiency in our industry, has been attended to with despatch by the government so far. The two sets of controls were mutually reinforcing. Equally, the removal of one without removing the other would have been generally infructuous: e.g. if raw material imports were allocated pro rata to capacity, and not allowed to be resold, then the more efficient producers could not expand production and drive out the less efficient ones even if industrial licensing preventing production expansion (and hence such competition) were abolished.

In the same way, the reform that has led to the rupee's trade account convertibility is also critical. If exchange controls continue while import controls are eliminated, the former can create the same restraints as the latter. For, imports can be as readily prevented by exchange controls as by import controls. Thus, the removal of industrial and trade licensing must be seen in conjunction with the restoration of the rupee's (trade account) convertibility as having jointly resulted in a freeing of India's economy.

Yet, important qualifications must be attended to forthwith if these reforms are to be truly effective.In particular, four important problems need to be addressed: (1) the bureaucracy should not become an obstacle to the intended reforms; (2) the State-level restrictions on economic decision-making, once the center-level restrictions are largely removed, should not become the new, effective constraints now; (3) the remaining controls, in particular the virtually blanket restraints on consumer goods imports, must be tackled; and (4) institutional changes must be made to support the general freeing of imports that we are moving to.

1. The Bureaucratic Problem

The dismantling of licensing by the government may be meaningless if the bureaucrats, down the line, continue to act as if controls are still in place. We have found numerous instances of bureaucratic inertia, at best, and obstructionism, at worst, which strongly suggests that the government needs to confront this issue frontally. Old habits die hard; and they linger on longer if they are also lucrative to stick to.

In regard to the licensing system, both domestic and in foreign trade and investment, it is necessary to systematically alert the bureaucracy to the new changes and to instruct it firmly (with prospect of penalties under due process of law) to prevent continuing roadblocks to production and investment decisions. In those instances where the bureaucracy no longer has a role in the new policy framework, the best policy would be to apply to it the "exit policy" that must now be embraced as part of the additional, new steps towards economic reforms that have to be taken by the government.

In this regard, it is also important that there be continual interaction, in an *institutionalised form*, between industry and the government so that efficient channels are established for rapid communication to the government of implementation roadblocks as the bureaucracy copes with the new changes that are aimed at greatly restricting its role. This also requires a change in the old, inherited style of operation where the government was in an adversarial role to industry[29]. That attitude, and the institutional structure, have to be changed quickly and comprehensively to make industry a creative and respectable partner both in implementing the reforms and in playing a central role in India's economic development. This is, in fact, the trend everywhere, including in the United States and in Great Britain where the adversarial attitudes to business and industry were long fashionable but have now lost ground.

Such institutional changes would also accelerate reform in new areas where residual controls and restrictions remain but have no good justification. Thus, for instance, in a most useful and revealing *Report on Administrative Reforms* produced by the Confederation of Indian Inudstry's National Task Force on Administrative Reforms, there are excellent suggestions for streamlining the clearance procedures that still remain for industrial undertakings.

It turns out, for instance, that there are 13 agencies which must be approached even today for clearance. Many of these permissions are, of course, necessary: some relate to polllution control, others to town planning and other reasonable requirements that have counterparts in most countries. The problem, however, is that because we do not have Single Window Clearance, each of the 13 clearances takes its own time. Besides, there is no effective time constraint on each agency's decision. Since time is money, it would surely make sense (as the CII Task Force recommends) to have Single Window Clearance by a designated authority which, in turn, ensures that the required 13 clearances are obtained within, say, 1.5 months. In Singapore, the Task Force notes, the Government grants clearance in less than two weeks.

2. State-level Restrictions

The delicensing is also at the central level and numerous restrictions continue at the state level. This again poses the question: since virtually any industrial plant must be physically located in a state, how can effective delicensing be achieved if state-level restrictions continue in place?

Of course, once central licensing is removed, states can no longer use political clout to have industries allocated by the licensing authorities to them. The allocation of industries among the states now comes about through competition among states. In consequence, states will now have an incentive to offer relief from the tyranny of their own restrictions to industrialists seeking to find the most favourable location of industry. We have been informed by industrialists that this is already beginning to happen. If so, the inefficient state-level restrictions will begin to disappear simply because the central licensing-cum-statewise-allocation system has been dismantled[30].

But this only represents a slow scenario and besides it works for large firms rather than for small firms without political access. There is thus room for accelerating the process through initiative by the central government to educate the state governments into simultaneous dismantling of state-level restrictions.

Equally, the central government should consider introducing "conditionality" in its allocation of revenues to the states: the level of such allocations could be made a function, not merely of "needs", but also of "rewards" for pursuit of designated policies such as delicensing that complement rather than frustrate the nation's economic reforms. This would be an extension of the principle that the Finance Commission and the Planning Commission already uses in rewarding the states for their resource mobilisation efforts. While this can only be a "medium-run" political process, it should be initiated at the earliest as its importance is undeniable.

3. Liberalising Imports

Imports have been largely liberalised, compared to pre-1991. But tariffs are still high and non-uniform and, in particular, a major qualification to the liberalization of the trade sector continues to be the extensive restrictions on consumer goods imports. Thus, the 1991 non-food consumer goods imports (at 1980-81 prices) were $650 million, of which $280 million were for personal baggage, $220 million for audio and visual equipment, $110 million for textiles and garments, and $40 million for sports goods, the total amounting to about 2.5% of the total imports. By contrast, in many developing countries with more liberal trade policies, the ratio of such imports to total imports ranges between 5 and 15%.

We believe that the hesitation in liberalizing consumer good imports is a hangover from earlier, fallacious modes of reasoning and that policy needs to be changed in this regard. We proceed to argue for such liberalization first by describing the current situation regarding import tariffs and quantitative restrictions on imports generally and on comsumer goods imports in particular, second by arguing at length why the arguments usually marshalled against consumer goods import liberalization are wrong, third by considering the way in which such reform should be undertaken.[31]

(a) The Current Situation Regarding All Imports:

QRs and Tariffs

The restraint on imports, once exchange controls are eased, is essentially defined by either quantitative restrictions (QRs) or by tariffs.

Currently, the imports of capital goods and of intermediates are mostly freed from exchange controls: in particular, the imports of capital goods worth up to Rs.2 crores were fully liberalised by last year, whereas the imports of intermediates have been liberalised (except for a few exceptions carried on the Negative List mentioned below) through the new ability to import them freely even if one is not an Actual User (though, foreign exchange for all imports can only be bought from authorised dealers which include the large commercial banks).

By contrast, the imports of consumer goods are severely constrained by QRs, coming principally under the so-called Negative List under our Import Policy. In essence, as the conventional usage goes, the list is Positive, in the sense that the Policy document specifies that, except for a few items altogether prohibited and a few others which are exempted, the imports of any consumer goods would require an import license.

Thus, on average, consumer goods imports are constrained by QRs whereas capital goods and intermediate good imports can be regarded as being constrained by tariffs.

Tariffs therefore have a predominantly revenue-generating effect, rather than a resource-allocational effect, in the consumer goods sector whereas they also have a significant resource-allocational effect in the capital and intermediate goods sectors. But if (as we argue below) consumer goods imports are liberalised as part of our next set of reforms, through the removal or enlargement of QRs, the consumer goods tariffs would become the binding, effective constraint on them as well. In that case, it becomes important to examine what the *tariff structure* is, since the resource-allocational effects of trade policy will then be determined by the tariff policy: and reform in tariffs, both in their structure and level, would acquire yet greater importance and urgency.

(i) *The Tariff Structure:* The tariff structure currently has a bias against consumer goods as does the QR policy structure, but in a much diminished fashion. Thus, if one looks at the available data, consumer goods have the highest range of duties whereas capital goods have the least.

But the range of duties can be misleading. The highest rates may apply to a few imports whereas the lowest rates may apply to many more. At minimum, we should look at the average duty rates calculated as a simple average. Preferably, we should look at import-weighted averages (though, even that has the problem that high duty rates lead to low imports and hence we would understate the restrictiveness of duties by using import weights). If we then look at the averages of the duties levied, what do we find?

Drawing on the Chelliah Committee's calculations, we can broadly infer that, in 1990, the consumer goods imports carried import duties that were at least as high as those on capital goods whereas the manufactured intermediate goods imports were taxed at lower rates. This is evident from Table 1 which shows that, in 1989-90, the import-weighted average duties on manufactured consumer goods were almost the same as on manufactured capital goods and lower than on intermediate manufactures. But if the non-manufactured intermediates, which must be the main component of the other groups such as Agricultural Products and Mineral Products are taken into account, the average duty on intermediates must surely lie below that of the consumer and capital goods imports. However, other estimates suggest that by the end of 1992, consumer goods did have the highest import-weighted average duty at 86%, with 69% for intermediates in general, and capital goods at below 55%. This trend towards reducing the capital goods tariffs and thus leaving consumer goods with the highest tariffs was continued in the 1993 budget.

For instance, the Finance Minister brought the duty on project imports and general machinery imports down yet further to 35%. Import duty in projects in priority sectors such as coal-mining and petroleum refining were brought down yet further to 25%, and in power projects to 20%. On machine tools, duties had varied between 60 and 110% but were reduced now to three rates: 40, 60 and 80%. Some of the duty reductions were extended simultaneously to intermediates used in the production of such capital goods in India so as to prevent adverse effects on their production from higher duties on their inputs than on their outputs. On the average, therefore, the consumer goods imports wound up carrying broadly higher rates than capital goods and intermediate imports.

Economists also distinguish between "nominal" protection, i.e. protection by item or commodity, and "effective" protection, i.e. protection to a process of production or to "value added" in an activity. The latter, effective rate of protection (ERP) is a better index of resource-allocational pulls created by the tariff structure and hence also to the actual such effects provided, of course, that these effects are allowed to operate and are not frustrated by an industrial licensing system that restricts and guides investments.

In general, one can argue that lower rates on capital goods and intermediates than on final goods would imply that the ERPs would be even higher than the nominal tariffs. Since the average official tariff rates on consumer and capital goods are roughly similar (see Table 1) and on intermediates are mildly below for manufactures and significantly below for other goods such as metals and agro-products, the net effect of the nominal tariff structure would appear to be to yield ERPs that should mildly exceed the nominal tariffs in most cases. The Chelliah Committee's calculations confirm this outcome (see Table 2) for nearly all major groups of imports.[32]

Table 1:
Average Tariff Rates for Broad Commodity Groups

Group	Weight (import based)	1989-90 Import	
		Simple Average	Weighted average
Agricultural prod.	0.03	99	46
Coal, crude oil, and natural gas	0.16	82	54
Other mineral prod.	0.03	98	20
Manufactured prod.	0.78	123	98
Of which-			
Consumer goods	0.87	138	89
Intermediate goods	0.47	125	103
Capital goods	0.24	94	91
Aggregate	1.00	121	87

Source: Chelliah Committee's Interim Report, op. cit., Table 8.2

Other aspects of the tariff structure also need to be noted before we discuss the question of liberalization of consumer goods and of the general trade policy reform within which that liberalization must be set:

(ii) *Revenue Collection:* The duty rates, discussed above, are not the same as the effective duty rates implied by actual revenue collections. This is because there are many exemptions from the duty rates, depending frequently on the user (e.g. drawbacks are granted to exporters)[33], and because the high tariff rates as in India lead to significant self-serving reclassification of imports, with suitable incentives provided to the customs authorities by the importers, such that these exemptions become applicable, pulling the average duty collected within a class of imports down to the below-mean levels.[34]

Table 2:

Nominal and Effective Rates of Protection Based on Simple Averages and Import-Weighted Averages in 1989-90 According to Major Groups.

Major Groups	Simple averages		Import-weighted avg.	
	NRP	NRP	NRP	NRP
Agro-based				
Mean	134	161	131	160
Standard dev.	26	65	49	91
Weighted avg.*	134	160	133	160
Chemicals				
Mean	117	120	115	131
Standard dev.	49	79	48	74
Weighted avg.*	105	101	104	114
Metals				
Mean	131	143	123	136
Standard dev.	16	32	26	50
Weighted avg.*	128	132	126	136
Machinery				
Mean	103	87	98	84
Standard dev.	25	42	29	47
Weighted avg.*	100	82	97	82
Manufacturing				
Mean	119	125	109	115
Standard dev.	33	63	50	88
Weighted avg.*	121	130	113	113

Note :   *Value-added weights.

Source: Chelliah Committee's *Interim Report, op. cit.,* page 184, Table IV.2.

In India, as elsewhere, therefore, there is a discrepancy between the official duty rates and the collection rates. Thus, the Chelliah Committee has estimated that: "In 1980-81, the import-weighted average rate of nominal tariff (with quantifiable exemptions) was 38 per cent. In 1989-90, it rose to 87 per cent. The collection rate of duty increased in this period from about 20 per cent to about 44 per cent."[35]

An added point needs to be made. It is most likely that, as evidenced in other countries, this discrepancy between the legal duty and that implied by the revenues collected, rises with the duty charged. In short, the exemptions tend to increase de jure and also to be increasingly exploited de facto, the greater the incentive to do so that is provided by higher duties. As for the actual revenues collected, they tend to fall additionally because of increased evasion through smuggling and through underinvoicing, both of which mean that the duty fails to apply to the true level of imports.

Studies of other developing countries' duty collections show conclusively what we can guess at from our own anecdotal evidence, that the revenues do not rise proportionately to the duty rates. Thus, a fine study of the problem by the economists Pritchet and Sethi calculates that[36] : "The mean collected rate in Pakistan for items with 60% tariff is 40%. For items with 80% tariff the collected rate increases only to 51% and then is roughly the same 52% and 54% for items with official rates of 100 and 125 percent. In Kenya, the mean collection rate decreases from 43% at 60% official to 31% at 80% and 36% at 100%." Their estimated equation regressing the collection rate on the official rate of duty shows that: "An increase of ten percentage points of the official rates produces an increase of only 3.3 percentage points in the collected rate for Pakistan, 4.9 percentage points for Kenya and roughly 4.7% for Jamaica."

Since our average tariff rate is very high , and this is yet more so for consumer goods imports, it is important to remember therefore that the impact of substantial liberalisation of consumer goods imports along with the rest of our imports, via tariff reductions, will not necessarily have large adverse effects on our revenue position. With QRs liberalised and tariffs coming down from what would be highly-restrictive levels, we may expect the volume response to liberalisation to be large. Further steps by the government to reduce the average tariff level are therefore not to be feared because of their revenue implications.

(iii) *The Tariff Structure: Multiplicity of Rates:* Yet another aspect of the tariff structure must be considered since it is in necessity of bold reform as much as the liberalisation of consumer goods imports. The tariff structure is characterised by a multiplicity of rates. There are currently more than 20 ad valorem tariff rates and numerous specific tariffs as well.

In theory, non-uniform tariff rates can be justified on several grounds, including distributional objectives that cannot be met in more efficient ways and on efficiency grounds such as when different commodities enjoy different degrees of market power in world markets. In reality, there is little correspondence between such reasons and the actual policy choices as revealed in the tariffs in place.[37] The multiplicity of rates also implies that protectionist lobbies find it easier to lobby for tariffs whereas, if uniformity was adopted as a policy, it would become relatively unprofitable to lobby for one's tariff because of two reasons: the government could always argue that a specific demand for higher tariff could not be met because it would involve raising all other tariffs which the government cannot do; and the lobby's advantage from getting the higher rate, thanks to its own lobbying (which costs money), would be reduced since other tariffs, including of its inputs, would rise equally.[38]

The recommendations of the Chelliah committee now, and of the Alexander Committee and the Long Term Fiscal Policy document earlier in the mid-1980s, to simplify the tariff structure are therefore both sensible and in need of implementation at the earliest. However, they do not go far enough, in accepting the notions that "universal intermediates [should] be subject to a duty rate less than that for raw materials and other intermediate goods", that these, in turn, should have a rate "lower than that for capital goods", that "non-essential" consumer goods should carry the "highest duty rate", in the end there being a five-tier duty structure.[39]

We see little logic for these distinctions that would permit differential rates by broad groups so defined. For instance, reducing the input duties while maintaining the output duties on "nonessential" consumer goods would only increase the effective protection for such consumer goods, drawing resources towards their production, especially when industrial licensing has been effectively removed as a regulating device. It is more sensible, if the consumption of certain luxuries is to be curtailed, that this be done by taxing them, regardless of whether they are imported or home-produced, rather than by taxing only their imports and therewith creating an added incentive to produce them at home.

While the 1993 budget took several commendable steps towards reducing the rate structure, several were necessarily *ad hoc*, reflecting the production needs of domestic industry. It is time to look at the entire tariff structure in totality and to bring substantial uniformity into it, now that the Finance Minister has already made the idea of tariff rate simplification familiar to the public.

(b) Why Consumer Goods Ought also to be Liberalised?

The question of liberalisation of consumer goods imports (consistent, of course, with taxes on the consumption of luxuries and of "bads" through what are popularly called "sin taxes") is a particularly difficult one in India for several reasons. These reasons consist of misconceptions, fears, and lack of appreciation of the positive benefits to be derived from such liberalisation. Since they define politically powerful objections to completion of the trade policy reforms by extending the reforms to consumer goods, and they should evidently be confronted and contained, we consider these reasons now in some depth, warning the reader that the added space devoted by us in consequence to liberalisation of consumer goods imports, relative to the space allotted to other elements of reform, is no indication of the relative urgency and importance of these different reforms.

(i) *Misconceptions:* The misconceptions are longstanding on the Indian scene.

Two are particularly potent:

First, a common fallacy is that the removal of consumer goods import restrictions will lower the savings rate. But, in general, the effect will be to shift the consumption to other types of consumer goods, domestically-produced tradeables and nontraded goods.

Second, it is feared that consumer goods imports will increase the availability of luxuries. But this is wrong on several counts:

* "Luxuries" are a nebulous concept under whose rubric lie goods that reflect the cultural mores prevalent at any point of time in a society. Yet, the concept has been used in practice in India by bureaucrats in charge of licensing to categorise goods which, for one reason or another (whether their own preferences and prejudice), they would like to exclude from the consumption basket. Thus, in the 1950s and 1960s, cosmetics, refrigerators, airconditioners, cars and consumer electronics fell into this category. Today, with the growth of the middle class to over 100 million, it is hard to think of "luxuries" in the same way; most of these goods are now part of widespread consumption.

* Again, we must admit that some of these goods also have productive aspects. Electronic goods such as personal computers for instance are useable for fun and games, but are also clearly producer goods in the home. Our conventional tendency during nearly four decades of planning to look wholly upon such goods as "nonessential" or "luxuries" disregards the dual (consumption and investment) aspects of many such goods today, falsely forcing us into restrictive policies that can be harmful to productivity and to a growth-oriented modernisation of the economy.

* Moreover, if "luxury" imports of traded goods are curbed, and there are import-competing products available from domestic production, then the effect of such import curbs will be largely to substitute domestically produced "luxuries" for imported ones: e.g. Marutis replacing Hondas and Volkswagens. The objective of restraining luxury consumption will not have been served by such an import policy.[40] The correct policy to restrain consumption of any good or "bad" (e.g. heroin) is to tax it, regardless of whether the item is imported or domestically produced.

* If the demand shifts from restricted imports of luxuries to nontradeables, the results are likely to be deleterious in our context. Suppose, as is likely, that demand shifts to expenditures on housing, a nontradeable. This is likely to be conspicuous consumption, perhaps making the task of managing the politics of inequality more unmanageable. Moreover, an increase in demand for nontradeables such as housing will raise their prices, because the elasticity of supply is likely to be much lower than that of world tradeables, both feeding inflationary wage demands and also impacting adversely on the real incomes of the middle class.

(ii) *Fears:* Then, there are fears that the liberalization of consumer goods imports will harm the economy by reducing the governmental revenues, and by creating a balance of payments crisis.

(i) We have already indicated above that the fear of a substantial loss of revenue from such liberalization is exaggerated and that the problem is manageable. To recapitulate more cogently, a change in the trade policy to liberalise consumer goods imports would mean liberalising the QRs which are currently the real restraint on such imports. This itself, at the current high tariff rates, would generate added revenue, not diminish it.

But any added liberalization which effectively requires tariff cuts will also likely meet with a significant response for reasons suggested above. In fact, it seems very reasonable to argue that revenues may even rise in view of the extremely high tariffs now. Thus, in Figure 3, which is the so-called Laffer curve, the horizontal axis measures the average tariff rate and the vertical axis measures revenues collected. When the tariff rates are prohibitive, nothing gets imported, and there is no revenue. When the rates are zero, no revenue gets raised either. So, the curve meets the horizontal axis at the origin and at the high tariff that eliminates imports. In between, it rises and must fall. Assuming only a single peak, we can then plausibly assume that we are to the right of this peak and will therefore increase tariff revenues by liberalising consumer goods imports with QR expansions and tariff reductions.

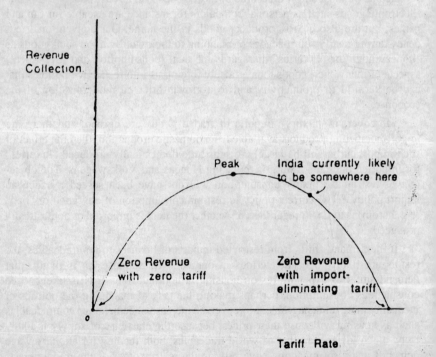

Figure 3: Tariff Rates and Revenue Collection

(ii) There is also the "macroeconomic" worry that liberalising consumer goods imports (and indeed other imports too) will create a balance of payments crisis because imports will then increase greatly owing to speculation, on the self-fulfilling assumption that the import liberalisation cannot be sustained and will be reversed. But there is little reason to believe that a balance of payments crisis should develop, given the prudence with which the government has proceeded in fact to reduce the budget deficit and to exercise monetary restraint. The substantial reduction in the real exchange rate since the reforms started has also made less credible the scenario that significant further depreciation will take place in the shortrun, a scenario which can (if credible) precipitate outflows and a crisis.

(iii) *Positive Arguments:* We should also stress several "positive" arguments which make the liberalisation of consumer goods imports desirable:

* The protection of consumer goods production is as harmful, from an efficiency viewpoint, as the protection of any other kind of production: it diverts resources to inefficient production. It would be desirable for any particular production only if economists could convincingly argue that there are uncompensated, beneficial spillover effects that this particular production generates, and these too more significantly than other production from which resources will be diverted. It is hard to imagine that case being successfully made for the bulk of consumer goods production as a class.

* Then there is the usual loss to consumers from the higher prices of consumer goods that protection implies. Modern economic theory shows how this loss arises also in the form of reduced variety of goods that are available in the economy.

* The lack of such quality and variety in imports also, in turn, leads to the loss of quality upgrading that international competition provides and which is necessary eventually for successful and sustained export of manufactures.

(c) How Consumer Goods Imports Should be Liberalised?

Essentially, since both QRs and tariffs are involved, and since QRs are generally the effective restraint on imports of consumer goods, the liberalisation of these imports must first involve the moderation or removal of the QRs and, second, as soon as tariffs begin to bite, the progressive reduction of the generally high tariffs as well.

The liberalisation of consumer goods therefore can proceed in alternative ways that involve different ways of dismantling QRs and of lowering tariff barriers, and different sequences in which these two may be combined. The important issue relates however to the choice of the methods by which QRs will be dismantled. The experience of other countries that have liberalised imports in the past suggests several ways in which QRs on consumer goods imports could be liberalised in India now:

(i) *Outright Abolition of QRs:* As in Greece (1953-55) and in Chile which abolished QRs within a year, we could simply "light a bonfire" of the QRs on consumer goods imports. This is certainly an idea worth considering since the existing tariffs are so high that our import-competing consumer goods industries will remain well protected anyway, with the impact of the QR abolition limited in consequence.

The further and truly difficult bite would come rather when we begin lowering the tariffs thereafter: this tariff reduction can be gradual, in a preannounced step-by-step programme. In addition, the depreciation of the real exchange rate has already made our tradeable goods internationally more competitive than prior to the reforms, and so has the reduction of the duties introduced in the last budget on imports of intermediates and capital goods.

If we put institutional machinery in place then (as proposed in subsection 4 below) to handle market-disruption complaints and to adopt temporary "safe-guards", as do many countries (e.g. Section 201 of the US trade law), we should have no problem with the adoption of such a policy. And we could substitute, in case of goods whose consumption we badly want to restrain, consumption taxes that do not discriminate against imports in favour of domestic production.

We would therefore recommend this option of outright abolition of the QRs on consumer goods imports, with the institutional safeguards and policy changes indicated, for the government to adopt at the earliest. But if gradualist solutions are desired from excessive caution, whether political or economic, then other solutions can be considered.

(ii) *Radial Expansion of QRs:* Imports could, for instance, be expanded, from an initial quantity established in case of altogether-prohibited imports as a small fraction of existing domestic production if any, at a certain rate annually. This method, which has the advantage of simplicity but has little economic rationale, was adopted by the European Community. As recorded by the economist Wendy Tackacs, the EC having aggregated all the bilateral QRs of the members into a total QR, for a commodity, the total quota was increased by no less than 10%, and quotas for items without any existing imports, the initial 1959 quota were set so as not to fall below 3% of domestic EC production at the time.

If such a scheme were adopted in preference to the scheme for outright abolition of QRs, the expanding QRs would have to be allocated to importers. Since they carry a premium which will continue in many cases, and for some time, the question will arise: who should get the benefit of obtaining the QR licenses? The obvious answer is: auction off the QRs so that the government earns the premium, this amounting of course to added revenue for the government at a time of macroeconomic pressure to reduce the budget deficit.

(iii) *Selective Reform:* On the other hand, the expansion of quotas, or even their abolition, could be done selectively by sectors or groups of commodities, as was done in South Korea between 1978 and 1988 by expanding the coverage of items on the automatic list of approval steadily from 53.8% to 95.2%.

It is hard to imagine, however, that this is a desirable method since a great deal of hassle and political bargaining would go into the choice of the sectors whose head would go on the block earlier rather than later.

(iv) *Tariffication:* In lieu of a simple abolition of QRs, a more cautious policy that is used sometimes is to seek to convert them into equivalent tariffs. This has, for instance, been suggested for Japanese rice quotas at the Uruguay Round of multilateral trade negotiations. It is also the method used variously by many liberalising countries: e.g. Israel, Ghana, the Philippines and Spain. Tariffication does not, of course, reduce the protection that the earlier QRs provided: the protection might, in some cases, even increase though that is not intended.[41] The only advantage is that the tariffication makes the protective effect more transparent and that, insofar as the implied tariffs are usually excessively high, this transparency assists the cause of those who want to reduce the protection being provided.

If this course of action is followed, the QRs would indeed be abolished outright and they would be replaced by added tariffs which would then define a higher set of tariffs from which to begin the task of reducing tariffs. This may lead to problems with the GATT where some of our tariffs are bound. But there is little doubt that if QRs, which are the effective constraint, were being converted to tariffs, no Contracting Party at the GATT is likely to act perversely and to object to our tariffication.

In practice, there are numerous variations on how QRs might be mitigated or removed. The only serious alternative which might be considered appealing is to build on current practice by using the fact that the government has already eased up a little on consumer goods imports by introducing in October 1992 the Special Import Licenses, SILs, which permit a small single-digit fraction of the export earnings by certain classes of exporters to be used to import consumer goods on the Positive List of restricted consumer goods imports. Since these imports fetch premia, though the premia have not always been large because of the high tariffs that must be paid, these schemes (like many Export Bonus Voucher and Exchange Retention schemes of yesteryear and even now in other developing countries) utilise the scarcity premium on consumer goods imports to subsidise exports. This tie-up between what are, for the erroneous reasons analysed above, considered to be undersirable imports and the desirable objective of promoting exports may ease the politics of liberalising consumer goods imports by steadily increasing the fraction of foreign earnings to be so utilised and by increasing also the number of consumer goods eligible for such imports. But this is a small gain in our view.

A cleaner and deeper surgical strike on consumer goods import restrictions would be our preference. It would also imply that the "bias against exports" that such restrictions inevitably provide would be reduced simultaneously (continuing then only insofar as tariffs provide them), though the expansion-of-the-SILs approach would provide an added export incentive. But such an added incentive would, in the nature of the case, be unstable, varying with the premium and the rates of retention provided. We doubt that this would provide the sustained incentive to make the investment and marketing decisions to enter foreign markets on a longrun basis.

Beyond QR-removal to Tariff Reduction: Once the QRs are virtually removed, and tariffs become the relevant restraints, the government needs to proceed quickly to simplification of the tariff structure and to step-by-step reduction of the tariff level as well. We can proceed simultaneously to binding the tariffs at the GATT and making significant tariff concessions at the Uruguay Round itself this year so as to take credit for such tariff changes in the game of reciprocal concessions and thereby earning some concessions in return for doing what is good for us anyway.[42]

4. Institutional Changes to Accompany Trade Liberalisation

As we liberalise trade policy, freeing imports of all types of goods, making international competition an increasing reality on the Indian scene, we also need to make institutional changes to accompany and support the new regime.

(a) *Anti-dumping:* While antidumping institutions and practices are nowadays being misused for protectionist purposes in the EC and in the United States, the underlying notion that predation needs to be avoided for free trade to assure mutual gain for the trading nations is not without merit. As we enter freer trade, we must therefore create the necessary antidumping procedures and institutions to implement them.

But we should also learn from the grossly abusive practices of the United States and of the EC to devise procedures which will truly assure fair trade instead of being captured by protectionists for their own use. In doing this, we must remember of course that it is difficult for the government to set standards which others do not care to observe. But we must remember that our protection hurts us as it hurts others, and that the use of antidumping actions fairly is as much in our interest as in that of our trading rivals.

Since, however, it is difficult to adhere to higher standards than others do when our industry complains, it is important that we also work energetically, joining forces with other developing countries such as Singapore and Hong Kong and with Japan, to oppose the weakening of the antidumping discipline at the Uruguay Round that is sought currently by countries capitulating to their protectionist lobbies.

(b) *"Safeguard" Actions:* Like other countries with freer trade, we will also have to handle the market-disruption problems that can arise when imports are freed from restraints. Procedures and institutions again will have to be put in place, taking international experience into account, so that complaints concerning injury from "import surges" (as they are called in the new context of negotiations for the North American Free Trade Area where the US fears market disruption to its industries from rapidly expanding Mexican exports) are investigated and determined upon, and relief offered in a way that does not lead to interminable or discriminatory protection.

Towards these ends, we will need to re-examine and redefine the role of institutions such as the Tariff Commission whose role was earlier circumscribed to merely calculating the protection needed to protect an industry from competition rather than judging whether such protection was justified in light of some objective criteria!

B. Direct Foreign Investment

The question of direct foreign investment (DFI) is related to the question of trade and industrial policy, reforms in one suggesting and even requiring reforms in the other.

Thus, for instance, inward oriented trade policies lead to DFI which is aimed at the domestic market whereas outward oriented trade policies encourage DFI which seeks global markets. The former then leads to inefficiencies which are similar to those that afflict domestic investments: small scale, lack of effective competition, and bias against exports, whereas the latter leads to efficiencies which are similar to those that accrue to the domestic investments and firms in these economies. Thus, as we have been forced to do in the past, under inward oriented trade policies the DFI policy is geared to *forcing* the foreign firms to export as a *precondition* for investing in India, since the incentives work against producing in India for export markets. Once the bias against exports is eliminated, we then do not need to produce these artificial inducements to offset the adverse anti-export disincentives of our own making. Thus, these "export performance requirements" which have contributed to the relative unattractiveness of India as a host country for DFI can be eliminated now that we are turning rapidly to an outward oriented set of trade and industrial policies.[45]

Indeed, the outward orientation of our trade and industrial policies, belated as it is, should also help us to attract more DFI since DFI is not merely less productive in an inward oriented policy framework but also because the flows of DFI are likely to be limited when only aimed at the domestic market and hence coterminus with the size and growth of that market. On the other hand, outward oriented economies attracting DFI aimed at global markets have the world for their market.[46]

Our DFI policy, embodied in the FERA Act of 1975 but in making before that time, was itself dictated by the view, widely prevalent at the time, that regarded DFI as capable of malign impact on the economy. Indeed, policy inclined to the view that this possibility was also probable and that extensive regulation was the only way to tame DFI into a benign influx. This was part of the general revisionism which argued with the conventional view that the world economy, and integration into it, would be to mutual advantage of the developing and the developed countries. It argued forcefully instead that the interaction could be malign, the effect being to create predation, not gain, for the weaker countries of the South. If unchecked and unregulated, DFI would inhibit the growth of domestic entrepreneurship; it would stifle the growth of domestic technology; it would create balance of payments difficulties, contributing to the natural proclivity of DFI to result in a loss of political and economic independence.

Needless to say, specific instances can be cited that would illustrate each of these concerns. Indeed, flagrant use of political muscle by foreign multinationals in their host countries was manifest in the overthrow of President Allende in Chile and in the downfall of Mr. Lumumba in the Belgian Congo (though, the factors that led to these political events were quite complex and domestic disaffection produced by unsustainable policies cannot be underestimated).

But several observations must be made. First, the accumulation of evidence in the postwar period shows that the malign-impact scenarios have not proven to be the dominant experience with DFI in the developing countries. DFI has been mainly associated, for instance, with substantial technology diffusion, with dissemination of better management practices, with increased competition that has stimulated local firms into producing higher-quality products that facilitate entry into export markets, and with substantial contributions of its own to the host country's export performance.[47] Where DFI has failed to achieve these beneficial effects in a substantial way is precisely where the policy framework has tended to restrict and regulate with a view to inhibiting these effects from arising.

Second, for India itself, our longstanding policy of inhibiting DFI has been associated with a general decline in the technological capability of our industry on average[48], though that failure is attributable to the whole complex of policies that must include also the licensing framework that, by severely restricting the ability to diversify output and to invest, made the entrepreneurial absorption (and invention) of new technology a relatively unremunerative activity. Indeed, studies of the technological backwardness of the former Soviet Union, now abundantly in evidence, had long argued that similar restrictions on production and investment, endemic to the communist scene but reproduced ingeniously in ours by the policy framework we now seek to discard, had inevitably led to this astonishingly bad outcome. [49]

Third, while we are moving in that direction through successive measures of liberalisation, it is important to clear away the debris left by the old-fashioned thinking (endemic in trade policy as well, as we have just seen) that somehow consumer goods are not an appropriate area for DFI inflows. Producing consumer goods efficiently "saves foreign exchange" as much as producing other goods that are equally efficiently produced. The successful export performance in manufactures by Japan and other Far Eastern economies was led at the outset by light consumer goods whose production had not been hampered by restrictions on absorption of technology, on production levels, on investment and on product diversification. It is noteworthy that Toyota and Hindustan Motors started production of cars in the same year, and witness the contrast today! Is there any doubt that, allowed to expand freely and with export disincentives absent, the Birlas could not have done what the Toyodas did? To have restrictions on DFI in consumer goods per se, no matter what they are, is to commit the fallacy of characterising commodities as "good" or "bad", depending only on their role as consumer or other goods. We recommend therefore that these ways of restricting DFI be done away with.

This policy decision would be compatible with giving *positive* incentives for DFI in areas where, for say security or other demonstrated reasons for prioritising the investment, we seek immediate DFI which would otherwise not be forthcoming.

Fourth, since attracting DFI has now become a policy adopted worldwide, by the developing countries of Latin America, the "newly exporting countries" (NECs) of Asia, the former Soviet Union, Eastern Europe and China — not to mention the same game being played by the EC and the United States as well vis-a-vis each other —, the restrictions on the sectors where DFI can flow in India, especially ones that have no rationale, are likely to hurt our competitive efforts at getting the DFI flows up. More than even before, the competition for DFI has become a very difficult one today.

Fifth, it is in this light also that we ought to consider modifying our opposition to the proposed intellectual property rules at the GATT under the Uruguay Round. Yes, the theoretical classroom case on our side is strong. But the reality is that such protection has now become identified in the multinational circles and lobbies with whether a developing country is serious about attracting foreign investment. Mexico, recognising this reality, has thrown in the sponge, accepting extremely stringent intellectual property protection rules so as to win US consent on the NAFTA accord and therewith to attract DFI. Making a shrewd cost-benefit calculation, we need to do more or less the same linking this explicitly to policy statements and public relations efforts to advertise our determination to attract DFI.

Sixth, the continuation in place of FERA and COFEPOSA, with the machinery for control and many controls still present, remains a standing reminder to foreign investors of the ambivalence that continues in regard to DFI in India. If these cannot be removed, with the exception of regulations that simply require attendance to our necessary legislation regarding environment, for instance, (legislation which most nations have or ought to), the least we can do is to minimise the bureuacratic hurdles by reducing the large number of permissions and clearances to be still sought to a quick-acting, single-stop clearance system.

Seventh, as we discuss in detail in Section V, we need to examine forthwith the options before us in light of the ongoing regionalisation of the world economy, so as to access (through Association agreements or membership) the trade blocs already formed and likely to form. Such access gives the developing countries which enjoy it the ability to divert DFI away from developing countries that do not have such access. We cannot afford to sit idly by while this happens.

C. Public Sector Enterprises: Privatisation and Competition

Among the major reforms still awaiting a forceful solution is the reform of India's immense, and immensely inefficient, sector comprising enterprises engaged in "productive" activity. It would be tedious to repeat here the well known facts concerning these enterprises. We concentrate therefore on the remedies.

The problem has arisen in two different ways:

* Under SICA, the government has traditionally acquired several "sick" units, thus avoiding the bankruptcy of failing enterprises and ironically extending to private enterprises the disincentives that operate on public enterprises!

* For public enterprises started as such, the inefficiencies and the losses met by subsidies have been the major problems.

In principle, the former policy can simply be stopped and the bankruptcy laws, duly reformed, can be applied to any new enterprises that are failing the market test so that no new enterprises are taken on as sick units. [In practice, whether this can be credibly done depends on whether the government is seen to have the determination to withstand political pressures to take over such units so as to protect the jobs of their workers. This credibility will increase with the establishment of the new institutions such as the National Renewal Fund which ease the exit of workers from failing units.]

We should also insist, in light of the experience we have had with the working of the public sector enterprises in the last four decades, on fully renouncing the creation of any new public sector enterprises in areas where the private sector will invest and where "security" considerations do not require governmental ownership. It is not enough to "dereserve" the sectors held exclusively for the public sector (reduced from 17 to 8 in 1991, with the possibility of case-by-case exceptions); instead, the presumption now should be universally in favour of the private sector.

When it comes to enterprises already under governmental ownership and care, there are of course several options which the government has already been considering and, in some cases, even adopting.The central policy in this regard was laid down well in the Industrial Policy Statement of 24th July 1991 where a number of different approaches were distinguished. While the government has pursued several of them, and we believe that governmental policy so as to achieve management efficiency in the public sector enterprises is finally on track and should be steadily acquiring the necessary momentum, we consider here the broad dimensions of different policy options and their desirability.

1. Privatisation

Two main approaches need to be distinguished: sale of fractional equity in the public sector enterprise to private parties, while retaining controlling ownership and management in the pubic sector and true privatisation that transfers control and management to the private sector (though some governmental equity holding, without managerial intervention, may continue).

(a) A main thrust of the early privatisation efforts was to disinvest in public enterprise shares. But, instead of considering the matter to be one of genuine conversion of the public sector enterprises to private sector ownership and management, as should have been the objective of policy, the programme offered only fractions of total equity in the chosen enterprises to the private sector.

Unless there was a "signalling" effect that further and fuller privatisation was in the works and therfore the management had better shape up or be prepared to ship out — a signal we suspect, was not being conveyed —, the programme offered only a marginal stake in public sector enterprises to the private sector without any efficiency implications.

The best defense that one might make of this policy was that the government may have been moving cautiously in the matter of genuine fullscale privatisation because of the complexity of the matter in view of the fact that the public sector had become a sacred cow in the political arena and partly perhaps because it wanted to gain some experience with disinvestment on a limited scale before moving full speed ahead in a more substantive way. It is perhaps more likely that the government found virtue in the fact that the sales proceeds could be used as revenues targeted at reducing the budget deficit as required by both necessity and by broad conditionality. In that case, the policy raised the further question (discussed in Section III. 1. (d)) as to whether such use of the sales proceeds may not have meant that the necessary effort at raising revenue or cutting expenditure was not compromised.

As is wellknown, the policy involving disinvestment upto only 25% of equity in 30 profitmaking enterprises was made in three successive sales: December 1991, February 1992 and October 1992.[50] The method used in the first two sales was to offer "packets" containing shares of the enterprises for sale only to financial institutions, banks and mutual funds, in a bidding process with reservation prices, and with the restriction that the bundles could not be unbundled and the shares traded individually until 3-6 months. In the third sale, there were important changes: packets were absent and the auctions were open to bids by private individuals. In short, the process of disinvestment was already being changed in a more efficient direction, in light of both experience and criticism.

The realization of proceeds from these sales exceeded anticipations in the first two sales, however, while falling under in the third (despite the unbundling and the opening of the bidding process to private parties). The question that created controversy, therefore, is whether the procedures chosen to disinvest led to underpricing of the sales price of the equity and hence to an unintended transfer of wealth to the buyers. Drawing on British experience, studied by the economists Vickers and Yarrow[51], adapting their methods of analysis to the Indian situation as necessary, and analysing the behaviour of share prices when traded alongside the methods of the sales used by the government, the economist Rajendra Vaidya has concluded that the listing of shares prior to sale and the underwriting of shares are two ways in which the underpricing of the equity being sold can be avoided. Doubtless, these lessons have been drawn by the government as well now.

(ii) But the main option, from the viewpoint of efficient management, has to be privatisation that transfers control and management to the erstwhile public sector enterprises. Sale of fractional equity to the private sector in enterprises that continue to be essentially owned and managed by the public sector cannot address the efficiency question meaningfully. The government is moving, quite properly, in this direction with the active exploration currently of the restructuring of Hindustan Machine Tools Limited, Bharat Bhari Udyog Nigam Limited, and Bharat Yantra Nigam Limited, preliminary to promoting their eventual privatisation. We endorse these moves and only make three observations.

First, the idea of restructuring before privatisation is desirable simply because it would, by exploiting any efficiencies that can be implemented, improve the proceeds that the government can secure from privatisation. On the other hand, the best restructuring may materialise from the actions of the private investors who would have the incentive to restructure in order to improve the returns from the enterprises they have bought.[52]

Second, the restructuring that would be truly useful prior to privatisation has to be the change of labour laws and the creation of institutions to ease the adjustment problems of labour when retrenched, the freeing of restrictions on price-policy and of other restraints on efficient functioning, and the like. These changes would enhance the ability of the private investors to make improvements in management and efficiency, which would enable them to earn more in the marketplace and hence to offer better terms to the government for the enterprises they are buying. These changes would have a beneficial impact on the working of not merely the public sector enterprises to be privatised but indeed for all economic activity in every sector.

We, therefore, support the establishment of the National Renewal Fund, though it has limited funds, as it will ease somewhat the adjustment problems associated with retrenching labour as restructuring proceeds in the public sector (as also for retraining, placement services etc. for labour being displaced in the organised sector). We urge however that we learn from the experience of the developed countries such as the United States where the Adjustment Assistance schemes (introduced in the context of trade liberalisation) effectively turned into instruments for financially supporting labour and enabling it to stay on in sectors that ought to be winding down when the true objective was to get the labour to retrain and get out more quickly from these sectors.

Third, the sale of lossmaking enterprises without any attempts at possible restructuring could lead to their being taken over at prices that reflect a decision by the private investor simply to dismantle them for what they are worth in their component assets, provided that this is politically and legally feasible. In that case, however, there could be serious adjustment problems for infrastructure-supplying sectors: the closure of an inefficient airline when others more efficient are not in a position to fill the gap in the service, for instance, may lead to immediate dislocations that could be quite damaging to the privatisation effort.

2. Competition

From this perspective, it is important to understand that the introduction of effective competition for the existing public sector enterprises would be valuable in itself so that, where it is particularly successful in turning a public sector enterprise into a highly-efficient undertaking, it may even justify a decision at times not to privatise (since the essential aim of the reforms must be to improve the efficiency of operation and management, not a shift to private sector ownership per se). But in other cases also, as the privatisation proceeds, the introduction of efficiency-prompting competition can only help the government to realise better returns from the privatisation if the enterprises are in better operational shape.

The Indian Public already knows what the effect of allowing the introduction of private airlines, however modest, has been on the Indian Airlines: the sheer ability to compare the two sectors has put some pressure on the IAC, though much more awaits being done. Similarly, the effect of letting in CNN and BBC, for example, and destroying the erstwhile monopoly of Doordarshan has permitted the viewers to vote with their feet, or rather with their remote controls, and is forcing changes in the latter.

The dismantling of industrial licensing, the ability of the private sector to invest in areas reserved for the public sector: these policies have changed. But the government needs to ensure that these changes are truly effective instead of becoming frustrated by continuing administrative obstacles (as noted by us earlier in this Report in regard to industrial delicensing, for example). Furthermore, the entry of the private sector requires also that the ability to deter entry be carefully examined: thus for example, in power generation, access to the electricity grid has to be effective for entry to occur. Then again, price controls may render profitable operation impossible, deterring entry into a sector that is technically open to entry now.

The government also needs to make clear that the existing public sector enterprises will not automatically be subsidised out of their losses into continuing operation.[53] The combination of such a clear policy, of what economists now call "hard budget constraints" with truly effective dismantling of barriers to private entry, would mean a pincer-movement type of attack on public sector inefficiency: the entry of better-managed and efficient private competition would put pressure on the public sector enterprises and that pressure would then translate, in the presence of hard budget constraints, into the option to perform or to fail into bankruptcy.

While the government, thanks to the macroeconomic measures which we have reviewed, is currently wedded to dismantling subsidies and will introduce a measure of hard budget constraints, we suspect that the continued easing of the macroeconomic crisis could lead to a weakening of the political ability to stay the course. Hence, our preference is to go ahead with privatisation plans, preparing to shed most of the public sector enterprises from the custody of the government even as we implement speedily the institutional changes (such as the National Renewal Fund) that would make competition an increasing reality in much of the public sector.

We also suspect that, since many public sector enterprises impinge directly on the consumers, the demand for privatisation and for competition regardless is currently ahead of the supply, and that the hesitation of the government to proceed more expeditiously with the task reflects excessive caution. We know that the demand for serious reforms in delicensing was undercut because the elites who made policy were insulated from the effects of bad policy by being able to jump ahead of the queue. But, this is not always true for infrastructure-supplying public sector enterprises that impinge on all. Thus, when IAC service breaks down, it affects indiscriminately. Power failure also affects all (though the rich can take defensive action through their own mini-scale and expensive generators whose multiplication is an indictment of our policy to date). Thus, we suspect that the outrage over the failure of power, airlines, telephones and communications to function with efficiency has grown, especially as the possibility of alternatives has become a reality thanks to the reforms to date. The worldwide movement towards privatisation also reflects similar experience, and is based on pragmatic experience rather than on an ideological preference for the private sector.

3. Infrastructure

While we have argued for reform of the public sector enterprises, partly because of their importance in supplying the infrastructue without which the response to the reforms to date will be inadequate, infrastructure is supplied by the government in other ways as well (e.g. through Departmental undertakings). Thus, the total public sector spending on infrastructure in the Eighth Plan (on power, transport, telecommunications, and urban water and sewage provision) accounted for roughly a third of the total public sector outlays.

We would then be remiss if we ignored this critical area that requires attention from the government. However, the problems that attend the sectors in infrastructure are complex and difficult because of several reasons. For instance, they produce output that is often not traded internationally.[54] So, opening of the market to international competition to introduce efficiency is not a policy that is available. Then again, these sectors are often characterised by scale economies, network externalities, long gestation lags in investment, and public-goods aspects in their output, raising familiar but policywise difficult problems.

Hence, an agenda for improvement of efficiency, and for increase in the supply (given the serious current shortages), needs to be developed for each sector, keeping its special characteristics in view. This goes beyond the terms of our reference. We therefore confine ourselves mainly to drawing the government's attention to a few salient issues that the available studies have highlighted.[55]

(a) In the *transport* sector, railways and airlines (until recently, as already noted) have been state monopolies, the former organised as a departmental enterprise and the latter as a public sector corporation. In road transport, however, goods transport is almost entirely private while a mix of public and private operations exists for passenger transport.

In *road* transport, then, indicators such as the number of employees or the profits per vehicle are cited to suggest that the state transport agencies are overstaffed relative to the private firms. But this may be an overstatement of the problem since the private firms are exempt from some of the labour laws that state agencies must conform to, while they also have profit-related incentives to evade the labour laws they are subject to whereas the state agencies have no profitmaking to worry about!

We suspect that the real problem with the efficiency of the road system lies in its role vis-a-vis the competing rail system: for, freight can be often carried by either. In particular, railway passenger fares and freight rates are *administered* prices; and studies suggest that cross-subsidisation of passenger fares at the expense of freight rates is significant. At the same time, railways are required to favour the movement of freight by other sector agencies (e.g. the Food Corporation of India) over the movement of private freight when it comes to allocating scarce wagons. It is certainly likely that the phenomenal growth of private movement of freight over long distances in lorries reflects to a great extent the cost, uncertainties and other impediments associated with private freight movement on the railways.

Again, we only have a system of motor vehicle taxes, and no tolls are levied on the use of the highway system. As a result, there is no link between the revenue from these taxes and the cost of investment and maintenance of the highway network.

What is clearly necessary in the road-surface transport sector is an integrated analysis which would provide a systematic basis for determining the rate structure, the tax structure, and the level as also the modal and spatial distribution of highways and rail tracks.

In regard to the *airlines*, we have already indicated that competition through the encouragement of new entry by private, domestic, and foreign, airlines would shape up the IAC.[56] At the same time, we see no reason why the IAC should not be privatised in the foreseeable future, even as the competition is intensified so as to improve its efficiency.

(b) *Power generation* is an area that has already been opened up for private investors, domestic and foreign. However, until the issues relating to the administered prices of fuels (such as coal and natural gas) and to controls on prices charged to various users of electricity are resolved, the response is likely to be limited.

Then again, efficient *telecommunications* remain a major problem on the Indian scene. This sector is also being opened up to more private entry. But the issues relating to pricing, and to the regulatory regime we will work with, will have to be quickly resolved if new investments are to be attracted and the working of the old ones induced to become more efficient.

China and Latin America are moving ahead with major foreign investors to modernise their telecommunications. If we fall seriously behind, we will be handicapped in our competition for the world's markets for sure.

D. Financial Sector Reform

The role of financial sector reforms is equally well understood by the government presently. In essence, this is a part of the new institutional setup that is necessary once the old system of licensed and controlled allocation of investible resources among different activities is abandoned. The essential questions should relate, not to whether we should have these reforms (a question we have answered in the affirmative since the excellent 1991 Narsimham Committee Report), but to how rapidly to proceed on the different dimensions of the necessary reforms.

Some general observations may be made. First, the financial scandal that burst on the Indian scene nearly a year ago, understandably slowed down the pace of financial reforms. Quite aside from underlining the need to improve the regulatory regime, many thought that the liberalization in the financial sector was responsible for the scandal. In reality, this was not so. Nothing that happened could not, in principle, have occurred a few years ago when we were still in the old regime. If anything, the old regime had meant that the ability to earn decent profits was seriously compromised by measures such as the forced purchase of low-yielding governmental liabilities and this may have made banks hungry to earn profits even by cutting corners (as noted by us earlier). While the government did argue this, it carried less weight than it should, simply because it was in the dock and politics is often the art of pressing an advantage even when objective analysis shows otherwise. Nonetheless, it is necessary to understand that the scandal was not a product of the financial sector reforms that were beginning to be made.

Second, there is nothing exceptional in the fact that the financial sector will show occasional excesses that even the best regulatory regime may fail to detect. The BCCI scandal, which was far greater than our homemade variety , escaped some of the best regulatory agencies in the world, deceiving the formidable Bank of England and the US authorities. Perhaps some sectors are more prone to abuse than others. The financial sector presents the greatest opportunities for skulduggery, leading to the rise of major criminal figures and scandals; the industrial sector throws up fewer robber barons; and the agricultural sector usually presents the fewest opportunities for ill-gotten wealth.[57]

Third, therefore, governments typically tend to swing from excessive regulation, often moved by such excesses and scandals, to excessive deregulation which then, because of the excesses it encourages, leads back to excessive regulation. These cycles exist in all regulatory activity, to some extent, but are exaggerated in the financial sector everywhere.

Fourth, the government also needs then to distinguish between desirable and undesirable regulation. The financial liberalization, that the government is embarking on, is deregulation of the right kind: removing the features that have seriously reduced the efficiency of the financial sector and which must be eliminated to make the financial sector play the role it must now in the new regime. Deregulation of the wrong kind was the one that removed the restraints on the US banks' activities that led to the enormous S&L crisis (as was in fact predicted by several economists at the time that the restraints were being removed).

The government must, therefore, proceed expeditiously with financial sector reforms, to facilitate an efficient flow of resources into our industry and trade, and also (as noted above) to establish the instrumentalities that constrain the government's ability under the old regime to finance inflationary financing by commercial banks and by a compliant central bank.

The creation of an efficient mechanism to ensure the flow of resources into the industries and activities that are most promising by the market-test requires action on several fronts that the Narasimham Committee ably laid out.[58] In particular, the Committee wanted interest rates to be freely determined by market forces, and to reduce the role of the government in the allocation of credit by (i) reducing the so-called priority sector lending from 40% to 10% of total bank loans within a period of three years, and eventually down to zero %; and (ii) reducing the Statutory

Liquidity Requirement from 38.5% to 25% of the bank deposits and reducing also the "cash reserve" requirement that similarly taxes the banks in favour of the government. In addition, the Committee urged the reduction of entry barriers on private and foreign banks so as to improve efficiency through competition, and it proposed also financial opening to the world by permitting private capital inflows.

. We endorse these proposals (while recognizing the well known problems of moral hazard and adverse selection in letting interest rates be market-determined). If anything, there needs to be faster progress on proposals such as reducing priority sector lending and, during the transition to such lending to government being eliminated, raising the cost of such credit in any event to normal commercial rates (as has been done by several developing embarking on financial reforms).[59]

The government is aware, but we might reiterate, that rapid financial sector liberalization in the matter of allowing private (non-equity) capital inflows, in pursuit of higher real interest rates resulting from the freeing up of interest rates, created severe problems in some developing countries. Thus, in Chile, Argentina, Uruguay and the Philippines, the freeing up of the interest rates led to extremely high real interest rates, exceeding at times 25% in real terms, thanks to destabilising demands on bank credit from several sources with pent-up demands that had been frustrated before the financial liberalization.[60] At the same time, of course, there is much evidence of artificially low real interest rates leading also to adverse effects on economic growth. The answer, therefore, seems to be to ensure that there is close monitoring of the interest rates and of bank lending as also reasonable limits on deposit insurance so as to ensure that speculative borrowing is not financed by banks (as the US banks did, given that their deposits were guaranteed without effective limits by the Federal Deposit Insurance Corporation, contributing to the creation of the S&L crisis).[61]

In view of the limited nature of our experience with many of these matters, given the old regime, it is important that the government draw extensively on both academic and practical expertise in the area of financial liberalization. The (necessary) regulatory structure that we finally put in place, including the guidelines under which, say, SEBI will operate, will also require expert processing of ideas and information about other countries' experience which we should freely draw upon. This should be standard practice in any case; but it is all the more important when we start from an institutional setup where such expertise has not developed in India because it had no place.[62]

E. Agriculture

We have decided to treat reforms in Agriculture separately, even though the specific measures we recommend belong to areas such as Foreign Trade and Macroeconomic Reforms (e.g. the proposals to curtail drastically the input subsidies and to reform the Public Distribution System), largely with a view to emphasising that this sector remains critical to the overall health of the economy and both efficiency and equity considerations demand that the reform effort be focused squarely on it as much as on other important areas such as the reform of the public sector enterprises. In particular, we urge the government to address the following areas with concrete policy reforms:

* Foreign trade in agricultural outputs and inputs

* Public distribution system (PDS) with respect to foodgrains, edible oils and sugar

* Subsidisation (explicit and implicit) of agricultural inputs: fertilisers, irrigation and electricity

* Agricultural credit

1. Foreign Trade in Agricultural Goods

Foreign trade in most of the agricultural goods is currently subject to QRs or canalisation or other restrictions such as minimum price requirements, and has not been covered by the trade liberalization measures of 1991 and 1992 to date. The effect of the traditional trade policy in regard to agricultural goods is evident from the fact that, until recently, the border prices of rice and wheat were about twice the domestic price whereas the domestic edible oil prices were more than twice the world market prices, these price disparities between domestic and world prices reflecting export and import restraints.

At the same time, inputs into agriculture, such as fertilizers, irrigation water and electricity are heavily subsidised (and agricultural income is still not subject to income tax). If the total effect of all implicit and explicit taxes and subsidies, including the protective effect for manufactures (relative to agriculture broadly speaking) that the overvaluation of the rupee implied until recently, were calculated, we would find that the effect has been to bias the government-provided incentives against agriculture. Hence, a broadbased sweeping set of reforms would favour, rather than harm, agriculture on the average.[63] Within agriculture, of course, some items (e.g. rice and cotton) are deprotected by the full set of current policy measures while others (e.g. oilseeds and sugracane) receive high protection.

We see no reason for this continued reliance on QRs and on canalisation of agricultural goods to continue under the new regime of liberal trade that the economic reforms plan to implement. It is now time to abolish canalisation altogether and also to convert the QRs into equivalent export and import tariffs, next turning to a phased, preannounced set of reductions of these tariffs down to much lower levels. [Where there is reason to maintain higher tariffs, as in the few cases when India has a sizeable influence in the long run on prices in the world markets (e.g. tea, basmati rice and jute), this could be done consistently with the general reform we advocate in shape of removal of the QRs and the canalisation process.]

2. The Public Distribution System

We now turn to the pressing question of reform of the Public Distribution System which has distributional-equity objectives. This system requires immediate reform because, as currently constituted, it is inefficient in targeting the poor effectively, so that is has soaked up largescale governmental revenues (adding to the problem of the budget deficit) while producing limited results. The macroeconomic necessity to rein in subsidies and to protect the poor effectively during the necessary macroeconomic adjustment doubly requires therefore that the reform of the PDS be undertaken as an urgent task.

The PDS supplies specified quantities of rice, wheat, coarse cereals, edible oils, kerosene and sugar at prices below ruling retail market prices to holders of ration cards through the Fair Price shops. Although the PDS initially covered (except in Kerala) only urban areas, at present rural areas also are covered.

The supplies of cereals and sugar for the PDS are obtained through domestic purchases and imports by the Food Corporation of India (FCI), a central government enterprise, and by state governments. Edible oils are imported by the canalising agencies, viz. the State Trading Corporation of India (STC) and Hindustan Vegetables Oils Corporation Limited. Since kerosene is a petroleum product, it is handled by the state monopoly, Indian Oil Corporation. If edible oil imports are freely permitted, the domestic price is likely to fall; in any event, a good case does not exist for subsidising edible oil prices below import price levels.

The domestic purchases are made at "procurement" prices from wholesale traders in wheat and from rice millers. A specified proportion (the so-called 'levy') of sugar output is bought from sugar mills at the levy price below the open market price at which the rest of the sugar output is sold. The FCI and other relevant state government agencies thus purchase, transport and store the commodities included in the PDS. In the triennium ending in 1988-99, about 16.5% of domestic wheat output and 13.2% of rice output were procured on the average.[64] The pressure for increasing procurement prices year after year has proved politically irresistible: in 1992-93 they were raised by over 15% in the case of rice, wheat and coarse cereals.

The direct budgetary cost of PDS (i.e. the difference between the revenues from sales and the cost of purchase, transport, storage and establishment) has been growing. In 1990-91, the central government alone spent Rs. 25 billion (or 3.5% of its total revenue expenditure of Rs. 735 billion) on food subsidies. However one should not view these subsidies exclusively as consumer subsidies, or as representing the total economic cost (over the prices paid by consumers) of the operation of the PDS, for two reasons.

First, the cost of the inefficiency of FCI (its excessive staffing, inefficiencies in its purchase, storage and transport operations) is reflected in the budgetary subsidy. According to one estimate, FCI overhead and storage cost have recently risen at annual rates exceeding 20% and together accounted for half of the total food subsidy in 1990. Second, there are non-bugetary costs such as the cost of the preference given to FCI relative to private traders in the transportation of agricultural commodities by the railways, concessions in the interest rate charged to FCI by the banking system for credit, etc.

Ostensibly, the PDS is meant to be part of a 'safety net' for the poor. According to estimates by the economist Subbarao, however, while 50% of India's poor live in Bihar, Madhya Pradesh, Rajasthan and Uttar Pradesh, they received only 10% of PDS supplies in 1990. Minhas has also estimated that more than a third of rice and wheat, 40% of edible oil and as much as 73% of sugar sold through the PDS in rural areas were bought by the richest 40%. In urban areas, however, the poorest 40% managed to buy about the same proportion of wheat, edible oil and sugar, and about 50% of the rice sold through PDS. Thus the PDS did reach the poorest 40% (at least in the country as a whole) while at the same time supplying the non-poor the same commodities at prices below those ruling in the market. PDS is thus poorly targeted to the poor: the leakage to the non poor is really very high.[65]

Apart from poor targeting, the PDS also suffers from leakage of supplies to the open market. Some estimates put such leakages at a third of the rice, wheat and sugar offtake from the PDS and over half of edible oil. Presumably these leakages are effected through sales by fair-price shopkeepers to bogus ration card holders. The shopkeepers earn the difference between the open market price and the sale price to card holders. Thus the leakage is an unintended transfer to the shopkeepers.

These problems of the PDS have of course been clearly recognized by the government. Indeed the Economic Survey 1992-93 points out that:

"The PDS supplies no doubt have contained the vigour of inflation but part of their impact has been offset by monetisation of budgetary deficit to meet food subsidies. Maintaining supplies to PDS involves continuation of food procurement, grant of subsidies, and reintroduction and perpetuation of some controls. But several weaknesses have emerged in the distribution system which have diluted the essence of the system to benefit the vulnerable sections. The financial liabilities of the state governments in maintaining this system have increased. Leakage and black marketing in PDS supplies have also reduced the full impact of PDS in containing inflation." [paragraph 4.51]

In reforming the PDS system, however, different alternatives may be considered. First, consider alternative ways of targeting the poor more effectively.

(i) Better targeting of the poor may be achieved through a means test. It is often argued however that a cheaply administered, reliable means test is administratively infeasible in the Indian context. Possibly this is so; but we doubt that this option has been effectively explored.

(ii) Better targeting may also be achieved by entrusting the task of identifying the poor to the local bodies (at the block or village level), with possibly social action groups co-opted into the task, through some centrally-defined transparent procedure. Kerala has had some success with this approach and it would be worth exploring it thoroughly to see if it can be transplanted effectively elsewhere in

India.

(iii) Yet another approach would be through commodity-based targeting. For example, a PDS confined to the distribution only of coarse cereals is most likely to be used only by the poor. The case for supplying sugar and vegetable oil through the PDS is extremely weak anyway. As such, even if the PDS is not confined to coarse cereals, sugar and edible oils should be excluded from it altogether.

Next, consider the design of the PDS more generally. Is the chosen method of distribution, assuming even efficient targeting, the least-cost way of achieving the objective of supporting the consumption of the poor? We do not think so.

(i) *Food Stamps*: Thus, we could move to a system of food stamps which enables the holders of these stamps to pay for part of the cost of their purchase (from the open market) of commodities covered by this alternative PDS.

If the issue of the food stamps could not be effectively targeted at the poor and if the use of stamps could not be effectively confined to the puchase of PDS food commodities, such a scheme in effect becomes an undifferentiated income subsidy. At the other extreme, full effectiveness in targeting and purchases would provide the poor, and only the poor, with additional income to buy essential PDS food commodities.

In either case, with the poor buying from the market, the government would not be involved in the purchase, transport and storage of commodities. Thus the FCI could be dismantled.

The Sri Lankan experience with food stamps might be worth examining in this context. If there is significant inflation in food prices, as was the case in Sri Lanka, food stamps of fixed nominal face value would obviously fetch less food and amount to less of a real income subsidy. But with flexibility in the design of the scheme (for example, one could consider indexing the value of the stamps by the prices of coarse grains or other such commodities bought only by the poor), such problems could be effectively tackled.

A move to food stamps away from the present PDS seems to us therefore to be an attractive policy option for the government to embrace as part of the continuing reforms.

(ii) *Bids*: If the changeover to a food stamps system is somehow deemed no feasible, it is still desirable to do away with the inefficient FCI by letting the private sector supply the quantity of grains needed for the PDS, at the place and time needed, by calling for bids. By making the entire process of the call, receipt, opening and acceptance of bids as transparent and open as possible, abuses of the system could be minimized.

Admittedly neither the food stamp system nor the bid system takes into account the possible implicit taxation involved in the purchase of grain at procurement prices for the PDS. If the very operation of the PDS, by effectively removing the poor from the open market and leaving only those with an inelastic demand in it, does not raise the open market prices sufficiently above procurement prices so that the weighted average of procurement and open market price is below the open market price that would have prevailed in the absence of a PDS, this taxation could be significant. But in recent years, with effective lobbying by farm interests, the procurement prices have not deviated much from the open market prices. As such, the cost of operating the PDS has not been reduced by such implicit taxation of producers.

3. Subsidies on Agricultural Inputs

There is also an excellent case for removing the existing subsidies on the three major agricultural inputs: fertilizers, irrigation water and electricity.[66] This is necessary because they add to the budget deficit in a big way and they must distort the choice of technology in agricultural production as well. If, further, these subsidies are removed in tandem with the changes in the import regime that are discussed earlier, it is also likely that agriculture, on the average, will benefit from the reforms instead of being harmed incentivewise.

(a) Fertilizers

In 1990-91, fertilizer subsidies amounted to as much as Rs. 44 billion as compared to the total revenue expenditure of Rs. 735 billion. Although, on the average, the issue price of fertilizers has been increased by 30 percent since August 1991, there is still room for further increases since, even with this increase, the considerable gap between domestic and import parity price has not been closed. There is much evidence that the marginal returns on fertilizer use would be attractive to farmers even with an increase in fertilizer price to import parity levels.

(b) Irrigation

The situation with respect to irrigation charges is also abysmal. In 1989-90, even without providing for capital costs, current expenditure on the irrigation system exceeded revenues from the water charges by over Rs. 23 billion, the revenues as a proportion of current expenditures amounting only to 7.5% in 1988-89. Since the current irrigation charges as a proportion of marginal returns from irrigation are almost negligible for most crops, it follows that raising them would not significantly reduce the net returns from cultivation of irrigated crops at the outset, while it would raise revenues significantly.

There are also many serious problems with the planning and implementation of irrigation investments and with the operation, maintenance and management of irrigation capacity once created. Irrigation departments are widely understood to be overstaffed, inefficient and uninterested in recovering irrigation costs since they have no access to the use of irrigation revenues. A number of studies have already identified many of these problems and have made recommendations for their correction. Since irrigation is the responsibility of state governments and since their capacity (administrative and political) to reform the irrigation system management is limited, not much can be expected in the short to medium run by way of major reforms. But the centre needs to push for these reforms in all possible ways, while insisting at least on having irrigation charges raised immediately.

(c) Electricity

Agricultural use of electricity has grown rapidly from less than 5% of total consumption in 1960-61 to about 20% in 1990-91. In the 1980s the average annual rate of growth was about 15%. Estimates by World Bank economists suggest that both farmers and other consumers have been heavily subsidized at a price that is less than half of the long-term marginal cost of supply. Moreover, only two-thirds of the amounts billed are recovered.

Thus, electricity generation (other than self-generation by the railways and by some industries and the limited output of private utilities) and distribution are the responsibilities of State Electricity Boards (SEB's). The Economic Survey of 1991-92 projected the commercial losses of all SEB's to be Rs. 48.5 billion. Although the supplying of power to widely-scattered irrigation pumps is costly, it is supplied free of charge in some states such as Tamil Nadu or at a very low price in almost all others. Thus the losses in sales to agriculturists account for a significant proportion of the total losses of SEB's (which, ofcourse, reflect other factors such as inefficiency in operation and in the maintenance of generation and transmission facilities).

Power generation has now been opened for domestic and foreign investors. Yet, as long as the price which private producers will receive is controlled by the state, it is likely that the response by private investors will be disappointing. Indeed, the price guarantees reportedly demanded by foreign investors who have shown an interest in power generation testifies to this. This can be calamitious for the success of the entire reform effort since power is clearly an important bottleneck right now. Therefore, the entire gamut of issues relating to power generation and distribution such as the scale of investment in generation and transmission, the composition of the generating capacity in terms of thermal, hydro and nuclear, the choice of fuel for thermal plants (i.e. coal, lignite, fuel oil and natural gas), and above all the extent of state involvement in the energy sector as a whole and particularly in the generation, transmission and pricing of electricity also need now to be thoroughly reviewed.

New institutional arrangements should also be examined. For example, scale economies in generation are apparently not significant in some new technologies. In the absence of significant scale economies and externalities in generation and distribution (which require public ownership or preferably public regulation), these activities could be privatized, while long-distance transmission through an inter-state grid in which network externalities are important could be in the public sector or alternatively be operated as a regulated private monopoly. The grid would then purchase power from private generators and sell to private distributors.

4. Agricultural Credit

We finally turn to the question of agricultural credit. The major, declared objective of agricultural credit policy has been to enable farmers, especially small and marginal farmers, to adopt modern technology and improved agricultural practices. However, "Despite a substantial increase in the overall agricultural credit, the problem of mounting overdues has slowed credit expansion. Overdues have been around 40-42 percent during the last 3-4 years," (*Economic Survey* 1991-92).

While the decennial rural debt surveys of the Reserve Bank of India suggest that the share of institutional credit in total rural credit has increased substantially from 20% in 1951 to over 80% in 1981, there are reasons to believe that these data overstate the increase and that informal credit continues to be very significant in rural areas. At the same time, there are substantial regional variations in institutional credit use. The World Bank estimates that in the mid-1980s an average of only 27% of India's farmers used co-operative credit, varying from 9% in West Bengal to 90% in Punjab. Besides, only 4% of the farmers used credit from commercial banks and two-thirds of term credit went to the large farms.

Thus it is an open question whether the objectives of the agricultural credit policy are being achieved. The World Bank estimates that farmers cultivating over 5 acres receive an interest rate subsidy on term loans of about Rs. 1 billion per annum. If one realistically assumed that their annual overdues would never be cleared, they in effect received a further subsidy of over Rs. 2 billion.

Given then the scale of the problem, the situation calls for a corrective policy. It must be understood that the credit subsidies are of little value to the poor farmers since most of them do not get access to credit in the first place; access to credit is really the problem faced by the poor (a problem that can be attacked along the lines suggested by the Grameen Bank in Bangladesh). The reform of the agriculture credit system, as we have now inherited it, should in fact be regarded as an important part of the financial sector reforms whose urgency we discussed earlier in this Report.

V. Looking Ahead: Trading Choices

If we make a successful transition from an essentially inward-looking posture to an outward-oriented economy, exploiting foreign trade and investment opportunities fully, we have to examine how we can position ourselves so that these opportunities are maximally available to us. Else, we will be working with one blade of the scissors, ignoring the other.

This requires that we now begin to appraise the trends in the world trading system realistically and formulate policies that will prepare us to exploit these trends to our best advantage.

A. Supporting the GATT and Closing the Uruguay Round

The ability to exploit the trading opportunity in the world economy requires that our access to world markets is secure. While world markets can absorb our increasing exports, if these markets are kept open, it is not certain that they will be left open as effectively as when the trading nations agree to binding rules and disciplines. This discipline is provided by the GATT (the General Agreement on Tariffs and Trade) in Geneva.

If the GATT is wounded and weakened by the failure to conclude the seven-year old multilateral trade negotiations, then the effect will be to pull the world yet more towards unilateral actions by the economically stronger trading nations. A telling example is provided by the United States in its use of Section 301 policies aimed at unilaterally imposing its own demands on other trading nations through threats to otherwise close its own markets. Such a demand was indeed made on us on 25 May 1989, when the US invoked Super 301 provisions of its 1988 Trade Act to indict us for trading practices defined as unfair by the US unilaterally and not constituting a violation by us of any treaty-defined obligations. The Clinton administration currently intends to revive the now-lapsed Super 301 legislation. This will certainly be aimed at Japan; but, as in 1989, it can be expected to be aimed at other countries.

Since the US has asymmetric economic power, the result will certainly be to create unilateral demands on us and others. This cannot but lead to disruption of our trade access from time to time. If the US revives Super 301, then the EC can also be expected to follow suit. In Japan also, there is increasing concern about this use of aggressive unilateralism and therefore a segment of opinion suggests that Japan acquire a similar legal instrument to respond to US actions. This too can have prospective spillover onto other nations.

It is therefore in our interest to support the emerging efforts by the United States and the EC to close the Uruguay Round of multilateral trade negotiations, since a strengthened GATT means a greater worldwide, multilateral discipline that could contain the outbreak of unilateralism by the stronger trading nations. Multilateralism is the best defense of the weak.

Since there will be efforts by the US to exempt the use of 301 actions from any GATT discipline, as a part of the last-minute demands before closing the Round, India should actively join the world community in refusing to concede such demands, while being flexible on many other matters. Else, a central benefit to us of multilateral discipline in the world trading system will have been nullified.

India's ability to play a significant role in the Uruguay Round negotiations at this stage is strictly limited, of course. But our views today, precisely because of our changed image thanks to the reforms and also greater flexibility at the trade talks, are listened to with greater respect and attention than during the 1980s. Our role in the final lap of the Uruguay Round negotiations must be reckoned therefore to be non-negligible, especially if we back agendas that are clearly to strengthen, rather than weaken, the GATT system.

B. Regionalism: India's Options

The wounding of the GATT through protracted and continuing negotiations of the Uruguay Round has accentuated the existing trend towards the formation of regional blocks. The failure of the EC (European Community) to respond to the US demands to start multilateral trade negotiations in 1982 was a principal factor in turning US trade policy towards the US-Canada free trade agreement. That, in turn, triggered the further extension of the regional arrangement to include Mexico under the now-impending North-American Free Trade Area (NAFTA).

This tendency to build FTAs is now creating its own momentum. With the earlier Bush decision to extend the NAFTA to South America, as part of the Enterprise for the Americas Initiative, and President Clinton's increasingly likely endorsement of such an initiative, there is now strong likelihood that a regional Americaswide NAFTA will materialise and therefore that there will be some momentum for a defensive response in Asia, with Japan at the centre of such a free trading area.

If this happens, as is increasingly likely, then the world trading system may soon be fragmented into four "blocs": the (enlarged) EC, the NAFTA extending into South America and becoming an "Americas" bloc, an Asian bloc, and the "bloc" of marginalised non-member nations that are not part of any of the former three blocs.

If India is left out of membership in any of these trading blocs, and becomes a member of the fourth "bloc" of marginalised non-members, she will be deprived of the maximal trading and (inward) foreign investment opportunity that she can otherwise enjoy. For, access to one of these large blocs can be a powerful way of attracting foreign investment which will go where the markets are. Indeed, the Mexican President Salinas's decision to seek to join NAFTA with the US and Canada was prompted largely by a desire to attract foreign investment in this way.

Our diplomacy should therefore now be geared immediately to seeking membership in one or more of these blocs. As of now, only the EC exists and NAFTA (embracing Mexico) is nearly born. Nothing precludes membership or quasi-membership in both.

(i) We should forthwith begin therefore formal approaches to the EC to explore an Association agreement such as the many that the EC has already signed with foreign nations, including in Africa. More cannot be expected because full membership is regionally constrained to Europeans. Our special relationship with Great Britain and generally excellent relations with France, Germany, the Netherlands and other European nations, as also the growing attractiveness of India as a market and as a sourcing country for foreign firms, should also predispose the EC towards a favourable response.

(ii) Equally, we should explore the possibility of a free trade agreement with NAFTA. Towards this end, we could exploit out Commonwealth relationship with Canada, encouraging it to seek our membership just as the US (not Canada) sought successfully to bring in Mexico (and Canada went along). It may not be too ambitious to get the Canadian government to play an initiating role in seeking new members for NAFTA, drawing upon Canada's external alliances and political affiliations (such as the Commonwealth), instead of relying only on the US for choice of new NAFTA members.

This does not preclude our simultaneously approaching the US itself for NAFTA membership. The nearly-million strong Indian community in the US provides the possibility of mobilization by us of political force that can get attention in Washington D.C.. This also requires that our objectives be totally clear and firm and that India be represented in Washington by an energetic and visionary Mission that acts so as to mobilize this political potential for the economic objectives, just as Mexico has done effectively with its more numerous nationals in the US in creating support for NAFTA in the US Congress. This also implies that voting rights of the Indians in the US become critical: unlike any other democracy, the US legislates primarily to benefit those who voice their concerns rather than for generalized benefits that accrue to all even if demanded by a few. In turn, this means that India should now go full speed ahead with permitting dual citizenship, enabling many in the US (and elsewhere) to gain voting rights that they can get only if they renounce Indian citizenship.

(iii) The possibility that we should explore with the greatest energy, however, is with Asia. At the moment, there is no Asian bloc, and many in the West think that one may not materialise. On the other hand, it is hard to imagine anyone taking seriously the formation of the US-Canada free trade area over a decade ago, and its extension to Mexico would have been regarded as altogether utopian. The speed with which old assumptions are shifted by new possibilities and realities is truly dazzling.

As it happens, the sense that the world trading system is being already "carved up" into blocs by the EC and the United States is already leading Malaysia to sponsor such an Asian bloc. The anti-American rhetoric in which such a proposal tends to emanate from Malaysia handicaps the acceptance of the idea by Japan. For, Japan has naturally no desire to make the Asian bloc an offensive rather than a defensive move: Japan cannot afford to, and sensibly will not wish to, alienate the United States.

But the sentiment for an Asian bloc is now stronger and growing. India must become an active proponent of the idea, seeking membership as and when the idea materialises. This will need patient diplomacy since the current position is that India is not perceived as a "natural" member of such an Asian bloc and our membership even of the APEC, which is only a looser body of Asian and Pacific nations for economic cooperation, is still pending.

We will need to woo the ASEAN nations which were earlier turned off by our pro-Soviet positions on Vietnam, and we will also need to work actively on Japan itself, using both economic and political carrots to do so. Essential to our success will be commitment to an Asian identity (which need not exclude multiple affiliations and identities). Without this commitment, our membership may run into difficulty just as Britain's less-than-total enthusiasm for entry into the EC contributed to repeated French vetoes on the British application for membership.

Only by getting ready diplomatically for exploring these policy options, and pursuing them urgently, can we expect to safeguard our economic interests in the evolving economy. Our thinking and polices have to be reshaped to suit the rapidly changing world economic scene.

The active exploration of these trading possibilities and choices would also make more credible our commitment to the reforms initiated since 1991, both at home and abroad. In turn, that would benefit the reform process itself, creating a virtuous circle where reforms lead to intimate engagement into the evolving trade regimes and that engagement in turn encourages foreign investment and interest in India's economy and reinforces the success of the reforms in providing benefits.

VI. CONCLUDING REMARKS

In conclusion, while the Rao government must be congratulated for boldness of the reforms to date, the time has now come to consolidate the reforms attempted already and to extend them boldly in several new directions.

In this report, we have argued why it is now necessary to take these further steps, we have highlighted the key areas in which these new steps must be taken, and we have spelled out these steps as well.

In essence, the productivity of the reforms to date depends critically on initiating and completing quickly the added reforms: they hang together in an integral way. Without the new steps, such as public sector privatisation and the breaking of important infrastructure bottlenecks for example, export performance and domestic productivity cannot respond significantly to the extensive delicensing and trade account convertibility that have been steadfastly implemented, thus putting these reforms at risk by preventing them from leading to significant results. For, the critics will point to the reforms in place and charge that the proponents had exaggerated their necessity.

The entire set of reforms, old and the new we propose, represents the creation of a sweeping, new institutional framework. With it, however, we will only rejoin the rest of the world in how we run our economy.

The full dividends from the reforms will come only when the transition is largely complete. The next, major steps we propose are what will complete the transition. The government has no time to lose.

FOOTNOTES

1. In particular, in the absence of public sector reforms, freeing up the infrastructure bottlenecks, the supply responses to the borrowing and the freeing of trade could be so limited as to cause acute problems with servicing the debt and sustaining these reforms.

2. The microeconomic inefficiencies can be aruged to have contributed to the macroeconomic crises in important ways, though. On this question, see Jugdish Bhagwati's 1991 Radhakrishnan Lectures, to be published as *India in Transition: Freeing the Economy*, by Clarendon Press: Oxford, 1993; and especially Vijay Joshi and Ian Little, *India: Macroeconomics and Political Economy, 1964-1991*, Oxford University Press: 1993. We return to this question later, in section IV.

3. The contrast between the actual outcomes and the plans and expectation embodied in the still-earlier and seminal work of the National Planning Committee of the Indian National Congress, constituted under the chairmanship of Pandit Nehru in 1938 is considered at length by T.N. Srinivasan in "Indian Economic Reforms : Background, Rationale, and Next Steps, "Economic Growth Center, Yale University (mimeo), April 1993. This paper also illuminates how longstanding the beliefs are about the earlier developmental strategy which the reforms seek to abandon in light of experience, and hence also the passion with which some critics object to the reforms. We have drawn on this paper in writing several sections of this report.

4. The comparative growth rates are assessed more carefully in Bhagwati, *ibid*.

5. This is manifest also from the deliberations of the 1938 Nehru Committee, referred to in Srinivasan, *ibid*.

6. This is not to say, of course, that those among the poor who are weakly connected with the growth process because of their social or economic circumstances would not be left poor despite growth. Our planners equally recognized the need for special measures to assist these groups.

7. Cf. Bhagwati, *ibid*. 1993, for further details.

8. While agriculture has been generally successful in India with the average growth rates being 2.5% and 3.1% per annum in 1965-80 and 1981-1990 respectively, performance has been better in other countries, e.g. Kenya, Pakistan, Indonesia. Our success rather has been in the dramatic increase in the output of wheat since the adoption of the green-revolution technology in the mid-60s.

9. The issue of credibility in ensuring the success of economic reforms has now been studied extensively and is recognized as a key component of successful reforms. See, for instance, the excellent discussion of the issue in Dani Rodrik, "Promises, Promises: Credible Policy Reform Via Signalling", *Economic Journal*, vol. 99 (1989), pp. 756-772.

11. For a fuller analysis of the Soviet experience, see Padma Desai, *Perestroika in Perspective*, Princeton University Press: Princeton, Updated Paperback Edition, 1990, page 154.

12. At the same time, of course, microeconomic reforms without macro-economic stability are unlikely to be productive and unlikely therefore to take hold.

13. Exceptions will typically arise, however, when the initial inefficiency in a sector being reformed is very high and the reform removes that inefficiency directly, as happened with the effects of Chinese decollectivisation of communes.

14. An analysis of our public finances, and their contribution to the crisis that engulfed India, can be found in Joshi and Little, 1993, *op. cit.*, and Bhagwati, 1993, *op. cit.* The barest essentials are treated here.

15. More detail on the budget deficit is provided below where we discuss the stabilization effort since 1991.

16. The reason to address this question is that some leftwing criticism of the new reforms

tends to assert that microeconomic inefficiencies are being exaggerated and liberalisation is being smuggled in under the misperception that the old micro policies caused a crisis. Cf. Deepak Nayyar, "Indian Economy at the Crossroads: Illusions and Realities:, *Economic and Political Weekly*, April 10, 1993 and the forceful critique of it by Manu Shroff, "Indian Economy at the Crossroads", *Economic and Political Weekly* May 8, 1993.

17. Cf. Willem Buiter and Urjit Patel, "Debt, Deficits and Inflation. An Application to the Public Finances of India", *Journal of Public Economics*, 47 (1992), pp. 171-205; and also Bhagwati, 1993, *ibid.* and Joshi and Little, *ibid.*

18. One can legitimately ask whether the inflow of foreign capital was "exogenous" and "primary", leading to an "accommodating" *ex post* current-account deficit and excess of domestic investment over savings, just as the Reagan administration claimed that the US payments deficit reflected capital inflow that came in because of confidence in the US rather than was driven by excess spending, primarily fuelled by the budget deficit. Our view is that, while our long-term foreign aid inflows are properly considered to be exogenous in this sense, the foreign borrowings in the 1980s, as by the public sectors noted in the next, were in the main reflective of the governmental excessive spending we focus on below. Even the NRI loans, attracted by offering generous returns that exceeded the rates in capital markets, can be viewed as reflecting the increasing inability of the government to balance the budget and hence to dampen the resulting pressures on inflation and on the balance of payments.

19. We consider below the question of addressing the interest cost of the debt (a problem afflicting many countries, including the United States, currently), in the context of the question as to how to use the proceeds from selling equity in the public enterprises that are being privatised.

20. This was demonstrated in T.N. Srinivasan and N.S.S. Narayana, "Economic Performance since the Third Plan", *Economic and Political Weekly*, Annual Number, 1977.

21. Of course, if such spending is highly unproductive in any particular segment of the public sector, then that consideration should override what we argue above, in favour of a high-priority shift to the private sector through privatisation and other policies encouraging private entry.

22. We might stress here itself that the cuts in the PDS can be made as part of a sweeping reform of the system so that it is much better targeted to the poor whom we seek to support. This is spelled out at length in our treatment of the PDS and its reforms below.

23. See, in particular, Sanjaya Baru, "New Economic Policy: Efficiency, Equity and Fiscal Stabilisation", *Economic and Political Weekly*, April 10, 1993: "Having chanted the 'safety net' mantra, Singh's letter [to the IMF] proceeds to focus the entire attention on the programme of action on fiscal, trade and tax reform." (page 715).

24. In this context, the establishment of the National Renewal Fund also needs to be cited as an institutional innovation designed to ease the adjustment problems of the workers as stabilisation and microeconomic restructuring prompt the laying off of workers from enterprises that must close or retrench. We might also remind ourselves that, as Professor P.C. Mahalanobis noted long ago ("The Asian Drama: An Indian View", *Sankhya,* Series B. Vol. 31, 1969), the welfare benefits extended to organised-sector urban workers under our labour laws accrue to a very small fraction of the work force and could operate both to introduce inequality and to inhibit growth that would benefit those not coverd by these labour laws. His remarks on the absence of a link in India

between productivity and wage as well as the excessive fringe benefits enjoyed by civil servants continue to be relevant. His proposal for a Labour Reserve Service is worth considering.

25. This alternative has been suggested most forcefully by the economist Deena Khatkhate.

26. We need however to keep in mind the fact that a significant proportion of the internal public debt is held by nationalised banks.

27. We should adjust further for any terms-of-trade losses that would arise from amortisation and interest payments in foreign exchange. But so would benefits change from the terms-of-trade gain from the loan inflow. We ignore this complication, whose empirical importance we doubt anyway, in the argument in the text.

28. Of course, the margin for the borrowing could be different from this measure if the borrowing for instance was wholly wasteful or was accompanied by improved efficiency in the economy. In the former case the return to the borrowing would be lower, in the latter case, higher, than our estimate. See our discussion below.

29. This is not to deny that, under the licensing system, influential and large business groups had a preferential access to licensing authorities.

30. State-level competition that takes the form of competitive relaxation of desirable regulations would however be deplorable. To avoid that, we also would need to coordinate and harmonise such desirable regulation, as is done in the European Community for instance.

31. We also recommend in subsection 4 some critical, accommodating institutional changes to go with the import liberalization of all goods.

32. The earliest calculations of ERPs for India were made By Dr. V.R. Panchamukhi and can be found in Jagdish Bhagwati and Padma Desai, *India*, Oxford University Press, 1970. The usual calculations distinguish between ERPs based on QRs when these are the effective constraints on imports and those based on tariffs as in the Chelliah Committee Report.

33. The discrepancy arises because the calculations of the (legal) duty cannot usually be adjusted effectively for the exemptions available and therefore, in practice, are always largely unaccounted for.

34. On the other hand, the collection of revenues, as distinct from the discrepancy between the official duty and the duty implied by the collections, will also be affected by high-tariffs-induced underinvoicing of imports and by outright smuggling outside of the customs and trade-accounting framework.

35. Ch. Chelliah Committee Interim Report on Tax Reforms, GOI, December 1991, page 94.

36. Lance Pritchett and Geeta Sethi, "Tariff Rates, Tariff Revenue and Tariff Reform: Some New Facts", mimeographed, Research Division, IBRD, Washington D.C., August 10, 1992.

37. Of course, when ERPs are calculated, the analyst finds a substantial degree of dispersion among these tariff rates (see Table 4). Total uniformity of tariffs would eliminate this phenomenon, of course.

38. The economists Arvind Panagariya and Dani Rodrik have recently explored a number of such arguments for adopting a policy of uniform tariffs.

39. Cf. Chelliah Committee Report, *op. cit.* (p. 94), citing the Long Term Fiscal Policy document of 1985, with apparent approval.

40. If it is thought that such domestic production "saves foreign exchange", that is still another fallacy. Resources used in such domestic production could be used to produce for exports, or to produce non-tradeables which then absorb domestic expenditure and hence reduce the demand for imports, for instance.

41. This may be because of shifts in supply and demand that would have reduced the protective effect of the replaced QR.

42. We have already dealt earlier with the problem of the effect of tariff cuts on revenue collection and discounted it.

43. In these and other ways, including GATT negotiations and law, we need considerably more expertise than we possess simply because we have not engaged forcefully in trade to date and the reforms make this neglect a shortfall that we must urgently repair. The immediate expansion of teaching and research programmes in international trade law where we can train lawyers, bureaucrats and economists who become experts on whom the government can draw as we transit to more integration into the world economy, is now of the utmost importance.

44. For an early analysis of this uncritical role played by the Tariff Commission, not because of its own fault but because of a faulty conception of its role by the government, see Padma Desai, *Tariff Protection in India 1947-1965*, Hindustan Publishing Corporation: New Delhi, 1970.

45. Since the conclusion of the Uruguay Round is likely to include proscription of such requirements as part of the agreement on Trade-related Investment Measures (TRIMs), as does the December 1991 "Dunkel Draft", our logical abandonment of such a policy, in view of our reforms, would also be timely. It is also not prudent to expend our limited bargaining power at the Round on fighting such a proscription which has little adverse effect on us in view of our trade reforms and also because few other developing countries are likely to join us in such an effort.

46. For evidence on this hypothesis about the relationship between outward and inward oriented trade policies and the magnitude of DFI inflows, see V.N. Balasubramanyam, "EP, IS and Foreign Direct Investment in LDCs", in A.D. Koekkoek and C.B.M. Mennes (Eds.), *International Trade and Global Development: Essays in Honour of Jagdish Bhagwati*, Routledge: London, 1991.

47. See, for instance, the various writings of Magnus Blomstrom of the Stockholm School of Economics and Robert Lipsey of the National Bureau of Economic Research, and other evidence cited in Veena Mishra's fine contribution on DFI to *Policy Options for Economic Reform*, Indian Merchants' Chamber and Indira Gandhi Institute for Development Research, IMC IGIDR Series, Vol. 1, April 1992, Bombay.

48. We deliberately say "on the average" because, as with the former Soviet Union, specific technical objectives can always be achieved, and have been in India, when resources are concentrated on a well-defined target. That fact is compatible with the failure of the system to produce technical capability and innovativeness over a wider spectrum of activity owing to policy-created disincentives.

49. Cf. Joseph Berliner, *The Innovation Decision in Soviety Industry*, MIT Press: Cambridge, Mass., 1976.

50. The economics of this disinvestment has been studied insightfully at our request by Rajendra Vaidya, "Disinvestment of Public Enterprise Shares", Indira Gandhi Institute for Development Research, Bombay, 1992, mimeo.

51. J. Vickers and G. Yarrow, *Privatization: An Economic Analysis*, MIT Press: Cambridge, Mass., 1988.

52. An excellent treatment of the question as to when privatization should be preceded by restructuring is provided by Paul Seabright, "Infrastructure and Industrial Policy in South Asia: Achieving the Transition to a New Regulatory Environment", The World Bank, June, 1993; see especially Box D.

53. This again can be done more credibly if the National Renewal Fund, and even a limited unemployment insurance scheme, are successfully established.

54. Power, of course, can be traded across borders but, in our case, is not traded. Then again, there is already some international competition for the market for international travel, though much more will prevail if the Uruguay Round talks succeed and concessions begin to be made to liberalise the service sectors.

55. In particular, we consider the transport sector, including road, rail and airlines.

56. The entry of foreign carriers can be part of the concessions we make at the Uruguay Round, earning reciprocal concessions in other sectors. Reciprocal concessions for Air India and other prospective new carriers down the road may also be put in place now, though our ability to profit from them would depend on our ability to come up with competitive airlines once we shift to a more competitive framework at home.

57. Governmental intervention such as the price support programmes for agriculture in the United States and the European Community do create opportunities for malfeasance as well; but the magnitudes involved are way below what can happen in the financial sector.

58. We have profited from the excellent treatment of the subject by Pradeep agarwal, "Financial Reforms", in *Policy Reforms for Economic Reform*, IMC IGIDR, 1992, op. cit.

59. For more detailed suggestions, see Agarwal, Ibid.

60. In the Chilean case, with the freeing of capital inflows, banks borrowed from abroad and lent at home at high interest rates with little consideration for potential default. When extensive defaults occurred, the government was forced by external lenders (using financial and political muscle) into accepting responsibility for these private debts even though the loans had not been guaranteed by the government!

61. In this regard, we should also stress that a careful policy reassessment is necessary in the matter of the treatment of "non-performing" loans in the bank portfolios. A significant part of these non-performing loans is attributable to the government's policy on priority lending (which we discussed earlier) without adequate scrutiny (at loan "melas", for instance), and to the fact that the waiving repayments (the so called loan "mafis") encourages imprudent borrowing.

62. We emphasise the obvious here, but it is necessary to do so. For instance, the non-negligible undervaluation of the equity sold under the first two rounds of sale in 1991 and 1992 could have been avoided, as we noted in the text, if the experience of the UK had been properly taken into account. Then again, the SEBI guidelines applying to investment and merchant banking services required for corporate issues of long-term securities in India could be improved and specific market mechanisms can be suggested which would be more effective than these guidelines. Cf. Sankar De and Sushil Khanna, "Merchant Banking under SEBI Guidelines: A Study of Regulations in Developing Capital Markets", Indian Institute of Management, Calcutta, April 1993, mimeo.

63. This conclusion is based on estimates made by the World Bank economists, Gulati and Purcell. The broad conclusion is also paralleled by the experience of many developing countries, as studied by a team of economists led by Anne Krueger of Duke University, at the World Bank.

64. Besides the procurement of foodstuffs for the PDS, the government buys raw cotton and natural rubber as well under its price support programme.

65. Also see a recent study by Kirit Parikh, "Who gets how much from PDS: How effectively does it reach the poor", Indira Gandhi Institute for Development Research, Bombay, undated. Parikh, using the data collected by the 42nd round of the NSS, reaches the same conclusion: in particular, that "the cost-effectiveness of reaching the poorest 20% of the households through PDS cereals is very small. For every rupee spent less than 20 paise reach the poor in all states, excepting in Kerala where 26 paise reach the poor".

66. It should not be inferred that it is the agriculturists who are being subsidised. Indeed, fertilizer subsidies reflect in part the high cost of fertilizers produced by some of the more inefficient domestic producers. Irrigation and electricity subsidies also reflect at least in part the overstaffing and other inefficiencies of state irrigation departments and electricity boards.

Prof. Jagdish Bhagwati and Prof. T.N. Srinivasan, two of India's outstanding and internationally recognised economists, were invited by Government of India, Minister of Finance, to study the current reforms underway in India and to make recommendations for future action. They submitted their report (reproduced here) in July, 1993.

3

An Interim Assessment of Economic Reforms in India

P.N. Dhar

Need for Reforms

We need economic reforms to achieve the objectives we set for ourselves more than seven five-year plans ago. Our objectives then were sustained economic growth, self-reliance, better income distribution and alleviation of poverty. Our economy, however, continues to be a low-income one; slow growing, vulnerable and saddled with the majority of the world's poor. With 14 per cent of the world's population, India accounts for nearly 30 per cent of its destitutes. However, when in the eighties, economic growth picked up and there was some reduction in the percentage of people below the poverty line, thanks largely to the loosening of some counter-productive controls on trade and industry, the economy found itself in an acute balance of payments crisis. It became obvious that a high growth rate could not be sustained without drastic changes in economic policies.

Why did this happen? Did India start on the wrong track? I think not. Things went wrong because we failed to adjust policies and institutions to emerging circumstances and opportunities. The Second Plan which laid the foundation of our planning had clearly stated that its objectives were not "rooted in any doctrine or dogma ... economic and social policy has to be shaped from time to time in the light of historical circumstances ... It is neither necessary nor desirable that the economy should become a monolithic type of organisation offering little play for experimentation either as to form or as to modes of functions." The Statement was reiterated in the third plan. This fundamental directive got ignored in actual practice. We chose not to learn from our experience. Worse still, we refused to learn from the experience of other countries whose performance continued to be better than ours. The countries, now known as Asian NICs, started their development with initial conditions which were more backward than ours. We let them overtake us and we continued to cling to policies and institutions long after they had served their purpose, regarding them as the goals rather than as means.[2]

Policy excesses

The failure to draw distinction between objectives and instruments is writ large on a whole range of our policies. For example, the process of import substitution was carried on far beyond the requirements of protecting infant and strategic industries. All late-comers, including the 'miracle' economies of East Asia have gone through a phase of import substitution in their drive for industrialisation. For example, the Korean state has been highly interventionist. But it pursued policies of import substitution and export promotion without giving up the norms of efficiency. This enabled Korean industry to compete successfully in international markets.[3]

In our case the policy not only continued unabated but was further reinforced by an over-valued exchange rate and import licensing till it reached autarkic levels. These policies eliminated all competitive pressures and created monopolistic industrial structures. These distortions were introduced initially by equating self-reliance with import substitution and later with self-sufficiency. In the process, we lost sight of the true meaning of self-reliance, viz., the ability to do without foreign assistance. The result has been indiscriminate protection leading to massive misallocation of resources to industries and enterprises which enjoy no inherent economic advantage and cannot survive competition in international markets. These uneconomic enterprises have actually eroded our capability to achieve self-reliance.

Again, the public sector has an essential role as an engine of growth. This is true especially in the early stages of development when capital is scarce and enterprise shy of entering into sectors with long gestation periods. In India the public sector lost its basic rationale when it went beyond its proper sphere and its extension became an end in itself. Its extension was looked upon as realisation of socialism. In the process, public sector absorbed about half of the total industrial investment, regardless of costs and returns.[4]

Small enterprises have played a very important role in industrial development. Support to such industries is warranted on several grounds. Small industries which are complementary to large industries such as ancillaries or those which use more labour than capital per unit of output or local resources for local use or specialised craft industries producing high value goods have inherent advantages and, therefore, deserve to be promoted. Moreover, they foster entrepreneurship and expand its social base. The establishment of industrial estates, technical assistance, hire purchase facilities, subsidised bank finance, and marketing assistance have provided a powerful stimulus for their development. These industries have also contributed their share to the expansion of industrial employment and exports.

But in this case too, our policies went far beyond promotion and development and extended protection to small industries against even domestic competition by reserving hundreds of products for them exclusively. Besides this protection, small enterprises enjoy large subsidies by way of excise duty concessions, preferential import allocations, cheaper credit and sales tax exemptions. These policies have motivated many small enterprises to stay small; if they increase their operations, they do so by establishing more small units. This is more advantageous for them than to strive for a larger scale and more efficient operation. The benefits to small enterprises proliferated in a manner that gains could be made even without any production. According to the latest official estimate, there are 3.5 lakh units which are registered but do not actually exist or operate.[5] This is a device to take advantage of input subsidies and other benefits. "Smallness" thus became an end in itself regardless of the burden it placed on the economy.

Similarly, the protection of workers against exploitation by the employers is a recognised principle that informs labour legislation of all enlightened governments. In India, organised industrial labour accounting for less than 5 per cent of the total workforce, under militant union leadership and permissive legislation and indulgent interpretation of law by the judiciary, has itself become an exploitative class. Under our system, wages in the organised sector are unrelated to productivity and, what is worse, have become a fixed instead of a variable cost.

Labour legislation has implicitly condoned trade union practices which are extremely coercive in their effect. This is especially true of the better paid white collar workers. Such irresponsible trade unionism has prevented the necessary modernisation and expansion of critical sectors like banking and telecommunications. This has had a deleterious effect on growth of income and employment in the country. The militant leadership of the unions has prevented the emergence of a stable system of industrial relations which has directly hit the growth of productivity in the economy. Indirectly, it has induced employers in industry and agriculture to substitute capital for labour wherever they can and thereby retarded the growth of employment which is the most effective instrument of poverty alleviation.

The security of employment and wages exceeding marginal productivity in the organised sector was combined with protection from internal and external competition to ensure adequate profits. And if, after all this, some businesses failed, they were subsidised or nationalised. As against unionised labour, there is a very large and increasing pool of exploited workers in the so-called informal sector who are neglected by the union leadership as well as by the state. They bear the brunt of inflation and recession. Together, the state and the union leadership have created, sustained and strengthened a dual labour market with a labour aristocracy on the one side, and a more numerous but defenceless and exploited class of workers, on the other.

The Green Revolution is another area where we have erred on the side of policy excesses. Rich and middle-income farmers have ushered in the revolution which reduced the country's food deficit, and gave her much-needed food security.[6] In the process, however, these farmers have become used to subsidies (which were necessary at some earlier stage) and also become more and more demanding in this matter. The range of these subsidies has widened steadily and become more and more of a burden on the budget, accounting for nearly 15 per cent of total budget outlays.

The political clout of the beneficiaries has, however, secured them powerful support even from the so-called radical parties. The 'radicals' ignore the fact that the medium and large farm households constitute about 10 per cent of total rural households but own about 50 per cent of the cultivated area.[7]

The fertiliser, power and irrigation subsidies mostly benefit a minority of the rural rich. It is estimated that the subsidies on agricultural inputs rose from about one-third of the combined Plan expenditure on agriculture, irrigation and special area programmes in the early eighties to 90 per cent by the end of the decade.[8]

An argument frequently used to justify the fertiliser subsidy is that its withdrawal will drastically reduce the demand and hence the use of fertilisers with damaging consequences on agricultural productivity. The exaggerated nature of this argument was well-established when the 30-per cent increase in fertiliser prices in July 1991 did not lead to any fall in their use. This was due to the fact that the demand for fertilisers responds more to the availability of water than to prices. This is because the ratio of fertiliser costs to total farm costs is very low – less than 10 per cent even for Punjab wheat. The expansion of direct and indirect subsidies to agriculture has reduced government resources and has resulted in an overall decline in capital formation in this sector during the eighties. This decline has very grave consequences for the future growth of agricultural output and productivity.

The inflexibility of our policies continued even in areas where it was clear that the premises of those policies were no longer valid. Our export pessimism remained undiminished even when world trade was expanding at an unprecedented. Thus the great boom in trade, which lasted a quarter of a century ending in 1973, bypassed us. Nor did we change our attitude to foreign equity capital when it was available on easier terms. This type of insularity is responsible for India being a very minor player in the world economy. The Indian share in world trade which was very meagre to begin with (2 per cent in 1950) has steadily come down (0.5 per cent in 1988). As a result, India's standing is reduced in the global economy. Our marginalisation is visible in the on-going round of multilateral trade negotiations in the GATT.

Politics of Economic Policies

How does one explain the continuation of such institutionalised inefficiency and the system of continuing subsidies resulting in low growth for such a long time ? The answer lies in the dynamics of our policital economy which has enabled the beneficiaries of old policies to dominate the political system. The core element of this system consists of the rich and middle farmers from the dominant, land owning castes. They have replaced the old and historically entrenched zamindars and substituted their old institutionalised inequality by their own variety of dominance over the rural poor. They have achieved this astonishing success through a combination of caste linkages and populist programmes and slogans and by the use of caste tensions in their own favour in the elections, especially in the state assembly elections. They have in this way secured the support of the social strata of the rural society whose interests are otherwise opposed to theirs. In fact, they are against Scheduled Castes and Scheduled Tribes and they often gather benefits from programmes meant for poverty alleviation in rural areas.

The more affluent sections of the dominant land owning castes have shifted to urban areas where they join the new urban middle class groups which have emerged as a result of the growth of small scale industries, trade, commerce, construction and services in the towns. These groups are in alliance with the rich and middle peasantry with whom they share their antipathy against large scale industry and big business.[9]

They may not share the social mores or cultural traits of their rural allies, but they find the alliance politically most rewarding. Together they form very powerful groupings whose views and interests have exerted considerable influence on the country's policy agenda. The leadership of these groups has acquired a radical vocabulary which has secured them the support of the intelligentsia and political parties and functions professing radical economic ideologies.

There was a time when India was regarded as a new model for economic development and social change. In the early phase of Cold War, the Indian model was often presented by some in the western world as a counterpoint to the Chinese model for other developing countries. But after the mid-sixties, India lost that appeal, primarily because of its economy's lacklustre performance. Meanwhile, East Asian economies developed at spectacular rates which, in our smugness we dismissed as small country phenomena. However, since 1978, China too has changed its economic gears and has demonstrated how increased participation in international trade can boost domestic economic growth even in a large economy. While China has been able to attract an average inflow of about 3 billion US dollars per year for the past few years, India has managed a bare 150 million.

While Chinese exports have grown to 60 billion US dollars, ours are languishing at 18 billion. China is integrating with the world economy at a faster rate: its average effective tariffs are in the range of 15-20 per cent while ours are nearer 60 per cent. As a result of its concentrated effort at export promotion, China's foreign exchange reserves stand at 45 billion US dollars, compared to India's 6 billion. To stimulate economic growth, China is changing even its much cherished labour policies. The new policies are replacing the old Job-for-life system by contract jobs. The latter system is considered essential for the success of the reforms. The new policy has been justified on the ground that "the permanent employment system which provides 'iron rice bowls' and 'iron chairs' or secure jobs for cadres, is now considered a major obstacle for economic reform."

India, on the other hand, persisted with its policies without revising them in the light of emerging circumstances and opportunities as adumbrated by the Second Plan directive. The policies became doctrines in support of political radicalism even as they became less and less relevant to the solution of basic problems. In actual fact, the so-called radicalism merely provided an ideological justification for the structures of privilege and protection that the excesses of policy had created. The really poor have been used as an incantation for the ideology; their reward being token gestures like anti-poverty schemes. This low-growth based political equilibrium could rest undisturbed only as long as the rival claims could be met through the resolution of conflicts by the state rather than the market.

The system of subsidies and patronage has assumed a size where it is no longer possible for all rival claims to grow further without making the arrangement untenable. Furthermore, over the years, due to increasing corruption and competitive populism, the state itself has lost the credibility and legitimacy which permitted it to reconcile rival claims.

In fact, the low-growth political equilibrium has already become untenable, considering the fact that the subsidies (explicit and implicit) add up to 15 per cent of the GDP in a situation in which the ratio of tax revenue to GDP is just a little ahead of the subsidies at 17 per cent.[10]

In the fiscal year 1988-89, "the three components of non-plan expenditure, viz, defence, interest payment and major subsidies alone pre-empted about 105 per cent of the Centre's net tax revenue."[11]

Thus there is no 'invisible hand' in the political market which can assure adjustments. There is nothing to prevent the rivalry of dominant and coercive groups reaching a stage where non-negotiable claims add up to more than the total national product.

The beginning of reforms

The fact that the economy as it has evolved is no longer able to meet the growing internal challenges and external shocks has gained acceptance gradually. With small beginnings in policy changes required to absorb the first oil shock in 1973 to experiments with selective deregulation of industrial and import licensing since the early 1980s, the process of economic reform has continued, though at a slow and halting pace. The government set up several committees to examine its fiscal, monetary, industrial and trade policies during this period.[12]

On the basis of this extensive policy review, it was recognised that the regulatory regime imposed on industry and trade had lasted much longer than was required and that the public sector could no longer function on the basis of a soft budget constraint. By mid-eighties, the reform movement gained further strength.

The budgets of 1985-86 and 1986-87 introduced some important changes in policy and several others were announced in broad terms in the documents of the Seventh Plan and the Long Term Fiscal Policy. There were also some important changes in industrial policies whereby 'broadbanding', i.e. greater freedom in the choice of product mix was permitted and some MRTP provisions were relaxed.

Entry conditions in some industries were also made easier.

Reforms slow down

Tragically, the reforms lost virtually all momentum when it was most needed and when they could have been more effective and less painful. By mid-1987, clouds of uncertainty appeared on the political horizon, the government weakened and further reform became a hostage to political rivalries. Fiscal indiscipline increased.

The Seventh Plan was financed by domestic borrowing and deficit budgeting to a much greater extent than was targeted. A similar pattern operated in the financing of the current account deficit. The decline in multilateral and bilateral assistance was replaced by sharp increases in commercial borrowing and non-resident short term deposits. As a percentage of the current account deficit, aid declined from 55 per cent during the Sixth Plan to 29 per cent in the Seventh, while commercial borrowing and non-resident deposits increased to 25 per cent and 23 per cent respectively.

While discussing the deterioration in the balance of payments situation, it is necessary to get a red herring out of the way. Several critics have argued that the deterioration in the balance of payments since' 1985 has been due to import liberalisation.[13]

This has been found to be factually incorrect. The deterioration was caused by increase in non-customable/non-commercial imports (which include fertiliser, POL and defence supplies), interest payments on foreign debt and decline in private remittances and net earnings from invisible services.[14]

The general elections of 1989 with their inconclusive results further encouraged competitive populism rather than the implementation of measures to reduce the budgetary and balance of payments deficits. For example, soon after it was installed the Janata Dal government announced agricultual loan waivers resulting in a new burden of Rs. 8,000 crore on the exchequer.

Again, while the procurement price of wheat and rice was raised twice in 1990-91, no attempt was made to raise the fertiliser prices which had remained unchanged since 1981 with the result that the burden of fertiliser subsidy stood at Rs. 8,400 crore in 1990-91.

Financial Crisis

These and similar policies led to widening fiscal deficits. The Ninth Finance Commission had projected the Centre's revenue deficit at the level of Rs. 8,500 crore for 1990-91 and 1991-92. The actual figures turned out to be twice as high with the inevitable increase in inflationary pressures which spilled over and aggravated the balance of payments deficits. By the beginning of 1989, the balance of payments situation was serious enough to require the government to seek IMF assistance.

For political reasons, a recourse to IMF was avoided in favour of short-term commercial borrowing, a decision which boomeranged when the situation deteriorated further due to the Gulf crisis.

The Gulf crisis resulted in a substantial loss of remittances from the area and of exports to the countries of the region and increase in the import bill for crude oil and petroleum products. These developments resulted in a sharp decline in foreign exchange reserves from Rs. 5,050 crore in August 1990 to Rs. 4,388 crore at the end of the fiscal year 1990-91 despite two IMF loans totalling Rs. 4,517 crore during this period!

The postponement of the budget in February 1991 further delayed the implementation of corrective measures. It also generated a crisis of confidence in world capital markets about India's credit worthiness and political will to discharge its debt obligations. As a result, access to external commercial credit was effectively denied. Evidently, the balance of payments situation was extremely precarious.

This fact, combined with political uncertainty, brought down India's credit rating in financial markets abroad and among non-resident Indian depositors. The banks decided to stop roll overs of the short term debt and a default on international obligations became a possibility.

It was in these grim circumstances that the present government took office in June 1991.

Thus, the task before the present government was twofold:

(i) to restore macroeconomic stability by reducing fiscal and balance of payments deficits, and

(ii) to complete the process of economic reforms which had for the last ten years been conducted intermittently.

Resumption of reforms

It is thus obvious that the interruption of the process of reforms since 1987 and the financial profligacy of the intervening unstable regimes made it obligatory for the government to implement the package of stabilisation and structural adjustment policies advocated by the IMF and the World Bank.

These policies address the problems which were perceived by our own policy-makers earlier.[15]

Their main purpose is to pull the economy out of the tight spot in which it has been placed by the recent financial crisis and set it on a long-term high-growth path which was the purpose of the policy changes initiated since early eighties.

The case for additional reforms rests on the proposition that their implementation will increase the economy's growth potential, increase its capacity and resilience to respond to future shocks successfully, increase employment, and reduce poverty. These results are expected to be achieved by policy instruments that will lead to better allocation of resources, elimination of public sector inefficiencies, better industrial relations and so on. In other words, the new policies will realise the old objectives with which we started our developmental effort.

The new policies constitute a more genuine radical programme and are more relevant to the solution of our problems than the policies of yesteryears.

The implementation of structural reforms requires a stable macroeconomic environment which, as we have seen above, has been deteriorating for the last several years. The restoration of macroeconomic stability requires reduction of fiscal and balance-of-payments deficits. Reducing these deficits and keeping the rate of inflation under control would necessarily involve contraction of domestic demand and economic activity in the short run. This would involve hardships and social costs which will be acceptable if they are, and are seen to be, equitably shared. This can be achieved only in a framework of political stability and a broad based national consensus which goes beyond partisan interests.

While adjustments are being carried out, their adverse impact can be softened by resorting to external concessional finance which would enable the government to maintain a larger external deficit than would be possible without it during the transitional period. It is, however, important to realise that external finance can at best provide a breathing time and cannot be a substitute for our efforts in the direction of adjustment or the solution to our problems. But this breathing time can be valuable and hence the recourse to the IMF for loan assistance. Without this facility, the contraction of economic activity and the resultant deprivation would be far greater. As is usual, it is the poorest who are the worst affected in any such eventuality.

The IMF conditionalities certainly involve policy changes and reform of institutions. But then why should we cavil at these conditionalities so long as they are congruent with our own programme of reforms, which as we have seen above, was interrupted by political instability. There need not be a one to one correspondence between IMF conditionalities and our reform programme. There can be differences on precise magnitudes such as the extent to which the budget deficit needs to be reduced; or, on the sequencing of various measures or their comprehensiveness. These differences can be of a technical or of a political nature. Technical differences are for experts to sort out, but where political judgments matter, the last word has to be with the government of India.

Unfortunately, the public debate on the IMF conditionalities and the involvement of the World Bank in the reform process is vitiated by the visceral feelings of the ideologues and the opposition of special interests who fear loss of privilege and power. These two multilateral agencies are supposed to be eroding the economic sovereignty of the country.[16] This has prevented the transmission of the true meaning and purpose of economic reforms to the people at large. The government, barring the Finance Minister, Dr. Manmohan Singh, and the erstwhile Commerce Minister, Mr. Chidambaram, have made no special effort to convey to the people that the reforms are not being adopted merely because the IMF wants them, but because India needs them. The countries that have carried out adjustment programmes successfully during the latter half of the eighties are the ones that undertook them out of their own conviction, for example, Chile, Mexico, Turkey and Indonesia.

The principal weakness of the Indian reforms has been the absence of a powerful constituency to support them. Their natural constituency consists of the poor multitudes who have been left out of the development process so far.

The poor have not as yet thrown up a leadership which can articulate their genuine demands. Nor has India produced a far-seeing elite which could mobilise the poor in their own interest and in the interest of creating a modern, vibrant and prosperous economy.

Even the reformers have not put before the public the linkages between economic reforms and the reduction of poverty convincingly. The Indian political elite has not been able to overcome the limits imposed by special interests which support it.

The Indian attempts at economic reforms have, therefore, been half-hearted and fitful. Till July 1991, the reforms that were introduced were meant either to relax the rigours of counter productive licensing procedures or as measures for crisis management or as administrative/technocratic measures to lessen the burden on administration.

Even though these have been helpful improvements in policy, they have amounted to no more than minor reforms. However, these measures have never been presented as a package with their expected consequences spelled out so that they could be judged as a whole. It is possible that someone in the government had a notion of the programme in its entirety and did not want to reveal it because of the fear of opposition from vested interests. But it is extremely naive to believe that a thorough-going reform which the Indian economy needs could have been pushed through stealthily. This approach has delayed the process of adjustment and has made the political management of the latest and most important policy changes and institutional reforms even more difficult than it would otherwise have been. People must know where the economy stands today and how it came to this pass and where it will be when the reforms are completed. This task is yet to be undertaken.

Current Phase of Reforms

As noted above, the current phase of the reforms started under the shadow of the balance of payments crisis. It is unfortunate, but perhaps inevitable under the Indian political conditions, that sharp policy changes can take place only in a crisis situation. For the first time, India is now making a serious and comprehensive effort to stabilise and reform the economy. Along with the measures to reverse the trend of fiscal expansionism to restore macroeconomic balance in the economy, sweeping measures have been adopted to remove distortions and inefficiencies that have prevented the economy from realizing its full potential.

The reform strategy of the government aims at achieving, in the course of next five years;

(a) a liberalised trade regime with tariff rates comparable to those of other industrialising developing countries and the absence of discretionary import licensing (with the exception of a small negative list);

(b) an exchange rate system which is free of allocative restrictions for trade;

(c) a financial system operating in a competitive market environment and regulated by sound prudential norms and standards;

(d) an efficient and dynamic industrial sector subject only to regulations relating to environment security, strategic concerns, industrial safety, and unfair trading and monopolistic practices; and

(e) an autonomous, competitive and streamlined public sector, geared to the provision of essential infrastructure goods and services, the development of key natural resources and areas of strategic concern and development of crucial social sectors like education, health and R&D which normally remain underfunded/underinvested in a market dominated economy.[17]

In pursuit of some of these objectives, new initiatives were taken in trade policy to stimulate exports. Besides, exchange rate adjustment to a more realistic level coupled with drastic reduction of export subsidies measures were taken to eliminate quantitative restrictions on import of intermediate and capital goods. Imports of consumer goods, however, remain under severe restriction which means effective protection of about 45 per cent of manufactured tradeables produced in the country. With improvement in the balance of payments situation, the ban on imports of consumer goods also is expected to be lifted. Tariffs have been lowered even though they still remain high. The maximum tariff was lowered to 110 per cent from the earlier level of 150 per cent. For capital goods, tariffs have been reduced to 55 per cent and for some items related to coal mining, petroleum refining and power projects, the rate has been lowered to 30 per cent.

Further reduction in tariffs is dependent on the success in reducing fiscal deficit. The dual exchange rate system introduced with eximscript scheme has been further simplified and made transparent under the new dual exchange rate management system popularly described as partial convertibility.

Although there are restrictions on some exports, their range has been reduced. The number of items banned for exports has been reduced to 7 from 68. The ban on the remaining items, such as wild animals, birds and human products is based on ethical and ecological grounds. Restrictions on most manufactured items have been removed. Much more significant are the restrictions on agricultural products like rice or cotton whose prices are lower than the international prices. The removal of restrictions on their exports is not feasible immediately but from a longer term point of view of efficient allocation of resources, the problem will have to be addressed.

To complement the new trade and fiscal policies, the new industrial policy has substantially deregulated industry. Industrial licensing has been abolished for all projects except in 18 industries where strategic or environmental concerns are paramount. It is estimated that 80 per cent of industry is now outside licensing system.

The need for large companies to seek prior approval for capacity expansion or diversification has been eliminated. The phased manufacturing programme is no longer required for new projects. Greater participation of private sector in core and basic industries is now permitted while the areas reserved for the public sector have been reduced from 17 to 8, mostly for strategic and security reasons. Even in these 8 private investment for oil exploration and captive coal mines refining have now been permitted. Small scale enterprises are now permitted to offer 24 per cent of their equity to large-scale and other industrial undertakings. Financial institutions are no longer required to provide for their right to convert loans to private companies into equity. The government approval for foreign investments up to 51 per cent of equity and foreign technology agreements in selected sectors has been made automatic. The Foreign Investment Promotion Board has been set up to negotiate with large international companies and also consider cases involving foreign equity participation over 51 per cent.

Next phase of reforms

The reforms introduced so far make an impressive list and mark a decisive break with some of the old policies that held the Indian economy back. But what remains to be done is even more important and crucial to the success of the reforms. At the same time, it is politically more difficult to manage. To impart dynamism to the economy, it is necessary to drastically reform the public sector, revamp the financial sector and create a healthy and stable industrial relations system. Additionally, further improvements in the fiscal, trade and industrial policies will be required to consolidate and improve upon the changes already introduced. This is a formidable agenda.

The part of the reform programme which is already completed was easier to implement because it was undertaken in an atmosphere of crisis that had a sobering effect on political wranglings. And despite their broad sweep and radical nature, the reforms did not hurt the entrenched interests. The reforms that are due now will take place under more 'normal' economic circumstances and hurt powerful vested interests to some extent. Their implementation will, therefore, demand better technical and political skills than those required earlier. The next phase of reforms will thus be a testing time for the government, in particular, and the political class of India, in general. It will test the government's commitment to reforms and the goal of transforming the economy into a dynamic one. It will also signal to the world the place and role India's political class envisages for the country in the global economy.

If the reforms are allowed to succeed India will rank among the most dynamic economies around the turn of the century.

Prospects of reforms

Given these circumstances, what then are the prospects of the reforms? The success of the reforms will depend on their political feasibility which, in turn, will depend on the length of the transitional period, the nature of the transitional costs and the manner in which these costs are shared. Most important, it is the understanding of the people about the actual nature and purpose of these reforms which will determine their success. Public support for reforms will also depend on their perception of its success. The more the reforms appear to be succeeding the more they will succeed on the ground.

The full impact of economic reforms will be known only after they have been implemented fully. The manner and the sequence of implementation programme is equally important in determining the final results. It is, however, important to monitor the effects of the reforms as they are being implemented. This will help in the early rectification of mistakes as they arise.

How does the economy look today, after a year and a half of reforms? The immediate threat to balance of payments has receded; and there is a perceptible improvement in international confidence in the economy. India has been removed from the watch list of the leading credit agencies though its credit rating has not been upgraded. The question of credit rating remains tied up with the problem of India's foreign debt which will be discussed later. Within the country it is now widely recognised that a better environment has been created for further growth of industry, trade and investment.

How are these perceptions translating in terms of hard economic indicators? To be sure, the initial period of adjustment of the sort Indian economy requires was expected to be harsh.

And it has indeed been so. The GDP growth rate for the fiscal year 1991-92 is estimated to be about 1.7 per cent, which is a steep drop from the previous year's figure of 5.6 per cent. This is as expected in view of the strong deflationary measures the government had to adopt to restore some order in macroeconomic balances.

Measures like drastic import restrictions and a tight monetary policy were bound to decelerate the economy. The process of deceleration was reinforced by the negative growth (0.5 per cent) of the agricultural sector due to adverse weather conditions and decline in exports due primarily to the sudden collapse of Soviet and the East European markets which accounted for 20 per cent of our exports. The high rate of inflation reduced the advantage of the devaluation of the rupee. The recession in the U.S. reduced the demand for some important Indian exports like gems and jewellery. Even so, the exports outside the rupee payment area increased by 6 per cent in dollar terms, but the overall result was disappointing; exports fell by 1.9 per cent. The tertiary sector, which has been a high growth sector, was also affected adversely by the decline in commodity sectors and reduced public expenditures. In sum, the year 1991-92, the first year of the structural adjustment programme, was, as expected, a difficult year.

According to the World Bank experience, adjustment programmes for which external funding is considered necessary are expected to last five to seven years; in some cases even ten years. Luckily for India, the period is not likely to be prolonged because, despite our many weaknesses, we have some advantages too. India, unlike some other developing countries and the reforming economies of the Central Europe and Russia, started the process of reforms much before it was hit by the financial crisis. In the year of the crisis itself India registered a growth rate of 5.6 per cent because the crisis was essentially financial in nature. India has other advantages, such as a large private sector and a class of dynamic entrepreneurs who has so far been constrained by a restrictive policy frame-work. It also has the institutions of the market economy and a high domestic rate of savings.

Evidence has started coming in, which suggests that the fiscal year, starting from March 1993 will see the beginning of a modest recovery. The GDP growth rate is expected to be around 4 per cent. The forebodings about the monsoons having proved wrong, the growth of the agricultural sector may turn out to be much higher than the expected 1.3 per cent. The easing of the tight monetary policy and the reduction of import restrictions have revived industrial growth in recent weeks. It is estimated to be about three to four per cent for the current year as against zero per cent last year. In recent months, exports have started picking up. For the period April-September, exports have gone up by 5.4 per cent and to the general currency area by about 12 per cent.

It also seems that the first round of reforms is resulting in a pick-up of private corporate investment.[18] The Reserve Bank of India has forecast an 11 per cent increase in total capital expenditure over the previous year.

These facts seem to suggest that India's period of adjustments is likely to be of a shorter duration. The sharp fall in foreign exchange reserves to 1.1 billion U.S. dollars, which triggered the crisis in June, 1991, has been reversed. A year later (8 July, 1992) the reserves climbed back to about 6.8 billion U.S. dollars.

This reversal is impressive and will greatly ease the adjustment process. At the same time, however, it must be noted that the improved foreign exchange reserve position is mainly the result of the IMF/World Bank loans, increase in foreign aid and its quicker disbursement. The financial inflows on account of India Development Bond and Immunity Schemes have further strengthened the reserves. However, aid and loans add to our foreign debt, which has to be served, and inflow of funds under Immunity Schemes are once-over episodes. The ultimate success of the reforms in this area will depend on our ability to move away from loans and aid to foreign direct investment and exports.

Debt Problem

Most of the criticism against economic reforms emanates from the advocates of the adversely affected interests or ideologues whose mind-set is against changes in old policies. But there is a genuine fear among many people that structural adjustment might lead to an increasing debt burden and ultimately to a debt trap of Latin American dimensions. This is a fear that needs to be allayed if the reforms are to gather greater public support.

Before addressing the main issue, viz., our ability to cope with the growing foreign debt, some preliminary remarks are in order. The big jump in our foreign debt during the past 10 years was the result of massive mismanagement that preceded the June 1991 crisis. The problem India faced then was not only of short-term external disequilibrium but also of long entrenched and policy-induced malaise which kept its economy hobbled on to a low growth path and foreign exchange shortage. The government's task was not only to manage the immediate balance of payments crisis but also to exercise the spectre of foreign exchange shortage, which has been hovering over the economy since 1956-57.

In the summer of 1991, the country desperately needed foreign exchange to meet the immediate payment obligations to avoid default. It also needed an assured foreign exchange support to bridge over the period during which the economy would be reformed enough to pay for its imports and debt service requirements in the future. For both of these purposes the only source of funds available was the IMF and the World Bank. It is the indebtedness to these institutions that has increased significantly during the past two years. Since the repayment schedule for their loans has to be adhered to strictly, questions are raised by critics about India's ability to meet these and other obligations without running into another crisis of the 1991 variety. The credibility of the reform programme thus hinges on the management of the debt problem. In this context, it is important to have first an accurate idea of the size and structure of India's foreign debt.

There has been a lot of confusion on this account because of discrepancy in the data provided by the Reserve Bank, the government and the international agencies, like the World Bank, the IMF and the Bank of International Settlements. Now that the exercise to streamline the statistics on external debt have completed, the picture is much clearer. According to the exercise, the external debt of India on 31 December, 1991, was about 66 billion U.S. dollars.[19]. To this should be added three billion non-rouble defence-related debt, which raises the total to 69 billion U.S. dollars. This, however, excludes the debt we owe to the former Soviet Union.

In the next three years, the total figure of India's foreign debt is likely to increase by another 10 to 15 billion dollars on account of exceptional financing requirements. This will pose problems of repayment in 1995-96 because of the bunching of repayments. By that year exports may not have increased to a level which will enable a normal servicing of the debt. This is a problem that requires serious thinking even at this stage.

India's external debt is now comparable to that of the heavily indebted Latin American countries and makes India rank among the largest debtors in the developing world. However, from the point of view of debt servicing, the composition of the debt is as important as it's size. In this respect, India is better placed than middle income debtor countries. About 28 billion of India's debt is on concessional terms: interest rates average 2.2 per cent and maturities average about 35 years. India, however, cannot afford to repeat the profligacy of the last decade, when an increasing proportion of debt was contracted on hard conditions because of easy recourse to commercial borrowing which increased from 9.8 per cent in 1980-81 to about 41 per cent in 1990-91. The management of foreign debt is, therefore, a crucial task. It involves avoidance of commercial borrowing, encouragement of non-debt sources of capital like foreign private capital, and a concentrated attention on promotion of exports, all the things that were neglected in the past. Above all, it involves the use to which the debt is put. If it is used to implement the reforms and to build export capacity, it will be self-liquidating. The economic reforms are expected to give a competitive edge to our exports, but that may not be enough. Trade policy changes are necessary but not a sufficient condition for high growth of exports. These policies will have to be reinforced by product-specific and country-specific marketing and promotional measures. Korea and Taiwan did not succeed in their export drive because of simple liberalisation, but rather as a result of planned strategy.

Foreign investment has started picking up though the pace has yet to accelerate significantly to fulfill India's requirements. During May-August, 1992, the number of foreign collaboration approvals increased by 184 per cent as compared to the corresponding period last year (i.e. from 457 to 1298). The amount of foreign equity involved also increased by about 12 times during this period.

Financial Stabilisation Programme

Since financial stabilisation is an overriding requirement for the success of the reforms, containment and reduction of the rate of inflation from the high levels of 1991-92 was an important objective of the new policies. If the fiscal deficit comes down and inflation is reduced, exports too have a better chance of expansion. On a point-to-point basis, the weekly price index on December 15 was only 8.6 per cent above the corresponding week last year. On an annualised basis, the rate of price increase for the current year is likely to be around 10 per cent.

The fiscal deficit has been brought down to 6.2 per cent of GDP from 8.4 per cent of the previous year and may be brought down further to 5 per cent in the current year, but the control over inflationary forces will continue to pose problems for policy makers. The reduction of fiscal deficit by more than two percentage points has come primarily from cuts in capital expenditures on infrastructure and reduction of outlays on social sectors. Such cuts are likely to hurt future growth and the poor. These actions go against the fundamental purposes of the reforms and should be avoided.

From an economic point of view, the cuts should have been made in the revenue expenditure as it was indeed postulated in the budget presented in July, 1991. The budget had announced a deficit of Rs 13,850 crore for the year 1991-92. The revised estimate turned out to be of the order of Rs. 17,080 crore. The government explanation for its inability to bring down the revenue deficit to the targeted figure is that it had to meet arrears due to previous commitments on account of export and fertiliser subsidies and farm loan waivers. This, however, is not an adequate explanation. The unstated part of the explanation is the inability of the government to reduce its personnel made redundant by the reforms. Worse still, it has failed to make public services and public sector employees to share even in a small measure the burden of the adjustment programmes. This inability of the government has been dramatised by its unilateral announcement, in September 1992, of the latest instalment of dearness allowance which goes against the suggestions of the sub-committee of the National Development Council, chaired by the Chief Minister of Orissa, Mr. Biju Patnaik.

The sub-committee had recommended a one-year freeze on wage increases and additional dearness allowance, bonus and leave travel grants for government employees at the Centre and States. If these recommendations had been implemented, it would have committed the states to greater fiscal responsibility and helped in the stabilisation of state finances.

The implementation of such policies would, no doubt, have been strongly resisted by the trade unions and some political parties, but the government of India has by its action prevented these issues to become even a matter of public debate. In a much less serious economic crisis in 1973-74, in the wake of first oil price hike, the government did implement similar measures successfully.

The government has by this single act undermined the usefulness of National Development Council as a forum for securing concensual political support for the reforms and encouraged its unionised employees and industrial workers in their dog-in-the-manger attitudes. Since the budget has no provision for dearness allowance, the government will have either to raise more revenue to meet its self-inflicted new obligations or to divert funds from productive uses to meet the demands of what Mr. Patnaik has correctly described as "the two per cent of the relatively better-off population".

It must, however, be recognised that though there is a general consensus about the need to reduce fiscal deficit to more manageable levels, there are wide differences on how to go about it. The differences are basically of a political nature. Ideally, the guiding principle should be to raise revenue from those who have, for one reason or another, escaped their share of the burden lightly and to reduce expenditures which are manifestly wasteful or unproductive. While the principle is acceptable in the abstract, it's application runs to counter entrenched interests. Take the case of income tax. Even after excluding agriculturists who are exempted from income tax, there are about 44 million urban families and only 7 million income tax payers.

There are two reasons for this low figure. First, the exemption limit for income tax is high, if allowance is made for the various tax concessions given. By raising the exemption limit further in the last budget, 8 lakh assesses have been left out of the income tax net.

Our idea of progressivity in the past has been to raise tax rates, which has resulted in large scale tax evasion. But then, the right course to adopt is to reduce the rates especially in the lower income brackets rather than reduce the number of income tax payers. The second reason is that a very large number of self-employed professionals, traders and small businessmen evade income tax on a massive scale.

With a low share of direct taxes, our revenue structure has become both regressive and distortionary. High incidence of excise duties is regressive. Import duties of 110 per cent and above distorted investment patterns and make Indian products uncompetitive.

Again, a very large part of the industrial output produced by small scale industries is either exempted from excise duties or is subject to concessional rates. These are only a few instances to indicate the laxity of our tax system, which needs a thorough overhaul. Our tax system has not been systematically reviewed since the Taxation Enquiry Commission of 1952. The changes since then have been of an adhoc nature which have made matters even more chaotic. With the appointment of Raja Chelliah Committee, the tax system is being reformed. The first set of recommendations of the Committee were incorporated in the budget for the fiscal year 1992-93.

Beginning of Tax Reforms

The recommendations introduced are the first steps towards the reform of the tax system, which aims at reduction of present dependence on customs duties, broadening of the tax base, and replacement of the existing chaotic excise duties by a broad-based value-added system.

In pursuit of these objectives, the present income tax rates were reduced by 10 percentage points to 40 per cent and some tax exemptions meant earlier to stimulate savings were either eliminated or reduced. Capital gains tax will now be adjusted for inflation and equities, bonds and deposits removed from items subjected to wealth tax. A presumptive tax is to be levied on people having income from retail trade. A similar tax is to be levied on people engaged in vocations. These changes have started the process of simplification and rationalisation of the tax structure but for the present they are largely tax neutral. Meanwhile, the reduction of the fiscal deficit is an immediate necessity. Since the prospects of raising revenue are not bright in the immediate future, the emphasis in government pronouncements and in public debate is on reduction of expenditure. The government, however, has not undertaken any systematic review of public expenditure.

The reduction of subsidies is the most favoured and, at the same time, the most resisted recommendation for closing the budgetary gap. Substantial reduction in the export subsidies and some reduction in the fertiliser and containment of food subsidies has started the process, but it is clear that the process will be very slow. The elimination of fertiliser subsidy affects interests that enjoy powerful political support. It also requires reorganisation of the fertiliser industry. Some kind of a compromise solution has been arrived at by the Joint Parliamentary Committee, which has tried to accommodate the need to cut the subsidy and pacify the farm lobby. It's recommendation of partial decontrol of fertiliser prices has been quickly implemented, not because it was the best solution, but because it was politically feasible. All that partial decontrol has achieved is to keep the amount of subsidy within the budgetary provision of Rs. 5,000 crore!

Similarly, nothing much can be done about the food subsidy, which is required to cushion the impact of higher food prices on the poor. It certainly needs to be better targeted, but that is something more easily said then done. Better targeting is likely to impose additional administrative costs and open new avenues for corruption.

The extension of public distribution system is often abused for populist reasons. For example, in Andhra Pradesh, 80 per cent of the population is covered by the rice subsidy even though only 30 per cent are below the poverty line. The Government of Kerala had, in a similar populist fashion, decided to spend Rs. 180

crore from state funds on food subsidy. However, they found it difficult to sustain the subsidy at that level and had to reduce it by half. In both the cases, the motivation of the state government has been to gain partisan political advantage and not the welfare of the poor.

There is no way out of the political murk which envelops subsidy schemes meant for the poor but to find more effective solutions. These solutions will have to be productive, employment schemes which provide work and income for the really needy rather than for those whom insensitive and corrupt agencies define as poor for the express purpose of doling out subsidy.

Agricultural Development

The problem of poverty, employment and growth cannot be solved effectively without recasting the strategy for agricultural development. The policy of protection to industry is inherently biased against agriculture: the relative price of industry and agriculture favours the former when compared with world prices. Consequently, investment flows to agriculture from private as well as public resources have tended to decline, particularly during the past 10 years. The result has been a stagnation of foodgrain output.

Policy measures are needed to reverse this trend. In this connection, the recent reduction in protection to Indian industry should be seen as a step in favour of agriculture.

The earlier approach of budgetary support via direct and indirect subsidies to agriculture is neither desirable nor sustainable in view of the urgent need to reduce fiscal deficit. New policies are required, which should enourage greater flow of investment resources based on more realistic relative prices and gradual elimination of subsidies for inputs.

The withdrawal of agricultural subsidies will release resources which will enable the government to raise its outlay on the much-needed public investment in this sector.

Equally important for agricultural development is the revamping of the rural banking system. The system of rural credit has almost broken down. The cooperative credit system has been rendered unviable by the imposition of unrealistically low interest rates. The availability of the institutional credit which, at present, is mostly used by the better off farmers is far more important for the poor farmers than the artificially low interest rates. Measures to improve access to institutional credit will also widen the social base of investors in agriculture. Again, there has been a visible decline in the agricultural research system. It needs to be revived and its linkage to seed production and productivity firmly established. All these problems in this vital sector of the economy require a thorough review of current policies, particularly those pertaining to subsidised inputs and control on output prices.[20]

The foregoing discussion on the problem of subsidies makes it clear that it is not a simple matter of budgetary cuts. It also involves formulation of policies which will take care of the side effects of these cuts. It also involves some reshuffle of the beneficiaries and the victims of the old policy, which makes it a thorny political question.

Subsidies and Consensus

The subsidies can be reduced effectively only on the basis of a political consensus. This is particularly true of the hidden subsidies, such as those of electricity, irrigation and higher education. Given the nature of resistance to the reduction of subsidies, policies have to be designed in a manner which will link their reduction to concrete counter-balancing advantages. Such trade-offs will create constituencies for reform which at the moment are either non-existent or inarticulate.

For example, it has been demonstrated that the reduction of fertiliser subsidy and allocation of a part of the savings on rural works programmes and the rest on additional investment for irrigation is a policy that will benefit landless workers, poor farmers as well as urban consumers and lead to higher economic growth.[21]

Again, if power and irrigation rates were raised to the level that would yield a reasonable return on capital invested in these undertakings, resources will become available to provide irrigation and power facilities to the poorer farmers. A smooth flow of supplies of fertiliser, water and power at market prices may be much more profitable than inadequate, interrupted and uncertain availability at subsidised prices. In this connection, it has to be borne in mind that the inefficiency of the operations of the government agencies and public sector enterprises justifies demands of farmers for subsidies in several cases.

The inefficiencies of the public sector and multiplying subsidies have reinforced each other at public cost. Costs of fertilisers, irrigation water and electricity could be lowered substantially by improved efficiency in their production. For example, an increase of just one per cent in the plant load factor will yield an additional output of 500 MW of power from the existing capacity or save about 700 crore rupees worth of new investment. Similarly, greater cost effectiveness of the public distribution system would yield savings which would reduce its burden. The reduction of subsidies on higher education will release resources which can be used for providing scholarships and financial assistance to the needy but deserving students and for improving the quality of teaching and research in the universities and so on.

Disinvestment by Public Sector Units

The fair sharing of the burden of the stabilisation programme will, therefore, mean that part of the funds saved by expenditure cuts are allocated to other productive programmes. Thus, the net savings are likely to be less than the total of expenditure cuts. In view of this, other measures need to be explored to reduce the fiscal deficit. One such measure that could reduce fiscal deficit without any harmful side-effect is disinvestment of part of the public sector enterprises. The government initially decided to disinvest up to 20 per cent of the equity of a few such enterprises. This was expected to fetch Rs. 2,500 crore. The percentage has now been raised to 49 and the government expects to raise Rs. 3,500 crore from the sales of public sector equity in 1992-93.

The advantage of disinvestment is that it generates ready cash for the treasury, which should be used to retire debt with the consequence of reducing interest burden. This burden today accounts for nearly 20 per cent of the budgetary outlays. Public shareholding will also enforce public scrutiny and accountability, which will enhance efficiency of the enterprises. It will also broaden the shareholding base in the stock market and open up a new source of funds. All this is, of course, based on the hope that the funds thus raised will not be squandered by the government on unproductive current expenditures.

If the disinvestment programme is implemented successfully, it will help the government in its effort to reduce the fiscal deficit. More importantly, it may enable the government to overcome it's political inhibitions and proceed more boldly to privatise those public sector enterprises where it is necessary. Privatisation has been a complex, cumbersome and time-consuming process wherever it has been undertaken. It has given rise to trade union resistance, complicated legal problems and accusations of corrupt practices. But it has yielded beneficial results in the form of increased productivity and enhanced revenue for the state. The government will have to assemble a great deal of expertise, all of which may not be domestically available, to undertake the privatisation exercise. Even in the case of the modest disinvestment carried out so far, the government has been accused of selling equity at a price lower than what it could have fetched.

Besides disinvestment in public enterprises, suggestions have been made about the sale of a part of the land that the government owns. Here again, the sale of this asset could be linked directly to investment in infrastructure or debt   reduction.

Concluding Observations

The successful implementation of reforms is expected to increase efficiency and growth. As a consequence, employment will expand and poverty will decline. But that is a medium-term perspective. Currently, the measures required to curtail fiscal deficit which has led to a demand squeeze and lower growth as was noted above. This has hit the workers in the informal sector and the rural poor. While it is true that the economy is showing signs of recovery in the current year, the real recovery is at least a couple of years off. This will mean continuation of hardships for them and other vulnerable sections. The alleviation of their hardship is necessary for it's own sake as well as for the acceptance of the reform in general.

Vigorous efforts are, therefore, needed to make the existing anti-poverty programmes more cost-effective and strengthen the self-targeting programmes such as Jawahar Rozgar Yojana and Maharashtra-type employment guarantee schemes. The populist urge to raise the wages in these schemes above the market-determined minimum wages will have to be resisted to ensure that the schemes operate for the really needy. It is also necessary to expand the primary educational and health facilities for the poor in a big way. These measures will lend credibility to the claims of the Eighth Plan that high priority has been given to human resource development and reduction of poverty.

The longer-term impact of liberalisation on industry in the public and private sector leading to retrenchment/redeployment of excess labour poses the most formidable problem for the success of the reforms. This problem cannot be solved only by establishing a fund to finance the terminal benefits or retraining costs of surplus labour. The so-called exit policy will have to be woven into a larger programme of industrial reorganisation – something of the kind that the Japanese did through their famed Ministry of International Trade and Industry. The government has not so far outlined its role in terms of strategic intervention in key areas of industry, trade and technology. Hopefully, this question will be taken up along with the reorganisation of the Planning Commission.

Finally, when all the sums regarding the expenditure cuts and additional expenditures to contain their undesirable economic and social effects are done, it may turn out that the fiscal deficit is not reduced to figures to which the government is publicly committed. There is nothing sacrosanct about a particular figure so long as the trend is in the right direction and there are other advantages favouring growth and more equitable burden-sharing to be gained in the bargain. This position should be acceptable to the IMF and the World Bank. These institutions are themselves showing greater understanding of the costs of adjustment programmes than they used to. They have learnt this from their international experience.

Since 1987, World Bank staff guidelines concerning adjustment lending and social welfare have required that policy framework papers for low-income countries include a "brief description and assessment ... of the social impact of the government's intended adjustment programme" and that the President's Report on structural adjustment loans and credits (SALS) analyse the "short-term impact of the adjustment programme on the urban and rural poor, and the measures proposed to alleviate negative effects". An increasing number of these reports now estimate the expected impact on the 'new poor' – those impoverished by adjustment programmes in the short term, such as retrenched public sector employees.[22]

Thus, the implementation of targets for the reduction of fiscal deficits cannot be a mechanical exercise of numbers. If the deficit is reduced at the cost of future growth or at the cost of the poor, it will defeat the main purpose of the reform. If, therefore, shortfalls in deficit reductions take place without any counterbalancing gains, it will be a compounded folly. Such an outcome will be a triumph of special interests over general welfare. This is the challenge that India poses today to the influential segments of it's political elite, who have been too spellbound in the past by their narrowly conceived interests to focus on national progress and prosperity.

Notes and References

1. See Second Five Year Plan, Planning Commission, Government of India, p. 23 and Third Five Year Plan, p. 5.

2. "Had India's GDP grown as rapidly from 1960 to 1980 as South Korea's, it would stand at $ 531 billion today rather than $ 150 billion – surpassing that of the U.K., equal to that of France, and more then twice that of China. India's per capita income would have been $ 740 instead of $ 260; even with the benefit of growth inequitably distributed, it is not unreasonable to believe that most of the poor would have been substantially better off. India's standing in the world economy and as a world power would have been quite different ..." Myron Weiner, Political Economy of Industrial Growth in India, *World Politics*, 38 (4), 1986. p. 597.

3. See M.K. Datta-Chaudhuri on "Industrialisation and Foreign Trade: The Development Experience of South Korea and the Philippines" in *Export-led Industrialisation and Development*, edited by Eddy Lee, 1981.

4. The rate of return (measured by the ratio of net profit to capital employed) of 236 Central Government public enterprises that were in operation in 1990-91 was 2.3 per cent. The working results of departmentally-run commercial undertakings of States and Union Territories are worse. Their losses for the year 1991-92 were estimated to be of the order of Rs. 1,827 crore. *Economic Survey*, Part II, 1991-92, Government of India, Ministry of Finance, p. 20-21.

5. *Report on the Second All-India Census of Small Scale Industrial Units (registered up to 31st March, 1988)*, Development Commissioner of Small Scale Industries, Ministry of Industry, Government of India, 1992, p. 2.

6. "The Green Revolution changed the agenda of development pertaining to agriculture. Supply of inputs and farm prices took priority over issues of land reform. Since the institutional reordering of agriculture was proving to be politically difficult, the obvious way to increase domestic food supplies was to provide incentives (through guaranteed support prices for major foodgrains and large subsidies for fertilisers). Thus, it was a system of subsidies that made the technocratic solution possible. However, the techno-cratic approach emphasised the favourably placed regions, crops and farmers and left out the marginal farmer and the landless out of it's pale. To prevent any political fall-out from this phenomenon, it became necessary to work out direct assistance programmes which could create additional employment through subsidised loans, integrated rural develop-ment programmes, food for work programmes and so on". See P.N. Dhar, The Political Economy of Development in India. *Indian Economy Review*, Vol. XXII, Number 1, January-June, 1987, p. 11.

7. *All India Report on Agricultural Census*, Ministry of Agriculture, Government of India, 1992, p. 10.

8. C.H.H. Rao estimated that "the subsidies on agricultural inputs rose from about one-third of the combined plan expenditure by the Central and State governments on agriculture, irrigation and Special Area Programmes in the early eighties to 90 per cent towards the close of eighties. The beneficial effects of subsidies seem to be outweighted now by the adverse effects in terms of macroeconomic imbalances, slowing down of investment in agriculture, inefficient use of resources at the farm level and adverse impact on environ-ment and employment of labour". *Economic Reforms and Agriculture*, mimeo. p. 25, 1992.

   According to C.H.H. Rao, "The annual subsidy on fertilisers alone amounts to nearly as much as the annual Plan outlay on agriculture by the Centre and the States put together." Agriculture Policy and Performance in *Indian Economy, Problem and Prospects*, edited by Bimal Jalan 1992, p. 132.

9. The most influential and articulate leader and ideologue of the dominant peasant castes was Chaudury Charan Singh. It was he who evolved a comprehensive public philosophy and policy framework of these groups. See his book: *Economic Nightmare of India, Its Cause and Cure,* National Publishing House, New Delhi, 1981.

10. See, Mundle, S. and Govinda Rao, M., "Volume and Composition of government subsidies in India, 1987-88", *Economic and Political Weekly,* Bombay, May 4, 1991.

11. Reserve Bank of India, *Annual Report, 1988-89,* p. 75.

12. *Report of the Committee to Examine Principles of a Possible Shift from Physical to Financial Controls.* Narasimhan, Chairman (New Delhi: Government of India, 1985); *Report of the Committee on Trade Policies,* Hussain, Chairman (New Delhi: Government of India, Ministry of Commerce, 1984); *Report of the Committee to Review the Working of the Monetary System,* Chakravarty, Chairman (New Delhi: Reserve Bank of India, 1985); and *Long Term Fiscal Policy,* (New Delhi: Government of India, Ministry of Finance, 1985).

13. A. Singh and J. Ghosh, "Import Liberalisation and the New Industrial Strategy: An Analysis of their impact on output and Employment", *Economic and Political Weekly,* Special Number, 1988.

    See also BM, "Liberalisation Road to Economic Ruination", *Economic and Political Weekly,* August 19, 1989.

14. Arvind Virmani, "Trends in Current Account Deficit and the Balance of Trade: Separating Facts from Prejudices", *Economic Research Paper No. 6,* Planning Commission, 1989.

15. The Economic Advisory Council, under the Chairmanship of late Professor Sukhmoy Chakravarty had submitted two reports in January and April, 1990 in which the Council had amply brought out the extent of macro-imbalances in the economy and the need to take corrective measures.

16. The fear about the erosion of economic sovereignty in the wake of the implementation of economic reforms has been repeatedly expressed in Parliament and in the media. For an analysis of this issue, see Appendix 1.

17. This is an extract from the text of Finance Minister's letter to the President, World Bank, dated November 11, 1991, laid on the table of Parliament on February 26, 1992.

18. Non-governmental companies mobilised total investible capital of Rs. 9,846 crore during April-October, 1992 from the capital market through 383 issues of equity and 96 debenture floatations. This is five times larger than the collection for the same period in 1991.

19. For the revised classification of the external debt, see: *The Report of the Policy Group on External Debt Statistics of India,* Reserve Bank of India, 1992. The details are presented in Appendix II.

20. Ray provides an outline of policy requirements and tasks ahead for modernising Indian agriculture. He observes: "Strengthening agricultural research, promoting a distribution and marketing system organised on the basis of rural centering, and ensuring an economic environment to stimulate growth-oriented production and marketing decisions are the basic requirements for progressive modernisation of agriculture. -- Furthermore, active efforts should be encouraged to increase the employment content of agricultural programmes. However, in the short run, these efforts should not divert attention from the primary aim. In the long-run, it is difficult to see how the employment and equity problems will be solved without getting production on a firm footing'. See S.K. Ray, *Progress in Modernising Indian Agriculture,* paper presented at India-China seminar held at New Delhi, 16-18 December, 1982, mimeo, pp. 21-22 (forthcoming in a volume co-edited by D.N. Dhanagare and Huan Xinchvan).

21. See Kirit S. Parikh and M.H. Surayanarayana, *Food and Agricultural Subsidies: Incidence and Welfare under Alternative Schemes,* Indira Gandhi Institute of Development Research, Bombay, 1990, mimeo.

22. See Elaine Zukerman on Social Costs of Adjustment in *Restructuring Economies in Distress:* Policy Reform and the World Bank, edited by Vinod Thomas, Ajay Chibber, Mansoor Dailami, Jaime de Melo, Oxford University Press, 1991, p. 247.

Appendix I

Globalised Economy: much ado about sovereignty

We are all aware of the dramatic changes in world politics during the last couple of years, but the same awareness does not encompass the fundamental changes that have taken place in international economic relations during the last two decades.

These changes are generally subsumed under the term 'inter-dependence' and cover a steadily lengthening list of national problems which can no longer be solved by domestic national policies alone. Problems like environmental hazards, drug trafficking, terrorism, and the movements of people in pursuit of economic opportunity or political refuge are readily seen to fall into this category. But what is less readily recognised is that the problems of economic growth and welfare in individual countries are increasingly forming a major part of the agenda of interdependence.

The qualitative change in international economic relations is reflected in many ways. A large volume of economic and financial transactions now take place outside the network of government agencies. While this has reduced the role of agencies like the Central banks, the role of the multinational has increased. A sizeable volume of financial transfers across national frontiers constitute the internal accounts of multinationals in which they take the key decisions. Revolutionary changes in transport and communications systems, liberalised trading arrangements, the relaxation of foreign exchange controls in most industrialised and some newly industrialising economies, and the diffusion of new technology have dramatically increased the degree of interdependence among these countries. This has led to an unprecedented increase in international trade in goods and services, and in the volume of capital and technology flows benefitting the participating countries enormously.

At the same time, this interdependence has reduced the area over which domestic policy used to exercise sole control. In other words, the individual countries have become more amenable or, if you like, more vulnerable to external influences. Even the most powerful economies find that there are limits upon governmental action. That explains why, for example, the finance ministers of the USA, Japan and Germany meet so often. In practice then, economic sovereignty boils down to relative autonomy in decision making. The major players have greater autonomy than minor ones who are generally at the receiving end, either directly or indirectly, through the impact of the domestic decisions of the major players on the rest of the world. In these circumstances, commonsense and national interest demand that we accept the world as it is and look for opportunities to strengthen our economy and gradually outgrow the league of minor players.

Until recently, our response to the global economy has been reactive and negative. Our national economy has stayed too long on the fringes. We participated in international trade at the minimum, unavoidable level, importing only what we could not produce domestically and exporting just enough to pay for these imports. This is not quite accurate because more was imported than exported and the difference for most of the time was financed by foreign aid. This arrangement left India less vulnerable to external influences but made it poorer and more slow growing.

India's arms-length relationship with global economy, however, could not continue indefinitely. The decline in foreign aid and the need to accelerate growth have together created pressure on India to seek foreign markets for its goods and services and explore ways ad means of attracting foreign capital and technology. In other words, India's own needs necessitated further linkages with the rest of the world. The recent financial crisis dramatised the urgency for such linkages. Obviously, greater participation in the global economy means that we have to learn the rules of the game and use them to our greatest advantage.

It is against this background that we need to examine the appropriateness of our finance minister's letter to the World Bank, which has been debated so acrimoniously. Given the financial situation prevailing in the country last year, it was the finance minister's duty to explore all available means to stave-off bankruptcy and set the country's financial house in order. That is precisely what he is attempting and something in addition: he is also resuming the implementation of reforms, a process which was interrupted by the political instability of the last few years. In this he has utilised the only facilities available to us, namely, the IMF and the World Bank.

Some critics have suggested that the government should have sought the help of non-resident Indians instead. It is true that NRIs love India, but they love their money too. Last year, when India's credit rating went down, NRIs withdrew about a billion dollars from their Indian accounts. They were understandably as concerned about the safety of their money as the foreign commercial banks which refused to roll over the short-term loans they had advanced to India.

During the decade of the eighties, concern for the heavy indebtedness of the developing countries persuaded the IMF to be more flexible in the formation of their conditionalities. Similarly, the World Bank has stepped out of its traditional groove of project lending into the sphere of balance of payment's support and policy reform. The dichotomy between the Bank and the Fund has narrowed down and the two now work in tandem. The Fund assistance to India would not have been available without the structural adjustment loan. The assistance from the two institutions goes hand in hand.

When some people talk disdainfully about a mere £500 million loan assistance from the Bank, they forget that without it the Fund would not have provided its contribution, which raises the total to 2.2 billion.

Where exactly does the finance minister's 'letter of development policy' fit in these loan transactions? It fits in precisely the same manner as a project report for a project loan which provides the details of a project along with its overall rationale.

The Bank has to be persuaded about the soundness of the project. It may make suggestions for alternations to make the project fundable. These then become a matter for negotiations. Similarly, for a structural adjustment loan which is sought to support a programme of policy reform, the borrower provides the new policy design in outline and the sequence in which it is to be implemented.

That is what the finance minister's letter was all about. It was a part of the 'policy dialogue' or negotiations between the government and the Bank or the Fund.

The letter reflects the changes in trade, industry and fiscal policies that the government has been advocating since it was established in July 1991. the proposed policy changes were also mentioned in the memorandum of understanding with the Fund. It is true, however, that unlike a project loan, a new policy design does sometimes involve very sensitive political issues. On such issues, the judgement of the government has to prevail. The Bank itself has found that the programme has to have domestic political support if it is to succeed. This is amply borne out in a comprehensive assessment of its structural lending programme covering 51 countries.

The Bank and the Fund should be seen for what they are – not adversaries, but multi-lateral agencies set up to assist economies in distress. They too want the programmes they support to succeed. Their style can sometimes be overbearing but a self-confident government that knows its mind looks upon the role of these institutions as a supportive one.

The growing interdependence among countries has abridged every one's sovereignty to a smaller or larger extent. This can happen either voluntarily as in the case of the European Economic Community or under duress as in some small and weak economies in Africa and Latin America. India's economy is not small or inherently weak. But at this time, it is in distress. It is also under duress, but at the hands of special internal interests rather than of the World Bank.

Appendix II
EXTERNAL DEBT OF INDIA
(Revised Classification)

(US $ Million)

		31 March 1991	31 December 1991
I	**Multilateral**	20,900	22,595
A	Government Borrowing		
	i) Concessional		
	a) IDA	13,052	13,931
	b) Others	325	309
	ii) Non-Concessional		
	a) IBRD	6,293	6,500
	b) Others	217	466
B	Non-Government Borrowing		
	i) Concessional	-	-
	ii) Non-Concessional	1,013	1,389
	a) Public Sector		
	1) IBRD	157	N/A
	2) Others	-	
	b) Financial Institutions		
	1) IBRD	451	N/A
	2) Others	206	
	c) Private Sector		
	1) IBRD	171	N/A
	2) Others	28	
II	**Bilateral**	14,195	16,159
A	Government Borrowing		
	i) Concessional	11,963	13,693
	ii) Non-Concessional	-	-
B	Non-Government Borrowing		
	i) Concessional		
	a) Public Sector	-	-
	b) Financial Institutional	266	336
	c) Private Sector	-	-
	ii) Non-Concessional		
	a) Public Sector	1,530	1,549
	b) Financial Institutional	273	393
	c) Private Sector	163	188
III	**IMP** 2,623	3,470	

IV	**Export Credit**		2,356	2,523
	A	Buyers' Credit	1,154	1,184
	B	Suppliers' Credit	483	487
	C	Export Component of Bilateral Credit	719	842
V	**Commercial Borrowings**		10,209	10,538
	A	Commercial Bank Loans	6,831	6,920
	B	Securitised Borrowings	3,022	3,139
	C	Loans/Securitised Borrowings, etc. with Multinational/Bilateral Guarantee + IFC (W)	356	479
VI	NRI Deposits (above one year maturity)		7,012	5,765
	Total Long-Term Debt		57,295	61,050
VII	**Short Term**			
	A	Banks2,267		2,267*
	B	Export Credit		
	C	NRI Deposit (Upto one year maturity)	3,572	2,743
	Total Short Term Deposit		5,839	5,010
	Gross Total		63,134	66,060

Note: N/A = Not Available

* As short term figures for 31.12.1991 was not available, the previous figure of US $ 2,267 million is repeated. The status of short term debt is as per proposed definition which excludes all credits up to 180 day maturity with the exception of NRI deposits.

Memo: The total debt above excludes: (a) Rouble/Rupee bilateral credit of US $ 1,669 million and US $ 1,227 million for March 31, 1991 and December 31, 1991, respectively; (b) Rupee Suppliers' credits of US $ 352 million for March 31 and December 31, 1991; and (d) Short term credits (less than six months) of US $ 2,197 million for March 31 and December 31, 1991.

Source: Reports of Policy Group and Task Force on External Debt Statistics of India - Reserve Bank of India, Department of Economic Policy and Analysis, 1992.

Reprinted with permission from the author. Occasional Papers: 1993 - I, Observer Research Foundation, New Delhi.

Economic Reforms in India

MANMOHAN SINGH

N ow that the immediate economic crisis is well behind us, it is all too easy for us to sink back to 'business as usual'. But if we do so, we must be clear about the consequences. We will remain poor and weak and our neighbours in Asia will forge ahead. We will be left far behind. Our position in the comity of nations will sink to unacceptably low levels. We have, therefore, no choice but to persevere with our reform programme. This alone will enable us to achieve our basic goals of growth, self-reliance, modernisation, equity and raising the living standards of the poor people in our country. India has the talent and the genius to be the next "economic miracle". But it will not happen by itself. It requires all of us to dedicate ourselves to new ways of thought and action and make a success of new economic policies.

The decade of 1990s has begun with dramatic and momentous changes in the world. The old economic philosophies that guided the process of economic development are being discarded and several countries have launched ambitious reforms of their economic and political systems. It is now being increasingly realised that a development policy framework that constrains exercise of people's initiative and ingenuity limits utilisation of their full potential and results in unacceptably low levels of growth in output and employment. A consensus is now emerging that an economy that fails to reform itself would also fail to effectively tackle the problems of poverty and unemployment. A more open economy which does not suffer from excessive government control and regulations is necessary to bring about a rapid and sustained improvement in the quality of life of its people.

Although precipitated by an unprecedented economic crisis, the economic reforms we initiated in mid-1991 are the culmination of a long search to find a durable solution to the problems of poverty and unemployment. Endowed with considerable human and natural resources, India is certainly capable of achieving a higher growth rate than the 3.5 per cent growth in Gross Domestic Product per annum we achieved in the first three decades since our independence or even the 5.5 per cent growth rate we managed to achieve during the eighties. A large part of the blame for the huge gap between our potential and performance has to be put on our inability to change a highly regulatory and interventionist regime characterised by licences, quotas and price controls which distorted the incentive structure and choked the initiative of our entrepreneures and professionals. The ongoing economic reforms are designed to correct this.

The twentieth century has seen scientific discovery, technical innovation and technological advancement more than ever before. As a result, the nature of markets and institutions, industrial organisation and structures, and social relations of production have been transformed dramatically. India's role in the new world order is going to be decided by our response to these changes, particularly to the increasing globalisation of economic processes. Economics today is the driving force in international relations. The power and influence of nations today is directly proportional to the size of their GNP and prosperity of their people rather than the size of their defence budget. Our economy must, therefore, grow much faster if we are to play our rightful role in the emerging world order.

We have responded to these changes through a wide-ranging programme of economic reforms. In a short period of about two and a half years we have undertaken major reforms in our industrial policy, foreign trade and exchange rate policies, taxation policies and the financial sector. The basic medium-term objective of these policies is to lay the foundations for sustained growth of output and employment in the context of increasing global competitiveness of the Indian economy. A comprehensive review of our past policies has convinced us that we really have no alternative to economic reforms. We cannot continue with excessive Government revenue expenditure and high levels of fiscal deficit and still hope to control inflation. We cannot spend more on education, health and rural development if we do not improve the profitability of our public sector and reduce subsidies payable to loss making public sector units. We cannot continue to accord high protection to domestic industry and expect to be sufficiently competitive to secure rapid export growth needed for true self-reliance. We cannot afford to shackle foreign investment without losing the benefits of additional capital, technology, market access and growth that have been so successfully harnessed by our neighbours in East Asia. We cannot continue with detailed, discretionary licensing of imports and still expect to have sustained export growth. We cannot maintain the plethora of unnecessary Government controls, regulations and procedures and still expect the skills and potential dynamism of our entrepreneurs, professionals and workers to be fully exploited. We cannot postpone financial sector reforms without risking a serious banking crisis. We cannot continue to resist flexibility in employment policies in the organised sector and yet expect rapid growth of employment. We cannot deny our farmers access to export markets and yet hope for rapid growth of incomes in agriculture. We cannot eradicate illiteracy without redirecting our priorities within the education sector towards primary education and literacy. We cannot provide high quality infrastructure if the costs are not recovered from beneficiaries. We cannot build social infrastructure in the agricultural sector without reducing existing subsidies which benefit only a handful. It is simply not possible to spend our way to prosperity. Above all, we cannot expect to banish poverty without achieving sustained growth of output and employment.

Economic reforms must not be viewed as a package of rigid measures. They represent an open minded and flexible response to the changing economic environment, aimed at serving the best interests of our people. The Government recognise the importance of evolving a national consensus for the reform initiatives and it is reassuring that the positive early results of reforms have testified to the fundamental soundness of our policies. We are firmly of the view that the reform process must be so managed as to protect the interests of workers and other vulnerable sections of the population. The establishment of the National Renewal Fund and substantial increase in allocation for rural development, health and education in the budget for 1993-94 are indicative of Government's concern for reform with a human face. This has helped in forging a national consensus in their favour.

5

Indian Economy at Crossroads
Illusions and Realities

I. Introduction

The Indian economy has lived through difficult times in the past couple of years. Indeed, it would be no exaggeration to state that this crisis in the economy is the worst that we have experienced since independence. As a result, perhaps, problems of the economy which had been on the back-burner for a long time moved to occupy centre-stage, although Ayodhya and its aftermath may now change the focus of attention. There is, however, an irony in the situation that has probably escaped our attention but would immediately strike an outsider, say a visitor from Mars. In mid-1991, we were in the depths of despair. In mid-1992 we were at the heights of ecstasy. In this short span of time, there was a dramatic transformation in the characterisation of the economy, in the perception of the media and the Government or the literati and the influential. The dead-end came to be seen as a new horizon. The plodding elephant turned into an uncaged tiger. These are perceptions in the mind's eye: the extra-terrestrial, who read our minds at the two points in time, would certainly have wondered whether it is the same country. The reality, alas, is more complex and less certain! For those of us who are concerned citizens, the time has come for dispassionate analysis. The analyst, you would agree, cannot afford to be either an optimist or a pessimist but must endeavour to be a realist. In this spirit, the object of my lecture is to consider the macro-economics of stabilisation, adjustment and reform so as to provide an assessment of the problems and the prospects of the economy. In doing so, I claim no divine right to wisdom. Nor do I possess a crystal-ball. The disclaimer is important because economists sometimes fail to recognise, or admit, the limitations of their profession.

The structure of the paper is as follows. First, I shall consider the origins, the dimensions and the implications of the crisis: how did we get into this mess? Second, I shall outline the strategy of macro-economic stabilisation and structural reform adopted by the Government in terms of its rationale: where do we go from here? Third, I shall analyse the problems of adjustment and transition: what can we learn from elsewhere? Fourth, I shall examine the evidence on stabilisation, with a focus on the short-term, to consider inflation and the balance of payments: what can go wrong? Fifth, I shall explore the medium term consequences of fiscal adjustment and structural reform for output and employment: does the future promise stagnation and poverty or growth and prosperity? Sixth, I shall highlight and evaluate the assumptions implicit in the strategy adopted by the Government: what lies below the surface? Seventh, I shall draw together some conclusions that emerge in an attempt to outline the contours of an alternative view: what now?

II. The Crisis in the Economy

The economy is in a crisis and, for all the brave words, we are not out of the woods. The fiscal imbalances persist. The balance of payments situation is fragile. Inflationary pressures are considerable. It must be recognised that the situation is more stable than it was two years ago. However, we have only bought time, which has postponed the day of reckoning but not quite resolved the problem.

The origins of the crisis, which surfaced in early 1991, are directly attributable to the large and persistent macro-economic imbalances since the 1980s. The widening gap between the income and the expenditure of the Government led to mounting fiscal deficits, met by borrowing at home. The steady increase in the difference between the income and the expenditure of the economy as a whole led to persistent current account deficits in the balance of payments, inevitably financed by borrowing from abroad. The internal imbalance in the fiscal situation and the external imbalance in the payments situation were closely related, through the absence of prudence in the macro management of the economy. The macro economics of this relationship can be reduced to a simple proposition: *ex post*, the current account deficit in an economy is the sum of (a) the difference between investment and saving in the private sector and (b) the difference between expenditure and income of the Government sector.

The problems associated with these macro-economic imbalances were sharply accentuated, and brought forward in time, by the impact of the Gulf crisis on the economy in late 1990. This coincided with an uncertain and disturbed situation in the polity, which was followed by a prolonged political interregnum. Taken together, these developments led to a massive erosion of international confidence in India. Our credit rating in international capital markets plummeted, from where it has not recovered until now. It is clear, however, that the problems of the economy, which reached crisis proportions in 1991, did not come as a bolt from the blue. They accumulated over several years. The economy was able to cope with and adjust to much larger and more sustained oil shocks in 1973 and 1979. Yet, the minor oil shock of

1990 had a disproportionately large impact. In a sense, the Gulf crisis was like a virus that strikes a person who has lost immunity.

The fiscal crisis was neither an accident nor a coincidence. It was a direct consequence of financial profligacy on the part of the Government. The gross fiscal deficit of the Union Government, which measures the difference between revenue receipts plus grants and total expenditure plus net domestic lending, was 8.2 per cent of GDP during the second half of the 1980s, as compared with 6.3 per cent during the first half of the 1980s and 4 per cent in the mid-1970s.[1] This fiscal deficit had to be met by borrowing. As a result, internal debt of the Government accumulated rapidly, rising from 35 per cent of GDP at the end of 1980-81 to 53 per cent of GDP at the end of 1990-91.[2] It is not surprising that the burden of servicing the debt became onerous. Interest payments increased from 2 per cent of GDP and 10 per cent of total Central Government expenditure in 1980-81 to 4 per cent of GDP and 20 per cent of total Central Government expenditure in 1990-91.[3] The irony is that many of us, concerned scholars and concerned citizens, had warned that any growth process based on such borrowing was simply not sustainable as the balance of payments situation would become unmanageable and inflation would exceed limits of tolerance. The decision makers then, oblivious to criticism, were convinced that they could borrow and spend their way to prosperity. But the inevitable crunch did come. It is the people of India who have had to face the consequences.

The balance of payments situation came to the verge of collapse in 1991, but this was only to be expected. The current account deficit doubled from an annual average of $ 2.3 billion or 1.3 per cent of GDP during the first half of the 1980s, to an annual average of $ 5.5 billion or 2.2 per cent of GDP during the second half of the 1980s.[4] These persistent deficits which were inevitably financed by borrowing from abroad, led to a continuous increase in external debt of the nation which, including non-resident deposits, rose from 12 per cent of GDP at the end of 1980-81 to 23 per cent of GDP at the end of 1990-91.[5] Consequently, the debt service burden also rose from 10 per cent of current account receipts and 15 per cent of export earnings in 1980-81 to 22 per cent of current account receipts and 30 per cent of export earnings in 1990-91.[6] These strains, which mounted over the years, stretched to breaking point on account of the Gulf crisis. The balance of payments lurched from one liquidity crisis experienced in mid-January 1991 to another in late June 1991. The level of foreign exchange reserves, on both occasions, dropped to levels which would not even have sufficed to finance imports for ten days.

We thus came close to the default in terms of financing imports and meeting debt service obligations. But that is not all. The vulnerability of the balance of payments was accentuated by two other factors which were a function of perceptions and expectations. First, it became exceedingly difficult to roll over the existing short-term debt in the range of $ 5 billion because of adverse international perceptions of the situation, and our overnight borrowing in international capital markets was as much as $ 2 billion.[7] Second, non-resident deposits, where the outstanding amount then was more than $ 10 billion levelled off in September 1990, with net outflows that added up $ 330 million in the period October 1990-March 1991 and $ 1311 million in the period April 1991-September 1991.[8] If perceptions had worsened any further, our short-term debt would have been called in and there would have been a run on non-resident deposits. It would then have been impossible to avert default. We were indeed reduced to last-resort measures such as using stocks of gold to obtain foreign exchange, seeking emergency bilateral assistance from donor countries and borrowing under special facilities from multilateral financial institutions. It is obvious that the soft options adopted by the Government in the second half of the 1980s claimed their pound of flesh. The short-term debt was incurred to finance imports of crude oil and petroleum products, while non-resident deposits were used to finance the current account deficit, instead of introducing hard correctives.

The price situation also came under mounting pressure. During the second half of the 1980s, the average rate of inflation was 6.7 per cent per annum in terms of the wholesale price index and 8 per cent per annum in terms of the consumer price index. These rates climbed to 10.3 per cent and 11.2 per cent respectively in 1990-91.[9] What is more, the inflation was concentrated in essential commodities and prices of food rose in spite of three good monsoons in a row. It needs to be said that inflationary pressures in the economy did not surface out of the blue. The build-up was attributable to the large fiscal deficits, which were inevitably associated with a monetisation of budget deficts and an excessive growth in money supply. This liquidity overhang, in conjunction with real disproportionalities and underlying supply-demand imbalances, was bound to fuel inflation.

I would like to stress that the origins of the crisis lie in the cavalier macro-management of the economy during the 1980s and not, as claimed by some, in a misplaced strategy of development since the mid-1950s. Given the Indian development experience over the past four decades, it would be idle to pretend that everything we did was right but it would be naive to suggest that everything we did was wrong. The reality was a mix of the good, the bad and the indifferent. It was the fiscal mess which began in the mid-1980s and the debt crisis which surfaced in the early 1990s that pushed the economy into an awkward corner. For it is obvious that neither the Government nor the country could continue to live beyond its means year after year. The room for manoeuvre to live on borrowed money or borrowed time had been completely used up by early 1991. Any further postponement of macro-economic adjustment, long overdue, would have meant that the balance of payments situation, already exceedingly difficult, would have become unmanageable, and inflation, already high, would have exceeded limits of tolerance.

III. The Strategy of the Government

In response to the crisis situation, the Government sought to formulate and implement a strategy of stabilisation, adjustment and reform not simply to extricate the economy from the mess but also, it is argued by some, to catapult it into a golden age. For an assessment, it is necessary to set out the content and the rationale of this strategy.

In any programme of macro-economic stabilisation, there are two fundamental objectives. The first object is to pre-empt a collapse of the balance of payments situation in the short term and to reduce the current account deficit in the medium term.

The second object is to curb inflationary pressures or expectations in the short term and to reduce the rate of inflation as soon as possible thereafter. The principal instruments of stabilisation are fiscal policy and monetary policy, sometimes used in conjunction with an exchange rate adjustment, which seek to reduce the level of aggregate demand in the economy, on the presumption that the problems are attributable to rising fiscal deficits and the associated monetary expansion. This provides the rationale for reducing the fiscal deficit of the Government and adopting a tight monetary policy.

In contrast, a programme of structural adjustment, based on policy reform advocated by the multilateral financial institutions, is concerned with the supply side, in an endeavour to raise the rate of growth of output. Structural reform seeks to shift resources: (a) from the non-traded goods sector to the traded-goods sector and within the latter from import competing activities to export activities; and (b) from the Government sector to the private sector. Apart from resource allocation, structural reform seeks to improve resource utilisation by : (i) increasing the degree of openness of the economy, and (ii) changing the structure of incentives and institutions, which would reduce the role of State intervention to rely more on the market place, dismantle controls to rely more on prices, and wind down the public sector to rely more on the private sector. The underlying presumption is that industrialisation based on import substitution and State intervention leads to inefficient resource allocation and resource utilisation.

In the pursuit of these objectives, the Government has embarked on a wide ranging reform of the policy regime.[10] Trade policy reform has eliminated most quantitative restrictions on imports, except for consumer goods, and progressively reduced tariff levels. The desire to increase the degree of openness of the economy extends beyond trade flows to capital flows and technology flows. The liberalisation of the regimes for foreign investment and foreign technology is intended to expose domestic firms to international competition further. Industrial policy reform, which has removed barriers to entry for new firms and limits on growth in the size of existing firms, seeks to cut out State intervention in investment decisions. This process is sought to be reinforced by deregulation in the financial sector of the economy, so that the allocation and utilisation of investible resources is left to the market. Public sector reform is limited so far, and does not address any of the real maladies, but the intention to reduce its role is clear enough.

The resolution of the crisis in the short term requires a stabilisation of the balance of payments situation, so that the default is no longer a sword of Damocles, and a reduction in the rate of inflation so that inflationary expectations are curbed. Once this stabilisation is complete, the economy must return to a path of sustained growth combined with price stability. In my judgement, if everything went according to plan and fell into place, the probability of which was never high and now appears low, the process would have taken at least three years to complete. Even then, there would have been problems of adjustment and transition, the importance of which cannot and should not be minimised. If things go wrong and there is some evidence to suggest that this process may have begun, the economy would not be able to cope with the transition. It may, then, become necessary to analyse the macro-economics of destabilisation and stagflation as with the Latin America experience of the 1980s or the East European experience of the 1990s. The lessons that emerge from the experience of stabilisation and adjustment in Latin America and Sub-Saharan Africa during the 1980s, guided by IMF programmes of stabilisation and World Bank programmes of structural adjustment, provide us with some pointers to and understanding of problems of transition.

IV. Problems of Adjustment and Transition

It is possible to consider problems of adjustment and transition at two levels. First, in terms of analysis, we can consider problems that arise from the interaction between the demand side and the supply side, problems that arise on the demand side alone and problems that arise on the supply side alone. Second, in terms of actual experience, there are problems which emerge from the experience of IMF and World Bank programmes elsewhere. The distribution of the burden of adjustment, in the process of transition, is a problem that surfaces at both levels.

The fundamental problem of transition arises from the fact that the speeds of adjustment on the demand side and on the supply side are considerably different. Fiscal adjustment and monetary discipline can be used to squeeze aggregate demand, so that the speed of adjustment on the demand side is fast. On the other hand, the speed of adjustment on the supply side is inevitably slow, particularly in economies characterised by structural rigidities where resources are not easily mobile across sectors or perfectly substitutable in uses. This is so even if all the price incentives of a market economy can be brought to perfect function. Supply adjustment typically requires structural change through creation of capacity, alleviation of infrastructural bottlenecks, streamlining of input supplies, creation or reorientation of public utilities, and so on, all of which take time. The fast dynamics of demand and the slow dynamics of supply have four macro-economic implications which are crucial in the process of adjustment.

First, insofar as aggregate demand remains greater than aggregate supply, or the sectoral composition of demand does not match the sectoral composition of supply, and balance of payments constraints prevent excess demand from being met through imports, inflation persists. Second, stabilisation policies which are meant to reduce demand may, at the same time, reduce supply even more, for the simple reason that a substantial fiscal adjustment and a tight monetary policy squeeze both investible resources and working capital. Excess demand would, then, persist. As the economy contracts from both sides, the current account deficit in the balance of payments would probably be reduced but inflation would not be restrained. Third, the initial effects of structural reform, particularly in situations where the balance of payments constraint is binding, may lead to a contraction of output in some sectors before an expansion of output in other sectors. This tends to increase excess demand in the system and exacerbates the problem of inflation. Fourth, fiscal adjustment and monetary discipline which squeeze aggregate demand in the short term may constrain supply responses in the medium term. Yet without a foundation of macro-economic stabilisation in the short term, policy reform simply cannot produce the desired results in the medium term. This is the crux of the problem when economies begin on adjustment processes in a situation of deep macro-economic disequilibrium.

Even if we consider the demand side alone, the transition path of stabilisation adjustment is like walking a tight rope. The Achilles' heel of any such programme is the rate of inflation or the balance of payments. If inflation does not slow down or the balance of payments does not stabilise, the intended virtuous circle is easily transformed into an unintended vicious circle, as the exchange rate and the price level chase each other. The possibilities of what economists describe as stagflation are then considerable. This did happen in Latin America where the 1980s are, in retrospect, described as the lost decade. Economic stagnation, which led to rising levels of unemployment and falling per capita incomes, was juxtaposed with hyper inflation. Many countries in Eastern Europe, in their process of transition from planned systems to market economies, are experiencing similar difficulties.

On the supply side, structural reform may turn out to be a cause for concern and it may be wise to hasten slowly. The process of policy reform is sustainable only if two conditions are satisfied. First, the changes must be acceptable to polity and society. Second, the pace of the transition must be such that it can be absorbed by the economy. If this is not the case, things can go wrong and easily discredit even sensible reform. The experience from elsewhere suggests several examples, but these do not exhaust the reality. Trade policy reform can move an economy from a situation of too much protection to a situation of too little protection and the industrial sector may not be able to cope with such a rapid transition. Industrial de-regulation, which removes barriers to entry and limits on growth for firms often leads to retrenchment and closures but cannot wish away barriers to exit, particularly in economies where levels of income are low, levels of unemployment are high and social safety nets are absent. De-regulation in the financial sector, unless it is paced with care, can be perilous not just in terms of scams or scandals, but also if it diverts scarce resources to unproductive uses. Public sector reform, which is based on a sale of government assets and rudimentary forms of privatisation, may not resolve problems of efficiency or productivity but can end up socialising the costs and privatising the benefits. Given an unequal income distribution and the associated patterns of demand, industrial de-regulation, in conjunction with more open trade regimes and liberal foreign investment policies, may lead to a greater import intensity of domestic production and thus enlarge the current account deficit. If export performance is sluggish or does not respond fast enough, the economy may be forced into more borrowing or further deflation. In sum, the direction, the speed and the sequence of policy reform must be planned and calibrated in a careful manner, for an ailing and weak patient in need of gradual convalescence may not become healthy and strong with shock therapy.

The actual experience of stabilisation and adjustment programmes in Latin America and Sub-Saharan Africa, guided by the IMF and the World Bank in a medium term perspective, also reflects problems of transition. The critical evaluation of these programmes in the literature on the subject points to significant dangers.[11] First, almost without exception, there is an adverse impact on poverty insofar as the burden of adjustment is borne largely by the poor. Second, these programmes tend to stifle long-term growth prospects so that a return to the path of sustained growth is often a hope rather than a reality. Third, such programmes tend to over-estimate export prospects and the availability of external finance, and when this does not materialise, economies are forced into a deflation that imposes social costs and squeezes supply responses. Fourth, there is a steady externalisation of policy formulation. This has two implications: For one, responsiveness to changing and evolving situations is significantly reduced as policy prescriptions are characterised by an analytical absolutism: if you have a balance of payments problem the answer lies in liberalising trade, and if you have a fiscal crisis the answer lies in reducing tax rates. For another, sensitivity to social and political realities is sharply eroded, as national policies are shaped without reference to the context. In the policy based lending programmes of multilateral financial institutions, conditionalities begin with the classical areas of economic policy, although cuts in subsidies have both social and political implications, and then extend to political areas such as governance, military expenditure, human rights and democracy.[12]

Macro-economic adjustment and structural reform are not simply a matter for the drawing board. In the period of transition it imposes a burden of adjustment that is distributed in an asymmetric manner. Without correctives, the burden of adjustment is inevitably borne by the poor. For all the rhetoric about social safety nets, countries simply do not have the resources for this purpose. It cannot suffice to assert, as Governments often do, that the burden of such adjustment would have to be borne by the affluent simply because it is the rich who have the incomes to immunise themselves from the burdens of structural change. It is obvious that there can be no adjustment without pain, but pain for whom? Surely, in keeping with the equity principle, the costs must be borne by those who enjoyed the pleasures derived from profligacy. Reality turns out to be the opposite. Inflation tends to make the rich better off as it redistributes income from wages to profits and the poor worse off as it erodes their incomes which are not index-linked. The soft options in fiscal adjustment tend to squeeze public expenditure in social sectors where there are no vocal political constituencies, as the resources allocated for poverty alleviation, health care, education and welfare programmes decline in real terms. This can only hurt the poor. Restructuring on the supply side, which follows structural reform, inevitably imposes a burden on wage labour. The phrase 'adjustment with a human face' is then not just hollow.[13] It is deceptive.

V. The Evidence on Stabilisation

The evidence available in India so far is limited but there is some cause for concern about stabilisation, whether we consider the problem of inflation or the balance of payments situation.

The facts on inflation are less than assuring. There is a significant decline in the rate of inflation, on a point-to-point basis, in terms of both the wholesale price index and the consumer price index, which has been emphasised by the Government. But this must be interpreted with caution for two reasons. For one, the stabilisation policies introduced in July 1991 pushed up the rate of inflation in the second half of 1991 and the first half of 1992 so that point-to-point rates now show a decline in comparison with those high price levels. For another, the measurement of inflation on a point-to-point basis is somewhat deceptive because it tends to overstate both the acceleration and the deceleration in inflation. It would, therefore, be more appropriate to examine trends in inflation on an average-of-period basis. This does not suggest a real turn around. Consider the evidence for the financial years 1989-90, 1990-91, 1991-92 and, until end-December, 1992-93. The annual rates of inflation, on an average-of-period basis, were: (i) 7.5 per cent, 10.3 per cent, 13.7 per cent and 11.5 per cent respectively in terms of the wholesale price index; (ii) 6.6 per cent, 11.2 per cent, 13.5 per cent and 11.1 per cent respectively in terms of the consumer price index for industrial workers; and (iii) 5.4 per cent, 7.6 per cent, 19.3 per cent and 17.4 per cent respectively in terms of the consumer price index for agricultural labourers.[14] These figures show that the slow-down in the rate of inflation is much less than what point-to-point rates suggest. It is also worth noting that the decline in the average-of-period rate of inflation is largely attributable to the good monsoon and its impact on the prices of agricultural commodities.

The substantial fiscal adjustment together with the tight monetary policy should, of course, lead to a contraction of aggregate demand and thus dampen demand-pull inflation, though not cost-push inflation, but the impact would be limited insofar as the real disproportionalities underlying the inflationary pressures persist. But that is not all. The nature of fiscal adjustment itself tends to fuel cost-push inflation when subsidies are cut as on fertilisers, administered prices are raised as for petroleum products, or charges are hiked by public utilities as in railway freight and electricity. What is worse, the stop-go method of increasing administered prices adopted by the Government is likely to have accentuated inflationary expectations. The tariff reform, which has reduced customs duties across-the-board, is sought to be made revenue-neutral not through an increase in direct taxes that would reduce disposable incomes of the rich and dampen inflation but through increases in excise duties that fuel inflation and squeeze the real incomes of the poor. The exchange rate adjustments, followed by partial convertibility of the rupee, have obviously contributed to inflation by raising the cost of traded goods but have also generated inflationary expectations as the market speculates about a further depreciation. In the sphere of monetary policy, the liquidity overhang inherited from the past and the parallel economy are beyond the reach of discipline. What is more, monetary policy appears to be somewhat lax, for the increase in money supply, defined as M3, was 18.5 per cent in 1991-92 and is estimated to be in the range of 15 per cent in 1992-93;[15] the substantial accumulation of foreign exchange reserves may account for some part of monetary expansion in 1991-92 but there can be no such explanation for 1992-93. While credit is not so tight, interest rates are high and that does contribute to cost-push inflation.

The balance of payments situations, it must be recognised, is no longer precarious. The level of foreign exchange reserves climbed from a meagre $ 2.2 billion in end-March 1991 to a comfortable $ 5.6 billion in end-March 1992 and has remained in that range thereafter. This accumulation of foreign exchange reserves does not, however, mean that stabilisation is complete for the simple reason that one swallow does not make a summer. The build-up of reserves during 1991-92 (and the associated stabilisation) was attributable to three factors. First, the draconian import compression reduced the balance of trade deficit by as much as $ 4.3 billion, from $ 5.9 billion in

1990-91 to $ 1.6 billion in 1991-92, even though exports stagnated and the petroleum import bill did not register a significant decline;[16] this was, perhaps, the major factor underlying the reduction in the current account deficit from $ 8.4 billion in 1990-91 to $ 2.8 billion in 1991-92.[17] Second, special bilateral assistance from Japan and Germany ($ 355 million), structural adjustment loans from the World Bank and the Asian Development Bank ($ 580 million), and borrowing from the IMF ($ 1240 million), taken together, provided $ 2.2 billion of exceptional financing during 1991-92.[18] Third, the amnesties announced in the 1991-92 budget raised another $ 2.2 billion, largely in the form of borrowing from non-residents through bonds ($ 1374 million) and partly through remittances ($ 863 million).[19]

The extra-ordinary capital flows in the form of borrowing from multilateral financial institutions, or from non-residents through amnesties, is an once-and-for-all phenomenon. The import compression, which was within our control and provided a more sustainable means of managing the balance of trade situation, has been lifted altogether. But there is no evidence of a turn around in export performance which remains sluggish: the dollar value of exports decreased by 1.7 per cent in 1991-92, as compared with 1990-91, and increased by a mere 3.4 per cent in the first nine months of 1992-93, as compared with the corresponding period of 1991-92.[20] If the level of reserves has remained in the range of $ 5 billion despite the poor export performance, it is because imports are also sluggish on account of recession while exceptional financing made up entirely of borrowing from multilateral financial institutions and bilateral donors is, once again, about $ 2.5 billion for 1992-93. The reliance on borrowing abroad to support the balance of payments has led to a rapid accumulation of external debt, and evidence available suggests that the amount outstanding would have increased by about $ 10 billion during 1991-92 and 1992-93.[21] In fact, by the end of 1991-92, external debt was more than 27 per cent of GDP.[22]

It would appear that much of the stabilisation is now attributable to borrowing and, therefore, may not be sustainable in the long run. The world outside is obviously not (even if the Government is) convinced about the stabilisation in our balance of payments, for international credit ratings remain where they were, borrowing access to international capital markets is virtually closed, and there are no net inflows into non-resident deposits. The continuous chant about convertibility of the rupee on the part of the Government, almost as if it is a *mantra*, has certainly not helped the cause of stabilisation, since the market is bound to speculate about further depreciation. The medium-term borrowing, particularly from the IMF and non-residents, where repayments would commence soon, and the accumulation of external debt to buy time could unleash destabilising expectations whenever there is any crisis of confidence, irrespective of whether it originates in the economy or in the polity.

VI. The Medium Term Prospects

The short-term impact of macro-economic stabilisation on output and employment is almost always adverse. The stabilisation experience in India so far is no exception. In real terms, the growth in GDP in 1991-92, as compared with 1990-91, was definitely less than 2 per cent and perhaps closer to 1 per cent.[23] This was due, in part, to the uneven temporal and spatial distribution of the monsoon, which meant that agricultural output was 1 per cent lower than in the preceding year. But the aggregate demand management also had its impact. Industrial production registered a negligible growth of 0.1 per cent while manufacturing output declined by 1.4 per cent; within manufacturing, the production of capital goods dropped by 12.8 per cent and that of consumer durables by 12.5 per cent.[24] In 1992-93, real GDP growth is expected to revive on account of the good monsoon and a robust increase in agricultural output. Industrial production is also expected to revive and register a growth of about 3.5 per cent, but this does not mean much given that it reflects a comparison with the dismal performance in 1991-92.[25]

It would seem that the economy is in a recession. The industrial sector is obviously hurt by the deflation on the demand side and the high interest rates combined with a credit squeeze on the supply side. Firms with high debt-equity ratios and large working capital needs, particularly those in the small scale sector, have probably borne the brunt. In this context, it is not surprising that there is no upsurge in animal spirits of entrepreneurs which would lead to a step-up in investment. So much for the short-term. Let me now turn to the possible effects of fiscal adjustment and structural reform on output and employment in the medium term. It would also be essential to explore the probable distribution of the burden of adjustment.

Consider first, the fiscal adjustment. To begin with, it is worth noting that some of it is neither real nor sustainable. It is not real in so far as it relies on accounting devices such as technical credit to the erstwhile Soviet Union, or on window dressing which does not provide for, or under-estimates expenditure, say on fertiliser subsidies. DA payments and external debt servicing, and over-estimates revenue from direct taxes. It is not sustainable in so far as it relies on once-and-for-all mechanisms whether royalties from the ONGC, sale of confiscated gold by the Government, arrears of dividends from the railways and increasing dividend from the Reserve Bank of India by a multiple of five.

A substantial part of the fiscal adjustment, however, is both real and sustainable. Unfortunately, this adjustment is concentrated in two areas: public investment and social sectors. The evidence is clear enough, if we compare the period from 1987-88 to 1990-91, prior to the fiscal adjustment, with 1991-92 and 1992-93. The proportion of capital expenditure in total expenditure was, on an average, 31 per cent during the period 1987-88 to 1990-91 but dropped to 26 per cent in 1991-92 and 25 per cent in 1992-93. What is more, capital expenditure in the Central Plan outlay, which provides a better measure of resources made available for public investment, in 1991-92 and 1992-93 (at about Rs. 16,000 crores) was almost the same as in 1990-91 in nominal terms; it is obvious that the budget provisions did not even compensate for the exchange rate adjustment, let alone inflation, so that public investment certainly declined in real terms. Budget support for the infrastructure sectors - energy, transport and communications - was squeezed the most, because Plan expenditure on these sectors as a proportion of Central Plan outlay dropped from an average of 19 per cent during the period 1987-88 to 1990-91 to 14 per cent in 1991-92 and 12 per cent in 1992-93. Similarly, we find that the Plan expenditure allocations for rural development (used mostly in poverty alleviation programmes) and the social sectors (education, health, family welfare, water supply, sanitation, housing, urban development, labour, social welfare and nutrition), as a proportion of Central Plan outlay, declined from an average of 16.1 per cent during the period 1987-88 to 1990-91 to 15.7 per cent in 1991-92 and 14.1 per cent in 1992-93. As a proportion of GDP, the budget provisions for Plan expenditure on rural development and the social sectors declined from 1.2 per cent during the period 1987-88 to 1990-91 to 1 per cent in both 1991-92 and 1992-93.[26]

In my judgement, the quality of this fiscal adjustment is poor, particularly when situated in a medium-term perspective. First, it has relied on a surplus in the capital account to finance a deficit on the revenue account as the focus of the adjustment is on the fiscal deficit rather than the revenue deficit, which means that an important element of the fiscal crisis would persist in the medium term. Second, it has squeezed public investment, particularly in the infrastructure sectors, which is bound to constrain the supply response of the economy in the medium term, and the problem may be accentuated if public investment crowds-in rather than crowds-out private investment. Third, the distribution of the burden of adjustment has been, to say the least, unequal. A significant proportion of the expenditure adjustment is at the expense of social sectors which can only add to, rather than minimise, the burden on the poor. I believe that the fiscal adjustment should have come from a more appropriate mix of expenditure-cuts and revenue-raising instead of relying excessively on the former. In a period when we are imposing a substantial burden on the poor through expenditure adjustment, the equity principle demands that the rich in particular, and the non-poor in general, share in this burden through their contribution to direct taxes. For this, it is absolutely essential to broaden the base for direct taxes so that a larger number of people are brought into the net and to deepen the structure of direct taxation by increasing the average rates of tax. The adjustment so far, and the tax reform on the anvil, appear to be moving in the opposite direction. In caricature form, the underlying philosophy can be summed up as: comfort for the rich and hardship for the poor. It is important to stress that these patterns of adjustment are nothing new, for they have been reproduced time after time in developing countries that embarked on stabilisation and adjustment. Experience suggests that the squeeze on supply responses and the burden on the poor persist in the medium term.

Consider next, the structural reform. It is much too early to assess its impact on output and employment. But the problems associated with the direction, the speed and the sequence of policy reform, mentioned earlier, appear to have surfaced already in India. Industrial de-regulation has removed barriers to entry but the Government is unable to address problems associated with barriers to exit. De-regulation in the financial sector is being contemplated without putting in place prudential norms, institutional systems and legal frameworks which would provide adequate protection to savers or investors. Public sector reform has not extended beyond a sale of Government assets, which may imply selling the flag-ships and keeping the tramp-ships, while there is no systematic attempt to resolve the real problems in the spheres of efficiency and productivity. The Government is flirting with convertibility of the rupee without a sustainable stabilisation in the balance of payments. Indeed, even before attaining convertibility on current account, there is an endeavour to introduce convertibility on capital account in the form of portfolio investment without any lock-in period; given the speculation and the manipulation in our capital markets, this might lead to large de-stabilising capital outflows. Imports have been liberalised without establishing a comprehensive system of anti-dumping laws for domestic firms to invoke and to use whenever necessary. What is worse, the rapid liberalisation of the import regime has dismantled quantitative restrictions and reduced tariff levels, even before export growth has created an import capacity in the economy. It is obvious that the sequence and the speed of structural reform needs careful consideration to ensure a positive impact on output and employment in the medium term. It does become difficult to move forward if the cart is placed before the horse.

VII. The Underlying Assumptions

There are some important assumptions implicit in the strategy adopted by the Government. It is necessary to highlight and to evaluate these underlying assumptions if we wish to separate the illusions from the realities. The assumptions are : (a) the market mechanism would be a substitute for State intervention; (b) private investment would be a substitute for public investment and direct foreign investment would be a substitute for other forms of foreign capital inflows; (c) imports of technology would be a substitute for domestic technological capabilities; and (d) the agricultural sector would, somehow, take care of itself. In my judgement, these assumptions are not only heroic in nature but also suggest an inadequate understanding of reality. Consider each in turn.

The first assumption that State intervention does not matter, or is counterproductive, in the process of industrialisation, is ahistorical. Our experience in the second half of the twentieth century suggests that the guiding and the supportive role of the State has been at the foundations of successful development among late industrialisers. Even among the East Asian countries, which are often cited as success stories that depict the magic of the market place, the visible hand of the State is much more in evidence than the invisible hand of the market.[27] In the earlier stages of industrialisation, State intervention creates the conditions for the development of industrial capitalism by establishing a physical infrastructure through government investment, developing human resources through education, or facilitating institutional change through agrarian reform. In the later stages of industrialisation, State intervention is functional or strategic rather than conducive but remains crucial. At one level, functional State intervention may seek to correct for market failures, whether general or specific. At another level, strategic State intervention, interlinked across activities or sectors, may seek to attain broader, long term, objectives of development. It is possible to cite several examples. Exchange rate policy is not simply a tactical matter of getting-prices-right but may turn out to be a strategic matter if deliberately undervalued exchange rates, maintained over a period of time, provide an entry into the world market for differentiated manufactured goods. The structure of interest rates is not just about allowing market forces to determine the price of capital, but may be a strategic method of guiding the allocation of scarce investible resources. Restrictions on the use of foreign brand-names is not so much an inward-looking attitude, if it is perceived as a strategic means of buying time to develop national brand names that become acceptable in world markets after a lag. In this manner, State intervention may constitute an integral part of any strategy of industrialisation that endeavours to strengthen capabilities and develop institutions rather than rely on incentives or markets alone.[28] There is, of course, government failure just as much as market failure, for neither governments nor markets are, or can be, perfect.[29] In theory, it may be possible to remedy market failure by State intervention. In practice, governments may lack the ability or the willingness to intervene efficiently. It is the nature and the form of State intervention that matters. The experience of excessive State intervention associated with government failures, however, should not lead to the conclusion that minimal State intervention is the best or that market failures do not matter. We appear to have moved from a widespread belief, prevalent in the 1950s, that the State could do nothing wrong to a gathering conviction, fashionable in the 1990s, that the State can do nothing right. These are caricature perceptions. The reality is more complex than simplified paradigms that may be in or out of fashion. In a world of uneven development, characterised by rapid technical progress, ever-changing comparative advantage and imperfect market structures, the role of governments in the industrialisation process remains vital and could account for the difference between success and failure. For, industrialisation is not only about getting-prices-right; industrialisation is also about getting-state-intervention-right.

The second assumption has two components, both of which are open to question. For one, most of the evidence available in India suggests that the level of public investment in the economy has been an important determinant of the level of private investment in the economy. This is particularly so for the industrial sector, where public investment crowds-in, rather than crowds-out private investment.[30] Thus, a scaling down of public investment would squeeze supply responses in the medium term not only because it would cut back on infrastructure but also because it may dampen private investment. For another, given the relative magnitudes, it is most unlikely that direct foreign investment could substitute for other forms of foreign capital inflows, at least in the medium term. The open door policy may stimulate large inflows of direct foreign investment as compared with the recent past, but we must recognise that policy regimes are permissive and not causal. The perceptions of transnational corporations about India and a comparison with investment opportunities elsewhere would exercise a much more important influence. Even under the most optimistic scenario, however, direct foreign investment would be more important as a means of providing access to markets and technology, rather than as a means of financing the current account deficit.

The third assumption emphasises the importance of access to imports of technology and neglects the significance of domestic development of technology at the present stage of industrialisation in India. The liberalisation of technology imports would lead to a multiplicity of imports by several firms at a point in time and a recurrence of imports by the same firm over a period of time. The discipline of the market would, of course, place some limits on this process, but it is possible that domestic technological capabilities may be stifled. Yet, an economy that industrialises should be able to move from importation to absorption and adaptation of technology through to the stage of innovation, at least in some sectors, on the path to sustained industrialisation. In the pursuit of this objective, imports of technology and indigenous technological development need to be combined in a judicious mix. The industrialisation experience of India suggests that there are a number of sectors where the level of technological development is just not adequate. There are several examples of situations where technologies were imported for particular sectors at a point of time and the absorption of such technologies has been followed by stagnation rather than adaptation, diffusion and innovation. At the same time, in many cases, indigenous development of technology has not led to widespread diffusion, let alone technological upgradation. The underlying reasons are complex.[31] It is clear, however, that market structures and government policies have not combined to provide an environment which would accelerate the absorption of imported technology and foster the development of indigenous technology, or create a milieu which would be conducive to diffusion and innovation. Indeed, the R&D effort in the private corporate sector has been minimal. It needs to be stressed that, at a macro-level, the role of the government is crucial for planning technological development across sectors and over time. This means planning for the acquisition of technology where it is to be imported, setting aside resources for technology where it is to be produced at home, or even deciding to opt out of a technology where it is not needed. For this purpose, it is necessary to formulate a policy regime for the import of technology, allocate resources for R&D and evolve government procurement policies. Such a guiding and supportive role of the State has been a necessary condition for technological development among the latecomers to industrialisation, not only in Asia but also elsewhere.[32]

The fourth assumption is perhaps the most curious. It is striking that the entire discourse about structural reform proceeds as if the agricultural sector does not exist, or if it exists it does not matter. This is indeed puzzling in an economy where the agricultural sector contributes one-third of GDP and employs more than two-thirds of the work force. And it is not as if the agricultural sector is without structural rigidities or structural imbalances. The process of macro-economic stabilisation combined with fiscal adjustment and structural reform would, of course, be constrained by what happens in the agricultural sector. But this process would also have a significant impact on Indian agriculture inasmuch as it reduces fertiliser subsidies and priority sector lending, or insofar as it moves domestic prices of inputs and outputs closer to world prices. The increase in fertiliser prices and the possible increase in the price of credit are a cause of concern because, given the stagnation and decline of public investment in the agricultural sector which began in the late 1970s, the use of fertilisers and the availability of credit have been the most important determinants of the increase in yields per hectare and, hence, agricultural output. The trade policy reform in India, in the sphere in agriculture, which seeks to dismantle restrictions on trade other than tariffs and to bring domestic prices closer to world prices, represents a fundamental departure from the past. It may set in motion a sequence of changes large enough to reshape the parameters not simply for the agricultural sector but for the economy as a whole.[33] The impact would not be confined to trade flows. It would extend to output and prices. The changes in the distribution of agricultural output and incomes between regions may accentuate inequalities, which would have political implications. Increases in domestic prices of wage goods produced in the agricultural sector are bound to erode food security, which, in turn, would have social consequences. There may not be much comfort in the balance of payments either. Insofar as the volume of India's agricultural imports or exports would affect world prices, terms of trade are likely to worsen. The possibilities would be constrained further inasmuch as structural rigidities in the agricultural sector inhibit supply responses.

VIII. Concluding Observations

It is time to draw together some conclusions that emerge from the lecture, in an endeavour to highlight the contours of an alternative view. I would like to stress, however, that my observations only provide a modest beginning for a meaningful debate, which is essential at this critical juncture in our economy.

In a situation of deep disequilibrium, macro-economic stabilisation and structural reform or adjustment should not be simultaneous events. In my judgment, stabilisation must restore a semblance of equilibrium in the economy before policy reform is used to re-structure the economy. The simultaneous pursuit of stabilisation and adjustment is based on the orthodoxy of multilateral financial institutions. There are two dimensions to the logic underlying this prescription. In terms of economics, stabilisation policies on the demand side have some corollaries on the supply side. In terms of politics, a debt crisis accentuates vulnerability so much that unpalatable reforms can be imposed. Thus, bitter medicine is seen to be best administered in one swallow. However, there are good reasons why stabilisation and adjustment should not be implemented together, for the multiplicity of objectives and of time horizons tends to compound difficulties rather than resolve problems. For one, such an approach often leads to a situation where the economy achieves neither stabilisation nor adjustment, so that the outcome is stagflation and poverty. For another, if reform is not absorbed by the economy or is not acceptable to the polity, which is not uncommon in crisis situations, disillusionment sets in and even the necessary or desirable components of reform are discredited.

The choice of stabilisation policies is also crucial. So much so that it can account for the difference between success and failure. There are two points that deserve emphasis in this context. First, aggregate demand management should be used in conjunction with import controls, rather than by itself, since the combination can bring about an equivalent reduction in the current account deficit with less deflation or without as much sacrifice in terms of output and employment. Second, aggregate demand management through fiscal adjustment and monetary policy should squeeze imports and consumption of the non-poor, instead of investment and consumption of the poor. In other words, stabilisation policies must be formulated in such a manner that they do not impose a burden on the poor and do not choke supply responses. Then, growth and equity are not irreconcilable objectives.

The restructuring of the economy should be situated in a medium-term, preferably long-term, perspective because it is not a matter of here and now. What is more, structural reform should be perceived not as a fixed menu or display but as an *a la carte* menu where the choice of content is as important as the sequence and the speed. The process of economic reform must be responsive to evolving situations and sensitive to social or political realities, which means that it cannot be shaped by analytical absolutisms. For example, it is both necessary and desirable to reduce the degree of monopoly in the industrial sector and increase the degree of competition among firms, but the exposure to international competition must be introduced in a phased manner. Similarly, in terms of any rank ordering of priorities, public sector reform should precede trade policy reform. And public sector reform is not simply about the sale of assets or rudimentary forms of privatisation, just as premature trade policy reform cannot be sustained unless a robust export performance creates an import capacity in the economy. In sum, although it is necessary to rely more on market forces at the micro-level, State intervention cannot be dispensed with at the macro-level, for the market is a good servant but a bad master.

Last but not least, the strategy of the Government for the macro-management of the economy in the early 1990s resembles the strategy of the 1980s in one respect which is a cause for serious concern, and that is a reliance on borrowing abroad. Unfortunately, borrowing is only a tactic and not a strategy that can provide a sustainable solution to the problem. The analogy of a peasant household that can never borrow its way out of debt may be an exaggeration but it is not altogether inappropriate. In our economy, polity and society there is a real danger, borne out by earlier experience, that external resources may be transformed into a soft option, insofar as they become a substitute for, rather than an addition to, domestic resources, and are used to support consumption rather than investment. Therefore, in the medium-term, our strategy of planned structural adjustment at a macro-level should endeavour to raise the investment-GDP ratio, by raising the export-GDP ratio and the domestic savings-GDP ratio and not by allowing a compensating increase in the import-GDP ratio supported by borrowing abroad. In this strategy, the most important point of departure from the past and the present is that, in terms of macro-management, we stop using the current account deficit in the balance of payments as a means of financing the excess of investment over saving for the economy and the excess of expenditure over income for the Government. The basic objective should be to rely to our own resources to finance the process of development and to make a systematic effort to raise the productivity of investment through an appropriate restructuring of the economy.

To recapitulate, then, it is important to distinguish between illusions and realities apropos the Indian economy at the present conjuncture. But that is not all. It must also be ensured that there is no confusion between strategy and tactics or ends and means. For, the path that we have chosen at the crossroads needs careful consideration and substantial correctives. The implications are serious and the consequences may be far reaching, so that it cannot be left to economists alone. If things go wrong, we could end up globalising prices without globalising incomes. In the process, a narrow segment of our population may be integrated with the world economy but a large proportion of our population may be marginalised even further in India. Should this happen, and I sincerely hope that it does not, the grand illusions of a few may indeed be transformed into harsh realities for the many in our society.

Notes

1. *Economic Survey 1991-92*, Part II, Ministry of Finance, Government of India, New Delhi, p. 3.
2. *Ibid.*, p. 13

3. For data on interest payments, *Economic and Functional Classification of the Central Government Budget*, Ministry of Finance, New Delhi, annual issues; and for data on GDP at current market prices, CSO, *National Accounts Statistics,* Annual issues.

4. See Reserve Bank of India, *Report on Currency and Finance*, annual issues.

5. For 1980-81, Report of the Economic Advisory Council, *The Current Economic Situation and Priority Areas for Action*, New Delhi, December 1989. For 1990-91, *Economic Survey 1991-92,* Part II, *op.cit.*

6. *Ibid.*

7. *Report of Policy Group and Task Force on External Debt Statistics of India*, Reserve Bank of India, Bombay, 1992.

8. *Economic Survey 1991-92*, Part II, p. 61.

9. Reserve Bank of India, *Annual Report 1990-91*, p. 57.

10. The policy reform is described, at some length, in the *Economic Survey* published by the Ministry of Finance and the *Report on Currency and Finance* published by the Reserve Bank of India. See also, *Statement on Industrial Policy*, Ministry of Industry, New Delhi, 24 July 1991; *Statement on Trade Policy*, Ministry of Commerce, New Delhi, 13 August 1991; and *Export and Import Policy April 1992-March 1997*, Ministry of Commerce, New Delhi, 31 March 1992.

11. There is an extensive literature on this subject. See, for example, Lance Taylor, *Varieties of Stabilisation Experience*, Clarendon Press, Oxford, 1988; John Williamson, *ed. IMF Conditionality*, Institute for International Economics. Washington DC, 1983, Tony Killick ed., *The IMF and Stabilisation* and *The Quest for Economic Stabilisation*, Overseas Development Institute, London, 1984, and John Williamson *ed. Latin American Adjustment: How Much Has Happened?* Institute for International Economics, Washington DC, 1990.

12. Similar concerns are expressed in a paper which evaluates policy based assistance to developing countries led by the adjustment based lending of the World Bank: "Designing economic and social policies - an avocation which can also be called policy engineering provides immense satisfaction for all those interested in economics and politics....Soon, the policy engineer finds himself attempting to do nothing short of what political leaders of the country are supposed to do. This, of course, is a grave mistake....this can open the door to what some have called neo-colonialism and the imposition of external governance on what has to be national policies. "See Oktay Yenal, 'Development: A critical look at the consensus', *The Economic Times*, New Delhi, 30 January, 1992.

13. Cf. G.A. Cornia, R. Jolly and F. Stewart, *Adjustment with a Human Face*, Claredon Press, Oxford, 1987.

14. For data on 1989-90, 1990-91 and 1991-92, Reserve Bank of India, *Annual Reports*, 1990-91 and 1991-92. The data for the first nine months of 1992-93 are based on press releases about the wholesale price index and the consumer price index.

15. For 1991-92, Reserve Bank of India, *Annual Report 1991-92*, p. 49. The estimate for 1992-93 is based on information available for the period up to end-December 1992.

16. See *trade statistics* published by DGCIS, Calcutta.

17. These are provisional estimates for 1990-91 and quick estimates for 1991-92 reported by the Reserve Bank of India in its *Annual Report* for 1991-92 (p. 69).

18. Reserve Bank of India, *Annual Report 1991-92*, p. 71.

19. *Ibid.*

20. Statistics published by DGCIS, Calcutta.

21. The outstanding external debt, including external assistance on Government and non-Government account, external commercial borrowing, libilities to the IMF, non-resident deposits and short-term borrowing, increased from $ 63.4 billion in end-March 1991 to $ 71.4 billion in end-September 1992; see *Economic Survey 1992-93*, Ministry of Finance, New Delhi.

22. *Ibid.*

23. Reserve Bank of India estimates suggest that it was 2 per cent, whereas the quick

estimates released by CSO suggest that it was 1.2 per cent.

24. These estimates of growth in agricultural production and in industrial production and obtained from the Reserve Bank of India, *Annual Report 1991-92,*. pp. 34-37. The latter are based on the index numbers of industrial production.

25. The data for 1992-93 are based on CSO projections.

26. The proportions cited in this paragraph have been calculated from the Union Budget documents. The figures are based on actuals for the period from 1987-88 to 1990-91, revised estimates for 1991-92 and budget estimates for 1992-93 (cf. Expenditure Budget, 1992-93, Volume 1). After this lecture was delivered, the Union Budget for 1993-94 was presented in Parliament. In general, the same trends continue in the budget estimates for 1993-94. Capital expenditure as a proportion of total expenditure declines further to 22.5 per cent. Capital expenditure in the central plan outlay is budgeted to increase by less than 5 per cent in nominal terms which suggests a decline in real terms. Budget support for the infrastructure sectors - energy, transport and communication - is only 8.8 per cent of central plan outlay. However, the allocation for plan expenditure on rural development and the social sectors is significantly higher in nominal terms and is budgeted to consti-tute 15.4 per cent of central plan outlay (cf. Expenditure Budget, 1993-94, Volume I)

27. See Alice Amsden, *Asia's New Giant: South Korea and Late Industrialisation*, Oxforx University Press, New York, 1989 and Robert Wade, *Governing the Market*, Princeton University Press, Princeton, 1991.

28. Cf. Sanjaya Lall, *Building Industrial Competitiveness in Developing Countries* OECD Development Centre, Paris, 1990; J. Stiglitz et al, *The Economic Role of the State*, Basil Blackwell, Oxford, 1989; T. Killick, *A Reaction Too Far: Economic Theory and the Role of the State in Developing Countries*, Overseas Development Institute, London, 1990; and H. Shapiro and L. Taylor, 'The State and Industrial Strategy', *World Development*, 1990, pp. 861-878.

29. See J. Stiglitz, 'Markets, Market Failures and Development' *American Economic Review, Papers and Proceedings*, 1989, pp. 197-202, and A. Krueger, 'Government Failures in Development', *Journal of Economic Perspectives*, 1990, pp. 9-23.

30. Cf. T.N. Srinivasan and N.S.S. Narayana, 'Economic Performance since the Third Plan', *Economic and Political Weekly*, Annual Number, 1977; Prabhat Patnaik and S.K. Rao, 'Beginning of the End of Stagnation', *Social Scientist* January-February 1977; and C. Rangarajan, 'Industrial Growth: Another Look', *Economic and Political Weekly*, Annual Number, 1982.

31. For a discussion of the issues, see Sanjaya Lall, *Learning to Industrialise: The Acquistion of Technological Capability by India*, Macmillan, London, 1987.

32. The literature on this subject is vast. See, for example, H. Pack and L. Westphal, 'Industrial Strategy and Technological Change: Theory versus Reality', *Journal of Devel-opment Economics*, 1986, pp. 87-128; and C. Dahlman, B. Ross-Larson and L. Westphal, 'Managing Technological Development : Lessons from Newly Industrialising Countries', *World Development*, 1987, pp. 759-75.

33. For a detailed discussion, see Deepak Nayyar and Abhijit Sen, 'International Trade and the Agricultural Sector in India', Centre for economic Studies and Planning, Jawaharlal Nehru University, New Delhi, *mimeo*, January 1993.

This is the text of the Frontier Lecture delivered by the author at the Indian Institute of Science, Bangalore, on 25th February 1993. It has been published by the Indian Institute of Science and is reprinted here with permission from the author.

6

Economic Reforms in India in the Context of Emerging Global Economy

C.T. KURIEN

I

"The rapidly changing global economy' is frequently referred to as the compelling reason for the sweeping economic reforms initiated in the country and which have entered the third season, if not exactly the third year, with the presentation of the union budget at the end of February. The 'full convertibility' of the rupee on current account transactions, and the slashing of customs duties in particular, both of which emerged as the special features of the 1993-94 budget are meant to further integrate the Indian economy with the emerging global economy.

But what exactly is the nature of 'the global economy' out there? Who are the main participants in it? What are their agendas? How does a national economy get integrated with it? I do not believe that these questions have received the attention they deserve. In fact, even though the term 'the global economy' is of very recent vintage, there is not enough discussion as to what it is and whether it is only another name for the older and more familiar 'international economy'. Similarly, even when it is acknowledged to be rapidly changing, it is doubtful whether sufficient attention has been paid to the nature of that change and to draw out its implications. I am certainly not pretending that no work has been done in this area. On the contrary, there is a considerable body of literature on some aspects of it as, for instance, on transnational corporations (TNCs) or multinational corporations (MNCs) who, it is generally accepted, play a crucial role in the emerging global economy. But what is the nature of the engagement between these bodies and the national economies? Or consider the following claim that *The Economist's* special survey on the world economy made in September 1992: "Twenty years from now economists will think of the 1980s not as the decade of the international debt crisis, nor of the dollar's boom and bust, still less of Reaganomics and 'monetarism'. All these mattered, but none of them marked decisive change in the forces that drive the world economy. Yet, the 1980s did witness such a change. During these years many of the boundaries between national financial markets dissolved, and a truly global capital market began to emerge. It is for this that the past decade will be remembered".[1] Is this a valid claim? And, if an integrated global economy is emerging in the financial sphere, what are its implications for the 'real' economy?

These are some of the questions that I propose to examine in this paper so as to come to have a better understanding of the emerging global economy and then to consider what bearing it will have on the Indian economy and the reform measures in particular. The paper is essentially exploratory in nature.

II

Underlying an approach to something as abstract and complex as the global economy is the search for a conceptualisation of it. Part of the problem is that economists have a conceptualisation of it which may have been valid earlier on and for some limited purposes, but is totally inadequate for the set of questions raised above. Consider the Ricardian theory of comparative advantage. Certainly, the crucial aspects of that theory are not England and Portugal, the two countries that Ricardo wrote about of wine and cloth, the two goods that he dealt with. The basic premise of the theory is that the 'international economy' that Ricardo set up consists of two countries which are both interested in the use of goods, and the issue to be settled is whether the goods should be produced or purchased. To put it differently, the conceptualisation of the international economy underlying the Ricardian theory of comparative advantage is that it consists of similar units with similar agendas. If this basic premise is granted the theory can be 'generalised' to deal with 'n' countries and 'm' goods. Further modifications and extensions can also be made as has been done in what has come to be referred to as the Heckscher-Ohlin theory which took into account the possibility of the goods being produced not by labour alone (as Ricardo did) but by capital as well. But note again that the units are similar and their agendas are also similar. It can be claimed that not even the literature on 'optimum tariffs' which is sometimes considered as a departure from the Ricardian position rejects or escapes from what I have described as the basic postulate of the Ricardian theory. And, if there has been no departure from this basic postulate, it must be assumed that current discussions on the global economy, whether at the realm of 'pure theory' or in terms of the application of theory to policy matters, are still anchored on it.

A major issue to be considered, then, is whether that premise is compatible with what is generally referred to as the emerging global economy. Three reservations must be listed. The first is that in the context of the international economy the relationship of one of its units with others is of a 'between' nature as, for instance, the Indian economy in relation to the US economy or the Indian economy in relation to all other national economies. It is in this latter sense that the recommendation is being made that the Indian economy must be 'opened up' to the global economy out there. But the concept of the global economy is essentially an inclusive one: The Indian economy is within the global economy, and as such may share some of the characteristics of the global economy and the global economy may reflect some of the features of its constituent unit, the Indian economy. This relationship between the whole and the part cannot be captured by the concept of an international economy which, at best, only enumerates all its units.

The second reservation is that if the emerging global economy consists of (at least) national economies and multinational corporations, then its units cannot be treated as similar or homogeneous. In fact, an important feature of the emerging global economy is the rise to prominence of the MNCs who, in many fundamental respects, are very differnt from national economies. Hence, it is important that the global economy should be conceptualised as consisting of heterogeneous units which will then distinguish it clearly from the existing conceptualisation of the international economy as consisting of homogeneous units.

This distinction will become sharper if we take into account the third reservation which is related to what has already been referred to as the agenda of the units. Within the conceptualisation of the international economy which is concerned with trade, it may be legitimate (definitely convenient) to depict all units as having the same agenda, but intuitively one can see that national economies and MNCs cannot be treated as having similar agendas. This must be more adequately spelled out and I shall try to do so subsequently.

However, one aspect may be noted straightaway. The international economy of international trade theory is essentially a real economy construct of the movement of goods from one country to another. Of course, it is not pretended that international trade even when it is between two countries is barter trade (though that may also happen); it is recognised as part of multilateral trade made possible through the medium of money. But if it is not exchange of the C-C type, it is only of the C-M-C type with money assumed to play only the mediatory role of facilitating a real economy transaction. Even the balance of payments calculations are at that level. Conventional international trade theory does not move into the M-C-M level of analysis. In particular, it does not postulate the possibility of trade in money (different currencies) which today constitutes the major agenda of some of the units in the global economy.

Now if these three reservations are taken together, it will become evident that the conceptualisation of the global economy has to be distinctly different from the manner in which the international economy has been conceptualised in the Ricardian theory of comparative advantage. The global economy must be viewed as a collection of heterogeneous constituent units with different agendas interacting with one another in a variety of ways and thus changing its character over time.

III

The characterisation of the global economy given above is not an end in itself.

Its purpose is to serve as an aid to the understanding of what is happening around us. A quick review of the developments in the world economy since the end of the second world war may be helpful. Recalling the collapse of world trade, the competitive devaluations ('beggar thy neighbour' policy) and the spread of the depression of the inter-war period, that United States and the United Kingdom, as the emerging victors of the second world war set out to create "a world in which countries did not close their eyes to the repercussions of their actions on others" as an author subsequently expressed it.[2] That was the underlying principle of the Bretton Woods Conference of July 1944, which set up the International Monetary Fund (IMF) whose responsibility was to maintain a fixed exchange rate system with provisions for dealing with temporary balance of payments problems of member nations and the International Bank for Reconstruction and Development (World Bank) to provide long-term capital requirements. For the first time, therefore, two international agencies were set up followed by a third, the General Agreement on Tariff and Trade (GATT) in order to permit national economies to pursue domestic policies of their own almost autonomously, but providing for free trade and free flow of capital among them on the basis of fixed exchange rates.

The arrangement seemed to work successfully for the first decade and a half. However, it was not so much the setting up of these bodies that accounted for the smooth functioning of international economy at that time, but the dominating role of the US economy, the strength of the dollar which would, therefore, function as the international currency and the fact that the flow of capital was almost unilateral, from the US to Europe in the form of the Marshall Plan, to Japan and in small trickles also to what were then recognised as underdeveloped countries. "The American economy became the principal engine of world economic growth", recalled a commentator, "American monetary policy became world monetary policy, and the outflow of dollars provided the liquidity that greased commerce".[3] But the hegemonic role of the American economy and the standing of the dollar as international currency were to have other consequences which soon began to become evident. The United States needed foreign exchange to finance its global operations, especially the stationing of its forces in Europe and carrying out a prolonged war in Vietnam. But since the dollar was globally acceptable, the US was in a position to solve its balance of payments problems by issuing its own currency as and when the need arose leading to such situations as the proliferation of 'Euro-dollars'. For a short while the dollar reigned as the undisputed global currency (acceptable and highly in demand even in the Soviet bloc which, in many ways, stood out of the international economic system that was developing in the post-war period) as no other national currency had ever done.

One reason for this global acceptability of the dollar was, of course, that the US government had the legal obligation to convert the dollar into gold on demand. But this arrangement was not to last for long, both for global and domestic reasons. At the global level, both Japan and West Germany had a spectacular economic revival from the 1950s and throughout the 1960s and their currencies, mark and yen, emerged into the global scene. In the meanwhile, the massive escalation of the Vietnam War led to glaring deterioration in America's balance of payments and US domestic policies, particularly the Great Society programmes of the Johnson administration, generated huge budgetary deficits generating inflation in that country. These developments that began to show the vulnerability of the US economy and the steadily growing capital surplus of Japan started eroding the confidence of the world in the strength of the US economy and of the dollar. By 1971 the outflow of gold from the US had become massive and in August of that year Nixon was forced to announce the suspension of the convertibility of the dollar into gold, thereby abandoning the basis of the Bretton Woods system of fixed exchange rates, although the decision to move to an era of floating exchange rates was made only in 1973 and was ratified only in 1976.

The change in the status of the dollar and the first oil shock of 1973 resulting from the sharp hike in oil prices by the OPEC could have thrown the international economy into utter chaos. However, the willingness of the OPEC and Japan to continue to hold their surpluses in the form of dollar gave the dollar the status of *de facto* reserve currency.

The period from the end of the second world war, or the beginning of the 1950s till the oil shock of 1973, was also one of unprecedented growth in output in real terms in most countries of the world. The application of science and technology to production was the main reason for it which also linked up countries of the world closer together. There was very rapid expansion of international trade. Along with these changes a development of far-reaching consequences was also taking place. The political and economic clout that the United States had during this period was put to use to promote the global interests of the giant US corporations and to give them a new standing as transnational corporations active across national boundaries. From an accumulated direct investment of a little over $ 10 billion in 1950, American direct investment abroad had picked up rapidly and by the early 1970s the US had become more of a foreign investor than an exporter of domestically manufactured goods. These investments continued to some extent in traditional manufacturing industires, but the growth in direct foreign investment turned out to be in automobiles, chemicals and electronics. And by the early 1970s international production by American transnational corporations had surpassed trade as America's international economic exchange. Foreign production by the officials of the US corporations had grown nearly four times as large as American exports. Also, a substantial proportion of the US exports of manufactured goods was really transfer from an American branch to an overseas branch of a transnational corporation.[4] What was essentially a US phenomenon up to the 1970s became more widespread with European and Japanese transnationals also following the pattern set by the US transnationals. By the early 80s TNCs had emerged as a new set of units where, till the 1970s at least, national economies were the only entities.

The appearance of the TNCs, therefore, marks the first step in the transformation of what was the international economy into a global economy in the sense in which I have drawn the distinction between the two in the preceding section. It will be noticed that the transformation indicates not only the presence of new kinds of units in the system, but also a significant change in the nature of interactions among the units. What was considered as international trade now changes its character. Although, physically, there is still a movement of goods from one country to another, a significant part of this movement must now be considered as the internal movement of goods from one department of a corporation to another department. In other words, what was so far treated as movement between one set of units (countries) turns out to be to a large extent movements within another unit, a transnational corporation. And, if the former was based on 'market' transactions, the latter may have entirely different considerations behind it.

From the middle of the 1970s the transformation that was taking place came to have another dimension. In the 1950s and 1960s the major part of capital transfers from the richer countries of the world (north) to the poorer countries (south) was through official channels. But the surplus liquidity of the 1970s initiated the flow of funds from private sources in the north to countries of the south. Banks and other financial institutions were more than willing to lend their excess funds to anyone who was willing to borrow, and there were many takers, some for the purchase of armaments, some for importing oil at the higher global prices, some for financing prestigious projects, and some for backing developmental efforts. The decade of the 1970s, therefore, was one of closer financial links between countries of the north (or, to be more precise, between some units in countries of the north) and countries of the south, primarily through bank lending which increased by nearly 800 per cent during the decade.[5]

At the same time, the phenomenal growth of the 'golden decades' of the 1950s and 1960s began to slow down. The complexion of the global economy at the beginning of the 1980s was very different from what it was at the beginning of the 1970s. Gone was the optimism of the immediate post-war era of the possibilities of growth and co-operation among nations. The caution about continuing inflation was replaced by concern about a global recession. The early symptoms of the emergence of centres of economic power in Europe and in the Far East and the consequent challenge to American hegemony were quite evident. Consequently, in the 1980s leading national economies retreated from the earlier emphasis on global orientation and multilateralism into preoccupation with their own national economies, regionalism and 'minilateralism' becoming its corollaries. What has come to be known as 'new protectionism' became the unofficial creed among many national governments, especially the United States and several of the leading European countries, not to speak of Japan which always had an armoury of measures to keep its economy effectively closed to the rest of the world.

When national economies began to retreat from internationalism, leading private corporations the world over emerged as the champions of the concept of the 'global economy' and of free trade. The major ones among them, especially the transnational ones, had already come to view the world at large as the theatre of their operations. A study in the mid-1980s about the manufacture of Ford Escort which is assembled as a car in the UK and Germany showed that the manufacturing process was done in 15 different countries, each one of which supplied some component or the other of the final product.[6] (The increase in 'international trade' resulting from such activity can be easily inferred.) A more recent account puts it thus: "When an American buys a Pontiac Le Mans from General Motors, for example, he or she engages in an international transaction. Of the $ 20,000 paid to GM, about $ 6,000 goes to South Korea for routine labour and assembly operations, $ 3,500 to Japan for advanced components (engines, transaxles and electronics), $ 1,500 to West Germany for styling and design engineering, $ 800 to Taiwan, Singapore and Japan for small components, $ 500 to Britain for advertising and marketing services, and about $ 100 to Ireland and Barbados for data processing. The rest — less than $ 8,000 — goes to the strategists in Detroit, lawyers and bankers in New York, lobbyists in Washington, insurance and health-care workers all over the country, and General Motors shareholders — most of whom live in the United States, but an increasing number of whom are foreign nationals."[7]

Two aspects regarding the nature of corporations such as General Motors can be seen from this account. The first is the transnationalisation of production already referred to. Transnational corporations make decisions about the location of production, taking into account a wide range of considerations such as labour costs, transport costs, government subsidies and taxes, exchange rates and polit-ical climate, all governed by a single point agenda of maximising profits. Sure enough, comparative advantage of alternative locations is given careful consider-ation in arriving at a final decision, but these calculations are not of the kind that Ricardo had thought about. They frequently involve negotiations with the govern-ments of host countries about terms and conditions. These decisions are, there-fore, based to some extent on comparative costs, but they also alter comparative cost calculations. Secondly, and from an analytical point of view more signifi-cantly, the account given above also shows that what were considered as transnational corporations (with activities across national boundaries) are also becoming multinational in nature with their ownership belonging to people of different nationalities. This indicates the emergence of units in the global econ-omy relatively independent of national economies. This is a fairly new phenom-enon. An American writer says: "Beginning in 1991, Japan's Mazda would be producing Ford Probes at Mazda's plant at Flat Rock, Michigan. Some of these cars would be exported to Japan and sold there under Ford's trademark. A Mazda-designed compact utility vehicle would be built at a Ford plant in Louisville, Kentucky, and then sold at Mazda dealerships in the United States. Nissan, meanwhile, was designing a new light truck at its San Diego, California design centre. The truck would be assembled at Ford's Ohio truck plant, using panel parts fabricated by Nissan at its Tennessee factory, and then marketed by both Ford and Nissan in the United States and in Japan. Who is Ford? Nissan? Mazda?"[8]

The answer to that question is not easy. But the examples cited above will indicate why the TNCs and MNCs are becoming champions of the 'global econ-omy' and why they are turning out to be the most ardent advocates of 'free trade' even when many national governments, known to have been proponents of that doctrine, are retreating into various shades of protectionism. Freedom to operate in any part of the world is a necessary condition in terms of their agenda and the free movement of goods across national boundaries is a requirement for their operations.

But, of course, the free movement of goods is not so readily achieved in a global economy where national governments still make many crucial decisions and control many important activities. But there is one sphere where free and rapid movement is becoming the rule. This is the sphere of finance capital. And, as *The Economist's* survey of the world economy quoted in Section-I claims, the decisive changes in the global economy in the decade of the 1980s took place in this sphere. That survey gives the following figures to substantiate the claim:[9]

* In 1980 the stock of 'international' bank lending was $ 324 billion. By 1991, it had risen to $ 7.5 trillion. To put these figures in perspective, in 1990 it constituted 4 per cent of the GDP of OECD industrial countries; in 1991, 44 per cent.

* In 1982 the total of international bonds outstanding was $ 259 billion; by 1991 it was $ 1.65 trillion.

* In 1970 America's securities transactions with foreigners amounted to the equivalent of 3 per cent of the country's GDP; in 1980 the figure was 9 per cent; in 1990 it was 93 per cent. The corresponding figures for West Germany are 3 per cent, 8 per cent and 58 per cent; and for Japan, 2 per cent (1975), 7 per cent and 119 per cent.

* Currency trading in 1991 was estimated to be roughly $ 900 billion each day.

To these may be added information obtained from another source that foreign direct investment (i.e., capital invested throughout the world, crossing national boundaries) nearly tripled in the 1980s and by the end of 1990 stood at over $ 1.5 trillion in terms of book values.[10]

These changes, and in particular, the very short period in which they took place are, indeed, mind-boggling and support *The Economist's* claim that they have brought into the global economy a totally different dimension. What is the explanation for these changes? According to the survey, the financial transformation of the 1980s was just the newest phase of an old process: market-driven economic development brought about by innovation, technology and deregulation. This may be so, but it does not give enough clues to understand what happened and what has been going on. The survey also provides some more detailed explanations situating the new phenomenon in the context of the international economic relationships of the 1980s, especially among the big three, the US, Japan and Germany. At the beginning of the decade the US had a current account surplus of $ 1 billion which began to change into a deficit fairly soon mainly because of the policies pursued by the first Reagan administration. By 1987 the deficit had reached $ 160 billion. Since the US deficit was primarily in relation to Japan and West Germany, they moved into current account surplus. The surplus countries lent America the capital it needed to pay for its excess of imports over exports. Balance of payment statements of this kind are, of course, net figures, hiding the magnitude of gross transactions. In any case, they show the extent of financial transactions across national boundaries arising from such situations. There is also a related phenomenon. These transactions led to considerable exchange-rate volatility which become a regular feature in the 1980s. In turn exchange-rate volatility promoted rapid movements into and away from the leading currencies, thus adding to the volume of transactions. Such a climate also provided excellent opportunities for speculative transactions, again augmenting the flow of funds in different directions. Differences in interest rates in different parts of the world, especially in the leading countries, further stimulated these propensities. As the survey argues: "The higher the interest rates are, and the more interest rates and currencies move around, the greater the opportunities for profitable 'regulatory arbitrage' are likely to be." These movements were greatly facilitated by the dramatic changes in communications technology which made possible 24-hour financial trading and a vast range of new financial instruments for round-the-clock traders to buy and sell.

It is not surprising that TNCs and MNCs with their single point agenda to make profits and to make them quick found in these new developments a fresh avenue for their transactions. Shrewd financial transactions, buying and selling of shares, buying and selling of entreprises, take-overs, mergers and all forms of 'paper entrepreneurship' are becoming the best ways of making profits and hence this new segment of the global economy has come to be dominated by the TNCs and MNCs.

It must be noted too that while these spectacular changes were taking place in the financial realm, the performance of the global economy in real terms was moving in the opposite direction, especially in the north. The World Bank's *World Development Report 1991*, for instance, showed that the GDP per capita of the industrialised market economies grew at an annual average of 3.6 per cent from 1950 to 1973, but only by 2 per cent from 1973 to 1989. In fact, a comparison over time of industrial production of the leading countries substantiates this further as can be seen from the Table.[11]

Table : Industrial Production – Annual Average

(Per Cent)

	1960-70	1970-80	1980-90
United States	4.9	3.3	2.6
Japan	15.9	4.1	3.9
West Germany	5.2	2.3	1.8
France	6.0	3.0	1.3
Italy	7.3	3.3	1.3
United Kingdom	2.9	1.1	1.8

We must, therefore, infer that one of the striking aspects of the global economy is a palpable disjunction between the 'real' economy and the financial economy and the TNC's and MNC's may be largely responsible for this. As Peter Drucker has observed, "Ninety per cent or more of the transnational economy's financial transactions do not serve what economists would consider an economic function. They serve purely financial functions. These money flows have their own rationality, of course. But they are in large part political rationalities, anticipation of government decisions as to central bank interest rates or foreign exchange rates, taxes, government deficits and government borrowing, or political-risk assessment."[12] However, this does not mean that the real economy and the financial economy are distinct entities in the emerging global economy: They interact and intermesh, but not always in a predictable manner.

IV

The rather sketchy account of the salient aspects of the transformation that has been going on during the past four decades or so, evolving a global economy out of an international economy, it is hoped, is helpful to an understanding of the global economic context of the early 1990s which constitues the backdrop to Indian economic reforms. Let us try to capture its essential features:

(1) Relationships among national economies still play a major role in the contemporary global economy. But these relationships are not multilateral in any meaningful sense of that term. There are four distinct centres of the international economy: North America (led by the United States); Europe (with a unified Germany in the lead); the Far East (where Japan is the major actor followed by South Korea); and the People's Republic of China. These are the active agents of the international economy with other national economies being passive participants in it. Of the four, the last has special characteristics of its own and has not been drawn into the global system as much as the other three.

(2) In terms of economic activities -- production, trade and capital flows -- the first three account for a very high proportion. With respect to capital, Germany and Japan have emerged as surplus nations and the US as the largest deficit nation absorbing a major share of the capital available in the global system. For instance, in 1988 Japan had a surplus of some $ 80 billion, Germany $ 48 billion, and the NICs of Asia $ 26 billion. As against these (and smaller amounts from other countries) the US absorbed some $ 135 billion. In other words, "the US is now absorbing most of the capital exported by all the creditor nations of the world thereby crowding out other potential borrowers and increasing world real interest rates."[13]

(3) This situation has its bearing on the world's trading system. Let us note that in spite of all the trumpeting about 'free trade' as the natural corollary of the capitalist system, no leading capitalist country has really practised it. When GATT was established in 1948 to achieve a 'freer and fairer trade' through reduction of tariffs and diminution of other trade barriers, enough exceptions were provided, for instance, to keep agriculture entirely out of its purview at the insistence of the US and many European countries. As a recent study observes, "The [GATT] system was never based on standard economic arguments for free trade, but rather on a kind of managed mercantilism under which countries traded

'concessions' on imports in return for export opportunities."[14] This system of concessions has now run aground for a variety of reasons, the chief among them being the magnitude of current account deficits of the US which has led to increased pressures for protectionist policies in that country. The global trade regime has undergone major changes in the 1980s. In 1985 the Council of Economic Advisers of the President of the United States reported: "The world is moving away from, rather than toward, comprehensive free trade. In major industrialised countries, for example, the proportion of total manufacturing subject to non-tariff restrictions rose to about 30 per cent in 1983, up from 20 per cent just three years earlier."[15] This tendency has continued. *The Economist's* survey of World Trade in September 1990 gave the following information. Many new sorts of trade protection have been proliferating in recent years. One of these devices is what has come to be euphemistically referred to as 'voluntary' export restraint (VER). "Increasingly, if a powerful government is worried about the harm that imports are doing to its producers, especially if it happens to be the American government, it requires another government on pain of retaliation, to restrict its country's exports of the good in question."[16] This is an old practice going back to the 1970s when it was largely confined to textiles. But more recently VERs have spread to steel, cars, shoes, machinery, consumer electronics and more. The GATT's secretariat has counted nearly 300 VERs! In this connection *The Economist's* observations about 'Section 301' are worth repeating: "The crowbar in America's toolbox is the notorious Section 301 of its trade law. This gives the president broad authority to retaliate against foreign trade practices that unfairly discourage American exports. America decides what is unfair; the law is vague on the point."[17] The 'Super 301' was added in 1988 making it obligatory, again on pain of retaliation, for the 'named' countries to reach agreement with the US Trade Representative within 12 to 18 months. It may be recalled that India is one of the 'named' countries.

It is not only the US that tries to protect its trade. Japan is even more notorious with the difference that protectionism there is a domestic policy – the Japanese have 'voluntarily' agreed not to use foreign goods if these are produced in Japan also!

(4) In terms of national currencies, formally from 1971 and effectively from the second half of the 1980s the global economy has been functioning without any formally accepted standards or even a lead currency, taking the situation to the same kind of flux and uncertainty that prevailed after the collapse of the gold standard during the inter-war-period. This has led to exchange-rate volatility becoming the order of the day.

(5) Transnational and multinational corporations have emerged as powerful non-governmental agencies in the global economy. They operate with a single point agenda of maximising financial profits. They have transnationalised the production process with no long-term commitment to any particular global location and always ready to hop, step and jump to wherever they perceive their advantages to be. They exercise a great deal of control over capital movements, but, for reasons indicated, capital of this kind is essentially footloose, here today

and gone tomorrow. Increasingly the TNCs and MNCs are turning to financial activities and their actions have led to a substantial integration of the financial system in the global economy. They take full advantage of the exchange-rate volatility and, to a large extent, also generate such fluctuations. Exchange rates today are much more a reflection of global financial transactions than of trade. Because of their ability to influence exchange rates the TNCs and MNCs can greatly impact national economic policies, especially relating to monetary policies. In the emerging global economy, therefore, these non-governmental agencies have a profound influence, very evident in some respects, but subtly hidden in many other respects.

(6) In view of all these changes, the international economic agencies such as the IMF and the World Bank have lost much of their original mandates, but they now function primarily to protect 'global stability' which can mean only stability that favours those who control the physical and financial resources. In pretending to be guardians of 'global' interests, they become effective allies of those who are the *de facto* controllers of the system.

(7) Poorer countries of the world as a group – the "South" – have had a rough deal in the emerging new dispensation. On this, the best description is seen in the Report of the South Commission: "The widening disparities between south and north are attributable not merely to differences in economic progress, but also to an enlargement of the north's power *vis-a-vis* the rest of the world. The leading countries of the north now readily use that power in pursuit of their objectives. The 'gunboat' diplomacy of the nineteenth century still has its economic and political counterpart in the closing years of the twentieth. The fate of the south is increasingly dictated by the perceptions and policies of the governments in the north, of the multilateral institutions which a few of those governments control, and of the network of private institutions that are increasingly prominent."[18] And, "A network of relationships has been built up among private entities banks, investment houses, transnational companies in the leading developed countries. This has served to strengthen the influence of decisions made by private bodies on world economic activity, and to that extent to limit the effectiveness of governmental policy decisions. For the south the result is even further marginalisation and greater powerlessness."[19] Neither is this mere rhetoric. In terms of hard cash, for instance, the debt-related transfers of resources from 1984 turned out to be from the south to the north, the net amount being as high as $ 163 billion between 1984 and 1988. This reverse flow was not only from the south to the north. In 1986-88, net credits from the IMF to developing countries also turned out to be negative.

Such is the global economy to which through the reform measures initiated in July 1991 the Indian economy seeks greater integration. A number of questions need to be raised regarding this proposed integration even when the answers may not be readily available.

First, the timing. India has been under advice for many years to make its economic policies 'outward oriented' to 'open up' its economy to foreign goods and foreign investment and to join in the global movement towards liberalisation and privatisation. Apart from some 'theoretical' considerations, this advice was based on some empirical evidence, in particular, the experience of Singapore, Hong Kong, Taiwan and South Korea -the 'Asian tigers' -who took the advice a couple of decades ago and have shown excellent results in transforming their economies. This, of course, raises many questions such as repeatability of such experiences. But at least one of these is crucial. Does the global economy in the early 1990s provide the same kind of conditions as it did in the mid-1960s and even the early 1970s? The 1960s were years of rapid growth of the global economy as also of international trade. In sharp contrast, the World Bank's World Development Report, 1991 with 'the Challenge of Development' as its theme had this grim picture of the economic scene of the early 1990s:

A seven-year expansion in the world economy came almost to a halt in 1990. Signs of slowing economic activity in a number of large industrial countries became evident as monetary policies were tightened in response to production at near-capacity levels and rising inflation. The slow down became more widespread and pronounced with the Gulf crisis in August 1990. Increased uncertainty had adverse effects on consumer and business confidence, which in turn led to markedly lower growth of consumer spending and business investment in the industrial countries. The financial requirements of the unification of Germany and war-related reconstruction in the Middle East exerted upward pressures on short-term interest rates in Germany and Japan despite the economic slow down in 1990 and early 1991. Real GDP growth in industrial countries slowed down to about 2.6 per cent in 1990 compared with 3.3 per cent in 1989 and 4.5 per cent in 1988.

Canada, the United Kingdom, and the United states have been in recession. Growth has also slowed down elsewhere in Western Europe. Equity prices in Japan have fallen by about 50 per cent, and the quality of commercial bank portfolios in both Japan and the United States has deteriorated. Although the slow down of the industrial economies is likely to be short- lived and shallow, the recovery is expected to be only gradual.

In the developing countries, real GDP growth declined from 4.3 per cent in 1988 to 2.9 per cent in 1990, the lowest since 1986. The main reasons in addition to continuing macro economic instability and domestic policy weaknesses were falling non-oil commodity prices, high international (non-dollar) interest rates, and slower growth in world trade.[20] Surely, reasonable thinking would not have favoured greater integration with the global economy under such conditions.

Second, the diagnosis of the crisis of the Indian economy. The argument put forward when the reform measures were suddenly announced was that the prudent strategies of growth of the 1980s and the wise policies derived from them were reversed by two short-sighted governments that were in power from December 1989 to June 1991. On the contrary, even a cursory examination of the evidence available from official sources will show that the crisis was the direct consequence of the policies of the 1980s growth supported by mounting import surpluses and financed by reckless government deficits particularly on revenue account related to the political decision not to 'hurt' those able to pay direct taxes. These were very similar to what was being put into effect in the United states at the same time and, not surprisingly, with the same consequences, viz., alarmingly high debts, both internal and external. Unfortunately, however, while the creditors of the United States were ready to support the US position, no one appeared to be willing to lend support to a struggling India.

Third, if the diagnosis was wrong, were the remedies right? The capital flights of October 1990 to June 1991 and the consequent sharp fall in the foreign exchange reserves were mentioned as the immediate manifestations of the crisis for which remedial measures were needed. *The Economic Survey*, 1992-93 has now provided the figures: During those months a total amount of $ 1.33 billion was withdrawn from the Foreign Currency Non-Resident Accounts (FCNR), starting with $ 102 million in October, going down to $ 11 million in February, but picking up again, shooting up to $ 373 in April, then $ 228 in May and another $ 330 in June. Certainly, the cumulative impact of these flights would have been alarming, especially to new administration. But what was the nature of these capital flights? It has been pointed out that the capital flights started after the World Bank had strongly advocated a 20 per cent devaluation of the rupee in a report in October 1990.[21] Even if there is not enough evidence to suggest that the capital flight was thus engineered, it can be safely inferred that the learned arguments of the bank must have had a bearing on the decisions of the NRIs. In any case, if the crisis was precipitated by capital flight, was the devaluation of the rupee the first and best way to resolve it? The answer could be that the devaluation was a confidence restoring measure and it seemed to have worked because the capital flight was arrested. Perhaps yes; although the evidence is not very convincing. The FCNR flow turned positive in January 1992, but from there until September it was again negative. After that till January 1993 (the latest month for which figures are available) it remained positive. Will there be another outflow now that the interest rate has been brought down? In other words, how much can one rely on the NRI deposits? Are they being made for patriotic reasons, or are they part of the global phenomenon of transient capital resting in India for a while?

Fourth, other than as a temporary confidence restoring measure what is the devaluation expected to achieve? In the conventional theory of international trade, devaluation is expected to correct balance of payments problems by stimulating exports and curbing imports. The latter is almost sure to happen because devaluation will make imports costlier in terms of the domestic currency, but the former will depend very much on how price elastic a country's exports are and whether the increase in the volume of exports (if it happens) is sufficiently large to compensate for the higher exchange value of the foreign currency. Export and import figures are available only up to 1991-92 which show that exports fell to $ 18,135 million from the 1990-91 figure of $ 18,491 million, and that imports also declined from $ 26,241 million in 1990-91 to $ 21,213 million. Less than one year's figures are certainly not adequate to judge the issue. But the more important question is whether in the kind of global economy that has been emerging, a country like India has much of a chance to boost its exports through exchange rates adjustments alone.

Fifth, there is the related issue of the convertibility of the rupee. Here, again, convertibility will be a desirable objective to work towards if the external value of a national currency is determined primarily in terms of its 'real' transactions with the rest of the world. But in the global economy where financial transactions *per se*, including speculative buying and selling of currencies, are substantially the major component of transactions, is convertibility a virtue in itself? As of now the convertibility is limited to current account, but if and when it becomes effective on capital account too, will there not be speculative buying and selling of the rupee which may lead to violent fluctuations in its external value? Is it unreasonable to imagine that the rupee then will face problems similar to what has been happening to the British pound and the Italian lira?

Sixth, how realistic is it to expect that when the rupee is devalued and convertibility is established, there will be a significant flow of foreign capital into India? Some foreign capital will come in, as has happened in the food processing industry, for instance, to take advantage of India's big domestic market for such goods. But that would not lead to increase in exports and help to reduce the underlying balance of payments problems. On the contrary, to the extent that payments will have to be made in foreign currency, the balance of payments position may get aggravated. Some finance capital may also come in as has been happening. It has been observed that in 1991-92 foreign banks had made a profit of more than Rs. 1,000 crore in their Indian operations and that profits from Indian operations were far larger than the global rate of profits.[22] Is this all that the reforms can achieve? If more is to be expected, from which sources, for what reasons and on what terms?

These questions have been raised not to suggest that the Indian economy should delink itself from the global economy. That option does not exist. Neither is it implied that the Indian economy does not need reforms. Far from it. There is absolutely no doubt that a large measure of debureaucratisation and reduction of political meddling in day-to-day economic matters are both very much needed. But these cannot be achieved by divesting of the shares of public sector enterprises without a proper enquiry into their poor performance or by announcing tax concessions one after the other. If it is the case that in today's global economy no country has the option to contract out completely, it is equally the case that in no country can the state withdraw from economic activity.

Of course, in India even under the guise of liberalisation and privatisation there is no proposal for the state to retreat completely from the economic sphere. Political compulsions will not permit it. But that is not enough and that is not the issue. What is needed is for the state to define its economic agenda clearly. There has been no such thing so far. The reform measures so far have been a package of cliches and *ad hoc* 'adjustments' without any explicit statements about long-term objectives and steps to achieve them. That will not do.

In defining an economic agenda for the country it is important to note that in a very meaningful sense economic policies in India will have to be inward-oriented. The suggestion is not that we should go in for a further regime of import substitution without any consideration for the global situation. On the contrary what it does mean is that the Indian economy can expect to become an active player in the emerging global economy only to the extent that two basic internal issues are tackled. The first and most immediate is that there has to be a restructuring of the industrial economy of the country. It is totally unrealistic to suggest that the problem in the industrial structure is solely the poor performance of public sector enterprises. Basically, the problem to be resolved is in the private sector – the near total absence of innovative effort, in difference to qualitative orientation, attachment to the limited but readymade Indian market. It is futile to expect that opening up and liberalisation will automatically resolve these issues because they will bring in competition with them.[23] That is an assumption carried forward from the international economy of the Ricardian era. Without going into details, it can be argued that there is a good chance that the internal restructuring that will take place as a result of opening up without a conscious restructuring policy may be for Indian industrial enterprises to become subcontracting agents of global enterprises. That is the kind of restructuring that powerful MNCs are interested in and already there is tremendous eagerness in India to get on to the MNC bandwagon. It may yield some short-term financial benefits, but it is a poor policy if the intention is the strengthening of the real economy of India in the long run. A reorganisation of the industrial economy of India to achieve that long-term objective can come only through state initiative and monitoring. It has, therefore, to be a major item on the economic agenda of the state.

The second internal reorganisation that is required is more fundamental. A long-term industrial and developmental strategy in India can be sustained only to the extent that it succeeds in incorporating the masses into it. In the industrial sphere it must include the augmenting of the productivity of workers in what are described as the traditional village industries on which vast millions of people still depend for employment and livelihood, establishing closer links between them and the more dynamic sectors and carefully reorganising the market structure.[24] It must also take into account the role of the modern small-scale industries linking them effectively with the larger ones. Hence, this too must figure prominently in the economic agenda of the state. One of the major implications is that there will have to be a carefully organised training and retraining programme of massive dimensions. That is why the state will have to be an active agent in this sphere.

Another major area for state action is to ensure that the real economy and the monetary/financial economy do not get dissociated which is the distinct feature of the emerging global economy. At the global level this has happened because of the emergence of new units who can concentrate entirely on financial aspects and financial gains. No national economy can afford to do it. The agenda of national economies will have to be in the sphere of the real economy with money and finance being used to facilitate and co-ordinate the functioning of the real economy. All national economies now have to be alert to the activities of units in the global economy whose primary pre-occupation is with finance and whose involvement with the real economy is only to promote financial gains. Handling this situation is not easy because these new actors in the global economy are both within and without the territorial jurisdiction and legal controls of national governments. National economic policies all over the world have to reckon with this fact and decide, in terms of the specifics of each situation, how to deal with it. The stock exchange scam has already shown us what the pursuit of financial profits detached from the real economy component can lead to. In this sphere, certainly, complete abandon to private interests is not the answer and the state, as the guardian of larger social interests, has a decisive role to play.

In sum, the nature of restructuring and reforms that the emerging global economy makes necessary is not as simple as privatisation, liberalisation, marketisation, globalisation or whatever other slogan that is found attractive and marketable for the time being. It calls for a proper understanding of the far-reaching changes taking place in the global economy and intelligent responses to them with a clear perception of social priorities. Let the reader decide how the economic reform measures now being pushed measure up to these norms.

Notes

1. *The Economist*, September 19, 1992, Survey of World Economy.

2. Austin Robinson, "A Personal View' in Milo Keynes (ed) *Essays on John Maynard Keynes* (Cambridge, Cambridge University Press, 1975).

3. Robert Gilpin, *The Political Economy of International Relations* (Princeton, Princeton University Press, 1987), p. 133.

4. Ibid, p. 239.

5. The World Bank, *World Development Report, 1991*, p. 18.

6. The World Bank, *World Development Report, 1987*, p. 39.

7. Robert B Reich, *The Work of Nations* (New York, Alfred A Knopf, 1991), p. 113.

8. Ibid, p. 131.

9. *The Economist*, September 19, 1992, Survey of World Economy, pp. 6 and 9.

10. 'Globalisation: To What End?', Part I, *Monthly Review*, February 1992.

11. Loc cit, Table II. Basic sources of data are US, *Economic Report of the President*, 1986 and 1991.

12. Peter F Drucker, *The New Realities* (New Delhi, Asian Books, 1990), p. 127.

13. World Institute of Development Economics Research, *World Imbalances* (Helsinki, WIDER, 1989), p. 22.

14. Ibid, p. 114.

15. Quoted by Gilpia, op. cit., p. 192.

16. *The Economist*, September 22, 1991, Survey on World Trade, p. 8, **emphasis added**.

17. Loc cit, emphasis added.

18. *The Challenge to the South*, Report of the South Commission (Oxford, Oxford University Press, 1990), p. 3.

19. Op. cit, p. 5.

20. The World Bank, *World Development Report, 1991*, pp. 19-20.

21. See Arun Ghosh, *India in Transition-Economic Policy Options* (Allahabad, Wheeler Publishing, 1992), p. 127.

22. Ibid, p. 174, citing *The Economist*.

23. South Korea is often cited as an example of a national economy which opened itself up to the global economy and where the miracle of the market happened thereafter. More recent and comprehensive accounts show that there was a deliberate attempt to restructure the industrial economy of that country and that the state played a major role in that process. See Vittorio Corbo and Sang-Mok Suh (ed). *Structural Adjustment in a Newly Industrialised Country: The Korean Experience*, (A World Bank Book, Baltimore, The Johns Hopkins University Press, 1992). See also the growing literature on 'The New Competition' in Michael H. Best, *The New Competition: Institutions of Industrial Restructuring* (Cambridge, Polity Press, 1990) and the bibliography in it.

24. Elsewhere I have tried to bring out the role of the village industries in the restructuring of the Indian economy. See C.T. Kurien *Growth and Justice: Aspects of India's Development Experience* (Madras, Oxford University Press, 1992), Ch. 8, 'The Future of Village Industries'.

Reprinted with permission from the author. Economic and Political Weekly, April 10, 1993.

7

Economic Liberalisation : Lessons from China

ISHER JUDGE AHLUWALIA

The Chinese economic miracle has been the talk of the globe for some years. Of late the exuberance has been mixed with some anxiety over the sustainability of the high growth rates. Indeed, the high flying performance has brought with it a new set of problems. But as the new direction is firmly set, ideological prejudices are not allowed to stand in the way of the transition towards a socialist market economy.

The major dimensions of what is commonly described as the economic miracle of China are well-known, i.e., an average GDP growth rate of 9.5 per cent per annum during 1979-92 accelerating to 12.8 per cent in 1992 and 14 per cent in the first half of 1993; a six-fold increase in exports between 1979 and 1992; an investment rate which fluctuated around 35 per cent; and inflation rates of less than 10 per cent per annum for much of the period but shooting up to 25-30 per cent in more recent times.

In their zeal to bring about economic transformation in the shortest possible time the Chinese are being totally pragmatic. The constitution of the People's Republic of China has been repeatedly amended in recent years to accommodate the economic policy changes, the latest amendment being in 1993 which seeks to accelerate the separation of ownership and management in state enterprises.

1. Role of Foreign Investment

Foreign investment has played a very important role in the opening up and economic transformation of the Chinese economy. Call it "socialist market economy Chinese style" or whatever you like, but the only thing Red about Communist

China today is the red carpet that is laid out for the foreign investor. The socialist market economy is being built on the strength of massive foreign investment inflows, while we in India are still debating the pros and cons of foreign investment, worrying how it might affect the social fabric.

China had attracted by the end of 1992 foreign investments of the order of $ 40 billion. In 1992 itself $ 12 billion flowed in as actual foreign investment. In India, by comparison, total foreign investment in 1992-93 was around $ 0.5 billion and it is expected to be close to $ 1.5 billion in 1993-94.

The Chinese could attract foreign investment on a massive scale not only because there is the extended Chinese family residing in Hong Kong, Taiwan, Macao and even further off, but also because they have created conditions which make it possible for these investors to get very good returns on their investments while contributing to the process of development in China.

Incentives for foreign investment include preferential corporate tax rates (zero for the first two years, 7.5 per cent for the next three and 15 per cent thereafter in the special economic zones, compared with 24 per cent for joint ventures outside the zones, and 33 per cent for large state-owned enterprises), duty-free imports of materials except when the production is sold in domestic markets, and easy repatriation of profits, dividends and royalty.

Moreover, there are special provisions allowing foreign investors to sign labour contracts with their employees which give the investors the right to hire and fire. It takes two months from the time an application is made for foreign investment to the time that all clearances are obtained.

Be it a non-resident Chinese or any foreigner for that matter investing in consumer goods or any other industry, high-tech or low-tech, foreign investment is very welcome as long as it generates employment, economic activity and some exports.

In fact, foreign investment has played a significant role in fostering the growth of light industries through joint ventures in town-village enterprises. Agricultural surpluses and foreign investment have come together to provide employment and activity in low-tech, labour-intensive enterprises which have made significant contributions to the export boom. The boom was associated with a surge in imports but the trade account remained in surplus at rising levels of exports and imports.

Foreign investors are also allowed to sell upto a specified proportion (varying from 20 to 50 per cent) of their production in the domestic market. This introduces an element of competition and quality in the market for consumer goods in China. Shanghai is booming with newly set-up stores which are selling high-quality consumer goods, imported as well as domestically produced, to the Chinese consumers.

2. High Degree of Provincial Autonomy

A significant factor behind the success of the Chinese economic reforms has been the high degree of autonomy provided to the provinces in economic decision-making. For example, foreign investment projects upto $ 35 million are cleared by the provincial authorities without even making a reference to the centre. Taxes are also collected by the provinces and a certain agreed part of tax revenue is passed on to the centre. While fiscally not very efficient and/or equitable, this system ensures greater involvement on the part of the provinces in tax administration. More generally, the Chinese system ensures strong ground level participation. It has created a situation in which the provinces are competing with each other to push the economic reforms through and attract investment.

3. Emphasis on Change

The Chinese experience highlights the importance of openly admitting the need for a change in policies as well as in attitudes. Of course it will never be as easy in our open democratic system as it is in an authoritarian regime like China's. Not only will there be resistance from the vested interests, but also differences in policies and strategies will need to be openly debated. The adjustment is being made unnecessarily difficult by not admitting that we have made mistakes in our policies in the past and we need to change in a changing world.

Not only does the government feel compelled to talk of "continuity with change" rather than face the changing world squarely, but our intellectuals are also continually pondering over all kinds of problems that may possibly emerge as we tread the path of economic liberalisation.

4. Emerging Problems in China

No doubt the economic upsurge in China has brought with it a set of problems new to the communist nation. High rates of inflation, overheating, trade deficits, growing regional imbalances and rising tension between the Centre and the provinces are only some of the problems that have surfaced in the course of the transition from a centrally planned economy to a socialist market economy. But the resolve to manage the growing internal contradictions has also been growing.

High inflation

The overheating of the economy is reflected in high inflation rates of 20-25 per cent for China and even higher rates for the provinces that are growing faster. There are genuine apprehensions in Beijing about the sustainability of the high growth rates of GDP and the danger posed by the speculative boom in real estate and securities which has been fueled by unrestrained lending by local banks for speculative purposes.

The degree of provincial autonomy which has been a major strength in generating reforms from the ground will prove to be a hindrance when the Centre tries to generate overall macro-economic balance. Indeed, in 1993, the central authorities had set a target of lowering the growth rate of GDP from 12-13 per cent experienced in recent years to 8-9 per cent. In the event, in the first half of 1993, the growth rate of GDP accelerated to 14 per cent.

The heavily decentralised fiscal system is a source of growing tension between the Centre and the provinces. As of now, the Centre's share in total tax revenue comes to about 37 per cent. Beijing would like to see a substantial increase in this share but the provinces which actually collect these taxes, particularly the fast-growing ones, will hear nothing of this.

Trade deficit

The growing trade deficit during 1993 has also been a source of concern for the Chinese authorities. After four consecutive years of trade surplus, the first three quarters of 1993 have shown a cumulative trade deficit of almost $ 7 billion. Official sources attribute this to the decline in the exports of crude oil, finished oil, raw cotton and other raw materials, but over-heating of the economy must also have contributed to this development.

The strategy of pushing growth through attracting foreign investment in Special Economic Zones and Designated Development Areas in the South-East coastal region has meant that regional imbalances are growing in China. Mindful of the social tensions that this can generate even within an authoritarian regime, the Chinese authorities are now trying to extend reforms from the coastal region in the South East to the North and the interior. The red carpet for foreign investors in Special Economic Zones is being extended to new areas. The banks of the Yangtse river are the next focus for investment and economic activity.

During the first phase of opening up in the eighties, foreign investors came in droves to the light consumer goods industries which are labour intensive and low-technology, e.g., garments, toys, electronic assembly, etc. Having injected a spirit of quality and competition in light industries, the Chinese are now trying to attract foreign investment in high-tech industries by actively encouraging collaborations with major multinational corporations.

Reform of State-owned Enterprises

The reform of state-owned enterprises has been difficult even in an authoritarian regime like China's but they are now trying very hard to tie-up soft loans for upgrading the technology in many of these enterprises. In the first phase of reforms, flexibility to hire and fire labour was provided to foreign investors. When it comes to possible retrenchment in state-owned enterprises, they recognise the importance of a social security mechanism for effective restructuring through privatisation, liquidations and/or mergers. They are now gearing themselves up for this task.

Bureaucracy and Corruption

Interestingly, bureaucracy is no less in China than in India. The difference lies in the political message that has been delivered to the bureaucrats, i.e., that clearances must be fast and that the bureaucrats are accountable for any delays.

Corruption is also assuming serious proportions at all levels and stories of kickbacks and commissions abound. However, a major anti-corruption drive has been launched by the authorities. Of course, the Chinese are not burdened by the kind of judicial procedures which are the hallmark of a free democratic society.

The important lesson to learn from the Chinese experience is that there are no shortcuts nor clear cuts to economic prosperity. Pragmatism rather than ideolgy pays off. An important ingredient for success is the resolve to handle problems as they surface on the way rather than expect to anticipate all possible roadblocks before you start moving.

8

Banking Sector Reforms

C. Rangarajan

Assessment of Indian Banking System

The Indian financial sector today comprises an impressive network of banks and financial institutions and a wide range of financial instruments. All the indicators of financial development have significantly increased implying the growing importance of financial institutions in the economy and growth of financial flows in relation to economic activity, both in the form of direct and indirect finance. The extent of the growth of the Indian financial system, measured in terms of the "finance ratio", which is the ratio of total financial claims to national income, shows, that the ratio, which was less than 0.05 during 1951-55 and around 0.14 in the late 1960s, rose to reach as much as 0.44 by 1989-90. The "financial interrelation ratio" which is the ratio of financial assets to physical assets has also gone up from less than 0.1 in 1951-52 to 1.18 in 1970-71 and further to 2.50 in 1989-90, indicating that the financial structure in India has grown more rapidly than the national income. As at the end of March 1991, the total financial assets of all financial institutions, including banks, amounted to Rs. 3,54,039 crores of which the scheduled banks accounted for Rs. 2,22,613 crores or 62.9 per cent.

The Indian financial system is characterised by the predominance of public sector institutions and a high degree of regulation, motivated mainly by socio-economic considerations. Entry and expansion are controlled. There is an administered structure of interest rates, under which interest rates on deposits and credit are specified in detail. Besides there is a mandatory allocation of credit for specific sectors with varying degrees of concessionality in interest rates. Inevitably, such concessionality for some sectors pushes up the rates for those not so favoured.

The mid-1980's saw some movement away from this regulated regime. Commercial banks were permitted to undertake new activities. Several money market instruments were introduced and interest rates in the money market were freed from control. Greater flexibility was introduced in the administered structure of interest rates, with deposit rates made positive in real terms and the lending rates structure simplified.

There is no doubt that there has been a considerable widening and deepening of the financial system in the last two decades. The extension of banking and other financial facilities to a larger cross section of the people stands out as a significant achievement. Despite the overall progress made by the financial system, there has been a growing concern about the operational efficiency of the system. Low profitability, high and growing non-performing assets and relatively low capital base continue to cause anxiety. It is estimated that in 1991-92 gross profits of scheduled commercial banks (excluding RRBs) after provisions and contingencies were no more than 0.35 per cent of working funds, as compared with 0.4 per cent in 1969. In 1991-92, the spread between interest earned and paid as a proportion of working funds was 3.3 per cent. The proportion of 'other operating expenses' to working funds in the same year was 2.06 per cent. The rate of growth of earnings has been slower than the rate of growth of business and working funds. Profitability of banks has fluctuated rather than showing any consistent trend. With the decline in the quality of loan assets (domestic non-performing advances of all public sector banks formed 14.5 per cent of their total outstanding advances) the need for provisioning has become more urgent. Several banks are in fact not in a position to make adequate provisions for doubtful debts. The capital base — the ratio of paid up capital and reserves to deposits of Indian banks — at slightly over 2 per cent in 1991-92 is much lower by international standards and, in fact, has gone down over time. The attitude thus far that with government ownership there is little to worry about the ratio has resulted in a situation where the capital -deposit ratio has been falling. Lack of proper disclosure norms has led many banks to keep the problems under cover. The financial position of the Regional Rural Banks is far worse. The balance sheet of the performance of the banking sector is thus, mixed — strong in widening credit coverage but weak as far as viability and sustainability are concerned.

The present predicament of the Indian financial system is a result of combination of factors—both internal and external. Any reform of the financial sector must address both these factors. The ulitmate objective of financial sector reform in India should be to improve the operational and allocational efficiency of the system. Even from the point of view of meeting some of the socio-economic concerns, it is necessary that the viability of the system is maintained. While the thrust of the reform is to correct many of the endogenous, exogenous and structural factors affecting bank profitability, individual banks have to become conscious of efficiency focusing on balancing profitability with liquidity and servicing the necessary socio-economic objectives of our development efforts.

External Constraints

The external factors bearing on the profitability of the banking system have centered around pre-emptions in the form of Cash Reserve Ratio and the Statutory Liquidity Ratio and the administered structure of interest rates. In India the growth of high-powered money (reserve money) has been largely the result of increases in the net RBI credit to the Government. The inability of RBI to deny or regulate credit to Government due to both legal and practical reasons has been an important factor contributing to RBI's limited control over reserve money expansion. The high levels of SLR and CRR that were in operation till the end of 1991-92 stemmed from the need to moderate monetary growth in the context of high budget deficits and their automatic monetisation. There have, however, been important changes in this area. The Central Government is committed to reduce its fiscal deficit in the current year to 5.0 per cent of GDP from 6.5 per cent in the previous year. The Government has also expressed its intention to reduce the fiscal deficit further in the coming years. As fiscal and budget deficits come down, it will be possible to reduce the CRR and SLR and thus enable banks to provide larger amount of credit at their discretion. This has already happened. Because of the changes made in these ratios, pre-emption of incremental deposits which stood at 63.5 per cent in 1991-92 came down to 45 per cent in the first half of 1992-93 and will come down further to 25 per cent in the second half of the year. This implies that in the second half of the year, almost 75 per cent of incremental deposits are available for expanding credit.

A central feature of the Indian monetary and credit system is that the interest rates are administered. In the case of commercial banks, both the deposit rates and lending rates are regulated. Until recently the rate at which corporate entities could borrow in the form of debentures was also regulated. The rate of interest on the government securities can be maintained at lower levels because commercial banks and certain other institutions are required to invest a certain proportion of their liabilities in government securities. The purpose behind an administered structure of interest rates is to enable certain preferred or priority sectors to obtain funds at concessional rates of interest. An element of cross-subsidisation gets automatically built into the system if the concessional rates provided to some sector are to be compensated by higher rates charged to other non-concessional borrowers. Regulation of lending rates leads to the regulation of the deposit rates. If the average lending rate is to be maintained at a certain level, the deposit rate has to be accordingly adjusted. Over the years, the system of administered interest rate structure became complex as the number of sectors and segments to which concessional credit is to be provided proliferated.

The last few years have seen some important reforms in relation to administered structure of interest rates. These are: (a) considerable rationalisation has been effected in banks' lending rates with reduction in the number of concessional slabs and enhancement in some of the rates, thereby reducing the element of cross-subsidisation; (b) the regulated deposit rate structure has been replaced by a single prescription setting a maximum rate for maturities of 46 days and above; (c) rates of interest on government securities have been raised; and (d) for several instruments, such as Certificate of Deposits, the interest rates are freely determined by individual banks.

The broad outlines of the reform agenda in terms of the interest rate, as far as India is concerned, are quite clear. At least initially, from an elaborate administered structure of interest rates, we should move towards a more simplified system where only a few rates are specified. The Committee to review the Working of the Monetary System (1985) focused on three rates: (i) The maximum deposit rate; (ii) The minimum lending rate; and (iii) One concessional rate below the minimum lending rate. This may be a model towards which one can work.

Structural Reform of the Banking System

Even as the external constraints, such as the administered interest rates structure, reserve requirements, etc., are eased, the financial institutions must act as business units with full autonomy and transparency in operation, and by the same token, become fully responsible for their performance. There are instances of countries like France where the major banks are in the public sector but they are allowed to operate with a high degree of autonomy without any interference from Government.

The need for stringent prudential regulations in a more deregulated environment has already become apparent in many countries. The elements of prudential regulation are also well known. However, two aspects of prudential regulation which have assumed greater importance in the recent period relate to capital adequacy and provisioning. The Indian banking system, until recently, has been slack in relation to both these aspects. Capital adequacy did not perhaps receive adequate emphasis because of the false assumption that banks and financial institutions owned by Government cannot fail or cannot run into problems.

With major Indian banks now having branches operating in important money market centres of the world, this question can no longer be ignored. That apart, even banks operating domestically need to build an adequate capital base. The Bank for International Settlements has prescribed the norm for capital adequacy at 8 per cent of the risk-weighted assets. While there can be some variations in assigning weights to the various classes of assets in the Indian context, broadly speaking, the need for Indian banks to achieve the internationally accepted standards is absolutely essential. Obviously, this has to be a phased programme since the capital required to reach the desired level is quite large. What has been said about banks holds good in relation to term-lending institutions as well as other financial institutions. Whether they be leasing companies or hire purchase companies or investment companies, prescription of appropriate capital requirements is a must since capital is the last line of protection for all depositors.

Another important aspect of prudential regulations relates to adequate provisioning for bad and doubtful debts. If the profits of banks and other financial institutions are to be a true reflection of their functioning, loan losses must be adequately provided for. Both in relation to banks and the term-lending institutions, prescription of uniform accounting practices relating to income recognition and provisioning against doubtful debts has become imperative.

It is in this context that Reserve Bank introduced in April 1992 a capital risk-weighted asset ratio system for banks (including foreign banks) in India as a capital adequacy measure. Indian banks which have branches abroad will have to achieve the norm of 8 per cent as early as possible and in any case by March 31, 1994. Foreign banks operating in India will have to achieve this norm by March 31, 1993. Other banks will have to achieve a capital adequacy norm of 4 per cent by March 31, 1993 (Tier I or core capital having been set at not less than 50 per cent of total capital) and the 8 per cent norm by March 31, 1996. The total of Tier II elements will be limited to a maximum of 100 per cent of total of Tier I elements for the purpose of compliance with the norms. Banks have been advised to review the existing level of capital funds vis-a-vis the prescribed level and plan to increase funds in a phased manner to achieve the prescribed ratio by the end of the period stipulated.

The implementation of the norms for asset classification and income recognition introduces transparency in the profit and loss statements and balance sheets of commercial banks. Such a transparency has three distinct effects. To begin with, there is the liquidity effect. Where a bank does not really receive interest and is merely capitalising it in the borrower's account there is less of flexibility. In particular, the bank loses the opportunity to redeploy the income stream for a better purpose. Secondly, there is an effect on bank profitability. Unrealised interest receipts, when booked as income, cannot just be dismissed as harmless window dressing. It has important implications. Besides the loss of credibility of the financial statements, doctored declarations of profits can accelerate the erosion of a bank's capital base through unjustified tax and dividend payments. Thirdly, there is an effect on the balance sheet of the bank since non-performing loans need to be provided for and eventually written off against capital and reserves. If adequate provision is not made against non-performing assets it will impair the bank's capital base thus reducing the protection available to depositors and creditors of the bank.

Fortunately or unfortunately, there is by now extensive experience in both developed and developing countries in the context of workout programmes for commercial banks. Considerable ingenuity in financial engineering has been devoted to the restructuring of commercial banks, particularly to meet the Tier II requirements.

In the first place, to be meaningful, financial restructuring should be dovetailed to a wider programme of recoveries of bank dues. Such a programme needs to address a whole spectrum of issues for restoring viability: markets, product mix, quality of human resources, technology, cost structure and so on. Secondly, we have to examine which of the two alternatives is preferable – fresh injections of equity while leaving the doubtful assets in the books of the bank or replacing the latter with assets of better quality. The second alternative certainly reduces the encumbrances on the bank's capital and reserves. It may even improve liquidity and profitability depending on the yield and liquidity of the replacement assets. A similar approach was recommended by the Narasimham Committee when it suggested that doubtful assets of banks might be purchased by an Asset Reconstruction Fund (after being discounted to market value). It would then assume responsibility for recovery. Countries like Chile have preferred to purchase doubtful assets at par in exchange for government bonds but subject to the condition that the assets be repurchased as bank profits increased. So far as nationalised banks in India are concerned perhaps there is not much of a financial difference between topping of equity and asset exchange. The issue is more a behavioural one linked to the question of which approach is likely to maximise recovery of past loans and encourage sound credit assessment of future loans. What is, however, clear is that any such financial support should be given only against a well-designed strategic plan concurrent with legislation to speed up the recovery of collateral from delinquent debtors.

In relation to income recognition, Reserve Bank of India has instructed banks to treat an amount in respect of term loans, overdrafts and cash credit accounts, bill purchased and discounted and other accounts as "past due" when interest has not been paid 30 days from the due date. A "non-performing asset" has been defined as a credit facility in respect of which interest has remained unpaid for a period of four quarters from the date it has become "past due", during the year ending March 31, 1993, for three quarters from the date it has become "past due", during the year ending March 31, 1994 and for two quarters from the date it has become "past due", during the year ending March 31, 1995 and onwards. Banks have also been instructed that they should not charge and take to income account, interest on any non-performing assets. As compared with the existing system of eight health codes, banks are required to classify their advances into four broad groups: (i) standard assets, (ii) sub-standard assets, (iii) doubtful assets, and (iv) loss assets, by compressing the existing eight health codes. Broadly, classification of assets into these categories has to be done taking into account the degree of well-defined credit weaknesses and extent of dependence on collateral security for realisation of dues. The existing health code system of classification of assets would, however, continue as a management information tool. Banks have to make provisions on advances depending on the classification of assets ranging from 10 per cent to 100 per cent. Fifty percent of the aggregate provisioning required should be made by 31st March 1993 and balance amount of provisioning together with additional provisioning required should be made up by 31st March 1994.

Quite clearly there is a link between capital adequacy and provisioning. The criterion of capital adequacy will have to be met after ensuring that adequate provisions have been made. Thus, the task before the commercial banks in reaching capital adequacy is truly difficult. While the Government will have to come in a strong way to provide adequate capital, some of the stronger banks may be in a position to go to the capital market to raise funds on the strength of their balance sheets. Going to the capital market will require certain legislative changes except in the case of State Bank of India, where the existing provisions only specify that the share of the RBI will not go below 55 per cent.

Closely related to prudential guidelines is supervision. A strong system of supervision becomes necessary in order to ensure that the prudential regulations are followed faithfully by financial institutions. As the financial sector grows, it is quite possible to have different agencies supervising different segments of the market and institutions. In this background two issues arise. One relates to the co-ordination among supervisory agencies and the other regarding consolidated supervision. Financial institutions no longer operate in one segment of the market. Under the circumstances, the segmentation of the market for regulatory purposes can run into a number of difficulties. Apart from multiple authorities exercising control over one institution, differing prescriptions by different authorities can also lead to inconsistencies and conflicts. It is in this context that the concept of 'lead regulator' has emerged under which one authority is recognised as a primary regulator in relation to one type of institution. "Consolidated supervision" is also a related issue. With the entry of banks into a number of activities such as investment banking and merchant banking it is being stressed that the official oversight must be predicated on the principle of consolidated supervision. This will, in fact, mean looking at the entire gamut of activities of a bank and its affiliates so as to ensure that all their operations are conducted prudentially. It is some times argued that so long as the different functions are performed by separate entities there is no need for consolidated supervision. Some regard "fire walls", which is a term used for corporate separateness, as a substitute for consolidated supervision. "Fire walls" serve a useful purpose. They help guard against conflict of interests. They may also prevent the safety net facility from being abused. Corporate separateness may, however, not be of much use in times of crises. As the President of the Federal Reserve Bank of New York remarked: "when the temperature goes up, the fire wall stands to melt". A supervisory oversight of all institutions forming part of a single group may be necesary and useful.

Reform of supervisory practices can be effective and successful, if supervision is viewed as a backup support system for the banking industry. Banking supervision cannot be a substitute for prudent bank management. A strengthened supervisory system must be accompanied by an equally improved system of bank's own internal control. The first line of defence against financial distress and banking crisis is the quality and character of management within the bank. Strengthening of supervision policies and a vigilant internal control system together can ensure protection of the safety and soundness of the banking system and reduction of systemic risks.

While there exists a convergence of views on the goals of bank supervision, i.e., to promote a safe, stable and efficient financial system, supervisory structures vary across the world. Broadly, there are three approaches (i) separation between regulatory and supervisory bodies, like in Germany, (ii) regulatory and supervisory functions under the same agency such as in UK, USA and India and (iii) separate regulatory and supervisory institutions working in close coordination, such as, in France with on-site inspections carried out by the officials of the Central Bank.

In India's case, despite the recent events which have exposed the weaknesses of the existing supervisory system, I do not think we need to 'reinvent the supervisory wheel'. What is perhaps needed is the strengthening of the system in terms of supervisory policies, focus and skills. While retaining the strength of the central monetary authority, the revamped system of supervision should be able to devote exclusivity to the area of supervision and provide effective supervision in an integrated manner. Emphasis should be on compliance with various guidelines and directives as well as on prudential internal control and risk assessment systems within the different constituents of the financial system, viz., banks, financial institutions and non-banking financial intermediaries. Supervision should be based on expeditious on-site inspections as well as as off-site assessments. The information and reporting systems will have to improve.

Government and RBI are working towards determining an optimal model for supervision of the Indian financial system. A model, which is under active consideration, envisages the setting up of a Supervisory Board within RBI which would attend exclusively to supervisory functions. The board can have powers to ensure implementation of regulations in the areas of credit management, asset classification, income recognition, provisioning, capital adequacy and treasurey operations. Such a supervisory structure along with concomitant shifts in supervisory focus and policies could constitute a major step towards strengthening the institutional foundation of prudential regulation and supervision of the Indian financial system.

Two questions arise in relation to financial sector reform. The first relates to the implications of recent revelations with respect to gross irregularities in the securities operations for financial sector reform. The second question is whether the scheme of financial sector reform as adumbrated by the Government lacks social content. Scams occur in various types of situations. The only way to avoid scams is really to see that when a scam occurs the guilty are found out quickly and punished adequately and the system appropriately improved. The irregularities that have surfaced have caused a great public concern and, as the central regulatory authority, RBI has initiated several steps to fully comprehend the magnitude and dimension of the irregularities and follow up by taking several remedial actions to prevent the recurrence of similar lapses in the future. What has been revealed are gross violations of the guidelines issued by the Reserve Bank of India. Recent events have clearly underscored the need for a supervisory system that is efficient and prompt. But these events do not take away the need for banking sector reform aimed at improving the viability of the banks and at the same time ensuring their accountability. Banks should become both autonomous and accountable.

As regards the social content, it is not the contention of anybody that the special needs of the various sectors of the economy should not be adequately taken care of by the financial institutions. Banks and term-lending institutions are legitimate instruments of social and economic change. In fact during the 80's priority sector credit as a proportion of total net bank credit increased even beyond the stipulated 40 per cent. What is stressed is only that social responsibility must be balanced with the needs to ensure the viability of the financial institutions.

RBI's recent guidelines for the entry of new privately-owned domestic banks are aimed at fostering a healthy and competitive banking system. For well ove two decades, after the nationalisation of 14 larger banks in 1969, no banks have been allowed to be set up in the private sector. Progressively, over this period, the public sector banks have expanded their branch network considerably and catered to the socio-economic needs of large masses of the population, especially the weaker sections and those in the rural areas. The public sector banks have now 91 per cent of the total bank branches and handle 86 per cent of the total banking business in the country. While acknowledging the importance and the role of public sector banks, there is increasing recognition of the need to introduce greater competition, which can lead to higher productivity and efficiency of the banking system. Thus our financial system will now have room for both public and private sector banks, subserving the underlying goals of the financial sector reform. The guidelines aim at ensuring that the new entrants are financially viable. They also lay down norms to prevent concentration of credit, monopolisation of economic power and cross-holding with industrial groups. These are provisions that already form part of the Banking Regulation Act. The minimum paid-up capital of Rs. 100 crore, together with the 8 per cent capital adequacy ratio, will ensure entry of those who can lend strength to the financial system. With these stipulations, these banks can have a risk asset base of Rs. 1200 crore, which will accelerate the overall rate of growth of the banking industry. Insistence on the new private sector banks meeting the priority sector lending targets and other social obligations is in keeping with the principle of creating a level playing field for all banks. However, in recognition of the fact that new entrants may require some time to lend to all categories of the priority sector, modifications in the composition of the priority sector lending will be considered by RBI. Our expectation is that the entry of new banks will exert some degree of competitive pressure on the existing banks and lead to higher productivity and efficiency of the banking system as a whole.

Even as steps are being taken to improve the system in general, functional efficiency which is also an endogenous factor will require greater attention. Functional efficiency relates to the main economic functions of the financial sector, viz., administering the payments mechanism and intermediating between savers and investors. Banks must assess functional efficiency in terms of soundness of appraisals, resource cost of specific operations and the quality and speed of delivery of services. While it is true that the determinants of functional efficiency are the market structure and the regulatory framework within which a bank operates, easing of the external constraints must bring about commensurate changes in the approach of individual banks in their commitment to improve their functional efficiency.

Reprinted with permission from the author, Inaugural address, at the Sixteenth Bank Economists' Conference, January 28, 1993. Reserve Bank of India Bulletin March, 1993.

9

Reforming the Financial Sector

R.N. MALHOTRA

Financial sector reform is an integral part of the macro-economic stabilisation and structural change which has been in progress since June, 1991 with a view to raising the productivity of the economy. The financial system mobilises savings, intermediates between savers and investors and, especially through commercial banks, provides payments, clearance and settlement mechanisms to facilitate financial transactions. An efficient financial system is thus a necessary condition for higher savings, productive investment and healthy growth.

India has a large and varied financial system which comprises besides the Reserve Bank of India (RBI), numerous commercial and co-operative banks; specialised development banks for industry, agriculture, external trade and housing; social security institutions like insurance companies and pension and provident funds; collective investment institutions like the Unit Trust and mutual funds; merchant banks, leasing companies, housing finance companies, factoring outfits, venture capital funds, financial advisory services and rating agencies. Since 1980, the capital market has grown dramatically and there are at present as many as 23 stock exchanges. There has been considerable development of money and capital markets and numerous financial instruments have appeared on the scene.

The strong points of the financial system are its ability to mobilise savings, its vast geographical and functional reach and institutional diversity. Between 1965 and 1990, the household sector's gross savings in the form of financial assets rose from 5.5 per cent to 12.2 per cent of net domestic product. Since

1969 when major banks were nationalised, the number of commercial bank branches increased from about 8,300 to well over 60,000. The share of loans to the designated priority sectors, namely agriculture, small industry, other small businesses and weaker sections of society, in total bank credit, has risen remarkably. As against an annual average amount of Rs. 90 crores raised from the primary capital market during the 1970s, the 1994-95 level of issues could be around Rs. 30,000 crores. Between them the Unit Trust of India and other mutual funds handle a portfolio of around Rs. 65,000 crores. The number of companies listed on the stock exchanges now exceeds 6800 and it is estimated that there are upward of 15 million shareholders. More than 10 million new life policies were issued in 1993-94. General insurance business has also been growing rapidly. Despite this commendable progress and considerable talent, expertise and manpower, the financial system suffers from several weaknesses. Ongoing financial sector reforms as well as some that are on the anvil aim at addressing these deficiencies with a view to achieving systemic improvement on a wide front. Since financial sector reform is a very wide subject, I propose to limit my remarks here to the reform in the banking sector, including some important aspects of monetary policy and the external payments regime.

The Banking Sector: Major Deficiencies

The major deficiency of the banking industry is its low profitability and the consequent inability of several banks to provide adequately for loan losses and to build their capital. This is a serious drawback as only financially viable banks can serve their clients efficiently. The position, however, varies substantially from bank to bank. There are besides organisational inadequacies within banks due, *inter alia*, to their rapid expansion, weakening of management and control functions, excessive staff, growth of restrictive practices and erosion of work culture, flaws in credit management, and serious lags in introducing computer technology to handle the massive growth of banking transactions.

For almost four decades, Indian monetary and banking policies have been greatly influenced by the requirements of the Central and State Governments to borrow from the banking sector for bridging their fiscal deficits. Some aspects of the practices followed in effecting such borrowing deserve mention:

(a) With the launching of development planning in the 1950s, the use of bank resources was sought to be brought in line with plan priorities. Since a major part of the plan was in the sphere of the public sector which was financed through the Central and State budgets, pre-emption of resources of commercial banks (as well as those of insurance companies and provident funds) by the fiscal system rose progressively. The statutory liquidity requirement (SLR), which is a prudential stipulation for ensuring that a part of bank assets are held in liquid securities, became an easy device for statutorily compelling banks to invest rising proportions of their deposit liabilities in government and approved securities. The coupon rates on such paper were fixed well below market rates to contain official debt service. At its peak, the SLR was as high as 38.5 per cent of banks' net demand and time liabilities.

(b) Since the middle of 1950s, the Central Government began borrowing from the Reserve Bank of India (RBI) for covering its budget deficit (i.e. the deficit which remained after accounting for government's borrowings from sources other than RBI) through the issue of ad hoc treasury bills which carried very low interest rates (4.6 per cent for many years now) and were, therefore, not marketable. With increasing fiscal imbalances - the Centre's gross fiscal deficit rose from 3.5 per cent of GDP in 1970-71 to 8.4 per cent of GDP in 1990-91 - monetisation by the RBI also burgeoned, often resulting in excessive liquidity which had to be contained by compensatory increases in the cash reserve requirement (CRR). Again, for monetary policy reasons, the RBI gave a low average return on cash balances kept with it under the CRR. At their peak, in 1991-92, SLR and CRR together pre-empted 63.5 per cent of the incremental deposits of commercial banks.

(c) In pursuance of the government's socio-economic objectives, forty per cent of bank credit was provided to designated priority sectors, such as agriculture, small industries, other small businesses and weaker sections of society, mostly at concessional rates of interest.

The financial system was progressively nationalised, beginning with the conversion of the Imperial Bank to the State Bank of India in 1955. Fourteen major commercial banks were nationalised in 1969 and another six banks in 1980. Life insurance was nationalised in 1956 and general insurance in 1972. A number of development banks and the Unit Trust of India were also created as fully government owned institutions. Thus, the public sector acquired a dominant place in the financial sector. Between them, the State Bank of India and the nationalised banks account for 85 per cent of total bank deposits. Till recently, no new domestic private sector banks were licensed and the entry of new foreign banks was also restricted.

Some of the important implications of these developments were- First, automatic financing of the budgetary deficit by the RBI severely limited its control on the creation of primary liquidity and forced it to address the problems of excessive monetary growth and resultant pressure on prices through progressive increases in CRR and restrictions on bank credit to the enterprise sector.

Second, large pre-emption of bank resources through rising reserve requirements may have crowded out credit needed by the enterprise sector with possible adverse effects on growth.

Third, below-market coupon rates on government and approved securities, concessional lending to designated priority sectors and low returns on banks' cash balance with RBI increasingly constrained bank profitability as reserve requirements continued to rise to meet government deficits and reached unsustainable levels. Together with the excessive defaults in loan servicing, these strains resulted in several banks becoming financially weak. This situation was sought to be partially ameliorated through interest rates cross-subsidisation which, carried beyond a point, brought in its own distortions.

Fourth, a necessary concomitant of directed and concessional credit and cross-subsidisation of interest rates was a highly regulated and differentiated interest rates regime for bank deposits and loans. As a result, the system experienced a high degree of financial repression.

Fifth, since ad hoc treasury bills were not marketable and government's long-term securities carried below-market coupon rates and were held and traded within a captive market, the development of money and securities markets was greatly inhibited. This ruled out effective open-market operations by RBI.

Sixth, though bank nationalisation greatly succeeded in promoting the geographical spread of banking services, mobilisation of financial savings, and financing of designated priority sectors, it has also been accompanied by sharply reduced inter-bank competition, erosion of individual identities of banks, inhibition of innovation and flexibility, inadequate autonomy and accountability of managements, centralised practices of staff recruitment and wage setting, an ineffectual system of incentives and disincentives, and considerable increase in restrictive practices, including prolonged resistance to introduction of computerisation in banking operations.

It would, however, not be correct to attribute all the ills of the banking sector to the aforesaid policies. For one thing, performance varied considerably from bank to bank though all of them were subject to the same constraints, indicating that some managements and staff proved more effective than others, especially in management of their loan portfolios. There is a vast pool of talent and trained manpower in Indian banking. Nevertheless, it was becoming increasingly clear that major changes in monetary and banking policy were necessary with a view to -

Banking Reforms

i phasing out automatic monetisation of the Central Government's budget deficits by the RBI so that it regains control over primary creation of money;

ii reducing reserve requirements substantially to help bank profitability and release more resources for lending to the enterprise sector;

iii bringing down the proportion of mandated credit, especially the associated concessionality of interest rates;

iv liberalising interest rates;

v developing the money market as well as a market in long-term securities so that the RBI would increasingly depend on indirect regulation of money supply through open market operations in securities rather than on reserve requirements and credit allocation;

vi   Strengthening the banking system through enforcement of prudential norms relating to capital adequacy, income recognition, asset classification, loan-loss provisions and transparency of balance sheets; allowing greater discretion to banks in opening or closing their branches; providing banks more freedom regarding their deposits and lending rates; and permitting them to enter new areas of business such as merchant banking, underwriting and leasing for diversification of business, better interface with the capital market and for reducing market segmentation;

vii enhancing inter-bank competition by licensing new private sector banks, including foreign banks;

viii revamping RBI's regulation and supervision systems to drastically reduce, if not eliminate, credit allocation; emphasising compliance with prudential norms; and, considering the growth of non-banking financial companies, extending its oversight beyond commercial banks to other financial institutions; and

ix   ensuring viability of weak banks so that the banking system as a whole is strengthened to support economic activity.

The Committee on the Reform of the Financial System (Narasimham Committee) which was appointed by the Government of India dealt with most of the aforesaid issues in a report submitted in November 1991 (the Committee, however, did not deal with the question of monetisation of the budget deficit) and, barring a few, its recommendations have been accepted. Broadly, the Committee, inter alia, recommended that in light of government's stabilisation programme, reserve requirements (both SLR and CRR) be greatly reduced, that government should borrow at market rates, that weak banks be recapitalised, that capital adequacy norms adopted by the Bank of International Settlements be prescribed for Indian banks together with other internationally prevalent prudential norms, that interest rates be liberalised, that stipulations regarding the volume of priority sector credit be reduced and concessionality on such credit eliminated, that new private sector banks be allowed to enter the market, and that greater autonomy be permitted to public sector banks for their operational effectiveness.

Over the 1980s, several measures were taken by RBI to impart flexibility to the financial system and promote money and government securities markets. The maximum interest rate on government's long-term securities which was 6.5 per cent in 1977-78 was raised in stages to 11.5 per cent in 1985-86, and their maximum maturity was reduced from 30 years to 20 years. Later, in 1989, money market rates were fully freed and non-bank institutions were allowed to enter the money market. Several instruments were introduced to develop the money market. A 182-day treasury bill placed by auction, and not rediscountable with RBI, was introduced in 1986. Certificates of Deposit, commercial paper (without any interest rate stipulations on either of the two instruments) also appeared on the scene. The structure of interest rates was rationalised, reducing the number of regulated rates and realigning short-term and long-term rates in the system. For loans above Rs. 200,000 a minimum lending rate was prescribed and banks were given full freedom to charge that rate or higher rates in light of their risk perceptions on individual loans.

In 1985, RBI took the important measure of prohibiting overdrafts to the State governments. It also began suggesting that monetisation of the Central Government's budget should be phased out. It was, however, only after the adoption of the stabilisation programme that the government has agreed to this suggestion of the RBI. An agreement has been signed by the government and RBI under which monetisation of the budgetary deficit is to be phased out in three years beginning 1994-95. This fundamental change in fiscal-cum-monetary policy has far-reaching implications. First, it will restore RBI's control over creation of primary money, improve its ability to contain inflation and generally strengthen its autonomy as a monetary authority. Secondly, it would reduce resort by RBI to direct monetary controls which depress bank profitability and reduce the flow of credit to the enterprise sector. RBI would increasingly use open-market operations for reducing or increasing liquidity in pursuance of its monetary goals. Thirdly, a secondary market in government paper, and by extension, in other debt instruments would develop and complement the already active market in equities. This is because short-term and long-term government papers are being placed by RBI in the market through open auctions and a yield curve for various maturities is developing. Already, the interest rate on the 364-day treasury bill is emerging as an important reference rate.

In the absence of primary dealers in government securities, RBI underwrites the issue of government paper. It intends to develop such dealers which could underwrite such issues so that RBI operates only in the secondary markets. It has also been suggested that a statutory provision should be made for prohibiting monetisation of the budget deficit. At the same time, it is necessary that governments' borrowing requirements are contained at reasonable levels so as not to crowd out the requirements of the enterprise sector.

Progress

Considerable progress has been made in strengthening the banking system:

i   The SLR has already been brought down from 38.5 per cent to 31.5 per cent of net bank liabilities and the target of reducing it to 25 per cent in the next two years is on track. SLR on incremental bank deposits has already declined to 25 per cent. Besides, as new government securities are being issued at market rates, the strain on bank profitability on account of SLR has been substantially eased. However, the CRR is still as high as 16 per cent of net bank liabilities, mainly because large inflows of external capital in the last year and a half have been exerting inflationary pressure. As price pressures moderate and RBI increases its recourse to open-market operations, CRR should gradually decline. However, the government has not agreed to reduce stipulations regarding volume of priority sector credit. It also wishes to maintain at least one concessional rate on such lending. The real issue here is not so much the volume of priority sector lending as its price. Concessional interest rates inhibit lending and damage the profitability of banks. Timely and adequate availability of credit is more important than its price.

ii   Prudential norms of international standards have already been laid down and are to be achieved within a prescribed time schedule. Weak nationalised banks are being recapitalised by the Government but have to improve their performance according to programmes agreed with RBI. Two public sector banks have already accessed the market for strengthening their capital. The government has announced that it would not dilute its equity in such banks beyond 49 per cent. While this will help in putting pressure on banks for better performance and profitability, it may be necessary to consider whether some of the public sector banks should be privatised.

iii Ten new private sector banks have been cleared for entry into the market and half of them have begun operations. A few new foreign banks have also been licensed. This should increase inter-bank competition. However, for strengthening such competition it would be useful to privatise some public sector banks, as already suggested.

iv   Since the middle of the 1980s, several banks have established subsidiaries for leasing, housing finance, merchant banking, underwriting and mutual fund business. These subsidiaries have lean but professional staff and appropriate technology and should help banks diversify business in the face of some disintermediation which is underway.

v   Lending rates on bank loans above Rs. 200,000 have been fully deregulated. There is still one ceiling rate on bank deposits which is likely to be abolished soon. (Besides, other interest rates in the system, e.g. bonds and debentures rates and inter-company deposits have already been freed). Thus, interest rates in the system are now nearly freed. This should lead to better credit allocation and help productive forces in the economy. Cross-subsidisation would be considerably reduced and should bring down real interest rates for industry and trade.

vi   The new regulatory and supervision system being established by RBI should also enhance public confidence in the banking system.

vii Tribunals have been set up for quicker recovery of bank dues. However, for want of an effective exit policy, banks still repetitively finance sick (even non-viable) industrial units.

viii Some measures have been taken to enhance autonomy of banks. For instance, domestic banks can open or close urban branches on their own. However, systems of common recruitment and wage setting for nationalised banks continue. A great deal remains to be done in addressing the internal weaknesses of commercial banks such as technological lags, labour rigidities and inadequate systems of incentives and disincentives.

Another reform which has been a remarkable success relates to the foreign exchange regime and the balance of payments. There was a large devaluation (about 18 per cent) of the Indian rupee in July 1991 followed by its convertibility on current account. Devaluation is helping exports and the current account of the BOP has improved dramatically despite import liberalisation. The liberal regime now governing foreign direct investment, opening up the capital market to foreign institutional investors, permitting Indian corporates to raise funds through global depository receipts and Euro-convertible bonds, allowing gold imports, and progressive easing of other exchange controls have led to a large build-up of foreign currency reserves which now stand at over US$ 19 billion, equivalent to 9 months' imports.

The rapid inflow of foreign exchange has created some problems. The counterpart of foreign reserves accretion is the growth in high powered money which increases inflationary pressures in the economy. The RBI has been sterilising part of the money supply through open market operations with considerable success though the inflation rate is still hovering around 10 per cent going by the wholesale price index. As imports pick up in response to industrial recovery which is underway, reserves accretion is likely to get moderated. An increasingly open trade and payments regime - and this could become much more liberal if, in due course, rupee convertibility on capital account is achieved - underscores the need for looking at exchange rates and interest rates together and maintaining a stable macro-economic environment. To that end, and for reasons of social equity, it is essential to bring down the rate of inflation substantially. Over time, a measure of convergence between inflation rates in India and in its major trading partners would be necessary.

There has thus been considerable progress in the monetary policy area and the external payments regime. The policy constraints on the banking sector have been substantially reduced with the ongoing lowering of reserve requirements, market driven pricing of government securities, and liberalisation of interest rates. However, mandated concessional lending, continued financing of sick, often non-viable industrial units, and the still high cash reserve requirement would continue to strain bank profitability. With the strengthening of their capital base and compliance with an objective regime of prudential norms in a set time frame, commercial banks should emerge as financially strong institutions with transparent balance sheets. However, much more remains to be done in reinforcing the autonomy of bank managements, upgrading technology, addressing labour rigidities and improving customer services.

A more positive approach to privatisation of some of the nationalised banks is also called for.

Before concluding, I would like to refer briefly to the developments in the capital market which has grown remarkably in terms of annual capital raised, the number of companies listed on the stock exchanges, market capitalisation, and trading volumes. The number of shareholders is now placed at over 16 million. Some of the major developments in the recent years are (a) the entry of public sector companies in the market for raising both debt and equity capital leading to larger demand for capital as well as supply of stocks and bonds, (b) the massive growth in the funds handled by the Unit Trust of India and other public and private sector mutual funds providing greater scope for large, wholesale transactions, (c) the growth in the number of securities market intermediaries such as merchant banks, underwriters, custodians and share transfer agents, (d) the establishment and progress of rating agencies for evaluating debt to be floated in money and capital markets, and (e) proliferation of journals and magazines which seek to provide information on the performance of corporates and their securities.

The reform of the capital market required, on the one hand, a larger measure of liberalisation and, on the other, strengthening of its regulation. There has already been considerable liberalisation of the market. The Capital Issues (Control) Act, 1947 has been repealed and the office of the Controller of Capital Issues abolished. Companies are now free to issue capital and price their issues. Initially, this led to some overpricing of issues and excessive devolvement on underwriters. Market participants — companies, merchant banks, underwriters — soon learnt that the market can be a stern teacher. There were other problems such as issue of shares to promoters at prices way below market levels. These had to be resolved by intervention of regulatory authorities.

The Indian capital market has also been opened up to approved foreign institutional investors (FIIs) like pension funds, insurance funds, investment companies and other asset management outfits. Over 225 FIIs have been approved and 50 of them are reported to be quite active. At the same time, profitable Indian companies have been permitted to raise funds in foreign financial markets through modalities like global depository receipts and Euro-convertible bonds. Besides, a number of India country funds are already quoted in markets abroad. Thus the process of integrating the Indian capital market with foreign financial markets has begun. India is attracting substantial capital flows and there are apprehensions that some of these may prove volatile. The right answer to these fears is stable macro-economic policies which maintain confidence in the economy. An open regime which promotes capital inflow from abroad also increases pressures on the authorities for following sound policies.

As for regulation of the market, putting the Securities and Exchange Board of India (SEBI) on a statutory footing in 1992 has been a crucial advance. As a result, the stock exchanges, mutual funds and a host of market intermediaries including merchant banks, underwriters, brokers, custodians etc. are being subjected to fairly effective regulation. Insider trading has been prohibited. Rules governing substantial acquisition of company shares have been issued. The composition of stock exchange boards has been improved. Efforts are on to improve transparency of transactions through separation of brokers' own accounts from those of their clients.

An important development has been the stoppage of 'badla' trading which aggravated speculation and sometimes led to boom-bust cycles. Measures are also being taken to reduce the length of trade settlement periods. To strengthen investor protection, SEBI has been insisting on high disclosure standards in issue prospectuses. It has also been investigating investor complaints. What are the tasks of the future?

Basically, while the volume of primary capital has grown manifold, the infrastructure, technology, transparency of transactions, clearance and settlement of trades, and practices governing transfer of shares are inadequate. There is a shortage of brokerage services due to restrictive practices of stock exchanges and constraints of floor space. Share transfer is time consuming and sometimes not free of risk. It is necessary to upgrade technology in the stock exchanges, establish depositories, and gradually move over to a system of scripless trading. Besides, the inadequate liquidity of many registered stocks as well as that of debt instruments, including government paper, has to be addressed. In this context, the establishment of the Over-the Counter Exchange of India and the National Stock Exchange is a welcome development. These can, over time, help improve liquidity of stocks and bonds, bring about transparency and despatch in trades, assist in overcoming floor-space constraints and promote nation-wide screen-based trading. Besides, an options and futures market would have to be developed. These are indeed large and difficult tasks which can be implemented only over the next few years.

10

Indian Agriculture: Emerging Perspectives and Policy Issues*

C.H. Hanumantha Rao & Ashok Gulati

WINDS OF CHANGE

The Backdrop

Two major economic changes occurred during the early 1990s, which are likely to have far-reaching implications for India's economic development in general and agriculture in particular. Any strategy for the agricultural sector, if it is to be realistic, must pay due recognition to these economic changes.

First, India launched a process of economic reforms in July 1991.

* This paper draws heavily on the various research studies completed under a six-year collaborative project between the Indian Council of Agricultural Research and the International Food Policy Research Institute. The authors express sincere thanks to the researchers of various studies whose findings enabled them to draw some relevant policy implications for an accelerated and sustainable growth of Indian agriculture. A series of papers derived from this work is available from the International Food Policy Research Institute. The authors are also grateful to Per Pinstrup-Andersen, Peter Hazell, Gunvant Desai, Sudhir Wanmali, Mark Svendsen, Raisuddin Ahmed, Benoit Blarel, and Keith Oblitas for their comments on an earlier draft of this paper. The authors also acknowledge the benefit of comments from various participants in seminars that they gave at the International Food Policy Research Institute and the World Bank.

Besides macroeconomic stabilisation and structural reforms, these reforms are designed to integrate the domestic economy with the global economy. The process has already been initiated in the case of the industrial sector, and it would be naive to expect that the agricultural sector will remain insulated from the world economy much longer. What impact reforms in the industrial sector will have on agriculture and what is likely to happen when Indian agriculture is exposed to world agriculture are pertinent issues to keep in mind when delineating the broad contours of an agricultural strategy.

Second, the Uruguay Round of the GATT has been concluded with India as one of the signatories. Agriculture has been brought into the fold of the GATT for the first time, and its trading rules are being rewritten. It is likely to change the setting of world agriculture, having significant implications for the developed and developing world, including India, in the years to come. It is appropriate for India to assess the likely implications of such global changes and accordingly plan its agricultural strategy with a view to maximising gains from the new opportunities opened by trade under GATT.

It is against this backdrop that a modest attempt is made in this report to spell out the basic ingredients of such an agricultural strategy. A desirable strategy would be one that can make Indian agriculture a vibrant and cost-effective sector, boosting production of food and fiber, raising consumption levels through domestic production and exchange (exports/imports), generating productive employment, and thereby acting as an effective safety net and poverty alleviation programme, while also protecting the environment. It is this kind of a strategy that could put Indian agriculture and the overall growth of the economy on a sustainable path.

Changes and their Likely Impact on Agriculture

It is widely known that Indian industry enjoyed a high degree of protection (very high by world standards) for a long time after its stage of infancy through trade policy. What is less known is that Indian agriculture has been disprotected. Recent research relating to protection accorded to industry and agriculture, particularly during the post Green Revolution period, reveals that trade policies have favoured industry and discriminated against agriculture. The process of economic reforms begun in July 1991 is expected to correct this 'bias' by gradually globalising the two sectors. In essence, this implies that industrial prices in real terms will come down and agricultural prices will go up from their existing levels, leading to more favourable terms of trade for agriculture (Figure 1).

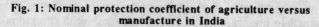

**Fig. 1: Nominal protection coefficient of agriculture versus
manufacture in India**

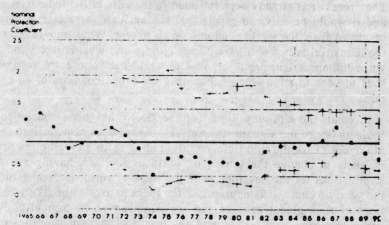

+ Aggregate Manufacture
0 · Aggregate Agriculture
+ Ratio of Agriculture to Manufacture

Source: Pursell, G. and A. Gulati. 1993. Liberalizing Indian agriculture: An agenda
for reform. WPS 1172. Washington, D.C.: World Bank.

Further, the overvalued exchange rate was corrected first by devaluing
the rupee by more than 20 per cent in July 1991 and then making it fully
convertible on current account. This has made much of agriculure a competitive export sector. Opening up of Indian agriculture under GATT, and
expected changes in world agriculture will most likely accelerate this
process of correction in terms of trade. The major implication of these
twin phenomena will be a change in the relative incentive structures in
the economy, with agriculture likely to attract more resources from the
private sector in the years to come.

The macroeconomic stabilisation process launched in July 1991 also
led to a fiscal squeeze in public sector investment in almost all sectors,
including agriculture. This is somewhat discomforting because it could
also act as a constraint to private investment, to the extent that the two
are complementary to each other. Thus, reduction in public sector investment could significantly curtail the potential for growth in Indian agriculture.

Another important point to be noted at this juncture is that for the
trade policy reforms to work their way fully through the incentive system,
domestic marketing reforms will also have to be carried out. This must
involve freer movement of agricultural commodities; gradual phasing out
of purchase levies (on, for example, rice and sugar); abolition of
monopsonistic procurements (as in the case of cotton in Maharashtra);
introduction of futures markets; and amendment or abolition of the Es-

sential Commodities Act to the extent that it imposes restrictions on the movement, stocking, and pricing of goods. These reforms are essential if the pull of demand-side factors are to be felt; otherwise changes in the incentive environment for investments in agriculture-related activities will remain only partial.

Given this background on likely policy and trade reforms at the main level, agricultural strategy must seek to exploit the growth opportunities that will arise, while also providing protective cover to the poor against any threat of unemployment following structural adjustment and inflation. It is here that the research undertaken under the IFPRI-ICAR collaborative research programme proves most timely and useful. It helps clarify the changes required in supply-side factors, including research and technology, irrigation, fertiliser, and rural infrastructure, critical for raising the aggregate supply response. Without the required changes in supply-side factors, it will be difficult for the nation to sustain growth in agriculture, and without this the overall growth of the national economy may prove disappointing in response to the policy reforms. In short, the desired impact of structural reforms on the demand side will largely depend on the degree of preparedness of supply-side factors, which ultimately may determine the pace of reforms in the economy.

EMERGING PERSPECTIVES AND GOALS OF AGRICULTURAL POLICY

Emerging Perspectives

An interesting feature of recent experience is a deceleration in the growth rate of demand for foodgrains, despite a rise in per capita income and a decline in the relative prices of foodgrains. The growth rate in foodgrain output has been steady at about 2.6 per cent per year. Within the post-green revolution period, some acceleration in the growth of foodgrains occurred during the 1980s (2.9 per cent compared with 2.3 per cent in the 1970s). Under the new scenario, wherein macro changes in the economy are likely to create a much better (relative) incentive environment for agriculture than has been the case so far, the likely growth rate in the production of foodgrains could increase further. On the other hand, the growth rate in demand for foodgrains may continue to decelerate, even after the demand for animal feed is taken into account. According to an IFPRI-ICAR study that assumes a 5 per cent growth rate in gross domestic product (GDP), the growth rate in demand is projected to decline during the period 2000-2010 from about 2.5 per cent per year during 1991-2000. If the GDP growth rate accelerates to 7 per cent per year, household demand for foodgrains is likely to decelerate further and the total demand growth, including that for animal feed, may rise but is unlikely to approach the observed long-term growth rate of 2.6 per cent in foodgrains output, let alone the 3.9 per cent growth rate in output envisaged in the Eighth Plan.

This downward shift in the demand for foodgrains can basically be attributed to changing consumer tastes and preferences as a result of the increasing availability of a wide variety of food items other than foodgrains. A wide range of nonagricultural goods and services are also now available in rural areas, within an institutional framework where there has not been any improvement in the distribution of income over a long period.

The significant decline in the per capita consumption of foodgrains in rural Punjab and Haryana, despite a high per capita income growth, dramatically illustrates this trend. In these states, the energy required to perform manual labour has declined due to the increasing mechanisation of agriculture, and the demand for and the availability of a wide variety of nonfoodgrain and nonagricultural consumption goods has increased because per capita incomes have risen. This change in the food balance opens up prospects for and indeed necessitates the export of food-grains, especially in view of the comparative advantage that the country enjoys in the production of rice and wheat. The export potential of foodgrains will further strengthen food security at home, since exports can always be adjusted to buffer fluctuations in production for the domestic market.

Achieving food security has so far been the overriding goal of agricultural policy in India. Opening up agricultural trade should now be seen as a major opportunity for raising the overall economic growth rate by exploiting India's comparative advantage in agriculture, for improving the efficiency of resource use in agriculture, and for technologically upgrading the rural sector. Trade could provide a much-needed safety net for the poor in the process of structural adjustment by increasing employment, generating income, and softening the rigours of inflation.

Opening up trade will improve incentives by raising producer prices, even after subsidies are reduced substantially. However, nonprice factors such as public investment in infrastructure, technological changes, human development, and institutional reforms are at least as important as prices in inducing an effective supply response, even after accounting for the effects of price-induced innovations. Therefore, a bigger public effort in overcoming supply-side constraints is called for, particularly in areas where there is strong complementarity between public and private investment. Indeed, the pace for freeing trade should bear some rational relationship to domestic supply augmentation, so that there is no undue rise in the domestic prices of essential food items. Such a sequencing is necessary to ensure equity, even when the public distribution of foodgrains is properly targeted, because consumer expenditure on food as a proportion of total expenditure is sizeable in a low-income country such as India. Further, such a policy is necessary to sustain the process of economic reform itself in a populous democratic polity where the incidence of absolute poverty is still quite high.

Goals of Agricultural Policy

Growth

Agricultural output needs to be stepped up by diversifying into areas such as dairy production and other animal products, horticulture, and floriculture, where demand is more elastic than that for foodgrains. Increased trade will help modernise production, processing, and marketing in these sectors. Agroprocessing and marketing should emerge as major rural activities providing linkages with industry and trade and enhancing opportunities for rural employment. Since rainfed or dryland areas in the country have a comparative advantage in animal husbandry, horticulture, and floriculture, agricultural diversification in the context of trade can benefit backward areas where poverty is widespread.

Efficiency

Export-orientation and removal of restrictions on the interregional movement of foodgrains will provide incentives for regional specialisation in crops according to their comparative advantage, thus improving the efficiency of resource use. For example, India largely achieved self-sufficiency in edible oils by 1993-94 by keeping domestic edible oil prices above world prices, thus attracting 6 million hectares of land into oilseed production that was previously in other crops. This clearly indicates allocative inefficiency in resource use, insofar as the area under oilseeds has expanded at the cost of other crops with better comparative advantage. Evolution of cost-effective technologies for oilseed production should, therefore, be accorded a much higher priority than protecting oilseed and edible oil prices.

More generally, agriculture growth during the 1980s was supported by ever-rising subsidies on critical inputs such as fertilisers, water, electricity, and credit. Removal of input subsidies, where they have outlived their usefulness, would promote their efficient allocation and give impetus to the evolution of cost-reducing innovations.

Equity

Employment generation per unit of incremental output has declined steeply and has even become negative in the irrigated Green Revolution belt. Substitution of capital for labour in high-wage areas has largely been responsible for the decline in employment per unit of output. In the wake of liberalisation, the prospects for employment generation do not appear to be bright in the nonagricultural sector, at least in the short run. Agriculture has the potential to serve as one of the biggest safety nets in this process of adjustment because the new activities that have a favourable export demand are also employment-intensive. Consequently, agriculture, on the whole, remains more labour-intensive than industry.

Sustainability

The unregulated exploitation of natural resources, caused among other things by the underpricing of inputs such as irrigation water and electricity for pumping ground-water, has contributed to degradation of the environment. Although, so far, use of chemicals in agriculture is not a serious environmental problem, the evolution of new biotechnologies to save on chemical inputs has to be accorded a high priority in agricultural research. In addition, efforts to conserve soil and water resources in dryland areas need to be stepped up, and this will require sustainable intensification through the application of yield-increasing technology.

It would appear that at present the complementarities between the goals of efficiency, equity, and sustainability in Indian agriculture outweigh the trade-offs, if any, between them. For example, one of the best prospects for improving the productivity of inputs is through dissemination of new technologies and inputs to the less developed areas. But these are areas where poverty and resource degradation are also widespread, so that growth, poverty alleviation, and improved resource management can all be improved together. Reduction of input subsidies, the benefits of which have so far accrued mainly to farmers in irrigated areas, will also contribute to the conservation of water and energy, resulting in greater output and employment per unit of such inputs, and less environmental damage.

AGRICULTURAL PERFORMANCE : GROWTH, INVESTMENT AND PRODUCTIVITY

Growth

The long-term growth of foodgrain output has been about 2.6 per cent per year in the post-Green Revolution period. There are indications of some improvement in this growth rate after the mid-1980s. The major intercrop imbalances in growth witnessed in the early years of the Green Revolution have been redressed to some extent in more recent years. For example, the growth rate in rice accelerated from about 2.2 per cent per year in the 1970s to 3.2 per cent per year in the 1980s. Further, after performing poorly during the early years of the Green Revolution, many of the states where poverty is widespread -- Assam, Bihar, Orissa, Madhya Pradesh, and West Bengal -- are now growing at rates close to or even higher than the all India average. In particular, these states have experienced an increase in rice production in recent years and some have recorded higher growth rates than the national average.

During the 1980s consumption of fertilisers increased faster in the eastern and western regions than in the northern and southern regions. Unlike the 1970s, fertilisers consumed in the kharif season have increased at a much faster rate than in the rabi season, particularly in the eastern region, which indicates the spread of new technology to rainfed and other unfavourable areas. Clearly, the importance of fertiliser relative to irrigation as a source of growth has increased considerably in recent years.

As a result of the higher foodgrain growth experienced by states in the eastern and central regions, their share in the country's total number of rural poor, which had gone up between 1970 and 1983, declined between 1983 and 1987, while the number of poor rose in some of the more developed states. The annual rate of decline in the rural poverty ratio among many of these eastern and central states was higher than the average for the country during this period. Also, the rate of decline in the rural poverty ratio in these states was more rapid in the 1980s than in the 1970s.

Investment

The most disquieting aspect of past agricultural performance is the significant decline in gross capital formation in agriculture at constant prices, by both the private and public sectors. Data up to 1990-91 show that, although real gross capital formation in agriculture by the private sector has increased since 1987-88, that by the public sector has continued to decline significantly, so that the total gross capital formation in agriculture is still lower than that achieved in the early 1980s (Figure 2). There are indications that gross fixed capital formation in agriculture by the public sector has been declining in all states, including the developed ones whose resource position is better.

The rising subsidies for agriculture during this period have made considerable inroads into the surpluses available for public investment in agriculture. These subsidies, open as well as hidden, on agricultural inputs such as fertiliser, irrigation, electricity, and credit rose from about 44 per cent of the combined plan expenditure by the central and state governments on agriculture, irrigation, and Special Area Programmes in the early 1980s (triennium ending [TE] 1983-84) to about 83 per cent toward the close of the 1980s (TE 1989-90)(Figure 3). In the light of subsequent developments, it appears that today for every rupee of public expenditure on agriculture, another rupee is spent on subsidies on inputs.

Fig. 2: Gross capital formation in agriculture (at 1980/81 prices)

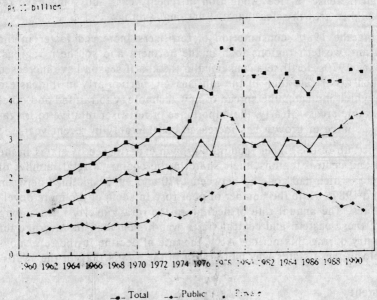

Source: Government of India (various years)

Fig. 3: Input subsidies as a share of plan expenditure on agriculture

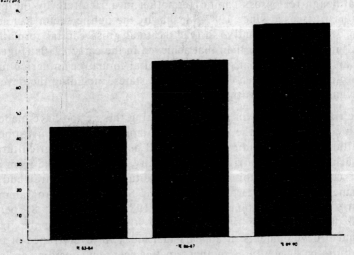

Source: C.H.H. Rao, Agricultural Growth, Rural Poverty and Environmental Degra-
          dation in India (Oxford: Oxford University Press, 1994).

Notes: TE is triennium ending.
          Input subsidies comprise subsidies on fertilizers, canal waters, electricity,
          and credit.

The high complementarity between public and private investment and the adverse terms of trade for agriculture in the 1980s may explain the decline in private investment. The recent recovery in private investment, despite the continued decline in public investment, can in part be attributed to the significant rise in agricultural prices in the last few years. However, it appears that the recovery in private investment is more significant in the eastern states, which may be due to the spread of high-yielding varieties (HYVs) and improved utilisation of the available infrastructure.

Agricultural investment in India is essentially determined at the state level. The recent reforms aimed at macroeconomic stabilisation, desirable in themselves, have nevertheless had a short-term adverse effect on capital expenditures on agriculture both by the central and state governments. The reduction in central tax revenues led to a significant decline in the revenues of the states, particularly of the less developed ones, as the statutory transfers to states, which have a significant built-in progressivity, account for a substantial proportion of these revenues. Moreover, central transfers to states -- both grants and loans -- as a proportion of GDP have also gone down significantly.

The observed decline in investment, unless reversed, may slow down the future growth of output and jeopardise food security as pressures on the available infrastructure increase and the productivity of current inputs begins to decline. In China, a big spurt in agricultural output over a long period following the opening up of the economy can largely be attributed to the high rate of investment in agriculture, realised in part by using surplus labour, over at least three decades, and the extreme misallocation of available capital and other resources under the communes and the collectives. The gains from the rise in the productivity of resources were thus considerable following structural adjustment in agriculture. In India, on the other hand, the rate of investment in agriculture rose for only a decade following the Green Revolution, and the development of human capital has been slow, with few inefficiencies in the allocation of resources at the farm level.

Productivity

The area planted in foodgrains declined somewhat during the 1980s. The entire increase in foodgrain output during that period is therefore the result of the rise in productivity per hectare; as a result of the increase in yield-raising inputs. There was a significant increase in the productivity of all inputs combined or total factor productivity (TFR). As the empirical studies of the IFPRI-ICAR programme show, TFP accounted for one-third of output growth during 1957-85. The contribution of TFP rose to over 50 per cent of output growth in the post-Green Revolution period. Public research and extension and private research were the major sources of increase in TFP; public research and extension accounted for more than two-thirds of the increase after 1975. Foreign and domestic inventions together accounted for more than 30 per cent of TFP growth, indicating the large impact of innovations in fertiliser, machinery, and chemicals, which have a high complementarity with public research. Apart from the market infrastructure, the effect of irrigation on TFP is strongly positive, indicating that irrigation had an impact on productivity over and above its contribution as an input. As expected, the effects of literacy are positive, showing the importance of human capital development in productivity growth.

This indicates that the rate of return to investment in public research and extension has been quite high 60 per cent for public research and more than 50 per cent for extension. These high rates of return on investments in research and extension can be attributed, in no small measure, ~ the spread of new technology to new regions and crops in the last decade. Indeed, the steadiness in the growth of foodgrain output despite falling investment can largely be explained by the improved utilisation of available infrastructure in new areas where the yield levels are low, and, therefore, the productivity of inputs at the margin can be expected to be high.

Corresponding to the increase in TFP has been a significant decline in the unit cost of production in both wheat and rice, the cost reduction being more significant in wheat. Since rice lagged behind wheat in application of HYV technology and since the growth in rice yields has only recently accelerated in such low-cost areas as the eastern region, a significant cost reduction in rice should also be expected. One must bear in mind, however, that part of the observed reduction in unit costs could be due to the rising subsidies on inputs, which have rendered them cheaper, albeit at a cost to society.

Even so, some interesting patterns seem to emerge from the observed trends in cost reduction. Farmers experiencing higher yields show a significant reduction in unit costs indicating the impact of the use of yield-raising technology on cost reduction. Further, over a period of time, the reduction in unit costs was widespread among different groups of farms within the states, indicating the diffusion of new technology. What is more, there are significant changes in the cost structure, the share of machinery and fertilisers increasing and that of labour declining.

It appears that input subsidies have in general had the effect of raising the share of capital costs and reducing the share of labour. The rise in capital-intensity may be due, in a significant measure, to the availability of capital on liberal terms, including concessional rates of interest even to large farmers. Also, the regional concentration of growth in output may have led to the rise in wages in high-growth pockets, providing impetus to mechanisation. These trends suggest a further scope for cost reduction as well as greater employment generation through appropriate pricing of inputs and the adoption of strategies for regionally broad-based growth.

It is interesting that the share of family labour has fallen more than that of hired labour, confirming that as incomes rise, family labour in the higher income groups tends to withdraw from manual labour, thus benefiting hired labour. It is also possible that seed-fertiliser technology has raised the dependence on hired labour because of the rising seasonal demand for labour.

PRIME MOVERS OF GROWTH

Development and Diffusion of Technology

Adequate funding of public research; appropriate economic signals for setting right priorities in research, whether public or private; and a favourable institutional framework providing for the absorption of new technology are the three basic pre-requisites for the proper development and diffusion of new technology.

These are best ensured by a rational demarcation of the relative roles of the state and markets and of the public and private sectors in agriculure. A number of studies have shown that a favourable macroeconomic environment, including openness in trade, is conducive to the development and diffusion of new cost-reducing technologies in agriculture. This occurs when the terms of trade for agriculture are favourable; when inducements are provided to improve quality and reduce costs in order to become internationally competitive; when prices truly reflect the scarcity of resources so that research is directed toward saving the scarce factors; and when allocation of resources -- public as well as private -- for research and extension is adequate.

Economic analysis has focused on the significance of relative prices of factors of production in inducing cost-reducing innovations directed toward saving scarce factors through greater use of abundant factors. For example, heavy subsidies on inputs such as chemical fertilisers, surface irrigation, electricity for pumping water, and on-farm credit discourage research in new areas and the development and adoption of innovations for the conservation of water and energy. In general, subsidies encourage capital-intensive techniques. Private research and extension, which is more responsive to user requirements that vary considerably across agroclimatic regions, is becoming increasingly important as a result of scientific breakthroughs such as the emergence of biotechnology. In such a situation, adequate intellectual property protection becomes necessary to provide incentives for private investment and effort in research.

So far, achievements of the Indian agricultural system in raising yields in the unirrigated and unfavourable agroclimatic regions are not comparable with those realised for the irrigated areas in the early years of the Green Revolution. Even in irrigated areas, yields from the seed-fertiliser technology have hovered around their peak for some time. The tools of emerging biotechnology, including genetic engineering and tissue culture, seem to offer significant possibilities for breaking these barriers. Although some advanced centres of research in biotechnology have been established in India, it is not clear how such priorities find their place in the existing agricultural research system. A fresh look at the priorities of the Indian agricultural research system is necessary in light of these emerging prospects, adequately taking into account the socio-economic factors relevant in the evolution of new technologies. India is currently investing only about 0.3 per cent of its agricultural GDP to agricultural research, as against 0.7 per cent in the developing countries as a whole and 2-3 per cent in the developed countries. Therefore, there is considerable scope for diverting incremental outlays to the priority areas in research.

As far as transfer of technology from research centres and agricultural universities to farmers is concerned, the system seems to have worked reasonably well in the sense that the levels of input use as well as the directions of change embodied in the recommendations are frequently reflected in farm-level practices. This is revealed by an examination of the normative enterprise budgets and the farm-level cost of cultivation data for Punjab -- the seat of the Green Revolution. However, the study indicates that economic evaluation and optimisation of the package as a whole through empirical analysis of experimental trials has been inadequate. And use of systematic evidence from farmers' fields on the practices actually followed by them and their consequences has been insufficient. The study suggests that evaluation of the package from the national or social perspectives of efficiency and sustainability is also inadequate.

In the case of wheat, for example, the recommended fertiliser rates have remained unchanged for the past 20 years in spite of expected changes in soil fertility from continuous intensive cultivation and evidence on imbalances in nutrient use. Similarly, the recommendations regarding the increase in mechanisation involve a significant reduction in the human labour requirement. There is a strong case for re-examination of many of these recommendations in the context of a changing policy environment, requiring greater efficiency in input use. For example, irrigation recommendations need to be re-evaluated from the viewpoint of water-use efficiency in the context of emerging water scarcities. To give another example, the recommendations regarding the variable costs need to be re-examined in the light of actual experiences in farmers' fields, where the variable cost per unit of output at constant prices has fallen considerably over time, so that the average unit cost is lower on farmers' fields than at the normative level. Overall, given the stagnation in yield potential, technical research, in the future, will have to deal with the more complex issues of efficient management of inputs and resource use at the farm level to keep up the momentum of growth. A careful economic evaluation of the recommended practices would be of considerable importance in this context, especially in view of the expected reduction in several input subsidies.

The studies for Bihar and Tamil Nadu on the workings of the regional research systems reveal that there is underinvestment in agricultural research, and allocation of resources to different enterprises is not in conformity with the importance of such activities in the agricultural economy of the regions. Further, the amount spent on scientific support for raising the quality of research is meagre. The regional research systems are far from meeting their avowed objectives of ensuring more flexible, imaginative, and innovative approaches. On-farm adaptive research is still weak and feedback linkages with farmers are poor, although the direct linkages between research and extension appear to be satisfactory. A large number of trials at the regional research stations are still decided centrally, and local problems and issues do not appear to be the main determinants of the research agenda. Consequently, on-farm research continues to be marginal. The evidence also suggests that communication with farmers through institutional innovations such as training and visit (T and V) extension is far from satisfactory; sources such as mass media are more important in disseminating new information. This situation calls for a fresh look at the functioning of the regional research systems, with a view to improving the relevance of their research to the areas in which they are located and strengthening communication with farmers as well as feedback from them. The existing research system needs to be made more flexible and accountable to farmers by developing appropriate linkages with user groups and the private sector engaged in research and extension and in the production and distribution of inputs.

Irrigation

Irrigation was the cradle where HYV seeds and fertiliser consumption thrived, bringing about the green revolution in Indian agriculture during the late 1960s and early 1970s. But even before that, development of irrigation was assigned a high priority by the government in its successive plans. In the early 1970s, north-west India experienced a 'tubewell explosion' in response to the first flush of profits accruing to farmers from the introduction of new technology in wheat production.

Between 1951 and 1990, India added about 55 million hectares of irrigated land to its existing 23 million irrigated hectares, taking the total to 78 million hectares in 1990. About 40 per cent of this additional irrigation was through major and medium schemes and the rest through minor schemes. This is only about half the ultimate irrigation potential of the country, indicating that the country has a long way to go on irrigation[2]. In the 1990s, looking ahead to the future growth of Indian agriculture and what role the irrigation sector will play, the following questions have to be addressed:

(1) Should more investment funds be allocated to major and medium irrigation schemes than has been the trend in the last decade and a half? During the 1980s, the irrigation potential created through major and medium schemes decelerated sharply in response to the shrinking real government expenditure on this sector. This has long-term implications for the growth of Indian agriculture.

(2) Should investments in major and medium irrigation works go to new schemes or to complete those already at hand? This is important because spreading resources too thin leads to long lags in completion of projects.

(3) Should canal waters be priced to cover at least operational and maintenance costs (and a part of the capital cost)? Cost recovery from the canal network has reached extremely low levels, leading to suboptimal use of water on the one hand and a financial crisis on the other. Research reveals that capital costs of major and medium irrigation schemes rose sharply during the 1980s due to larger concerns about rehabilitation and the environment and because more difficult sites were taken up. Operation and maintenance expenses have also gone up in real terms, and the share of management and administration costs has been increasing. As a result, a financial crisis is adversely affecting not only new construction activity but also proper maintenance of the existing systems. To imporve the efficiency and financial sustainability of major and medium schemes, drastic institutional reforms in management and ownership are needed in addition to corrections in the price of water.

(4) What institutional reforms need to be initiated in major and medium schemes to improve efficiency in resource use? More specifically, should farmers be involved in management (and ownership), by taking more 'bottom-up' rather than 'top-down' management approaches?

(5) How can the overexploitation of groundwater be curtailed? An important cause is the inappropriate pricing of electricity, which encourages excessive pumping. Ways to improve conjunctive use of ground and surface water are also crucial for reducing waterlogging and salinity in the command areas of major and medium irrigation schemes.

In terms of policy responses to these questions, the highest priority should be given, first, to maintaining the existing irrigation facilities and then to developing the rest of the irrigation potential in the country. This cannot be done without significantly stepping up the rate of investment in this sector. The largest chunk of this investment, however, should be directed to operating and maintaining the existing facilities and completing the projects already started. At current levels of investment, it is estimated that the projects in hand will take about 28 years to complete. This time span needs to be brought down to 10-15 years. To accomplish this, the rate of investment would have to almost double.

In order to generate resources to accomplish the above task, it is essential that pricing of canal waters be given due importance, along with institutional reforms in operation and management (O and M). Granting irrigation departments financial autonomy provided they recover O and M expenses from the beneficiaries is one way to proceed with reforms in this sector. Also, involvement of water users' associations (WUAs) in ownership and management of canal networks (starting with distributaries) through 'water bonds' or other mechanisms to transfer ownership should be placed high on the agenda for reforming the irrigation sector. An Expert Committee of the Government of India recently looked at the problem and suggested a two-part tariff system for pricing of canal waters. First, there should be a fixed charge to farmers who are in the command area of the canal, and second, there should be a volumetric price (in the long run) that depends on the quantities of water used by the farmers. If all O and M charges were recovered and 1 per cent of the capital cost, the charge to the farmers would not be more than 6 per cent of the gross output on their irrigated lands. This is within the charge of 5-12 per cent recommended by the Irrigation Commission of 1972.

In the case of groundwater, the prime concern remains that of depletion through overpumping, which is not a healthy sign, as the economy's capacity to depend upon this buffer during years of drought is adversely affected. An important step in checking overexploitation would be to introduce volumetric pricing of electricity, while involving farmers' organisations in the collection of electricity dues on a commission basis. If collection of electricity dues through farmers' organisations fails, it would be desirable to turn the problem over to private corporate bodies. While the government's proposed power sector reforms envisage a significantly larger role for the private sector in generation, it is more likely to remain partial without privatising electricity distribution. Ideally, privatisation of power distribution should have preceded privatisation of power generation. Another solution would be to evolve a proper institutional framework whereby surface and groundwater use could be monitored, and overdrafting of groundwater could be avoided or minimised through regulation.

Salinity and waterlogging problems in the commands of major irrigation schemes can be minimised by recognising them explicitly in the design stage and incorporating corrective measures into the scheme. Conjunctive use of surface and groundwater can go a long way in addressing this problem, and appropriate steps should be taken for its promotion. Appropriate pricing of water and electricity will also help in this direction. Further, proper drainage facilities, involving farmers' groups, need to be created where this problem has become acute.

Fertilisers

An overriding concern for removal of fertiliser subsidies, which has arisen during the past three years, emanates primarily from the subsidies' burden on the central budget, rather than from a desire to reform the fertiliser sector as such. By reviewing the major findings of research in this area, a way around present-day concerns without harming the long-term objectives of this sector may be found.

Empirical studies pertaining to the Indian fertiliser sector reveal that diffusion of fertiliser consumption has been quite widespread. Fertiliser was used on more than 85 per cent of irrigated land and about 50 per cent of unirrigated lands by 1988-89. During the last two decades (1970-71 to 1988-89), the growth rate of diffusion to the unirrigated land was much higher, taking the unirrigated land fertilised from 9 per cent to about 50 per cent, thus narrowing the irrigated-rainfed differential in fertiliser diffusion. Unirrigated areas, however, still suffer from discontinuity in the use of fertilisers.

The intensity of fertiliser use has gradually gone up from about 3 kilograms per hectare in the early 1960s to about 16 kilograms per hectare in the early 1970s to 34 kilograms per hectare in the early 1980s to more than 70 kilograms per hectare in the early 1990s. It has been relatively higher in irrigated regions (129 kilograms per hectare by 1988-89), which leads to skewed consumption of fertilisers in the country in favour of irrigated areas. Irrigated areas, which accounted for about 30 per cent of total crop area, used 69 per cent of fertilisers consumed in the country. Gujarat is perhaps the only state that, despite its low rainfall and low irrigation, had adopted fertiliser consumption on a sufficiently wide scale by the early 1980s. This success was primarily due to an efficient state machinery, which, in seeking to develop the fertiliser industry, streamlined transportation and stocking of fertilisers, and co-operative agencies, which distributed fertilisers.

The studies find that the rate of adoption of fertiliser use is somewhat lower among small farmers than large farmers, owing mainly to credit constraints, but those small farmers who do adopt tend to use higher doses of fertilisers than the large farmers. This relationship is more pronounced on unirrigated and partially irrigated plots, but breaks down on irrigated plots, where, in fact, farmers use higher doses of fertilisers. It is possible that small farmers improve the quality of their unirrigated plots through the use of surplus labour, whereas the quality of irrigation is better on large farms on account of higher investment in minor (controlled) irrigation.

Wheat and rice account for about 60 per cent of fertiliser consumption (NPK), and this ratio appears to have remained the same over the last decade. Irrigation and HYVs have played critical roles in promoting fertiliser consumption, supported by a widespread distribution network. The use of N,P, and K is quite unbalanced, not only in low consumption areas but even in high consuming and advanced areas. The responses (average and marginal) of wheat and rice to fertiliser consumption are highest in central (Madhya Pradesh and Rajasthan) and eastern regions (Bihar, Orissa, West Bengal, Assam, and other north-eastern states), and Uttar Pradesh. This indicates that there is sizeable scope for increasing wheat and rice production simply by inducing a redistribution in the consumption of fertilisers in favour of high-response regions, and by promoting balanced use of N,P, and K through appropriate policy measures. More specifically, research shows that, for wheat, a balanced use of NPK could increase production by about 2 million tons, and regional adjustment of fertiliser use to optimal levels with the existing mix could increase production by another 1.6 million tons. If the best mix of fertiliser is used at optimal levels, the current production of wheat could potentially rise as much as 12 per cent, with use of an additional 0.5 million tons of fertiliser. For rice, the potential is even greater, an increase of about 20 per cent over current production with an additional fertiliser consumption of 1.5 million tons.

Research elsewhere also shows that fertiliser consumption has lately become more sensitive to its real price than was the case two decades ago, presumably because fertiliser response is lower at higher levels of consumption. This is particularly true of those areas that use fertiliser very intensively and account for a substantial share of fertiliser consumption in India as a whole. But the elasticity of fertiliser consumption to its real price still remains far below its elasticity with respect to non-price variables.

The domestic production of fertilisers increased substantially, from less than 1 million tons in 1960 to more than 10 million tons by the early 1990s, thus India achieved a high degree of self-sufficiency. Growth was very rapid, especially during the 1980s, primarily for two reasons. First, the Retention Price Scheme launched in 1977 provided a good incentive environment for the industry, and second, the discovery of oil and gas fields at Bombay High contributed to the growth of gas-based fertiliser plants. However, by the late 1980s, it was increasingly realised that the cost of fertiliser production was becoming high at the margin, and that the Retention Price Scheme was inducing overcapitalisation of plants. This led to rapid growth in the fertiliser subsidy, making it an almost financially unsustainable part of the central budget.

Implications of these research findings for policy are clear:

(1) Wider distribution of fertilisers needs to be prompted by covering the regions that previously have used very low doses of fertilisers (for example, central and eastern regions and Uttar Pradesh in the case of wheat and rice). A precondition of the success of this policy is the launching of a massive drive toward both water conservation and drainage because a sizeable chunk of the irrigated tracts in this area suffer from waterlogging. Harvesting water in water-scarce regions and proper drainage, in waterlogged areas can set the ground for adoption of HYVs and increased demand for fertilisers. In addition, an extensive network of rural infrastructure needs to be created (including roads and credit) in these regions, which will facilitate timely and adequate supplies of fertilisers, particularly in the eastern states. Such a network of rural infrastructure will also help in establishing an appropriate interface of input markets with output markets in these regions.

(2) A boost to soil-testing facilities and extension efforts to educate farmers regarding the benefits of balanced use of fertilisers would go a long way. These efforts need to be reinforced by transmission of the right pricing signals (on the relative prices of N,P, and K), which have historically been distorted. There is a large scope to increase production simply by promoting balanced use of N,P, and K, and by correcting micronutrient deficiencies.

(3) Subsidies are not required to promote improved fertiliser management; if subsidies have to be given, they should be targeted to low-consumption areas where response is highest (for example, eastern and central regions, and Uttar Pradesh, especially for wheat and rice).

(4) Production of fertilisers has to be made efficient by gradually withdrawing the Retention Price Scheme and exposing domestic production to foreign competition by freeing imports of fertilisers. This must be accompanied by a variable import duty (to safeguard against dumping or an abrupt drop in international prices).

(5) The farmgate price of nitrogenous fertilisers needs to be gradually raised and then decontrolled, especially when P and K have been decontrolled. This could be done over two or three crop seasons (not years). It would give correct pricing signals for balanced use of N, P, and K, and thereby help raise agricultural production with the same amount of total fertiliser consumption.

(6) To minimise the possible adverse impact of this rise in the farmgate price of fertiliser, the savings from fertiliser subsidy should be ploughed back into basic agricultural infrastructure,

such as watershed programmes in moisture stress areas, which in turn will increase the demand for fertiliser in high-response regions. Further, organic manure should be accorded a high priority because it is environmentally friendly, compared with chemical fertilisers, and because it may be more attractive economically once subsidies on chemical fertilisers are phased out.

Strategies for Unfavourable Agroclimatic Regions

In the first decade of the Green Revolution, the new seed-fertiliser technology spread rapidly in agroclimatic regions with medium-to-low rainfall that had an adequate physical infrastructure (irrigation, roads, and a marketing network) as well as a favourable institutional framework (land tenure systems and credit institutions). Favourable agroclimatic factors such as abundant sunshine, irrigation, and low incidence of pests and diseases were extremely important in triggering the Green Revolution in these regions. On the other hand, regions with unfavourable agroclimatic factors such as too much, too little, or too variable rainfall; waterlogging; salinity; soil erosion; or moisture stress could not experience technological breakthrough.

The initial success of the Green Revolution in the favourable agroclimatic regions has undoubtedly led to the neglect of unfavourable areas, both with respect to the evolution of technologies suited to such regions and conservation of land and water resources. Moreover, the slow growth of income and widespread poverty in the dryland areas and the defective pricing of electricity for pumping water exerted further pressure on already fragile ecosystems, thus accentuating the depletion of land and water resources.

An IFPRI-ICAR study of 14 out of the 15 agroclimatic regions delineated by the Planning Commission shows that after the introduction of the Green Revolution technology, yield growth rates did not exceed the population growth rate of 2.2 per cent in 10 agroclimatic regions. All agroclimatic regions with high rainfall and subhumid to humid climates were in this category. Further, the three agroclimatic regions with less than 1 per cent growth per year in output per hectare had medium to very high rainfall and subhumid to humid climates. On the other hand, four out of five agroclimatic regions with annual growth rates of 2.0 – 4.5 per cent have very low to medium rainfall and arid to semi-arid climates. Also, the results clearly indicate that the output growth obtained from the use of irrigation and fertilisers was below average in agroclimatic regions with high rainfall and humid climates whereas it was above average in agroclimatic regions with low to medium rainfall and arid to semi-arid climates. Moreover, the productivity impact of growth in the use of irrigation and fertiliser was less than average in districts affected by waterlogging and salinity.

During the 1980s, among states with a substantial proportion of cropped area in agroclimatic regions with relatively low rainfall, there was marked improvement in the performance of all but two where overexploitation of groundwater was reported. Further, the 1980s growth performance of four agroclimatic regions with medium-to-high rainfall was also better than that in the previous two decades. Agricultural growth in West Bengal, Bihar, Uttar Pradesh, Orissa, Madhya Pradesh, Andhra Pradesh, and Tamil Nadu supports this.

It is incorrect to view resource degradation essentially as a consequence of technology-based growth. Rather, in some cases such as deforestation, ecological degradation itself is the consequence of insufficient progress in adopting land-augmenting technological change, leading to increased pressure on land. Indeed, in certain respects, technology-based growth has mitigated the resource-degrading effects that would otherwise have occurred. For example, tubewells have served as vertical drainage by arresting waterlogging and soil salinisation in the high rainfall areas and also in areas waterlogged as a result of canal irrigation.

Experience has shown that a critical minimum of favourable soil moisture is necessary to adopt technologies suited to the climatic conditions of these regions. Since favourable areas at present account for a small proportion of cultivated area in the country, broadening the geographical base of agricultural growth through the development of natural resources, infrastructure development, and the evolution of location-specific technologies for the hitherto unfavourable regions is essential for sustaining growth, improving the overall efficiency of resource use, reducing poverty, and protecting the environment.

Among the degraded areas, dryland areas with very low and uncertain rainfall and with low irrigation potential need to be given a high priority for soil and moisture conservation in view of their high geographical coverage, high rate of degradation, widespread poverty, and their comparative advantage for producing high value crops for export. The existing programmes for soil and moisture conservation have failed to make an impact because they are inadequately planned on a watershed basis; they have failed to integrate employment generation programmes into their works;they have failed to involve the beneficiaries and the voluntary organisations in the planning and implementation of programmes; and they lack co-ordination among the various departments concerned with these programmes. Therefore, to give high priority to soil and moisture conservation in the dryland areas, present strategies have to be revamped to create the necessary conditions for the adoption of improved practices.

Infrastructure

If Indian agriculture is opened up to international trade, and if the future growth of Indian agriculture is to be yield-based, requiring intensive use of inputs, development of infrastructure is necessary to support this growth. Infrastructure plays a critical role on both input and output sides. On the input front, it helps ensure timely and adequate delivery to farmers, which is essential in raising the aggregate supply response. On the output front, it helps integrate local markets with national and international markets so that the benefits of trade can percolate down to farmers. Without an adequate and efficient system of infrastructure, the real potential of Indian agriculture under the changing incentive environment cannot be realised.

Building infrastructure requires three-tier planning - at the national, state, and district/block levels. Ports (sea and air), railways, national highways, telecommunications, the national electrification grid, and so forth have to be planned at the national level. While the government may have to take the lead in giving a concrete shape to its needs and plans, private sector participation on a significant scale, particularly in construction and operation, would be welcome.

In creating a system of infrastructure at the second and third tiers (at state and lower levels), mostly in rural areas, regional characteristics become important at the planning stage. A thorough study and understanding of regional complexities, physical, economic, and social, is essential to ensure that the planned system of infrastructure of roads, markets, and other support services for agricultural development renders high returns. Empirical studies conducted at the state and substate levels in India note that when the infrastructural needs are identified on regional and crop-specific bases and are related to different social and economic groups, they are likely to gain most from investments in different types of activity-specific infrastructure. The basic policy thrust of these studies is that, at state and substate levels, planning for the system of rural infrastructure must involve local user groups, particularly farmers, traders, and non-governmental organisations (NGOs). Decentralisation in building, operating, and maintaining different components of infrastructure with the help of local people is a desirable policy direction for the future. This has the potential to change the entire system of planning rural infrastructure from a top-down to a bottom-up system, promoting better efficiency and maintenance of infrastructure.

Another policy conclusion from the rural infrastructure studies is the need for large-scale but low-cost housing schemes in the rural areas, replacing the temporary shacks of poor agricultural workers and marginal cultivators. Low-cost pucca housing, including community toilets, water supply, and electricity, should be given as high a priority as construction of roads, markets, and other support services for agricutlural development. Financial implications of such schemes, of course, need to be examined, especially because much of it would have to be subsidised. It would, therefore, be desirable to link the construction of such housing schemes with employment schemes, such as Jawahar Rozgar Yojana (JRY), in rural areas. Involvement of local people in deciding on the type of housing is essential. Further, the likely beneficiaries can be asked to contribute towards the costs by donating their labour. Such schemes can act as a protective cover for the rural poor by giving them employment during a period of structural adjustment when agricultural prices are likely to be rising. Further, employment for agricultural workers and marginal cultivators can also be provided under the JRY-type employment schemes. Land and water resources can be augmented through activities such as terracing, levelling, and bunding of fields; building and maintenance of village roads; and lining, deepening, and dredging of canals, wells, and tanks at the state and substate levels.

INSTITUTIONAL REFORMS

Credit Reforms

Credit for agriculture has to expand at a faster rate than before because of the need to step up agricultural growth to generate surpluses for exports, and also because of the change of the product mix toward animal husbandry, fisheries, horticulture, and so forth, which will necessitate larger investments. However, the rural credit system is now threatened by rising overdues and deficiencies in management. These can be attributed to a policy environment and political culture that encourages lending at subsidised rates, discourages a professional approach and necessary follow-up in lending, and promotes willful default on the part of those who have the capacity to repay. As a consequence, recycling of credit has become a major casualty, the losers being the prospective borrowers. Therefore, improving the economic viability of credit institutions has to be high on the policy agenda.

The existing large differential between the concessional rates of interest charged by institutional sources and market rates is responsible for rent-seeking by the middlemen who corner a good part of institutional credit at concessional rates and relend it to others, especially to the poorer farmers, at high rates of interest. Large farmers have been the major beneficiaries of the long-term loans advanced at a concessional rate of interest of 10 per cent. Their share in total institutional credit is significantly larger than their share in total operated farm area. The perpetuation of such concessional lending violates norms of equity as well as the viability of credit institutions. Also, this has had adverse allocational effects, resulting in high capital-intensity and slow employment generation in agriculture.

In view of the scarcity of credit and the very high rates of interest charged in the informal credit markets in rural areas, small and marginal farmers would benefit much more from easier and timely availability of credit from institutional sources than from the low subsidised rates of interest charged. It would, therefore, be desirable to phase out these concessional rates of interest. Such a step would improve the viability of rural banking, not only through increases in interest income but also by improving the repayment performance, as the cost of delayed repayment would rise. It is essential, however, to ensure the availability of institutional credit to farmers, particularly small and marginal farmers, by ensuring a stipulated share for agriculture, as is being done at present. Without such a stipulation, the well known tendency of bankers to reduce unit costs by serving a small number of big borrowers, rather than a large number of small borrowers, would result in a credit squeeze for needy borrowers.

Managers of credit institutions should be accorded greater autonomy; administrative and political interference in their day-to-day functioning should be eliminated. Managers and other staff need to be made more professional through appropriate recruitment and training. Loan advances should be based on the professional appraisal of investment projects, instead of being based on targets for the disbursement of credit, as is often the practice now. Loan sanctions should be accompanied by professional follow-up to ensure the profitability of investment by reducing the rate of mortality and sickness in these ventures.

The follow-up services for enhancing the productive utilisation of credit and repayment performance could be improved through group-lending schemes. Participation of groups such as voluntary agencies, women activists, and thrift societies, especially in the backward regions, would help reduce transaction costs to the banks as well as clients. This calls for a reorientation of the outlook of banks, posting of competent personnel in rural areas, and a system of incentives and rewards related to the performance of the specific tasks that have a bearing on long-term development as well as meeting the needs of the poor.

Agrarian Reforms

A ceiling on the ownership of land has served to limit the concentration of land ownership and, indeed, there is evidence of some decline in concentration. However, owing to population growth and subdivision of landholdings, the average size of both owned and operational holdings has decreased, even though the proportion of area held by small and marginal farmers has increased. The proportion of area held under tenancy, especially pure tenancy, has declined because the land has been resumed by the owners for self-cultivation. This resumption of farming was induced by technological change and impelled by tenancy legislation. This explains the rise in the concentration of operational holdings, although this concentration is still lower than that in ownership holdings because small and marginal holdings still lease in more area than they lease out and large holdings lease out more area than they lease in.

According to the empirical studies conducted under the IFPRI-ICAR research programme, where seed-fertiliser or land-augmenting technology has been adopted widely, the improved viability of small-holdings has helped reduce the incidence of landlessness. Also, in areas of technological dynamism, medium and large holdings have expanded their operated area significantly by leasing in land from the small and marginal holdings. Rural nonfarm employment opportunities and wages have increased in such high-growth areas, thus reducing rural poverty and relieving pressure on agricultural land.

What are the implications of this experience for policies on land tenure? With population pressure on agricultural land persisting, and there being, as yet, not enough evidence of economies of scale in Indian agriculture, there is little justification for doing away with the ceiling on the ownership of land at this stage, especially because farmers are able to ment their operational holdings in response to the changing technological and economic factors.

However, this experience also suggest that freeing the lease market for land may contribute to equity as well as efficiency of resource use. The pure tenants as well as the small and marginal farmers would be able to augment their operational holdings by leasing in area, where there is pressure on land and where wages are low and poverty is high. This may also contribute to the more efficient use of land, labour, and other resources. On the other hand, in areas experiencing technological change and high growth, where population pressure on land is low and wages are high, the marginal farmers may gain by leasing out their area and taking up non-farm employment. Where wages and the rate of mechanisation are high, the medium and large farmers who are leasing in area would be able to make a fuller use of their fixed equipment.

Experience also shows that consolidation of landholdings and improving land records will give a fillip to investment in irrigation by raising the profitability of such investment and by improving the creditworthiness of farmers.

Participation of Women

There has been an increase in the participation rate of female labour in agriculture. This is due to a rise in the seasonal demand for labour for operations traditionally performed by females following the spread of new seed-fertiliser technology, the rise in the demand for female labour in activities such as dairying, and to an increase in the employment of male labour in nonagricultural activities. As a result, there has been an increase in the real wages of female labour relative to those for male labour. However, the levels of labour input and wages are still lower for females than for males.

In addition to improving agricultural practices and protecting the environment, strengthening the position of female farmers and female labour can contribute significantly to the well-being of the household, as women allocate a greater part of their income for household expenditure than men do, thus improving the nutrition and care of children, particularly girls. Changing property rights in favour of women, evolving technologies to suit women farmers, increasing the number of women extension workers, educating and training women farmers, strengthening the thrift societies run by women, and other such measures may help them to better exploit the emerging opportunities.

POVERTY ALLEVIATION

The changes in rural poverty have been influenced by changes in agricultural output per head, changes in the prices of foodgrains, access to productive assets such as land, and the expansion of poverty alleviation programmes such as Jawahar Rozgar Yojana (JRY) and the Integrated Rural Development Programme (IRDP). Whether one considers the Planning Commission estimates or those of critics, there is a declining trend in the proportion of the rural population that is below the poverty line. This is consistent with the recent improvement in the growth rate of foodgrain output in the eastern states, where poverty has been widespread, and the rise in real wages in rural areas in most parts of the country. Another favourable development during the 1980s was the decline in the relative prices of foodgrain due to the rise in total factor productivity.

However, in view of the steep decline in the employment elasticity in agriculture, it appears that the indirect contribution of agriculture toward poverty reduction through the expansion of off-farm employment opportunities, achievement of food security, and the decline in the relative prices of foodgrains has become more important than agriculture's direct contribution by way of labour absorption. This experience does not imply that the potential for labour absorption in agriculture has been exhausted. On the other hand, the experience suggests that by focusing on public investment and on other appropriate technology packages for the low-wage areas, it should be possible to raise substantially employment and incomes of the rural poor. As mentioned earlier, the opening up of trade should give a further fillip to employment-intensive activities such as agroprocessing and marketing. The asset position of the small and marginal farmers and the landless can be improved by tilting the land market in their favour by extending long-term loans on liberal terms for the purchase of land.

Opening up of agricultural trade is likely to exert an upward pressure on the prices of foodgrains. The favourable incentive and allocational effects of trade liberalisation have, therefore, to be reconciled with the need to protect the vulnerable sections from rising food prices. This can be done by targeting food subsidies through the pubic distribution system strictly to the really needy, who should not constitute more than 35-40 per cent of the total population. Under the existing practice of providing subsidised grain to everyone, one cannot even be certain that the poor are benefiting because they still have to buy large quantities of foodgrains in the free market at higher prices. For example, the National Sample Survey data for 1986-87 show that in the case of rice, the share of purchases from the public distribution system to total purchases by the poor was less than 10 per cent in poorer states like Bihar, Madhya Pradesh, Orissa, Uttar Pradesh, and West Bengal. An attempt toward proper targeting is being made through the revamped public distribution system, recently launched in over 1,700 backward blocks, situated in drought-prone, desert, tribal, and hill areas.

A major challenge in the implementation of poverty alleviation programmes is to integrate them with measures for raising agricultural productivity by building up labour-intensive infrastructure, such as minor irrigation works and drainage, and also with those for protecting the environment, such as soil conservation and water harvesting on a watershed basis, and reforestation of degraded forests. Another major challenge is to improve the cost effectiveness of such works and maximise the benefits to the target groups. Unlike farm operations, the poverty alleviation programmes have remained essentially top-down ventures, heavily dependent on bureaucracy, resulting in inefficiencies and leakages to rent-seeking middlemen. Involvement of the beneficiaries in the design and implementation of poverty alleviation programmes through locally elected (panchayati raj) institutions, voluntary organisations, or NGOs seems to provide a workable alternative to bureaucratic management at this stage.

CONCLUDING REMARKS

The process of economic reforms, and the gradual opening up of Indian agriculture to world markets is likely to turn the terms of trade in favour of agriculture, creating a better incentive environment for agriculture than has been the case in preceding decades. To fully exploit this opportunity, a major reform in supply-side factors is needed as well as a clean sweep to dismantle all export controls on agricultural commodities, including foodgrains. It is these supply-side factors -- technology, fertilisers, irrigation, infrastructure, and credit -- that raise aggregate supply response and are the prime movers behind accelerated and sustainable growth of Indian agriculture. A neglect of these critical factors during the process of economic reforms has the potential to generate inflationary pressures in the economy.

A major revamping of the agricultural research system is required to enable it to better develop location-specific technologies, to upgrade the extension system, to become more accountable to farmers, and to set right priorities for research by placing due emphasis on biotechnologies. Greater flexibility in management and resource augmentation is also required.

Investments in public irrigation, which have been declining during the 1980s, need to be raised. But these must be combined with a drastic institutional reform in the canal irrigation system, ranging from financial autonomy of irrigation departments to making farmers co-managers and co-owners of these systems. In the case of groundwater, volumetric pricing of electricity is almost a necessity if this scarce resource is to be efficiently utilised and groundwater depletion reduced.

In the case of fertilisers, policies geared toward wider distribution would bring better results. Subsidies need to be gradually brought down, and domestic production exposed to foreign competition. Savings in subsidies can be plowed back into moisture conservation schemes and irrigation to minimise the adverse impact on crop production.

Development of infrastructure is critical to ensure that the farmers get their inputs in time and in adequate quantities, at lowest possible prices. On the output side, it ensures that they get the highest possible share in prices paid by consumers. It would be worth incorporating construction of low-cost housing, community toilets, and supply of electricity and water in rural areas as parts of an investment system which could be designed and developed with the help of local people, keeping in mind regional specificities at the substate level. These schemes could be integrated with employment generation and poverty alleviation programmes such as JRY and IRDP.

To get the maximum mileage out of reforms on the demand and supply sides, availability of credit becomes critical. To enable the banking system to respond to the needs of agriculture without any undue financial burden, concessional rates of interest to agriculture shold be withdrawn and repayment performance improved, while supplies of rural credit are augmented.

Broadening the geographical base of agricultural growth by spreading yield-raising technology to unfavourable agroclimatic regions is essential for sustaining high growth, improving the efficiency of resource use, reducing poverty, and protecting the environment. Toward this end, the ongoing programmes for soil and moisture conservation in drought-prone areas and those for arresting waterlogging and salinity in high rainfall areas need considerable strengthening. Further, rural infrastructure needs to be provided to facilitate the broadening of the geographical base of agricultural growth.

Since opening up trade in foodgrains is likely to raise their domestic prices, it is of utmost importance to build an adequate safety net for the poor by strengthening implementation of the existing poverty alleviation programmes and public distribution of foodgrains and other essential commodities by targeting them strictly to those who are genuinely needy.

With these broad policy changes in supply-side factors, India can feasibly benefit from the changing economic scene in India and abroad by accelerating the growth of her agricultural sector, thus providing momentum to overall growth of the economy. These policies will lead to greater employment, regional and sectoral equity, faster poverty reduction, more efficient resource use, and better protection of the environment than before.

NOTES

1. The demand for foodgrains is likely to range from 206 to 240 million metric tons by the end of the century under several alternative scenarios of overall growth and income distribution. The rapidly changing structure of demand, however, is likely to keep the demand for foodgrains nearer to the lower level of about 206 million metric tons.

2. The ultimate irrigation potential in the country remains a matter of debate. Earlier, about 113 million hectares were estimated as the ultimate irrigation potential by the government. Of this, about 40 million hectares were from groundwater and 73 million hectares from surface water. Recently, the government has revised the irrigation potential from groundwater to 80 million hectares, an amount that has been contested by some researchers.

These papers (December, 1994) are the outcome of a collaborative research programme conducted under a memorandum of understanding with the Indian Council of Agricultural Research, with funding from the United States Agency for International Development (International Food Policy Research Institute Washington, D.C., U.S.A.). The overall aim of the programme is to increase understanding of the options and complexities of future policies for agricultural growth. The opinions expressed in the papers are the views of the authors and do not necessarily represent those of the Indian Council of Agricultural Research or the Government of India.

This paper was first published in the form of an article in Economic & Political Weekly dated December 31, 1994. Reprinted here with permission from the authors and the journal.

11

Employment Situation: Some Emerging Perspectives

A VAIDYANATHAN

Creating adequate employment opportunities to absorb the existing unemployed and underemployed as well as the increase in labour force has been among the important and continuing concerns of Indian development policy throughout the post-independence period. Initially — and this is evident when we look at the debate in the early 50s - there was a great deal of interest on the possibilities of utilising 'disguised unemployment' for accelerated capital formation. The apparent success of China, following the communist revolution, in implementing such a programme was widely admired. But it was not considered feasible in the Indian context for several reasons: Withdrawal of 'surplus' labour would not automatically release the food they were consuming; nor would it be politically feasible to extract this food through coercive means. The employment of surplus labour in capital construction could therefore give rise to inflation and/or pressure on balance of payments. Secondly, releasing 'surplus' labour and mobilising it on a massive scale, as the Chinese did, could not be accomplished under the Indian political framework of parliamentary democracy. Full employment at rising levels of productivity and incomes would not in any case be feasible without growth and diversification of economic activity. This called for increasing the investment rate, a modern industrial base to produce equipment and material to complement labour, and improvement of technology all round [GOI, Planning Commission 1953]

The Mahalanobis strategy focused on the requisites for achieving and sustaining a rapid rate of growth in the long term. It recognised that in the transitional period employment may not keep pace with the growth of the labour force. The interests of employment in the medium term was sought to be balanced with those of long-term growth by a deliberate policy of producing mass consumption goods with labour-intensive techniques in the early stages of development. Discriminatory measures (differential taxation,reservation and subsidies)to protect, and positive measures (credit, marketing and technical help) to encourage, traditional and labour-intensive industry has been a continuing feature of policy throughout the last four decades.

By the end of the 50s, demographic growth was found to be much higher than expected even as the overall growth did not show much of an improvement. This led to fears that increases in job opportunities may not keep up with increase in population and labour force and that the problem of unemployment will be aggravated. The plan documents forecast an increasing 'backlog' of unemployment. The apprehensions were strengthened by other developments notably the increasing proletarianisation of rural labour and indications that the new agricultural technology did not increase employment in the same proportion as output. Data from the rural labour inquiries showed that even as dependence on wage labour was rising, employment per worker did not and real wage rates were stagnant or falling. The belief that growth would automatically lead to more employment and higher wages for everyone, everywhere was also beginning to wear thin.

The early 1970s witnessed an extensive debate on the 'trickle down' hypothesis, the nexus between unemployment and poverty and the need for special measures to alleviate the conditions of the poor and the unemployed who are by-passed by growth. There was near general agreement in the country, as indeed international bodies including the World Bank, that growth alone would not suffice to eliminate poverty and that special programmes designed to directly augment income and employment of the poor were essential. A special works programme of a rather modest scale had been included in the Third Plan; but the real fillip to the 'poverty alleviation' programmes came in the early 1970s with Indira Gandhi adopting 'Garibi Hatao' as the centre-piece of the government policy. Special employment schemes were an important component of this new programme. Over the years they have undergone various modifications culminating in the Jawahar Rozgar Yozana (JRY); more importantly the scale of outlays on these programmes has grown rapidly. By 1990-91 outlays on JRY exceeded Rs 2,600 crore and it was estimated to generate additional employment of nearly 870 million person days a year.

The continued expansion of special employment programmes and the fact that outlay on these will be further stepped up substantially in the Eighth Plan suggest that the perceptions regarding the employment problem have not changed much. The Eighth Plan document declares: " There has been a significant growth in employment over the years. However a relatively high growth of population and labour force had led to an increase in the volume of unemployment from one plan to another. The Eighth Plan aims at bringing employment into sharper focus in the medium term perspective with the goal of reducing unemployment to negligible levels within the next 10 years." The plan document notes with concern the relatively slow growth in agricultural employment and the declining elasticity of labour use with reference to output growth in agriculture. While recognising that non-agricultural employment has grown the document focuses on the declining rate of increase in successive quinquennia [GOI, Planning Commission 1992]. It also sees the growth of non-agricultural employment as reflecting the tendency for those who cannot find work in agriculture to take up any kind of non-agricultural work which is available. I would argue for a different reading of the experience.

Changes in Level and Structure of Employment

Let us look at the facts. We get a detailed picture of the growth of population, employment and unemployment, pattern of employment and wage rates in rural and urban India from the quinquennial surveys of employment and unemployment conducted by NSSO since 1972-73. These surveys have been designed after a great deal of careful study of conceptual and measurement problems in the light of experience gained by earlier surveys conducted by the NSS and other organisations. Since the early 1970s the NSS has taken care to ensure that successive rounds use comparable design, concepts and questionnaries. Unlike the census of population - the other important source of information on employment - the NSS enquiries are not only more frequent but have the advantage of providing far more detailed information collected by a professional organisation with long experience in conducting field surveys. There is good reason to suppose that the NSS is likely to be more reliable and sensitive in capturing the changes.

Population has grown by close to 40 per cent between 1972-73 and 1987-88; rural population by a little under 30 per cent and urban population by close to 70 per cent. Workforce participation rates (in terms of usual status) do not show any sustained trend (except among rural males where it shows a decline both during 1977 to 1983 and 1987-88). The current daily status emloyment rates show a decline from 1972-73 to 1983 but revived in 1987-88. The ratio of current to usual participation rates - which can be viewed as a rough measure of the number of days of work available per usual worker - also declined from 1972-73 to 1983 but recovered in 1987-88. In all cases, except rural males, this ratio in 1987-88 was lower than in 1972-73 suggesting a deterioration in the availablity of employment per worker. Overall unemployment rates in terms of usual status however do not show any sustained trend in any case except rural males (where it rose). In terms of current daily status, unemployment among rural male rose up to 1983 and then fell sharply; the rate among females has declined throughout and substantially; urban unemployment rate has declined since 1977-78 (Table 1).

Reported involuntary employment is systematically related to the status of the worker - it is highest among casual labourers and least among the self-employed. The NSS clearly shows a strong and sustained rise in the population of both male and female workers in rural areas working as wage labourers. In the urban areas the extent of self-employment has risen progressively among males implying a reduction in wage labour. But in both rural and urban areas there is a clear tendency for casualisation of male as well as female wage labour. With the rise in the importance of casual labour, one would expect a rise in the reported rate of involuntary unemployment. That this has not happened strengthens the inference suggested by the NSS data that employment opportunities have grown fast enough to absorb the increments in labour force.

The total number of persons usually employed (including marginal workers) has risen from an estimated 237 million in 1972-73 to 325 million in 1987-88. In percentage terms, total employment on this definition rose by 12.5-13 per cent each during the quinquennia ending 1977-78 and 1983; between 1983 and 1987-88 the increase was less than 8 per cent (Table 1). The rate of additions to employment shows a progressive fall in rural areas and a rise in the urban areas. This, however, is not wholly surprising in as much as there is a deceleration in the growth of rural population and a compensating quickening in urban population growth.

It is arguable that the actual number of days worked is a superior measure of employment than the number of workers. On this index (Table 2) there is no deceleration of employment growth either in rural or urban areas. The rate of increase in total employment shows a steep rise in the quinquennium ending 1983 compared to that ending in 1977-78; and a further, somewhat larger rise between 1983 and 1987-88. In rural areas the rate of increase in total employment rose progressively in the three successive quinquennia ending 1987-88. The impression of decelerating growth in employment is not quite supported by facts.

The more striking fact is that the total number of workers engaged in agriculture has increased by a mere 20 per cent between 1972 and 1987 while non-agricultural employment has risen by 80 per cent (Table 3). Nearly 60 per cent of the incremental employment is outside agriculture. The share of non-agricluture employment in the total has risen from 26.5 per cent in 1972-73 to 35 per cent in 1987-88. This reflects in part the growing urbanisation (90 per cent of the urban workers are non-agricultural compared to the mere 25 per cent in rural),but to an important degree it is due to the growing diversification of rural employment. Total rural workers rose by some 31 per cent between 1972 and 1987; those employed in agriculture rose by 20 per cent even as non-agricultural employment nearly doubled. The proportion of rural workers in non-agricultural activity has risen from 14-15 per cent in 1972-73 to 22 per cent by 1987-88 (Table 1) In terms of person days, the share of non-agricultural employment in total rural employment rose from 21-22 per cent to 27 per cent (Table 2).

Factors in Growth of Rural Non-Farm Employment

The increase in rural non-agricultural employment is both significant and distributed across a variety of activities including principally manufacturing, trade and services. Construction also shows a rather sharp rise between 1977 and 1987(Table 3). The phenomenon is seen nearly in all major states though the pace of change varies. It would further seem, on the basis of NSS data that prior to 1972-73 there was little change in the structure of rural employment, the relative shares of agriculture and non-agriculture in that year being actually somewhat higher than in 1959-60. The significance of the large and sustained change in the structure of rural employment since the early 1970s is not sufficiently recognised in current discussions of employment.

One of widely discussed explanations for the relatively rapid growth of rural non-agricultural employment is that it represents the inability of agriculture to absorb more labour. It is certainly true that agricultural employment has increased but slowly relative to the growth of output. A number of studies [Bhalla S 1993] have shown that the elasticity of employment relative to crop output is not only considerably below unity but also declining. While the spread of irrigation increases the labour requirements (both because of higher cropping intensity and of more intensive cultivation of land), the growing importance of chemical fertilisers (which is one of the most important sources of yield increase) and of weedicides tends to depress the requirement of human labour. Chemical fertilisers are a much more concentrated source of plant nutrients than farm yard manures: The latter involves handling a much larger volume of material per unit of plant nutrient; and weedicides clearly displace human labour used in weeding. It also seems likely that insofar as in productivity increases resulting from HYV are due to changes in straw-grain ratio, the volume of work involved in harvesting and transport may not rise at the same rate as yield. The rapid spread of tractors (for land preparation and transport) and mechanical harvesting and threshing are clearly labour displacing.

Slow growth of agricultural employment is however not exclusively attributable to the low elasticity of employment with reference to yield. The relatively slow pace of growth in yield and in overall output are also a contributing factor. The rate of growth in crop production varies a great deal; official data suggest that some states (e.g, Tamil Nadu) are experiencing a trend decline in agricultural output while some (e g, Punjab) are experiencing relatively rapid growth of 4 per cent a year or more. There are also indications that the overall output growth in irrigated agriculture is quite significant even as yields of rainfed agriculture seem to be more or less stagnant. A satisfactory analysis of the relative contributions of changes in employment elasticity and of slow growth in output in explaining the slow growth of the agricultural employment, as well as the considerable differences in this respect which seem to exist across states, remains to be done. Nevertheless, it is obvious that any quickening in the pace of agricultural growth and a greater spatial diffusion of such growth will mean larger labour absorption in agriculture.

The rapid growth of non-agricultural employment especially in rural areas tended to be underrated because it was accompanied by several other changes which were seen as unfavourable: the rise in the proportion of wage labour in total non-agricultural employment; the growing importance of casual labour; and the fact that much of the employment was in the unorganised sector. There has of course been a rise in the proportion of employees as distinct from self-employed (and employers), in the workforce. This however is an essentially rural phenomenon; the share of self-employment in fact shows a small rise in urban India. In both cases, however, an increasing proportion of the wage labour force consists of casual labour (Table 4).

Wage employment in the non-agricultural sector rose by nearly 27 million (from 39 m to 66 m) between 1972 to 1987-88. Organised sector employment rose by some 50 per cent (almost all of it in the public sector) while wage employment in the unorganised sector nearly doubled (Table 5). Thus, nearly 70 per cent of additional non-agricultural wage employment during this period is accounted by the unorganised sector. The latter's share in total wage employment outside agriculture has risen progresssively from 40 per cent during the quinquennium ending 1977-78, to 70 per cent in the next quinquennium and further to 87 per cent in the quinquennium ending 1987-88. Altogether the share of the informal sector in total non-agricultural wage employment rose from around 53 per cent in 1972-73 to 62 per cent in 1987-88.

The existence of a significant positive correlation between the share of non-agricultural sector in rural employment across states at 3 different points in time and between the extent of change in these two variables [Vaidyanathan 1986] to support the hypothesis that non-agricultural activities serve essentially as a residual absorber of labour in rural areas. There is however good reason to contest such an inference. The 'residual sector' Hypothesis holds that the rural economy is experiencing a growing excess supply of labour over demand from agriculture and that this excess is spilling into non-agricultural activities. If the real volume of activity in the latter is not increasing fast enough, this should lead to a depression of real wage rates overall or a widening disparity between agricultural and non-agricultural wage rates in rural areas. In point of fact, however, real wage rates have risen for both sexes and for both regular and casual workers, in both urban and rural areas, and in practically all states (Table 7 through 11).

The rise in rural real wage rates across the board, taken together with the rapid expansion of non-agricultural employment, strongly belies the residual sector hypothesis. The growth in non-agricultural employment does not seem to be a distress phenomenon; it reflects a real growth in the volume of rural non-farm activity whose underlying factors deserve closer examination. Much of the growth as pointed out earlier has occurred in four main sectors trade and transport, manufacturing, servicing and construction. Let us consider these in turn.

The growth of trade and transport in rural areas seems to reflect the growing commercialisation of the rural economy; the dependence of agriculture on fertilisers, electricity, diesel oil, pesticides and other non-agricultural inputs has greatly increased. The proportion of crop output which is sold in the market has increased for a variety of reasons: the relatively faster growth of crops other than foodgrains; the fact that output is rising faster than the cultivator population; the growing tendency for processing of farm products shifted out of the household into specialised enterprises; and the growing integration of village into the wider market economy as the modern transport system gets extended and improved. The penetration of modern means of transport and mass media into the countryside has probably changed rural consumption patterns in favour of non-traditional manufactures. The cumulative effect of all this is the expansion of rural trading activity - and associated activity of handling and transport of goods - at a much faster rate than production.

In the case of manufacturing, total employment rose by about 2 per cent a year (on the average) between 1961-81. Employment in the organised sector (namely, registered factories) rose considerably faster than in the unorganised (non-factory) sector. Within the latter, the household industry segment recorded a significant absolute decline (of nearly 20 per cent over the period) even as the non-household non-factory employment rose 2.4 times. During the decade 1977-87, while total manufacturing employment continued to rise somewhat faster than earlier, the expansion in factory employment slowed down. The tendency for household industries to decline and of non-household non-factory manufacturing to expand rapidly has continued.

Rural employment in manufacturing was roughly of the same order in 1972-73 and has also grown at more or less the same rate as in urban areas from that time to 1987-88. Since rural population and workforce are rising at a slower rate than in urban areas, the relative importance of manufacturing as a source of rural employment has increased significantly (from 5.7 per cent to 7.4 per cent of male workers and 4.7 per cent to 6.7 per cent of female workers), even as the comparable share in urban area has not changed much. By contrast, between 1959-60 and 1972-73 manufacturing employment as a proportion of the total seems to have declined appreciably in both rural and urban areas (Table 3).

The number of rural workers reporting employment in traditional rural industries like hand spinning, leather earthenware has declined or remained stagnant; there have been significant increases in bidi-making, food industry, textile products, and non-metallic mineral products other than earthenware. One of the largest increases has been in repair shops. Estimated employment of rural workers in relatively modern industries like rubber, plastic, chemical and metal products have also risen in several cases faster than the total employment in the industry [Vaidyanathan 1991; Bhalla 1993].

The decline in traditional industries has thus been more than made up by expansion in non-traditional sectors. In some cases (e.g. in the case of bidi), tax exemption to household industry, the high rural-urban differential in wages and the feasibility of operating an effective putting-out system have contributed to the growth of the latter. The rapid growth of employment in textile products most of which is probably in (tailoring) and of non-metallic mineral products (probably brick-making) responds to the growth in the rural demand partly from higher incomes and partly shifting consumer preferences. The growth of employment in repairs is directly related to the phenomenal increase in the stock of modern mechanical, electrical and electronic equipment used for transport, agriculture and domestic use. With improved transport, it is conceivable that more and more industries (e.g. some chemicals, food processing, pre-fabricated cement products), are finding it economical, and even attractive, to locate in rural areas. Part of the increases in the number of rural workers in manufacturing may also reflect a growing tendency for workers in urban industry to commute from their residence in nearby villages. The spread of the road network and motorised transport makes commuting quicker, affordable and economical especially when costs of setting up residence in urban are rising.

The growth of employment in the service sector is partly on account of the expansion of public employment in administration, defence and in various socio-economic development services (including education and health). But the major part of the increase (about two-thirds) is on account of community and personal services in the private sector. The nature and sources of the relatively rapid growth of employment in rural services deserve closer study.

Finally, there is construction. According to NSS, the number of workers normally employed in construction has almost trebled (from 4.3 to 12.1 million) between 1972-73 and 1987-88, the increase being somewhat larger in rural than in urban areas. This order of increase does not seem to be consistent with the behaviour of capital formation (which gives a rough measure of the volume of total construction activity) in the economy or the absorption to cement and other construction material. Total real capital formation is estimated to have only doubled between 1972 and 1987; the increase during 1977-87, when the steep rise in employment took place, being only 50 per cent. Special employment programmes, which started in the early 1970s and expanded rapidly since may have been a significant source of additions to rural employment in construction. The employment potential of the JRY in 1987-88 is placed at 670 million person days, equivalent to 3 million person years of nearly one-fourth of the rural workers reported to be engaged in construction as a usual activity. But given large and widespread leakages it is generally recognised that actual employment generated is unlikely to be as large as claimed. In any case special employment programmes cannot account for the reported rise in urban areas. The extraordinary expansion of construction employment, especially since 1977-87 needs closer scurtiny.

The above explanations of the sources of vigorous growth in rural non-farm employment are no more than suggestive. A definitive understanding requires a more detailed and disaggregated analysis of factors accounting for the wide inter-regional variations in the rate and pattern of changes in rural employment and wage rates. In so far as this is related to, and is the consequence of,the apparent quickening in the tempo of overall growth (at least during the 1980s), the sluggish response of the Indian economy to the recent structural reform and the marked slow down in the overall growth during the last 3 years is likely to have slowed down employment growth. Data of the 48th Round of the NSS, which should be available shortly, will verify this. If growth rates do not recover and the promised revival of growth to a much higher level than in the past does not materialise, the improvement in employment situation noticed in the 70s and 80s will not be sustained. Under these conditions the employment situation may very well deteriorate. Prudence therefore requires that special employment programmes continue to be given an important role.

However, it is not so much the scale of outlays on these progammes as their efficacy which deserves our attenion. Special employment programmes are but one of the numerous schemes which generate rural employment; moreover they have been far too concerned about creating immediate work unmindful of whether or not they help generate extra work on a continuing basis; and there is a great deal of leakage and mistargeting in their implementation.

The effectiveness of state intervention can be greatly improved and several concrete steps for this purpose can be suggested: (1) Instead of special programmes for employment, basic needs, backward areas and scheduled castes/tribes, the outlays for all local rural development activities should be combined into two pools - one for basic amenities and services and another for augmenting productive capacity of the local rural economy. (2) These pools should be allocated to states, and then on to districts, in proportion to the extent of deficiency in the current availability of services relative to an acceptable minimum (for basic amenities) and the number of poor and unemployed (in the case of productive works). (3) The deployment of these resources at the district level should be left to be decided in the light of local needs and possibilities. (4) In the process, not only will the resources be more effectively targeted to areas where the poor are concentrated but the efficacy of the programmes in terms of raising the productive capacity of the regions and laying the basis for increased employment on a sustained basis will be strengthened. (5) The introduction of democratically elected panchayat raj institutions has a key role in the whole process as it will release space for meaningful local planning and ensure greater accountability.

Wage rates

Between 1964-65 and 1974-75 rural wage rates of male agricultural labour declined as did the number of days of work per worker. This tendency was seen in all major states except UP, Punjab and Haryana. After 1974, real wage rates have risen progressively in practically all states. Available data suggest that employment per agricultural worker has also risen the level in 1983 being invariably higher than in 1974 and in 1977-78 (Table 6).

The data for 1964-65 and 1974-75 are from the rural labour inquiries, while for the latter two the source is the survey of employment and unemployment. Though these are wider in scope, the data relating to wage labour have been separately tabulated; both enquiries have been done by the same organisation (namely the NSS). The date are also more or less comparable in terms of concepts and coverage, at least in respect of rural labour households. Therefore, the apparent break around the mid-70s reflected in the relatively rapid expansion of non-agricultural employment and rise in real wages since that time, compared to the previous decade, deserves to be taken seriously and the underlying reasons examined.

Given that agricultural output and employment are liable to sizeable year to year fluctuations on account of variable weather conditions, we need to be cautious in using point to point comparisons for assessing 'trends'. For instance, it has been said that 1974-75 and 1987-88 being 'poor' agricultural years in terms of weather conditions, output, employment and wage rates would tend to be depressed. While this is true, it is noteworthy that (a) though 1974-75 was a 'below normal' year, output was higher by some 11-12 per cent than in 1974-75; (b) the decline in real wages and employment occurred even in states which had recorded significant increases in output; (c) 1977-78 being a good agriculture year (with output being 27 per cent higher than in 1974-75) should lead one to expect agricultural employment and wages in this year to be considerably better in 1974-75. By the same token since both 1983 and 1987-88 were poor agricultural years (1983 output was no higher and 1987 was barely 10 per cent more than the 1977-78), there should not have been much increase in employment in the subsequent two quinquennia. In point of fact the agricultural employment in 1987-88 was 16 per cent higher than in 1977-78. While employment per worker in 1983 was lower than in 1977-78, it staged a significant recovery in 1987-88 to above 1977-78 levels. Daily earnings on the other hand showed a rise in real terms throughout. Other evidence [Jose 1988] also suggests a general increase in real wage rates during the 70s and 80s after the relative stagnation in the previous decade. Something like a 'phase change' seems to have occurred from the early 1970s both in the structure of employment and in wage rates. This phemomenon deserves to be studied and explicated.

More detailed data on average daily earnings of different categories of wage labour by sex are now available separately for the three quinquennial surveys of employment and unemployment (namely, 1977-78, 1983 and 1987-88). These data have the merit of using an unambiguous concept of wage rate, namely, average daily earnings. In a situation where there are many different forms of labour contracts (cash and kind payments, time and piece rates, the basis on which piece rates are specified) it is impossible to arrive at a meaningful wage rate per unit of time from information regarding the prevailing rates for various types of work. One needs to know how much labour time of different types was spent on each type of work and how much was earned. This is what the NSS has done.

Taking the country as a whole, the average daily earnings (in real terms) of both male and female wage labourers has risen in all categories of employment. The increase between 1977 and 1987 ranged from 21 per cent in the case of casual non-agricultural workers in urban areas to 85 per cent for regular agricultural workers in rural areas. In the case of females, the increase ranges from 38 per cent for casual non-agricultural employment in urban areas to 63 per cent for regular non-agricultural employment in urban areas. The range of variation in the growth of average daily earning is much wider in the case of males than in the case of females (Table 7).

In most states rural wage rates for all categories of male labourers show a progressive rising trend; in the few which do not, the real earnings in 1987-88 are substantially higher than in 1977-78. The picture is similar in respect of rural females working as casual labourers. In urban areas caual wage rates of male workers in non-agricultural activity show a sustained rise only in 10 states; while the others show no sustained trend, the 1987-88 rates are generally higher than a decade earlier. Among regular workers in non-agricultural activities a sustained rise is seen in fewer cases (7 out of 16) but again in all cases the 1987-88 levels are higher than in 1977-78. Real earnings of female workers in regular non-agricultural employment also show a sustained rise in most states; but casual non-agricultural rates are more volatile. Indeed in a few cases 1987-88 rates are lower than in 1977-78 (Table 8 to 11).

The behaviour of the selected indicators of wage structure (namely, relative rates for different kinds of work and workers) shows widely divergent patterns (Table 12). In general the differential between regular and casual wage rates in 1987-88 are higher than in 1977-78 for practically all classes of labour; but only in the case of male agricultural workers in rural areas and urban female non-agricultural workers do we see a progressive rise between the three points of time. In others the ratio dipped in 1983 and rose in 1987-88 or rose in 1983 before dipping in 1987-88.

The time pattern of change is not the same in all cases as between agricultural and non-agricultural labour, or between males and females; much the same is true of the relative wage rates as between rural and urban areas. There is also considerable variation in the extent and even the pattern of changes in wage structure across states. All of which underscores the complexity and hetrogeneity of the labour market. Now that such a rich body of data has become available thanks to the NSS, one hopes that the factors responsible for the disparate behaviour of wages and employment as between different categories of work and workers and across regions will be studied in a systematic manner. We also need to study other changes which seem to be taking place in the labour market - the impact of faster, cheaper transport and the growing importance of casual labour in widening and integrating the rural labour market transcending village boundaries; the changing forms of labour contracts the terms and the mode of payment.

Educated Employment

The picture of overall employment trends contrasts however with a significant deterioration in educated employment. The estimated number of persons with matriculate level education or better is estimated to have risen more than eight-fold between 1961 and 1988. It is estimated that the total stock of this category has risen from 9.5 million to 79 million [Visaria and Minhas 1991]. The distribution of this stock between rural and urban areas has also shifted in favour of the former. The total number of matriculates and above in rural India has risen more than 10-fold, and its share in the country's stock of this category from 26-27 per cent to 40 per cent(Table 13). According to NSS, both the labour force participation rates and unemployment rates of educated persons in 1987-88 is considerably higher than in 1959-60 (Table 14): the number of educated unemployed must have risen considerably faster than the total stock in the country. Educated unemployment in rural areas must have risen considerabley faster than in urban areas. At present rural areas have about 40 per cent of the educated, but more than half of the educated unemployed (Table 15).

There are distinct differences in the job preference of educated workers. In rural areas the majority of them (62 per cent in the case of males and 58 per cent in the female) are self-employed; while in urban areas the large majority work for wages (Table 4). This difference may be partly due to the fact that a higher proportion of rural educated are from families with relatively large landholdings and engaged in cultivating own farms. The fact that they have alternative incomes perhaps also increases their 'reservation price' in respect of wage employment.

Those educated people who have regular wage/salary employment get much higher incomes than their less educated counterparts. In rural areas, the average daily earning of a regular male employee (with matriculation) is estimated at Rs 39.5 per day and that of a graduate Rs 52.3 compared to an average of Rs 17 for all regular employees who are literate up to middle standard. Similar differences are noticed in urban areas, except that the average earning of all classes of regular workers (including educated) is considerably higher than that of their rural counterparts. Much the same pattern is noticed in the case of females as well (Table 16.)

Regular employment is itself differentiated: There working in the organised 'sector' being unionised and also eligible for fringe benefits provided by law, have more secure and better paid jobs. On the average (assuming 250 worker earned in 1987-88 Rs 18,000 per annum (Rs 72 per day of work), and central government enterprise employee Rs 32,500 (Rs 130 per day) compared to an average daily earning of Rs 68 of a graduate with employment in urban areas. Those with regular jobs in the unorganised sector obviously earn considerably less.

The published tabulations of the NSS do not give us the data on organised and unorganised sector employees separately. Nor do they give the distribution of casual wage labourers or of self-employed by level of education and their average earnings. The expectation is that educated persons with casual wage employment will be earning even less than regular employees in the unorganised sector.

The average daily earning of educated regular non-agricultural employee in urban areas rose 2.7 times between 1977-78 and 1987-88; in the same period an annual earnings of a factory work rose 3.1 times, and of central public sector employee by 3.3 times (Table 17). Since the organised sector employment has slowed down in the 80s even as the stock of educated was growing unabated, it is reasonable to infer that employment and earnings of the educated class have been under increasing pressure. This would tend to accentuate the tendency for the educated currently employed in unorganised sector to register themselves with the employment exchanges in the hope of finding better jobs in the organised sector. This as well as the going number of educated unemployed accounts for the phenomenal growth in the number of educated on the live register of employment exchanges.

There are also indications that as the opportunities for wage salary employment are becoming scarcer relative to supply of job seekers, more and more of the educated persons tend to seek to go into self-employment. Thus among matriculate male workers resident in rural areas, the proportion reporting wage employment has fallen from 40 per cent in 1977-78 to 38 per cent in 1987-88; while in urban areas it has fallen from 69 per cent to 62 per cent. Among male graduates the comparable proportion fell from 63 to 52 per cent in urban areas, and from 78 to 71 per cent in rural areas. The increased incidence of self-employment in rural areas probably reflects the growing number of educated people in farming households. In urban areas on the other hand it probably reflects a genuine shift to self employment.

The government has also introduced special programmes to promote self-employment among educated youth and provide them with technical and financial assistance for the purpose. More important, several state governments have sought to accommodate unemployed educated youth by creating temporary jobs in the public sector. Though jobs are created initially on '*ad hoc* temporary' basis, pressures for granting permanent jobs and parity of emoluments with regular staff are generated and sooner or later the governments find it expedient to concede the demands.

The growth of jobs for the educated, as for the rest of the labour force has been mainly in the unorganised sector. The large gap between organised and unorganised sector wages makes the former 'coveted'.

As a consequence, 'market' for public sector jobs had developed and by all accounts become widespread. Educated people seeking such jobs are willing to pay substantial amounts and those responsible for providing them have come to actively seek such payments. The clamour for reservations can also be seen as a strategy on the part of the backward classes to get a fairer share of the jobs than they may get if 'merit' were the sole basis of selection.

Now that the fiscal squeeze has drastically reduced the scope for increasing public employment - if anything the compulsions are to reduce it - the 'market' for public sector jobs may become more active (so long as the differential between the earnings and benifits in public and unorganised sector remains as large as it is currently. However, as fresh recruitment is reduced, if not altogether stopped, the clamour for reservations in public sector jobs will tend to lose their edge. At the same time one may expect more intense agitation on the part of '*ad hoc* temporary' appointees to secure permanence. If liberslisation is sustained and succeeds, we may expect a rapid growth in job opporunities for the educated in the organised private sector. These jobs are currently cornered by the 'elite'among the educated(i.e, those who have the opportunity to get into better staffed, better equipped, more expensive and very likely English medium institutions). If they expand and public sector openings get scarcer, the tension between the educated elite in the urban areas and those who are kept out of this bonanza (mostly from the urban underclass and the rural areas) can be expected to increase. The focus of political agitation may shift to extending the reservation to the private sector. The beginnings of this tendency are manifest in the formulations of some of the political parties.

This tension can be eased only if economic growth is rapid, if education imparts skills which are needed in the economy and the educated overcome the strong cultural aversion for non-white collar work. A massive expansion of vocational education at the matriculate level and above is desirable. The other way to check potential social disruption - apart from rapid growth - is for those who are left out of wage employment seek to strike out on their own. That there are already signs of this happening is a good augury. It would be prudent for the state to follow policies which encourage this tendency. It is also just conceivable that the slack market for educated will dampen the demand for higher education - especially if higher education is made more expensive. Whether these measures will be taken and whether the effect will be large enough to contain the pressures which are building up among the educated classes is a moot question but it is a question which should worry us deeply.

The only effective and lasting solution, to repeat, lies in policies designed to stimulate faster overall development; in interventions (by way of training, credit, infrastrucfure support) to help educated people to take more and more to self-employment; and to pay far greater attention to improving the functional content of education both in terms of imparting skills which are needed in the growing economy, and also of equipping people to upgrade the skills or acquire new skill. The deeper problem of overcoming the strong preference of the educated classes of India for white collar jobs also needs grappling as does the deep and growing chasm among the educated between those who acquire higher education in well equipped institutions teaching in the Engilsh medium and the vast number of universities and teaching shops which are churning out graduates without any usable skills, and who are burdened with a strong sense of inferiority and deprivation.

References

Bhalla, Sheila (1987): 'Trends in Employment in Indian Agriculture, Land Use and Asset Distrubution', *Indian Journal of Agricultural Economics*, *Vol 28, No 38*.

——— (1993): 'Patterns of Employment Generations in India', *Indian Journal of Labour Economics*, *Vol 36 No 4*.

GOI, Planning Commission (1953): *The First Five-Year Plan, (Delhi)*.

——— (1992): *The Eighth Five-Year Plan, (Delhi)*.

GOI, National Sample Survey (1969): Fifteenth Round Report No 156, tables with note on Rural Employment and Unemployment, Delhi. Report No 157, tables with note on urban employment and unemployment, Delhi.

Lakdawala, D T (1977): 'Growth, Unemployment and poverty', presidential address, All-India Labour Economics Conference.

Jose, A V (1988): 'Agricultural Wages in India', *Economic and Political Weekly*, Vol 23, No 39.

Kundu, Amitabh (1993): 'Growth and Changing Structure of Employment in Urban India', *Indian Journal of Labour Econimics*, Vol 36, No 4.

Visaria, Pravin and B S Minhas (1991): 'Evolving an employment Policy for the 90s', *Economic and Political Weekly*, Vol 26, No 15.

Mahendra Dev S, Kirit S Parikh and M H Suryanarayana (1991): 'Rural Poverty in India Incidence, Issues and Policies', Indira Gandhi Institute of Development Research, Bombay.

Vaidyanathan, A (1986): 'Labour Use in Rural India', *Economic and Political Weekly*, Vol 21, No 52.

————— (1990): Cottage and Small Industries in India', Sir Purushothamdas Thakurdas Lecture 1990, Indian Institute of Bankers, Bombay.

TABLE - 1

Estimated Population and Number of Workers, India 1972-73 to 1987-88

	1972-73			1977-78			1983			1987-88		
	M	F	T	M	F	T	M	F	T	M	F	T
Population (10^6)												
Rural	231	220	451	254	241	497	280	266	546	305	288	593
Urban	63	53	116	73	63	137	91	80	171	104	93	197
Total	294	273	567	327	304	632	371	346	717	409	381	790
Unemployment as per cent of labour force												
Usual status												
Rural	1.2	.5		1.3	2.0		1.4	.7		1.8	2.4	
Urban	4.8	6.0		5.4	12.4		5.1	4.9		5.2	6.2	
Current daily status												
Rural	6.8	11.2		7.1	9.1		7.5	9.0		4.6	6.7	
Urban	8	13.7		9.4	14.5		9.2	11.0		8.8	12.0	
No of workers (10^6)												
Rural	126	70	196	140	80	220	153	90	243	164	93	257
Urban	31.6	9.4	41	37.1	9.8	46.9	46.6	12.1	58.7	52.6	14.1	16.7
Total	158	79	237	177	90	267	200	102	302	217	107	324
Non-agricultural workers (10^6)												
Rural	21.2	7.2	28.4	27.2	9.5	36.7	34.4	12.2	45.6	41.8	14.2	56
Urban	28.2	6.3	34.5	33.2	6.7	39.9	41.8	8.3	50.1	47.8	10	57.8
Total	49.5	13.5	62.9	60.4	16.2	76.6	76.2	19.5	95.7	98.1	113.8	

Note: These estimates are derived by applying the overall workforce participation ratio (by sex) in rural and urban areas reported in various rounds of the NSS to the official estimates of rural and urban populations, by sex for the corresponding years.

TABLE - 2

Estimated Person Days of Employment in India, 1972-73 to 1987-88

(10^9 persondays)

	1972-73	1977-78	1983	1987-88
All workers[1]				
Rural	60.8	62.3	68.5	77.6
Urban	13.1	15.0	18.8	21.8
Total	73.9	77.3	87.1	98.4
Rural workers 15-59				
Agriculture	40.3[2]	42.0[2]	49.1[3]	
Non-Agriculture	11.3	10.8	na	18.4
Total	51.6	52.8		67.5

Notes:

1 Estimated by applying current daily participation rates (which gives no of days employment per person) to the official population estimates for respective years.

2 Vaidyanathan (1986).

3 Computed from distribution of estimated person days, by age, sex and activity per 1,000 persons in 1987-88 as given in *Sarvekshana,* September 1990.

TABLE - 3

Sectoral Distribution Per 000 Workers in Rural and Urban Areas At Different Points of Time

	Male				Female			
	59-60	72-73	77-78	87-88	59-60	72-73	77-78	87-88
Rural								
Agriculture	787	832	806	745	8.21	897	881	847
Mining	12.1	.4	5	7	8.7	2	2	4
Manufacturing	74.4	57	64	74	82	47	59	69
Electricity	1.3	1	2	3	2.5	-	-	-
Construction	21.2	16	17	37	10.1	11	6	27
Trade	36.3	31	40	51	19.4	15	20	21
Transport	12	10	12	20	1.0	-	1	1
Services	40.6	48	53	62	40.9	28	30	30
Others[1]	15.1				18.4			
Urban								
Agriculture	134.7	107	106	91	249.7	328	319	294
Mining	4.6	10	9	13	6.2	7	5	8
Manufacturing	306.7	269	276	257	328.4	250	296	270
Electricity	5.1	8	11	12	8.1	1	1	2
Construction	35.9	43	42	58	22.5	33	22	37
Trade	170	201	216	215	53.4	94	87	98
Transport	89.2	90	98	97	7.5	9	10	9
Services	223.9	270	243	252	269.8	270	260	278
Others[1]	29.9				54.4			

Notes: 1 Not recorded or inadequately specified.

Source: 1959-60, NSSO report Nos 156, 157. Other years various issues of *Sarvekshana.*

TABLE - 4

Incidence of Wage Employment, India 1972-73 to 1987-88

	1972-73			1977-78			1983			1987-88		
	M	F	T	M	F	T	M	F	T	M	F	T
Wage and Salary employees as per cent of all workers												
Rural	34.7	34.5	34.6	37.2	37.9	37.5	37.6	38.1	39.0	41.2	39.1	40.6
Urban	61.8	51.6	59.0	59.6	50.5	57.6	59.1	54.2	58.1	58.4	52.9	57.2
Casual wage[1] labour as per cent of all wage and salary employment												
Rural	64.5	88.0	78.4	69.4	92.6	79.2	71.2	92.7	80.8	74.8	90.8	81.0
Urban	16.7	46.0	21.6	22.1	50.7	27.6	26.1	52.4	31.3	25.3	48.0	29.7
Wage and salary[2,3] employment among educated workers (percentage)												
Matriculates												
Rural	40	69	40	41	38	42						
Urban	69	86	65	75	62	67						
Graduates												
Rural	63	58	52									
Urban	78	74	71									

*Notes:*1 NSS, various reports.

2 Mahendra Dev et al(1991) and Kundu(1993).

3 In 1959-60, according to NSS, the percentage of workers with matriculation or higher education who were categorised as employees was:

	Rural	Urban
Male	50.0	61.3
Female	66.5	69.4
All	56.7	62.7

TABLE - 5

Distribution of Total Non-Agricultural Employment in Organised and Unorganised Sectors

(in million)

	1972-73	1977-78	1983	1987-88
Total workers[1]	63	77	96	114
Employees total	39	45	56	66
Organised	17.0	20.7	24.1	25.4
Public	11.3	13.8	16.5	18.0
Private	6.7	6.9	7.6	7.4

Notes: 1 See Table 1.

2 Estimated on the basis of data reproportion of rural and urban non-agricultural workers by sex reporting self-employment [Mahendra Dev et al 1991 and Kundu 1993].

TABLE - 6

Average Employment Per Year and Daily Earnings of Male Agricultural Workers, Major States 1964-65 to 1987-88

State	1964-65 Employment	RW	1974-75 Employment	RW	1977-78 Employment	RW	1983 Employment	RW	1987-88 Employment	RW
Andhra Pradesh	204	0.97	193	0.82	213	1.15	218	1.50		1.81
Assam	282	1.69	304	1.18	309	1.62	335	1.77		2.09
Bihar	198	0.93	186	0.82	265	1.03	258	1.15		1.45
Gujrat	278	1.11	206	1.02	234	1.44	251	1.79		1.57
Haryana	—	—	203	1.44	324	1.73	235	2.42		2.36
Jammu and Kashmir	—	—	189	1.59	201	1.83	216	2.21		2.45
Karnataka	228	0.83	204	0.83	—	1.00	226	1.12		1.47
Kerala	228	1.60	138	1.57	171	2.15	197	2.79		3.30
Madhya Pradesh	173	0.80	198	0.63	248	0.79	247	0.96		1.26
Maharashtra	212	0.97	221	0.72	229	0.98	211	1.30		1.53
Orissa	224	0.93	164	0.67	219	0.91	219	0.97		1.18
Punjab	282	1.53	233	1.91	260	2.20	245	2.53		2.75
Rajasthan	210	1.33	239	0.99	186	1.39	230	1.73		2.02
Tamil Nadu	194	1.01	148	0.90	193	1.26	188	1.42		1.70
Uttar Pradesh	189	0.67	200	0.84	213	1.06	232	1.22		1.48
West Bengal	269	1.33	210	1.03	242	1.32	216	1.66		1.92
All-India	217	1.00	193	0.88	229	1.16	227	1.39		1.72

Notes: RW- Real Wages Rs/day Employment: No of days of employment in agriculture per male agricultural worker.

Money wages at current prices have been deflated by CPIAL for these years to get real wages, at 1960-61 prices.

Punjab is inclusive of Haryana and HP 1964-65.

Similar Data suggest that in 4 out of 16 states real wage rates for female rose in a sustained way since 1974-75 and 7 others 1983 rates were higher than in 1974-75. No. of days worked per worker rose in 11 out of 16 states.

TABLE - 7

Trends in Average Daily Earnings of Different Categories of Wage Labourers, India

(Rs/day at 1960-61 prices)

Categories Of Labour	Adult Male			Adult Female		
	1977-78	*1983*	*1987-88*	*1977-78*	*1983*	*1987-88*
Regular						
Agriculture						
Rural	1.21	1.44	2.24	1.22	1.83	1.64
Non-agriculture						
Rural	3.25	3.08	5.37	2.49	2.08	4.04
Urban	4.70	4.46	5.85	3.07	3.26	4.85
Casual						
Agriculture						
Rural	1.18	1.38	1.73	0.82	0.94	1.14
Non-agriculture						
Rural	1.63	1.98	2.42	0.88	0.98	1.40
Urban	2.05	2.05	2.49	0.97	1.00	1.34

Notes: The estimates of average daily earnings in current prices are taken from NSS reports.

The nominal earnings in each year have been divided by the consumer price index for Agricultural labourers (1960-61 : 100) in the case of rural areas and cost of living index for industrial workers (base 1960-61) in the case of urban areas.

Note that regular employment is a relatively rare phenomena among rural females, in urban areas the incidence of both regular and casual wage employment in agriculture is very small for both sexes. For this reason we omit urban agriculture from the comparison. Comparisons with regular female agricultral workers in rural areas also calls for caution.

TABLE - 8
Average Wage/Salary Earnings Per Day Received by an Adult Male Labour

(Rs)

States	Agricultural Labour						Non-Agricultural Labour						Consumer Price Index for Agricultural Labour (Base: 1960-61=100)		
	Regular			Casual			Regular			Casual					
	77-78	83-84	87-88	77-78	83-84	87-88	77-78	83-84	87-88	77-78	83-84	87-88	77-78	83-84	87-88
	(1)	(2)	(3)	(4)	(5)	(6)	(7)	(8)	(9)	(10)	(11)	(12)			
Andhra Pradesh	3.11	5.01	11.54	3.64	6.47	9.73	8.60	11.38	37.72	4.42	8.08	13.47	2.97	4.36	5.37
Assam	5.17	10.42	17.28	5.23	10.81	13.77	12.55	22.78	40.39	5.50	17.20	17.25	3.15	5.37	6.64
Bihar	3.80	5.74	10.01	3.51	6.35	9.99	10.67	17.43	33.88	4.61	10.16	14.11	3.41	5.64	6.91
Gujarat	5.67	8.96	11.94	4.06	7.61	9.42	12.07	19.04	37.82	5.90	15.21	13.28	2.85	4.51	5.79
Haryana	5.64	10.14	16.32	5.99	11.95	16.40	9.85	25.31	36.78	6.03	12.68	17.31			
Himachal Pradesh	11.14	13.51	30.29	6.10	9.49	16.08	14.57	27.91	39.10	6.30	9.67	16.97			
Jammu and Kashmir	6.46	9.27	28.95	5.98	12.04	15.82	9.61	18.24	34.82	5.64	11.46	17.72	3.42	5.34	6.86
Karnataka	3.83	7.15	11.92	3.12	5.64	9.13	10.53	17.03	35.03	4.37	8.74	11.84	3.08	5.25	6.18
Kerala	7.02	13.34	28.58	6.73	14.94	23.34	11.54	22.99	40.34	6.89	16.25	25.79	3.17	5.85	7.06
Madhya Pradesh	2.79	5.12	8.42	2.90	4.94	8.16	9.63	10.59	29.84	7.20	7.49	11.48	3.45	5.26	6.53
Maharashtra	3.32	6.12	14.97	3.18	6.50	9.77	9.90	14.18	33.90	4.63	7.78	14.21	3.20	5.09	6.33
Orissa	3.02	5.38	10.54	3.14	5.89	8.47	9.39	12.02	30.87	3.80	6.84	10.04	3.51	6.01	7.18
Punjab	6.79	11.46	17.29	7.68	12.47	18.93	12.00	17.66	33.36	7.85	22.53	20.81	3.32	5.14	6.83
Rajasthan	4.49	7.97	12.96	4.56	7.88	13.48	11.24	17.47	33.26	5.44	13.53	12.60	3.26	4.72	6.64
Tamil Nadu	3.46	8.66	10.83	3.96	7.21	10.83	9.09	13.61	26.30	4.51	8.39	13.46	3.06	5.28	6.37
Uttar Pradesh	3.28	7.66	11.81	3.77	6.45	10.42	9.87	14.00	31.86	5.38	8.89	15.47	3.36	5.25	7.05
West Bengal	4.65	9.00	12.78	4.25	9.16	12.53	11.65	19.48	35.19	5.56	10.68	14.62	3.21	5.25	6.50
All-India	3.91	7.53	14.58	3.81	7.21	11.24	10.49	16.08	34.90	5.26	10.32	15.73	3.23	5.22	6.50

Source: National Sample Survey, various issues of *Sarvekshana*.

TABLE - 9

Average Wage/Salary Earnings Per Day Received by an Adult Female Labour

(Rs)

| States | Agricultural Labour | | | | | | Non-Agricultural Labour | | | | | | Consumer Price Index for Agricultural Labour (Base: 1960-61=100) | | |
| | Regular | | | Casual | | | Regular | | | Casual | | | | | |
	77-78 (1)	83-84 (2)	87-88 (3)	77-78 (4)	83-84 (5)	87-88 (6)	77-78 (7)	83-84 (8)	87-88 (9)	77-78 (10)	83-84 (11)	87-88 (12)	77-78	83-84	87-88
Andhra Pradesh	1.98	3.61	9.99	2.34	4.34	6.15	4.74	7.04	23.39	2.92	5.27	7.53	2.97	4.36	5.37
Assam	4.52	17.46	13.57	5.16	8.39	11.87	10.20	21.54	31.06	4.35	6.27	10.52	3.15	5.37	6.64
Bihar	2.97	4.20	9.29	3.17	5.53	8.41	5.76	11.60	33.37	2.88	4.90	9.23	3.41	5.64	6.91
Gujarat	2.33	5.98	10.40	3.61	6.62	8.96	36.73	12.00	30.64	3.62	7.41	9.34	2.85	4.51	5.79
Haryana	3.00	7.00	16.76	4.84	12.09	13.13	4.06	7.72	14.41	3.93	7.92	16.09			
Himachal Pradesh	0.00	6.84	0.00	4.35	6.28	13.71	13.34	28.76	34.93	4.62	8.20	17.12			
Jammu and Kashmir	10.00	21.40	20.93	4.30	5.79	17.04	8.92	32.25	30.12	5.57	11.27	11.73	3.42	5.34	6.86
Karnataka	4.59	5.55	7.71	2.03	4.02	5.81	6.41	6.24	22.84	2.76	4.14	7.65	3.08	5.25	6.18
Kerala	7.14	11.76	24.58	4.22	10.00	15.39	10.68	16.31	32.97	3.23	6.46	10.99	3.17	5.85	7.06
Madhya Pradesh	1.98	4.02	6.87	2.74	4.19	6.74	3.79	4.10	17.42	2.58	5.34	8.58	3.45	5.26	6.53
Maharashtra	2.23	3.64	8.23	1.99	3.80	5.96	6.01	10.66	23.79	2.40	4.59	7.68	3.20	5.09	6.33
Orissa	2.11	5.26	6.41	2.35	4.51	6.17	7.26	12.87	19.43	2.33	5.02	7.00	3.51	6.01	7.18
Punjab	2.64	4.04	10.81	5.09	9.70	14.51	9.18	10.56	29.36	4.59	6.65	10.73	3.32	5.14	6.83
Rajasthan	2.94	3.20	11.51	3.16	5.30	9.37	6.85	7.61	19.64	3.38	5.63	8.68	3.26	4.72	6.64
Tamil Nadu	2.98	8.35	6.53	2.29	3.93	6.14	7.23	9.61	13.91	2.39	3.82	6.77	3.06	5.28	6.37
Uttar Pradesh	2.29	4.59	6.85	2.73	5.08	7.79	6.63	7.39	21.72	3.26	5.01	9.43	3.36	5.25	7.05
West Bengal	5.70	8.19	13.81	3.46	7.79	10.76	4.20	8.00	15.20	2.61	5.33	8.02	3.21	5.25	6.50
All-India	3.94	9.53	10.65	2.64	4.89	7.43	8.05	10.85	26.28	2.83	5.10	9.11	3.23	5.22	6.50

Source: National Sample Survey, various issues of *Sarvekshana*.

TABLE - 10

Average Wage/Salary Earnings Per Day Received by an Adult Male Labour (Urban)

(Rs)

States	Agricultural Labour						Non-Agricultural Labour						Consumer Price Index for Agricultural Labour (Base: 1960-61=100)		
	Regular			Casual			Regular			Casual					
	77-78	83-84	87-88	77-78	83-84	87-88	77-78	83-84	87-88	77-78	83-84	87-88	77-78	83-84	87-88
	(1)	(2)	(3)	(4)	(5)	(6)	(7)	(8)	(9)	(10)	(11)	(12)			
Andhra Pradesh	5.05	4.72	31.08	3.90	7.44	10.70	13.72	20.37	37.75	5.25	9.58	14.22	3.29	5.14	7.05
Assam	10.99	18.01	45.87	5.31	10.00	15.70	15.65	25.21	46.25	6.90	8.97	23.08	2.87	4.53	5.89
Bihar	4.79	6.49	14.84	4.07	8.20	11.97	15.28	27.76	45.00	6.19	8.72	17.40	3.29	5.39	6.84
Gujarat	6.66	15.82	25.57	5.23	7.62	10.60	14.62	23.74	40.99	6.43	11.64	17.12	3.11	5.36	7.43
Haryana	6.32	19.86	32.73	5.30	10.54	15.67	12.82	23.54	41.69	7.80	12.51	19.03	3.44	5.43	7.31
Himachal Pradesh	4.76	19.83		11.00		18.57	18.51	31.80	55.64	7.23	13.66	22.52			
Jammu and Kashmir	12.99	20.81	39.67	7.11	14.09	21.22	12.52	23.33	39.84	6.77	12.89	22.75	3.18	5.60	7.97
Karnataka	6.72	6.82	18.95	3.55	7.08	10.05	14.35	23.90	42.12	5.05	9.54	15.76	3.35	5.44	7.31
Kerala	9.88	19.93	25.17	6.08	16.84	25.11	14.93	24.78	41.62	7.13	17.17	24.91	3.13	5.59	7.58
Madhya Pradesh	5.23	11.05	17.39	3.63	5.91	13.23	13.44	20.25	41.54	5.14	8.92	14.80	3.40	5.55	7.70
Maharashtra	5.25	12.45	18.36	3.62	7.37	10.33	17.30	26.26	44.48	6.69	10.65	17.16	3.16	5.51	7.39
Orissa	5.16	8.34	23.16	4.26	6.74	10.24	14.12	23.21	42.01	4.58	10.18	12.28	3.22	5.52	6.94
Punjab	8.57	16.17	25.82	8.12	15.84	22.99		21.88	38.48	14.17	14.51	22.51	3.36	5.26	7.18
Rajasthan	6.60	9.12	20.84	5.75	11.61	10.55	13.47	20.29	43.13	6.75	11.38	15.97	3.37	5.41	7.38
Tamil Nadu	5.65	10.95	19.78	4.76	8.69	12.73	13.23	21.19	32.98	5.49	11.50	16.92	3.16	5.63	7.50
Uttar Pradesh	8.47	16.64	25.60	5.24	7.81	11.91	14.14	21.58	38.72	6.20	10.01	17.15	3.43	5.48	7.47
West Bengal	6.02	8.98	29.15	4.88	11.19	14.79	15.21	26.43	42.16	7.33	10.47	17.36	3.07	4.78	6.50
All-India	6.28	12.59	27.57	4.47	8.54	13.08	15.10	23.72	42.07	6.57	10.89	17.89	3.21	5.32	7.19

Source: National Sample Survey, various issues of *Sarvekshana.*

TABLE - 11

Average Wage/Salary Earnings Per Day Received by an Adult Female Labour (Urban)

(Rs)

States	Agricultural Labour						Non-Agricultural Labour						Consumer Price Index for Agricultural Labour (Base: 1960-61=100)		
	Regular			Casual			Regular			Casual					
	77-78	83-84	87-88	77-78	83-84	87-88	77-78	83-84	87-88	77-78	83-84	87-88	77-78	83-84	87-88
	(1)	(2)	(3)	(4)	(5)	(6)	(7)	(8)	(9)	(10)	(11)	(12)			
Andhra Pradesh	2.46	3.49	7.14	2.65	4.48	6.38	7.18	14.98	26.94	3.29	5.04	7.29	3.29	5.14	7.05
Assam	4.86			4.04			12.84	21.08	33.62	6.40	6.12	12.29	2.87	4.53	5.89
Bihar	2.67		10.00	3.19	4.12	10.12	8.94	20.76	39.43	4.62	5.02	11.24	3.29	5.39	6.84
Gujarat	3.00	21.43	11.00	4.06	7.33	11.06	8.00	19.18	35.49	3.53	7.84	9.78	3.11	5.36	7.43
Haryana				4.52	11.10	12.00	10.34	21.91	37.85	3.73	6.78	9.61	3.44	5.43	7.31
Himachal Pradesh				2.00			14.70	32.16	47.92	3.33	8.20	10.00			
Jammu and Kashmir	4.10	7.50	45.38	3.97	14.59		11.01	23.05	40.40	3.99	11.54	9.88	3.18	5.60	7.97
Karnataka			8.00	2.37	4.22	6.34	9.48	16.17	35.42	2.73	4.74	7.54	3.35	5.44	7.31
Kerala			16.00	5.04	12.17	18.96	10.86	20.45	38.72	2.69	8.85	12.74	3.13	5.59	7.58
Madhya Pradesh	3.08	3.76	11.79	2.69	5.74	8.40	8.22	11.84	33.83	3.02	5.78	10.29	3.40	5.55	7.70
Maharashtra	4.06	10.47	8.89	1.94	4.05	6.46	11.07	20.78	34.80	3.05	4.39	10.75	3.16	5.51	7.39
Orissa	4.00	6.20		2.65	5.46	8.35	9.28	13.17	36.17	2.42	5.05	8.89	3.22	5.52	6.94
Punjab	0.52	15.00		5.36	7.10	15.43	13.13	22.03	37.98	3.64	10.50	12.33	3.36	5.26	7.18
Rajasthan	1.43	8.79	10.00	3.42	5.56	8.71	10.55	13.96	32.93	3.62	5.35	12.67	3.37	5.41	7.38
Tamil Nadu	5.88	11.55	18.48	2.97	4.78	7.23	9.62	13.40	21.19	2.59	4.51	8.08	3.16	5.63	7.50
Uttar Pradesh	6.00	9.36		3.13	6.05	7.63	9.17	14.82	32.24	3.22	5.27	10.19	3.43	5.48	7.47
West Bengal	3.21	6.46		3.96	8.09	8.57	8.19	15.20	31.75	3.47	6.31	8.12	3.07	4.78	6.50
All-India	5.32	9.79	19.05	2.81	5.03	7.63	9.87	17.36	34.90	3.12	5.30	9.65	3.21	5.32	7.19

Source: National Sample Survey, various issues of *Sarvekshana.*

TABLE - 12

Indicators of Changes in the Structure of Wage Rates

		Rural		
Relative Wage Rates		*1977-78*	*1983*	*1987-88*
Regular to causal				
Agriculture: rural	M	1.03	1.04	1.30
	F	1.49	1.95	1.43
Non-agriculture:rural	M	1.99	1.56	2.22
	F	2.84	2.13	2.88
Agriculture to non-agriculture	M	0.37	0.47	0.42
	F	0.49	0.88	0.41
Casual agriculture to casual				
non-agriculture: rural	M	0.72	0.70	0.71
	F	0.93	0.96	0.82
Regular to casual				
Urban Non-agriculture	M	2.3	2.18	2.35
	F	3.16	3.28	3.62
Wage rates in urban areas relative to rural areas				
Regular,non-agriculture	M	1.44	1.48	1.21
	F	1.23	1.60	1.33
Casual non-agriculture	M	1.25	1.06	1.14
	F	1.1	1.04	1.06
Relative wage rates of male to female				
Regular agriculture:rural	0.99		0.79	1.37
Regular non-agriculture:rural	1.3		1.48	1.33
Regular non-agriculture:urban	1.53		1.37	1.21
Casual agriculture:rural	1.44		1.47	1.51
Casual non-agriculture:rural	1.86		2.02	1.73
Casual non-agriculture:urban	2.11		2.05	1.85

TABLE - 13

Stock of Educated Persons in Rural and Urban India, 1961 and 1988

(10^6)

		Matriculates		degree Holders	
		1961	*1988*	*1961*	*1988*
Rural	Male	2.3	20.5	NA	3.6
	Female	0.2	6.3	na	0.9
	Total	2.5	27.1	na	4.5
Urban	Male	4.7	24.9	1.0	7.6
	Female	1.1	13.5	0.2	1.7
	Total	5.8	38.3	1.2	9.3

Note: According to NSS in 1959-60, the number of persons with education of matriculation and above level in rural areas accounted for 29 per cent of the total stock of this category in the country. The corresponding percentage in 1961 according to the census works out to 26 per cent.

Source: Visaria and Minhas (1991).

TABLE - 14

Unemployment Rates[1] by Education Level in Rural and Urban India 1987-88

		Not Literate	Literate					Total
			Primary	Middle	Secondary	Graduates		
Rural M	LPR	991	889	727	742	901		864
	UER	9	21.4	53.6	105.1	149.8		28.9
Rural F	LPR	424	284	204	263	399		377
	UER	24	35.2	37	335	373		36
Urban M	LPR	871	867	727	707	864		802
	UER	18	46	88	88	74		60
Urban F	LPR	235	141	102	162	377		192
	UER	21	64	216	228	210		89

Notes: 1. Relates to usual status and to persons aged 15 years or more. LPR - Labour force participation rate per 000 persons.

UER - Unemployment rate per 000 of those in the labour force.

2. According to NSS, the overall work participation rate of people with matriculation or higher level education and their unemployment rate (as per cent of the labour force in this category) in 1959-60 was as follows:

	Rural		Urban	
	M	F	M	F
WPR	65.1	35.4	66.9	21.9
UER	9.2	29.8	6.1	15.0

Source: *Sarvekshana*, September 1990.

TABLE - 15

Distribution of Educated Unemployed, 1987-88

(Million)

	Rural			Urban			Total
	Male	Female	Total	Male	Female	Total	
1987-88[1]							
Secondary	.85	.38	1.23	.71	.25	.96	2.19
Graduates	.31	.09	.40	.34	.21	.55	.95
Secondary plus graduates	1.16	.47	1.63	1.05	.46	1.51	3.14
1959-60[2]							
Matriculates+			0.145			.206	.351

Notes: 1. Computed from official population estimates and NSS estimates of unemployment rates by education level as reported in *Sarvekshana*, September 1990.

2. NSS report Nos 156 and 157

TABLE - 16

Average Daily Earning of Regular Employees by Level of Education, 1987-88

(Rs/day)

	Not Literate	Literate			Agri-culture	Non-Agriculture
		Up to Middle	Secondary	Graduates and above		
Rural male	15.0	25.2	39.5	52.3	14.6	34.9
Urban male	24.2	28.9	45.9	67.9		42.1
Rural female	9.7	17.2	35.2	45.7	10.6	26.3
Urban female	14.3	19.4	38.5	55.5		34.9

Source: Sarvekshana, special issue, September 1990.

TABLE - 17

Average Earnings of Different Categories of Non-Agricultural Workers with Regular Employment, India

(Rs at current prices)

	1977-78	1983	1987-88
Male workers Rural[1]	5.3	15.3	15.7
Urban[1]	6.6	10.9	17.9
Registered factory[2]	5900	11788	18076
Central public undertakings[2]	10048	24328	32537

Notes: 1. NSS from various issues of *Sarvekshana* earnings per day.

     2. Centre for Monitoring of Indian Economy relates to average annual earning.

This paper is the author's Professor Lakdawala Memorial Lecture delivered at the Gujarat Economic Association Annual Confernce in Valleb Vidya Nagar in May 1994.

12

10th Finance Commission Report (1995-2000)

I

FRAMEWORK AND APPROACH

Introduction

Our approach has been guided by the paramount need to restore fiscal equilibrium in the economy. Our recommendations have been in formed by our Constitutional responsibilities, the terms of reference, the budgetary scenario of the Centre and the States, the emerging issues in federal finance, and the evolving macroeconomic policy environment.

The period covered by our recommendations will witness the completion of half a century of fiscal federalism. Federal relations, as envisaged in the Constitution, have evolved over the years through political, institutional and functional changes. In this changing scenario, the Finance Commission, as an institution, has had an important role to play as resource sharing, based on a Constitutional division of functions and finances, is a critical element in the federal system.

While the charter of the Commission flows from the Constitution itself, the terms of references of each Commission have reflected some of the dominant concerns in the area of Centre-State relations and the emerging issues in national public finance. It is, therefore, not surprising that our terms of reference mirror the anxiety regarding the finances of the country and have been influenced by the systemic changes in the economic regime that have been initiated since 1991.

The whole gamut of policy changes is reflective of a change in the nature, content and extent of state intervention. The outcome of these changes will edge into view in the period which coincides with the period of our recommendations. Another dimension has been added by the 73rd and 74th amendments to the Constitution which have brought into being a third tier in the federal structure. It is these changes that provide the context for our recommendations and, in conjunction, with our concern for equity and efficiency, delineate the contours of our approach.

CENTRE AND STATE FINANCES: ANALYTICAL OVERVIEW

The macroeconomic vulnerability of the economy is linked in no small measure to the secular deterioration in its fiscal balance. The magnitude of aggregate deficits - revenue and fiscal - had reached levels in the late eighties that set the economy on a medium term path of stagflation and a recurring balance of payments problem.

From a revenue surplus the economy moved into a state of continuous deficit on revenue account in 1982-83. While in 1975-76 there was a revenue surplus of about 2.5 per cent of Gross Domestic Product (GDP), in 1990-91 revenue deficit reached 3.6 per cent and is estimated to be about 5 per cent of GDP in 1993-94. This rise has been even faster than that in the fiscal deficit which increased from 6 per cent in 1974-75 to about 12 per cent in 1990-91. It is estimated to be 11.5 per cent in 1993-94. A graphical presentation of the trends and pattern in the finances of the Centre and the States is at Appendix 1.

The change in the fiscal regime in 1982-83 - from revenue surplus to revenue deficit - has meant that what was earlier a non-debt creating source of financing has become a source of rising internal indebtedness. In other words, while revenue receipts used to cover a part of the capital expenditure, now an increasing part of the capital receipts are used to finance revenue expenditure. The consequent build up of public debt and the interest burden, which is now the largest and fastest growing item of expenditure, further fuelled the growth of revenue expenditure. This led to a spiral of growing deficits, rising debt, escalating interest costs, and further expansion of deficit.

The statement that deficits have emerged because of differential rates of growth of revenue receipts and expenditures is tautological. It is, however, of prescriptive value to note that the total revenue receipts as a proportion of GDP increased from about 12 per cent in 1960-61 to 27.4 per cent in 1987-88. Thereafter it has levelled off. A major part of the increase is accounted for by a sustained improvement in tax revenues while the potential for exploiting the sources of non-tax revenues has remained largely untapped. During the same period the tax/gdp ratio of the economy more than doubled from 8.3 per cent to 17 per cent which is impressive at the prevailing levels of per capita income. Thus, the principal factor underlying the fiscal imbalance is the unbridled growth of government expenditure.

The accelerating growth of revenue expenditure is a recent phenomenon. Till the mid-seventies revenue expenditure as a percentage of GDP remained constant at about 15 per cent. In fact, in the early seventies, aggregate government expenditure was actually declining in real terms. Thereafter, till 1987-88 it increased exponentially to reach 27 per cent of GDP - the real rate of growth being close to double digit during this period. After 1987-88 revenue expenditure as a percentage of GDP has remained stable at about 27 per cent. This appears to be in line with the behaviour of revenue expenditure over the last three decades during which it has increased in steps. The structure of expenditure has imparted downward rigidity and inflexibility to its level in recent years. Interest, and wages and salaries have emerged as the major components of expenditure as a direct result of the mode of financing of expenditure and the expansionary policies pursued by government. These two items are at any given point of time "committed expenditure" which can be curtailed only in the medium term. This has made expenditure more income elastic than revenue receipts thereby generating an in built tendency towards deficits. As a result the economy has moved away from resource based fiscal management to expenditure based budgeting.

From a diagnostic point of view, it is important to analyse the profile of deficits and their composition across levels of government. In the case of the Central Government, the revenue deficit increased from 0.2 per cent of GDP in 1981-82 to 3.5 per cent of GDP in 1990-91. It is estimated to be 4.3 per cent in 1994-95. The fiscal deficit for the corresponding period increased from 5.4 per cent to 8.4 per cent. Apart from the increase in magnitude, a disturbing aspect relates to the financing of fiscal deficit. Over the years, especially since 1991, the monetised deficit has been reduced significantly. Without a corresponding reduction in the fiscal deficit the proportion of other forms of borrowings has increased. The implication of this change is that the unit cost of financing government expenditure is increasing. This is of particular concern because revenue deficit as a proportion of fiscal deficit is also rising and this underlines the need for reducing the revenue deficit and the fiscal deficit along with a reduction in monetised deficit.

The higher cost of financing government expenditure will make its impact felt on expenditure by increasing the burden of interest payments. This is so because borrowings are financing such revenue expenditure as cannot possibly yield financial returns and a fair amount of capital expenditure which yields inadequate returns. In other words, it is the burden of interest payments arising out of the none too prudent use of borrowings that lies at the root of the fiscal malaise. This is borne out by the fact that the primary fiscal balance (i.e. fiscal balance net of interest payments) of the Central Government has turned surplus after 1991-92.

At the aggregate level, the combined accounts of the State Governments exhibit a similar picture of increasing revenue deficits though the deficits emerge on a secular basis from 1987-88. While the share of States in total revenue deficit of the economy has increased, its share in fiscal deficit has remained constant perhaps on account of their inability, unlike the Centre, to finance the expenditure-revenue gap through borrowings.

It is important to recognise that there is a pattern in the transition from healthy revenue surpluses that the system used to generate to chronic deficits. This becomes evident by disaggregating the revenue account into plan and non-plan. The plan revenue account has been in marginal deficit till the early eighties. Thereafter it has increased in response to the plan size. On the other hand, the non-plan account has been in surplus till 1990-91.

Almost all States have gone through a three phase deterioration in the revenue account balance. In the first phase up to 1986-87, the non-plan account surplus was larger than the plan deficit and to that the extent it was yielding an overall revenue surplus. Between 1986-87 and 1991-92 the magnitude of plan revenue deficit increased sharply and it became larger than the non-plan surplus which itself had been declining. The third and final phase started in 1991-92 when the non-plan revenue account went into deficit. That all States have had almost identical turning points seems to suggest that there are systemic factors underlying this deterioration rather than State specific reasons.

The magnitude of the fiscal problem can be gauged by the level of deficits projected in the Central and State forecasts submitted to us. It is significant to note that the Centre did not project a crisis of resource availability to the Ninth Commission. There was a clear break with the past when the Finance Ministry submitted a forecast which showed a pre-devolution deficit on the revenue account. Again, for the first time not a single State has submitted a forecast showing a pre-devolution surplus on the non-plan revenue account. Thus the problem posed to us was far worse than that faced by earlier Commissions.

Macroeconomic Stabilisation and Structural Reforms

The stabilisation and structural adjustment programme of the Centre was initiated in response to the situation of fiscal disequilibrium which reached crisis proportions in 1991. The components of the reform package are : deregulating industry, activist monetary management, gradual dismantling of the complex protective trade regime, a liberal policy towards foreign investment, strengthening the capital markets, restructuring the tax system, full convertibility on current account and an efficiency oriented hard budget approach towards the public sector. The overhauling and restructuring of the financial sector, which is the bridge between macro stabilisation and structural adjustment, is still under way.

The reforms aim at tackling a series of macroeconomic imbalances, both external and internal. The components of the reform, which are of particular relevance to government finances, are the policies relating to tax reform and reduction in fiscal deficit. Tax reform has revolved around simplification of procedures and reduction in rates of income and corporation tax, selective reduction in excise duties and a substantial reduction in customs duties. The premise is that the stimulus to growth provided by tax reforms and better compliance will more than offset the loss of revenues on account of lower rates.

The reduction in fiscal deficit was expected to come about both through improved revenue receipts and reduced revenue expenditure. However, in the face of temporary shortfalls in revenue and the inflexibility displayed by revenue expenditure in the short run, the fiscal deficit has been reduced primarily by compressing capital expenditure. Thus, contrary to expectation, the fall-out has been an increasing revenue deficit and reduced capital expenditure.

In the case of States, the rising revenue deficit has also cut into maintenance expenditure in the revenue budget. In order to accommodate the rising interest payments and the growth of wages and salaries, which have come to be regarded as committed expenditure, maintenance expenditure has been treated as a residual item. This has had a visible impact on infrastructure. The deteriorating conditions of roads, poorly maintained hospitals, neglected school and administrative buildings have together become a formidable supply side constraint on growth. Most assets like power stations, irrigation systems, and highways are operating at levels well below their capacity on account of poor maintenance and continual neglect.

Clearly, any attempt to curtail the growth of expenditure must be accompanied by measures to protect essential expenditure on maintenance of existing infrastructure and creation of new capacities. This requires a change in the emphasis and priorities of government expenditure. Development of physical and human infrastructure is also essential if the market oriented process of development, with its emphasis on competition and private investment, is not to bypass many States and sectors. If such development does not take place, regional inequalities are bound to accentuate. Quite paradoxically, expenditure priorities of States have in a number of ways tended to reinforce rather than reduce inter-regional disparities.

The long term implication of this will be that the resource raising capacity of States will be differentially affected. While to some extent this can be addressed through a greater degree of progressivity in transfers to States, the primary responsibility for strengthening the resource base is that of the States. The States will have to make continuous efforts to improve their revenue base, strengthen their capacity to provide better services and curtail expenditures.

As for receipts, States should initiate restructuring of the tax system through rationalisation of the complex multilayered sales tax system. The multiplicity of rates is counterproductive and can be rationalised by reducing dispersion in the rates. Inter-State variations in the rate and structure of taxes can be harmonised and move in the direction of uniformity. It would lead to an increase in the tax revenues of States as they will no longer be forced to indulge in unhealthy reduction of rates. If this is done, it would be an important step towards removing impediments to developing a common economic space which would give a substantial fillip to the rate of growth.

The potential of non-tax revenues as a buoyant source of revenue is virtually untapped by the States. Much greater attention must be focussed on non-tax receipts for resource mobilisation. There are two specific areas that merit attention viz. rates of return on investment and user charges. The total investment in public enterprises runs into thousands of crores of rupees but the rate of return is next to nothing. In many areas particularly power supply, transport services, irrigation, and higher education only a small portion of the expenditure incurred is recovered. It is important to reverse these trends not only for budgetary considerations but also for the overall growth of the economy.

The Approach

Given the evolving scenario, and the goals set out by our terms of reference—of not only balancing the revenue account but generating surplus for capital investment - the task before us was far from enviable. We could reach this objective for the States by recommending the requisite increase in transfers from the Centre but leave it with an unmanageable deficit. Alternatively, we could have left the States with an uncovered deficit. We have chosen not to do either because in doing so we would be just shifting the deficits while our aim was to arrive at a sustainable and healthy fiscal balance.

This concern would be fully tackled by taking a holistic view of government finances and looking for an integrated solution. It should be obvious that no policy prescription for the fiscal malaise can be given if a large component of the budget, viz. plan outlay, is left out of reckoning. Even if we leave out that part of the plan outlay which is financed by borrowings and is used for creating new capital assets which would eventually earn a return, there is a revenue plan which ought to covered by revenue receipts. The clubbing of the revenue and capital components in one category termed as plan outlay has generated a tendency to use borrowings to finance revenue expenditure. It is imperative to match the revenue resources separately with the revenue component of the plan. Failure to appreciate this basic requirement of fiscal discipline is one of the main causes of the endemic fiscal disequilibrium.

In an effort to project larger plan outlays, inadequate provision is made for crucial expenditures like the maintenance of existing assets which are, in current practice, regarded as non-plan expenditure and hence of lower priority. New schemes take priority over maintenance resulting in sub-optimal use of resources. We think that such a bias arises at least in part from the artificial classification of expenditures between plan and non-plan and the attitude of regarding all non-plan expenditure as of low priority. It needs to be appreciated that a large part of non-plan expenditure is of a developmental nature and should enjoy the same priority, if not higher, as new plan schemes.

We are of the view that there is a clear rationale for the Finance Commission to deal with the revenue account as a whole, and not merely the non-plan revenue expenditure. Our terms of reference require us to keep in view the objective of reducing fiscal deficit and generating surplus for capital investment which cannot be done adequately unless we reassess the projection of plan expenditure also. But our terms of reference also explicitly require us to assess non-plan revenue expenditure. Our period of recommendations not being co-terminus with the Eighth plan has further complicated the issue. The practical difficulties of making acceptable projections of plan outlay - even for the remaining two years of the plan - were brought to our notice by the representatives of the Planning Commission. Most States have also chosen not to hazard any estimates. In view of these constraints we have confined our reassessment to the non-plan revenue account.

We have, however, not lost sight of the need to reduce the fiscal deficit. Our approach to this issue has been based on the understanding that a reduction in fiscal deficit has to come about through improvements in the revenue account balance emanating from the non-plan revenue account. Accordingly, our attempt through the reassessment of Centre and State forecasts, has been to generate sustainable non-plan revenue surpluses. The premise is that a recurring revenue surplus is the basic prerequisite for achieving desirable macro fiscal balance.

In estimating the base and reassessing the non-plan revenue account of the Centre and States we have maintained, to the extent permitted by functional specificities and compositional differences, a uniform pattern of reassessment. The principles and methodology of the reassessment of Central and States forecasts is dealt with in detail in the subsequent chapters. Briefly, the reassessment of tax revenues is based on a study of the buoyancy of major taxes of the Centre and States with respect to the GDP and individual state domestic product. Non-tax revenues and some items of expenditure have been reassessed on a normative basis. Expenditure reassessment in general is based on price elasticity of expenditure besides allowing for a uniform 1.5 per cent rise in real terms independent of the rate of growth of nominal or real GDP. We have provided for higher real growth for priority sectors like elementary education, health, and family welfare. In contrast, we expect that even implicit subsidies in sectors like power, transport, and irrigation would be reduced greatly. Subsidies on food and fertilisers should be given on a uniform scale and pattern from a single source. We are of the view that the quantum of subsidies should progressively account for a smaller proportion of GDP.

In estimating revenues and expenditure a major determinant is the nominal GDP growth rate and its decomposition into real growth and inflation. In its forecast, the Ministry of Finance had assumed nominal GDP to grow at 11 per cent per annum comprising a rate of inflation of about 5 per cent and real growth of 6 per cent. While we accept the underlying premise of the medium term growth rate being around 11 per cent, we find it unrealistic that the rate of inflation will decline suddenly from about 10 per cent in the 1994-95 to 5 per cent next year. In an attempt to approximate reality we have assumed that the rate of inflation would decline gradually and reach a level of 5 per cent by the year 2000 A.D. At the same time the real rate of growth will increase in a secular manner. On this graduated basis we have assumed the nominal rate of growth to be 12.5, 12, 12, 11.5 and 11 per cent in successive years of the period 1995-2000.

The balance on the non-plan revenue account that we have sought to achieve is contingent on the profile of receipts and expenditure as reassessed by us. On this basis we have formulated our recommendations on vertical resource sharing and horizontal distribution. Our basic approach to vertical resource sharing has been influenced by the view that it would be in the interest of better Centre-State relations if all central taxes are pooled and a proportion devolved to the States. There is considerable merit in moving to such a system as it would make the vertical sharing simple and transparent. It also gives greater freedom to the Centre in choosing tax policy measures in an integrated manner. If a proportion of all taxes goes to the States, any apprehensions of bias in the choice of tax measures will be allayed. Therefore, we have proposed an alternative scheme of devolution.

We are conscious that moving over to such a system of pooling will require amendment of the Constitution. Our terms of reference do not require us to consider such a change. As such, we have made our recommendations in accordance with the existing provisions of the Constitution. The share of income tax and excise duty to be devolved has been recommended in a way that will facilitate a move towards the pooling of all central taxes and devolving a proportion to the States. We have reduced the gap between the percentage of income tax and excise duty shared with the States. This has been accompanied by uniform criteria for distribution of both the shareable taxes.

Our concern for equity and efficiency had been built into our criteria for horizontal distribution. We believe that the two are not mutually exclusive and we have in our devolution formula tried to blend equity with efficiency. Towards this end, tax effort - which represents fiscal efficiency on the revenue side - has been explicitly rewarded in our scheme. We have incorporated two new elements, area and infrastructure, keeping in view the spatial dimension of providing public services and the enhanced importance of infrastructure development across States.

A healthier fiscal attitude can be generated if the grants are not based only on the emerging picture of surpluses or deficits but also on the urgent needs and special problems of the States as identified on the basis of discussions and field visits in the States. In our scheme of transfers, we have used grants as an instrument for upgrading services and providing earmarked resources for some important purposes.

Following the 73rd and 74th amendments of the Constitution, enabling legislation has been enacted by all States and State Finance Commissions have been constituted by them. While our terms of reference do not require us to consider the financial needs of the third tier of the federal structure, we feel that the development of these institutions would be impaired if they are not put into funds at their inception. We are aware that a major part of their needs would come by transfers of functions and funds from the States, including plan funds, and central and centrally sponsored schemes. However, we still consider it important that initial funding of priority areas of basic services like drinking water, health facilities, and elementary education to our rural population and civic amenities to the huge population living in the slums in our megapolises, metropolises and other urban centres should be made. Accordingly, we have provided grants to all States for this purpose.

Our approach to the problem of the accumulating debt burden has been informed by the need for economy in expenditure and efficiency in raising resources. The solution to the problem of debt lies in restoring the revenue account balance and generating surpluses for investment. We are firmly of the view that debt relief offers only temporary reprieve and a long term solution to the problem lies in corrective measures discussed later. In line with our diagnosis we have tried to introduce an incentive based system of debt relief which is related to an improvement on the revenue account balance. We have, utilising the opportunities offered by the new economic environment, recommended a scheme of debt retirement from the proceeds of disinvestment of equity in the public sector enterprises. We have introduced an incentive scheme in this respect also.

Our projections of revenue and expenditure for the period 1995-96 to 1999-2000 set out the direction in which policies to restore fiscal balance have to move and provide a picture of what should happen in the five-year period if these are undertaken. Our projections, while showing an improvement over the present picture, are still far from the goal of having revenue surpluses for each State. It is not too much to expect that the measures we recommend would be implemented fully by the Centre and the States. If in actual practice the picture turns out to be worse than what is being projected, even our conservative assessment of what can realistically be done would have been proved wrong. It is a perpetual battle between hope and experience.

II

We have, through our reassessment and recommendations, tried to evolve a certain vision of the overall fiscal profile of the economy by 2000 A.D. In approaching our task and working out a design of resource sharing we have been guided by considerations of equity and efficiency. Our recommendations ranging from devolution to distribution and our method of balancing of revenue account take cognizance of the influence on and effect of macro-economic variables operating on the real and monetary sides of the economy. As indicated in Chapter II, to the extent possible, we have taken an integrated view of the finances of the country. If the fiscal profile envisaged by us is to be fully realised, the Centre and States would have to devote attention to certain areas which we have chosen to highlight in this Chapter. These areas relate to fiscal discipline; reform of the tax system; planning process and institutional changes in the context of economic reform; decentralisation of development. Each of these requires far-reaching changes in policies and attitudes and some of them point in the direction of changes in the relevant constitutional provisions. We now turn to a brief discussion of these issues.

Fiscal Discipline

The previous chapters of our Report have clearly brought out the sad story of rapid deterioration in the financial position of the Central and State Governments. While the potential for raising resources is inadequately utilised, expenditures have continued to mount. The report of the National Development Council Committee on Austerity contains many useful recommendations which still deserve consideration. We think it is of the utmost importance that the growth of expenditure on revenue account is curbed and a serious attempt made to contain it within revenue receipts so that governments do not incur additional debt, as they have been doing, to meet current expenditure which does not generate a return to service the debt. While borrowing for capital expenditure is in order, the projects for which such debts are incurred must earn adequate returns. It is is a matter of serious concern that investments in irrigation, power and road transport, which constitute the bulk of State Government investments do not yield enough returns. A shortsighted perception of political necessity, perhaps, has persuaded State after State to fix user charges in irrigation and power at levels which do not cover even the operation and maintenance expenditures in irrigation and generate meagre surpluses, if at all, in power. Several State Electricity Boards are over-staffed and run at substantial losses. The artificially depressed user charges result in a criminal waste of water and electricity - both very scarce resources. Several studies have shown that the marginal benefit of irrigation to the farmer far exceeds what he currently pays for water and even if the rates were raised to yield an adequate return on capital, they would still constitute only a small percentage of the additional production generated by irrigation. There is no justification that can be reasonably adduced for power and irrigation rates to be so heavily subsidised. We would recommend that a national consensus on irrigation and power rates should be evolved sooner rather than later to stem the rot in these sectors. No society can move forward if its citizens are encouraged to believe that costs of services do not have to be borne by those who benefit from them, especially when capacity to pay is not a constraint. Other central subsidies need to be phased out as quickly as possible, and those on food better targetted.

Fiscal discipline does not stop at bridging the revenue deficit, which in itself would be a very major step forward. Our forecasts do not suggest that this can be achieved by the year 2000, but every effort must be made to do so within the subsequent five years. This will require a careful look at both plan and non-plan expenditures. Equally important is to ensure that resources are not diverted from the purposes for which they are allocated. We came across a case of money meant for flood relief being used for building a sports stadium which exemplifies the extent to which fiscal discipline is eroded. The poor state of accounts in some States and the failure to complete accounts of State enterprises, for several years on end are other examples of such erosion. We would recommend that the Comptroller and Auditor General should constitute a task force to identify lapses from the prescribed norms and procedures and initiate corrective action. The report of the task force should be made public.

More generally, expenditure control should involve questioning every item of expenditure every year, rather than giving automatic approvals on the basis of continuity of schemes or projects. Over the years employment in government has grown manifold. There is scope for Central and State Governments to shed many an activity and absorb the staff rendered surplus in other activities and to encourage them to avail of retirement with attractive benefits. Viable methods of reducing the strength of government employment must be explored, otherwise, economic reform may lose its way in a new bureaucratic maze.

Economies in expenditure have many dimensions and we do not wish to deal with the matter in great detail. It is well known that there are leakages in many departments and schemes and only a part of the expenditure reaches the ultimate beneficiary. Accessibility to funds must be linked to performance. And a machinery must be established for close monitoring detecting leakages and punishing the guilty.

Selective privatisation of public enterprises will relieve the Governments of the burden of recurring losses while at the same time giving them the benefit of a one-time accretion to their resources. Privatisation should be viewed as a method of providing the same service in a cost-effective manner and raising resources which can be deployed to reduce the accumulated debt.

In the area of Centre-State relations, there is one specific matter to which we would like to draw attention. It is the persistence of a large number of centrally sponsored schemes. Although a number of them have been closed down following a review by a committee set up by the National Development Council, these were relatively small, representing an annual provision of only about Rs. 200 crores, as against a total for all centrally sponsored schemes of about Rs. 14,000 crores. Central intervention through such schemes is presumably acceptable to the States because they carry with them additional resources. Their continuance makes for large and sprawling bureaucracies at the Centre dealing with what are primarily State subjects - e.g. agriculture, rural development, education and public health. Given adequate decentralisation, it should be possible to effect considerable economies in such Ministries.

Reform of the Tax System

Centre-State financial relations will necessarily undergo a change with the progress of tax reform at the Centre and in the States. At the Centre, a major structural change which has occurred is the decline in the importance of customs as a source of revenue. This is a consequence of the opening up of the economy and the policy of progressively reducing customs duties on capital goods, raw materials and components. The policy of further liberalising imports, if necessary with a high customs tariff on sectors like consumer goods, will, apart from inducing greater efficiency in production, ensure that the growth in customs revenue does not decline rapidly. The reassessment of the Centre's revenues made by us (see Chapter IV) makes an implicit assumption that this will be the case.

As for excise duties, the Centre has adopted the policy of moving over to ad valorem rates and extension of MODVAT. Several variants of introducing a full-fledged value added tax (VAT) have also surfaced in discussions. One such is that the Centre would levy VAT upto the wholesale stage, leaving it to the States to move over from sales tax to VAT beyond the wholesale stage. Another is a comprehensive VAT levied by the Centre but collected by both the Centre and the States, the proceeds to be shared with the States. Whichever of the various versions is adopted eventually, it is clear that the system of indirect taxation comprising excise duties and sales taxes requires an overhaul in order to remove the deleterious impact it has on economic activity and exports through cascading and lack of transparency. Meanwhile, the widely varying sales tax rates and numerous exemptions and incentives announced by the State Governments to attract investment distort investment and production and result in an avoidable loss of revenue for the States. Harmonisation of rates and incentive structures should be brought about through agreement among the States. One possibility would be to evolve two or more broad bands for sales tax uniformly in all states.

Planning Process and Institutional Reform

We were considerably handicapped in our work by the fact that the period of our Report does not coincide with the period of the plan. The Eighth Plan runs from April 1992 to March 1997 whereas the period for which we are required to make our recommendations runs from April 1995 to March 2000, with an overlap with the Eighth Plan of two years. In the existing scheme of things, expenditures on plan schemes completed at the end of a plan are treated as committed non-plan expenditures in the subsequent plan period. Our terms of reference specifically require us to have regard to maintenance expenditure on plan schemes to be completed by 31st March, 1995. Since it is not the practice of the State Governments to move expenditures on completed schemes to the non-plan category until the end of the plan period, we have perforce had to take recourse to a broad estimation of such expenditures. In the absence of a common time-frame, we have not been able to take a view of the total revenue expenditure of the Centre and the States, both plan and non-plan, which would have been necessary for dealing fully with para 4(i) of our terms of reference. We believe it is important to synchronise the period of recommendations of a Finance Commission with that of a Five-Year Plan. In the past, due recognition was given to this factor and up to the Seventh Commission the periods were synchronised. The issue is urgent and should be dealt with while determining the period for the next plan.

It is becoming quite clear that the planning process will have to undergo a material change in the wake of the economic reforms now underway. The Planning Commission itself is conscious of this and has taken an initiative to start a debate on the subject. The greater market orientation of the economy and the enhanced role for private and foreign investment will put additional responsibility on the public sector to strengthen the economic and social infrastructure and reinforce the legislative, legal and judicial processes which make for good governance. In particular, public outlays on education and health will need to be increased substantially. This means a greater responsibility for State Governments whose resource base will have to be correspondingly augmented. Since the bulk of such outlays are on revenue account, we think that it should be the responsibility of future Finance Commissions to deal with them along with revenue receipts. It follows that the present artificial distinction between plan and non-plan expenditures, which runs across revenue and capital budgets shall be replaced by the simpler and conventionally well recognised distinction between revenue and capital. Future Finance Commissions may be required to examine the aggregate requirements on revenue account and recommend means to bridge the revenue gaps.

We are conscious that the current distinction between plan and non-plan expenditures serves the purpose of demarcating new from old schemes. We think, however, that the distinction may have had the perverse impact, as explained in an earlier chapter, of resulting in the neglect of maintenance of capital assets. The crucial point is the criterion of borrowing; it should be for activities which generate adequate return to service debt. Other activities must be a charge on current revenue or such funding as may be created from revenues from time to time to finance lumpy expenditures.

Decentralisation

Because of the 73rd and 74th amendments to the Constitution, Finance Commissions will be required in future to suggest measures in the light of the recommendations of the State Finance Commissions. We believe it is important that the panchayati raj institutions are firmly established and strengthened. Equally, we think it is necessary to guard against generation of dependency for resources at each sub-national level. The three-tier structure, with two layers of Finance Commissions, may generate expectations that in the end it will be the responsibility of the Centre to channel resources through the State Governments to the panchayats and urban local bodies. The fiscal system can scarcely meet such expectations. Panchayats and urban local bodies need to have well-defined sources of income and taxing powers. They must be encouraged to exploit them to the full, relying on transfers from the above only at the margin and preferably on a matching basis. Decentralisation of the development process is a desirable objective. But it can prove effective only if local resources are mobilised for local development, thus ensuring minimum leakage and cost-effective deployment.

We are of the view that in order to ensure continuity and advance preparations, a permanent Finance Commission Division may be created in the Ministry of Finance with an officer-oriented composition. We endorse the recommendations of the Eighth Finance Commission in this regard contained in para 16.12 of their report which reads:

The Division, which we propose, should have the following functions:-

(i) to watch the implementation of the recommendations of the Finance Commission;

(ii) to watch closely and analyse the trends in the receipts and non-plan expenditure of the State Governments and identify the reasons for variation between actuals and estimates made by the Finance Commission;

(iii) to monitor and evaluate the utilization of upgradation grants;

(iv) to preserve the records of the previous Commissions, and take such necessary action to obtain future information as might be of use to the future Commissions;

(v) to conduct studies and publish papers and data having a bearing on State finances.

The Division should be actively associated with the annual plan exercises of the Planning Commission so that the maintenance of assets already created does not suffer from either lack of attention or lack of resource-allocation because of the anxiety of the States to have progressively larger Plan."

We have noted that there is already a Finance Commission division in the Ministry of Finance. It is, however, no more than a cell. We are in full agreement with what the Eighth Commission had recommended and would urge that a fullfledged Division, appropriately staffed, and with adequate technical expertise, be created at the earliest under a senior officer and made to function within the Ministry of Finance so that it can discharge the functions indicated above. State Governments may also be asked to designate officers whose duty it would be to liaise with the Division to ensure continuity of contact and updating of information.

III

DEVOLUTION: AN ALTERNATIVE SCHEME

We have indicated earlier in our approach that we favour a system of vertical resource sharing in which central taxes are pooled and a proportion devolved to the States. In the context of the current economic reforms, this new arrangement is likely to have distinct advantages over the present system. We now set out our alternative scheme of devolution.

The main benefits resulting from this new arrangement may be listed as below:

a) With a given share being allotted to the States in the aggregate revenues from central taxes, States will be able to share the aggregate buoyancy of central taxes.

b) The Central Government can pursue tax reforms without the need to consider whether a tax is shareable with the States or not.

c) The impact of fluctuations in central tax revenues would be felt alike by the Central and State Governments.

d) Should the taxes mentioned in articles 268 and/or 269 form part of this arrangement, there will be a greater likelihood of their being tapped.

In the framework of cooperative federalism, the Constitution currently provides for sharing of two taxes, income tax and Union excise duties, with the States. India's economic space is occupied in common by the Centre and States. Recent economic reforms including tax reforms, have underlined this fact. The progress of reforms will be greatly facilitated if the ambit of tax sharing arrangement is enlarged so as to give greater certainty of resource flows to and increased flexibility in tax reform for, the two layers of government. The Indian tax system, heavily dependent on indirect taxes, with Union excises and State sales taxes comprising the core of the domestic trade taxes, suffers from many deficiencies like high and multiple tax rates, taxation of inputs and cascading, exclusion of services from the tax base, multiplicity of exemptions and concessions through notifications and lack of harmony in the tax systems of States. The country needs a climate in which there is greater harmonisation of State taxes in terms of their rates, structure and procedures as also greater Centre-State harmonisation in domestic trade taxes.

The relevant ratios determining the vertical allocation in tax devolution have remained at 85 per cent in the case of income tax and at 45 per cent for Union excise duties for the past ten years. As the share of the Central Government in income tax is only 15 per cent it has often been claimed that the Centre has shown lack of interest in tapping this source of revenue fully. A similar lack of interest is adduced as a reason for the tax sources under articles 268 and 269 remaining unexploited or underexploited. Similarly, it is believed that the large share of Union excise duties accruing to the States has reduced the flexibility of the Centre in the choice of tax measures. The Ministry of Finance itself has said in its memorandum: "If the Central Government raises more through personal income tax... as much as 85 per cent of the increase will go to the States. Similarly, in the case of the Union excise duty, 45 per cent of any increase in the yield will accrue to the States. Hence, if the Central Government wishes to raise Rs. 100 crores for itself, through Union excise duties, it would have to raise around Rs. 182 crores. To get the same Rs. 100 crores through a rise in the personal tax yield, the Central Government would have to raise Rs. 667 crores!"

Table 1
Revenues from Major Central Taxes: Growth Rates

	Average Annual Growth Rates		
	70/71-79/80	*80/81-89/90*	*70/71-89/90*
Corporation Tax	14.42	17.15	15.79
Income Tax other than Corporation tax	12.76	14.83	13.80
Customs Duties	20.96	20.03	20.49
Excise Duties	14.10	14.31	14.20

Source: Interim Report of the Tax Reforms Committee, Ministry of Finance, Government of India, page 24.

In their memoranda to us, States have generally urged us to move towards a larger pool of revenues from which they can be assigned a share. Many States have urged that corporation tax and income tax should be pooled together and then distributed. Orissa has suggested the inclusion of receipts from penalties, interest recoveries and surcharges on income tax in this pool. Rajasthan has suggested that capital receipts accruing from pre-emptive purchases and sale of immovable properties should form part of the income tax proceeds. Tamil Nadu has suggested that proceeds from the pre-emptive purchase of properties, penalties and interest recoveries, tax on Union emoluments, cost of collection and miscellaneous receipts should be included in the pool. Karnataka and Uttar Pradesh have suggested that all Central taxes should be made shareable.

The Ministry of Finance, Government of India, at one stage, made the suggestion that in the longer term context, we may wish to examine the desirability of changing the pattern of tax sharing such that the entire tax revenues of the Centre (except Union surcharges) become shareable. It also said, however, that the percentage may be pitched at 22-23 per cent and that it should remain fixed for 20 years.

Notwithstanding the present Constitutional position, Finance Commissions in the past have noted, with concern, that a share was not being assigned to the States in the proceeds of the corporation tax. The Third and Fourth Commissions took this factor into account for raising the States' share in income tax from 60 to 66 2/3, and to 75 per cent, respectively. The Third Commission had also raised the number of items of excise to be shared to compensate for the loss. The Sixth Commission had suggested a review of this issue by the National Development Council and the Seventh Commission had also suggested that the Centre may hold consultations with the States in order to settle the point finally. The Eighth Commission had expressed the view that since the corporation tax had shown a high elasticity, it would seem only fair that the States should have access to such a source of revenue.

The Sarkaria Commission had also examined this issue at length. It favoured bringing the corporation tax into the divisible pool as part of permissive participation like that of the Union excise duties. It suggested that this may be accomplished by a suitable Constitutional amendment.

The Chelliah Committee on Tax Reforms (1991) has expressed the view that the present Constitutional provisions regarding tax sharing need to be re-examined. In this context, the Committee observed in its Interim Report (p. 45) as follows: "The task of fiscal adjustment at the Centre has been rendered more difficult because of the compulsions arising from the formula of tax sharing with the States. ... The percentages of the taxes to be shared with the States are not specified in the Constitution, but are left to be decided by the President after he considers the recommendations of the Finance Commission in this regard. At present tax devolution to the States constitutes around 24 per cent of gross Central Government tax revenues. With the consent and cooperation of the States the relevant constitutional provisions could be amended to the effect that 25 per cent of the aggregate tax revenues of the Centre shall be shared with the States. There would be certainty then for the States and the Union regarding what revenues would accrue to their respective budgets and the Centre would not have to distort its pattern of taxation by being virtually compelled to raise non-shareable taxes."

The Constitution provides for the division of functions and sources of revenue between the Central and State Governments vide three-lists contained in the Seventh Schedule, viz. Union List, State List and Concurrent List. Article 270 makes it mandatory to share income tax with the States. Article 272 provides for a discretionary sharing of Union excise duties. The sharing of corporation tax has, however, been excluded by a specific provision in Article 270. In addition, the following proceeds of income tax are excluded from being shared with the States:

 i) proceeds attributable to the Union Territories;

 ii) taxes payable in respect of Union emoluments;

 iii) surcharge.

Duties set out in article 268 are such as may be levied by the Centre but the States collect and appropriate the proceeds within their respective areas. Article 269 specifies taxes that are to be levied and collected by the Government of India but the proceeds are wholly assigned to the States.

Assigning a share in the total proceeds from central taxes to the States would require suitable amendments to the Constitution. While doing so, the power of the Union to levy and collect all taxes in the Union list should not be qualified by the proposal to transfer a certain percentage of specified central taxes to the States. In other words, while all List I taxes remain Union taxes and the proceeds of no particular tax shall be deemed 'divisible', the States will be entitled to a prescribed percentage of the tax receipts of the Union.

We are proposing a share of the States based on the amounts currently accruing to the States. For this purpose we have distinguished between shares in income tax, basic excise duties and grants in lieu of tax on railway passenger fares as a proportion of central tax revenues (s1) on the one hand and the share of additional excise duties on the other (s2). The share of the States in these taxes is given in Table 2.

Table 2
Share of States in Aggregate Central Tax Revenues

	S1	S2	S
1979-80	25.66	2.92	28.58
1980-81	26.00	2.94	28.94
1981-82	24.11	3.00	27.11
1982-83	23.57	2.78	26.35
1983-84	22.27	3.16	25.43
1984-85	21.15	3.56	24.71
1985-86	23.26	3.20	26.46
1986-87	22.85	3.25	26.10
1987-88	22.53	3.20	25.73
1988-89	21.29	2.91	24.20
1989-90	22.77	3.04	25.81
1990-91	22.60	2.90	25.50
1991-92	22.90	2.85	25.75
1992-93	24.69	3.01	27.70
1993-94 (RE)	26.20	2.98	29.18
1994-95 (BE)	25.15	3.02	28.17
Average:			
1979-84	24.32	2.96	27.28
1984-89	22.22	3.22	25.44
1990-95	24.31	2.95	27.26

Notes: S1 = Share of States in income tax, Union excise duties, estate duty, and grant in lieu of tax on railway passenger fares as percentage of total Central tax revenues (incl. AED).

S2 = Revenue from additional excise duties transferred to the States as percentage of total Central tax revenues.

S = S1 + S2

Source: Finance Accounts, Government of India.
Receipts Budget, Central Government, 1994-95.

It will be noticed that during the period covered by the reports of the Seventh, Eighth and Nineth (1990-95) Commissions, the average value of s1 has been 24.32, 22.22 and 24.30 per cent and that of s2 2.96, 3.22 and 2.95. Having regard to these values, and the fact that we are recommending inclusion of some taxes under article 269 in the central pool, we recommend that the share of States in the gross receipts of central taxes shall be 26 per cent. We further recommend that the tax rental arrangement should be terminated, and additional excise duties merged with basic excise duties. These three commodities should not be subject to States sales tax. Having done so we recommend a further share of three per cent in the gross tax receipts of the Centre for the States in lieu of additional excise duties. These shares of twenty six and three per cent respectively should be suitably provided for in the Constitution and reviewed once in 15 years. We have used the perterion of revenue equivalence only for the intial fixing of the above ratios. We are not recommending revenue equivalence as a principle. It would not be relevant to consider in future what the share of the States would have been had they been getting shares individually in income tax and Union excise duties as at present.

The proceeds of taxes under articles 268 and 269, except in so far as they relate to the Union Territories, do not form part of the Consolidated Fund of India, and are wholly assignable to the States. There is a distinction between articles 268 and 269 in so far as this assignment is concerned. In article 268, the Constitution provides that the proceeds of taxes leviable within any State shall be assigned to that State. Article 269 provides that: "The net proceeds...shall be assigned to the States within which that duty or tax is leviable in that year, ans shall be distributed among those States in accordance with such principles of distribution as may be formulated by Parliament by law". Among the taxes covered by article 269, estate duty has now been abolished. The tax on railway passenger fares was also repealed in lieu of which the States are given a grant. The important taxes, from the viewpoint of revenue, are the central sales tax, and the consignment tax.

With the Central Sales Tax Act, 1956, the power to levy the tax on inter State sales has been effectively delegated to the States. A State levies tax on inter-State sales originating in its territory and retains the proceeds. The maximum rate of tax, currently 4 per cent, is prescribed by the Central Government. Such a tax is viewed as fragmenting the national market, and may be considered as an inefficient source of raising revenues. The consignment tax raises similar problems. The very reason why the power to levy these taxes was vested in the Centre was to avoid their misuse or overuse at the cost of fragmenting and distorting the domestic market.

We believe there is some advantage in retaining a system such as in article 268, where a tax is levied by the Union Government but collected and retained by the States, in the interest of uniformity of rates. Because Central sales tax, already being levied, and consignment tax, if and when levied, are similar to the taxes under article 268, we have decided to keep them out of the pool of central taxes. All other taxes in article 269 shall form part of the central pool.

In recommending that these taxes form part of the pool, we are guided by the consideration that this will induce the Centre to exploit these tax bases which are not currently being tapped. States will also benefit from such exploitation of tax basis. We are of the view that while article 268 taxes may be kept out of the arrangement of fixing a common share for all central taxes being suggested here, all article 269 taxes except Central sales tax and consignment tax should be brought within the purview of these arrangements.

There has been occasion in the past when the Centre had to augment its revenue for meeting emergent but temporary needs. In such circumstances a surcharge on income and corporation tax was imposed. Such occasions may arise in future also. The Centre should, therefore, continue to have the power to levy surcharges for the purposes of the Union and these should be excluded from the sharing arrangements with the States which are recommended above.

We have recommended the share of States in income tax, Union excise duties, additional excise duties and grants in lieu of tax on railway passenger fares in accordance with our terms of reference. However, we would recommend that the alternative scheme of resource sharing suggested by us may be brought into force with effect from 1st April, 1996 after necessary amendments to the Constitution. this should not affect the interest shares and grants recommended by us.

IV

SUMMARY OF RECOMMENDATIONS

Our important recommendations to the President are set out below.

Income Tax

We recommend that for each financial year in the period 1995-96 to 1999-2000 :

(a) Out of the net distributable proceeds of income tax, a sum equal to 0.927 per cent shall be deemed to represent the proceeds attributable to Union Territories.

(b) The share of the net proceeds of income tax assigned to the States shall be 77.5 per cent.

(c) The distribution among States of the share assigned to them in each financial year should be on the basis of the percentages shown in the Table below:

Income Tax: Shares of States 1995-2000

State	Per cent
Andhra Pradesh	8.465
Arunachal Pradesh	0.170
Assam	2.784
Bihar	12.861
Goa	0.180
Gujarat	4.046
Haryana	1.238
Himachal Pradesh	0.704
Jammu & Kashmir	1.097
Karnataka	5.339
Kerala	3.875
Madhya Pradesh	8.290
Maharashtra	6.126
Manipur	0.282
Meghalaya	0.283
Mizoram	0.149
Nagaland	0.181
Orissa	4.495
Punjab	1.461
Rajasthan	5.551
Sikkim	0.126
Tamil Nadu	6.637
Tripura	0.378
Uttar Pradesh	17.811
West Bengal	7.471
Total	**100.000**

Union Excise Duties

We recommend that 40 per cent of the net proceeds of Union excise duties during each financial year in the period 1995-96 to 1999-2000 should be distributed as per the shares in the Table below:

40 per cent of the net proceeds of Union Excise Duties: Shares of States 1995-2000

State	Per cent
Andhra Pradesh	8.465
Arunachal Pradesh	0.170
Assam	2.784
Bihar	12.861
Goa	0.180
Gujarat	4.046
Haryana	1.238
Himachal Pradesh	0.704
Jammu & Kashmir	1.097
Karnataka	5.339
Kerala	3.875
Madhya Pradesh	8.290
Maharashtra	6.126
Manipur	0.282
Meghalaya	0.283
Mizoram	0.149
Nagaland	0.181
Orissa	4.495
Punjab	1.461
Rajasthan	5.551
Sikkim	0.126
Tamil Nadu	6.637
Tripura	0.378
Uttar Pradesh	17.811
West Bengal	7.471
Total	**100.00**

We also recommend that the remaining 7.5 per cent of the net proceeds of Union excise duties be distributed among the States in accordance with the shares specified by us for each financial year in the period 1995-96 to 1999-2000 as given in the Table below.

Shares of States in 7.5 per cent of the net proceeds of Union Excise Duties

(per cent)

State	1995-96	1996-97	1997-98	1998-99	1999-2000
(1)	(2)	(3)	(4)	(5)	(6)
Andhra Pradesh	12.069	7.988	0.000	0.000	0.000
Arunachal Pradesh	3.410	4.300	5.871	6.224	6.667
Assam	8.543	9.836	11.849	10.748	9.290
Bihar	6.434	2.965	0.000	0.000	0.000
Goa	0.973	1.058	1.161	0.917	0.604
Himachal Pradesh	8.816	10.744	14.057	14.230	14.338
Jammu & Kashmir	13.366	16.491	21.985	22.741	23.700
Manipur	3.930	4.891	6.602	6.917	7.348
Meghalaya	3.590	4.403	5.815	5.994	6.130
Mizoram	3.676	4.628	6.278	6.784	7.074
Nagaland	5.818	7.417	10.247	11.072	12.025
Orissa	4.815	5.248	4.934	2.773	0.680
Rajasthan	0.835	0.000	0.000	0.000	0.000
Sikkim	1.199	1.473	1.938	1.982	2.055
Tripura	5.465	6.807	9.263	9.618	10.089
Uttar Pradesh	17.061	11.751	0.000	0.000	0.000
Total	**100.00**	**100.00**	**100.00**	**100.00**	**100.00**

Devolution : An Alternative Scheme

Having regard to the share of States in income tax, Union excise duties, and grant-in-lieu of tax on railway passenger fare in total central tax revenues (including additional excise duties), and the fact that we are recommending inclusion of some taxes under article 269 in the central pool, we recommend that the share of States in the gross receipts of central taxes shall be 26 per cent. We further recommend that the tax rental arrangement should be terminated, and additional excise duties merged with basic excise duties. These three commodities should not be subject to States sales tax. Having done so we recommend a further share of three per cent in the gross tax receipts of the Centre for the States in lieu of additional excise duties. These shares of twenty six and three per cent respectively should be suitably provided for in the Constitution and reviewed once in 15 years.

We believe there is some advantage in retaining a system such as in article 268, where a tax is levied by the Union Government but collected and retained by the States, in the interest of uniformity of rates. Because Central sales tax, already being levied, and consignment tax, if and when levied, are similar to the taxes under article 268, we have decided to keep them out of the pool of central taxes. All other taxes in article 269 shall form part of the central pool.

The Centre should continue to have the power to levy surcharges for the purposes of the Union and these should be excluded from the sharing arrangement with the States.

We would recommend that the alternative scheme of resource sharing suggested by us may be brought into force with effect from 1st April, 1996 after necessary amendments to the Constitution. This should not affect the inter-se shares and grants recommended by us.

Additional Duties of Excise

The share of Union territories amounting to 2.203 per cent should be retained by the Central Government. We recommend that the balance should be distributed among the States as shown in the Table below.

State	Per cent
Andhra Pradesh	7.820
Arunachal Pradesh	0.104
Assam	2.483
Bihar	7.944
Goa	0.232
Gujarat	5.995
Haryana	2.366
Himachal Pradesh	0.595
Jammu & Kashmir	0.856
Karnataka	5.744
Kerala	3.740
Madhya Pradesh	7.236
Maharashtra	12.027
Manipur	0.197
Meghalaya	0.188
Mizoram	0.079
Nagaland	0.137
Orissa	3.345
Punjab	3.422
Rajasthan	4.873
Sikkim	0.053
Tamil Nadu	7.669
Tripura	0.286
Uttar Pradesh	14.573
West Bengal	8.036
Total	100.000

Grants-in-lieu of Tax on Railway Passenger Fares

We recommend that:

i) The quantum of the grant in lieu of the Railway Passenger Fares Tax for 1995-2000 should be Rs. 380 crores annually.

ii) The shares of States in the grant would be as in the Table below:

State	Percentage share
Andhra Pradesh	8.345
Arunachal Pradesh	0.005
Assam	1.368
Bihar	9.326
Goa	0.194
Gujarat	6.901
Haryana	1.917
Himachal Pradesh	0.108
Jammu & Kashmir	0.728
Karnataka	3.388
Kerala	3.495
Madhya Pradesh	6.882
Maharashtra	17.548
Manipur	0.018
Meghalaya	0.034
Mizoram	0.001
Nagaland	0.145
Orissa	1.715
Punjab	3.280
Rajasthan	4.445
Sikkim	0.010
Tamil Nadu	6.458
Tripura	0.039
Uttar Pradesh	15.568
West Bengal	8.082
Total	100.000

Upgradation Grants

We recommend a total sum of Rs. 2,608.50 crores as grants for upgradation and special problems for the period 1995-2000.

Financing of Relief Expenditure

The amount worked out for all the States for the period of our Report is Rs. 6304.27 crores. Out of this, the Centre will be required to contribute Rs. 4728.19 crores (75 per cent) and the States Rs. 1576.08 crores (25 per cent). We recommend the continuation of the current scheme of the Calamity Relief Fund with modifications suggested by us.

We propose that in addition to the Calamity Relief Funds for States, a National Fund for Calamity Relief should be created to which the Centre and the States will contribute and which will be managed by a National Calamity Relief Committee on which both the Centre and the States would be represented.

The size of the National Fund for Calamity Relief would be Rs. 700 crores, to be built up over the period 1995-2000, with an initial corpus of Rs. 200 crores to which the Centre would contribute Rs. 150 crores and the States Rs. 50 crores in the proportion of 75:25. In addition, for each of the five years from 1995-96 to 1999-2000 the contributions of the Centre and the States would be Rs. 75 crores and Rs. 25 crores respectively. The contribution by both the Centre and the States would be made annually in the beginning of the financial year. Contribution of States *inter-se* would be in the same proportion as their estimated total tax receipts after devolution.

Grants for Local Bodies

A total grant of Rs. 5,380.93 crores should be made available to the States in four equal instalments commencing from 1996-97.

Grants-in-Aid

We recommend grants-in-aid, to be given to the States under the substantive portion of Article 275(1), equal to the amount of the deficits as estimated for each of the years during 1995-96 to 1999-2000. These amounts have been specified in the Table below:

	1995-96	*1996-97*	*1997-98*	*1998-99*	*1999-00*	*1995-2000*
Andhra Pradesh	483.47	202.98	0.00	0.00	0.00	686.45
Arunachal Pradesh	136.60	109.26	45.63	16.11	0.00	307.60
Assam	342.20	249.94	92.08	27.81	0.00	712.03
Bihar	257.72	75.34	0.00	0.00	0.00	333.06
Goa	38.98	26.88	9.03	2.37	0.00	77.26
Himachal Pradesh	353.11	273.00	109.25	36.82	0.00	772.18
Jammu and Kashmir	535.39	419.05	170.85	58.84	0.00	1184.13
Manipur	157.43	124.28	51.31	17.90	0.00	350.92
Meghalaya	143.83	111.89	45.19	15.51	0.00	316.42
Mizoram	147.25	117.60	48.79	17.55	0.00	331.19
Nagaland	233.04	188.46	79.63	28.65	0.00	529.78
Orissa	192.87	133.35	38.34	7.18	0.00	371.74
Rajasthan	33.45	0.00	0.00	0.00	0.00	33.45
Sikkim	48.05	37.45	15.06	5.13	0.00	105.69
Tripura	218.92	172.98	71.99	24.89	0.00	488.78
Uttar Pradesh	683.40	298.60	0.00	0.00	0.00	982.00
Total	**4005.71**	**2541.06**	**777.15**	**258.76**	**0.00**	**7582.68**

We recommend that in case the actual realisation of the concerned States from royalty is higher than that assumed in our estimates, it would be open to the Central Government to make suitable adjustments in the grants-in-aid under Article 275 recommended by us for meeting their non-plan revenue deficits.

Debt Relief

We have recommend a scheme for debt relief in two parts:

  i) a scheme for general debt relief for all States linked to fiscal performance; and

  ii) specific relief for States with high fiscal stress, special category States and States with debt problems warranting special attention.

In addition we recommend a scheme for encouraging retirement of debt from the proceeds of disinvestment of equity holdings of State Governments.

We recommend specific relief for all special category States, and three other States, viz. Orissa, Bihar and Uttar Pradesh, which are characterised by high fiscal stress. For these States we recommend writing-off of 5 per cent of repayment due with respect to fresh central loans given during 1989-95 and outstanding on 31st March, 1995.

We recommend the waiver of one third of the repayment of principal falling due during 1995-2000 on special term loans to Punjab in view of the special circumstances when these term loans were advanced and the need for the State to reinvigorate its development efforts.

Monitoring of Maintenance Expenditure

We recommend that the presentation of accounts should be redesigned in such a way that the expenditure on the works component and the establishment expenses get reflected separately and are easily accessible. We recommend that the Ministry of Finance, in consultation with the State Governments and with the concurrence of the Comptroller and Auditor General of India, should introduce appropriate changes in the accounting and reporting system in accordance with the scheme outlined by us.

We also recommend that the State Governments should ensure that the provisions for maintenance are made in accordance with our recommendations. We further recommend that a high powered committee chaired by the Chief Secretary and with secretaries of the State Governments concerned in the departments of Finance, Planning, irrigation and Public Works and the concerned chief engineers of the works departments should review every quarter the allocation and utilisation of funds provided for maintenance.

Finance Commission Division

We recommend that a full-fledged Division, appropriately staffed, and with adequate technical expertise, be created at the earliest under a senior officer and made to function within the Ministry of Finance so that it can discharge the functions assigned to it. State Governments may also be asked to designate officers whose duty it would be to liaise with the Division to ensure continuity of contact and updating of information.

Report of the Tenth Finance Commission, December, 1994 (excerpts).

13

Public Sector Commercial Banks and Financial Sector Reforms: Rebuilding for a Better Future

I. Introduction

The economic reforms launched by the Government more than two years ago are designed to accelerate overall growth and help India realise its full productive potential. The experience of successful developing countries indicates that rapid growth requires a sustained effort at mobilising savings and resources and deploying these in ways which encourage efficient production. The structural reforms in industry, trade and foreign investment, various policy initiatives in agriculture, and the continuing reform of the tax system, all form part of the strategy of improving efficiency by encouraging competitiveness of the system as a whole. These reforms, however, must be supported by reforms in the financial sector, particularly the banking system, which has the prime responsibility for mobilising and allocating financial resources.

Financial sector reform thus constitutes an important component of the programme of stabilisation and structural reform. At its very outset, the Government had recognised that financial sector reform was an integral part of the new economic policy. Less than five weeks after the new Government had assumed office, the Finance Minister announced the appointment of a High-Level Committee (the Narasimham Committee) to consider all relevant aspects of the structure, organisation, functions and procedures of the financial system. Following the Committee's report in November 1991, the Government embarked on a far-reaching process of reform covering both the banking system and the capital market. The need for a thorough-going reform of the financial system was further underscored by the securities irregularities in banks that were revealed in April 1992.

A large part of the agenda for reform of the financial system relates to the problems facing the public sector commercial banks, which have dominated commercial banking in India, since nationalisation in July 1969. The goal of nationalisation was to extend the reach of banking and financial services to all parts of the country and to all sections of the society. It also aimed at widening the net of resource mobilisation. There is no doubt that public sector banks have responded to these challenges and have built an impressive network, offering a wide range of financial instruments and services. Most indicators of financial development also point to significant progress. At the time of nationalisation, there were 8,321 bank branches of which only 23 per cent were rural. Today, the total number of bank branches (including RRBs) exceeds 60,000 of which about 58 per cent are in the rural areas. The public sector commercial banks (including RRBs) now account for 93 per cent of total bank offices and 87 per cent of banking system deposits (Table 1 & Fig. 1). Aggregate deposits of commercial banks have risen from 13 per cent of GDP in 1969 to approximately 37 per cent in 1993. The average population per bank branch, which was 65,000 at the time of nationalisation, came down to 11,000 at the end of March 1993. This quantitative expansion has helped mobilise a substantial portion of the savings of the community in the form of deposits and spread the banking habit throughout the country. In addition, the banking system has been a progressive force in widening the entrepreneurial base of the country.

Table 1
Scheduled Commercial Banks : Selected Indicators*
Business in India (March 1993)

	Deposits	Branches	
	(Rs. Crore)	Total Semi-Urban	Rural/
Public Sector Banks	239,361	57,198	44,177
	(87.3)	(93.4)	(94.6)
Regional Rural Banks	6,607	14,567	14,394
SBI Group	75,524	12,558	9,344
Nationalised Banks	157,230	30,073	20,439
Private Sector Banks	34,707	4,037	2,541
	(12.7)	(6.6)	(5.4)
Foreign Banks	21,957	138	3
Other Scheduled Banks	12,750	3,899	2,538
Total Scheduled	274,068	61,235	46,718
Commercial Banks	(100.0)	(100.0)	(100.0)

* Figures in brackets are percentage shares of total.

Source: Banking Statistics - Quarterly Handout, March 1993 (Reserve Bank of India)

Figure 1
Scheduled Commercial Banks
Deposits by Bank Type (percent)

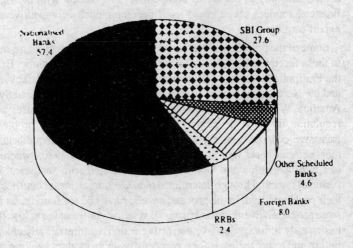

Nationalised Banks 57.4

SBI Group 27.6

Other Scheduled Banks 4.6

Foreign Banks 8.0

RRBs 2.4

While these are significant achievements, they have been accompanied by serious short-comings as well. The quality of customer service has not kept pace with modern standards and changing expectations. The time taken for processing and completing banking transactions is too long. The banks have also not kept pace with the revolutionary changes in computer and communication technologies. This has affected the speed and accuracy of service and the basic integrity of banking processes, such as internal controls and inter-branch reconciliation of accounts. It has also militated against prompt decision-making, and against improved productivity and profitability.

Equally significant is the poor financial condition of the banks, and the adverse impact this has had on the economy. This financial weakness reflects the impact of policies and practices pursued over a considerable period of time. The cumulative effect has been to leave many of the banks unprofitable and under-capitalised with a high proportion of bad debts among their advances. To cover their costs, banks have been compelled to raise interest rates to the commercial sector, with consequent effects on the competitiveness of their borrowers.

These difficulties are serious but not insuperable. They do, however, require immediate and continuous attention to ensure that the banking sector supports, rather than obstructs, improved efficiency and competitiveness of the economy, and that domestic and international confidence in our banks is maintained. As our exporters have found, reliable, efficient, low-cost financial services are an essential part of overall competitiveness. Even though India enjoys a high savings rate and an abundant supply of low-cost talented finance professionals, the sluggishness of our banks, their high cost structure, the weakness of our regulatory framework and persistent high fiscal deficits have all conspired to turn finance into a burden rather than a source of competitive advantage for our industry, which is now seeking low-cost financing abroad as a way to bolster its competitiveness. Indeed, with the right policies, the financial services sector could itself become globally competitive and a source of export earnings.

Some of the problems of our banks, particularly as regards loan quality, are similar to those faced in the 1980s by banking systems around the globe. Examples include the Philippines, Malaysia, Thailand and Indonesia in Asia, Turkey, Spain, Portugal and the Nordic countries in Europe; and the US Savings and Loan Systems in North America. While in the developed countries the underlying causes were inadequate regulation, in most developing countries, as in India, the problems arose from excessive economic intervention and macroeconomic disequilibrium. Perhaps the most extreme cases were in South America in the early 1980s, where banking crises in Chile, Argentina and Uruguay were associated with an overall collapse of the financial system. Through determined public action, all these countries have overcome their problems, and, in the process, several have laid the foundation for a sound and more progressive banking and financial systems. As discussed below, the Government has already initiated decisive corrective action, to forestall any chance of systemic failure and to lay the basis for a competitive and a modern banking system.

This paper presents an assessment of the current problems facing the public sector commercial banks and articulates the broad strategy being followed to overcome them in a phased manner, over the next three to four years. Given the complexity and importance of issues connected with rural finance, these are not dealt with in this paper. A problem area not covered in this paper relates to the Regional Rural Banks. Set up in 1976 as an alternative to the commercial and cooperative banks for lending to rural target groups, these banks have not been able to fulfil their objectives. They are in an extremely precarious financial position, with about 100 banks making losses continuously since 1983, and over 175 out of a total of 196 banks being in a loss in the current year. It is estimated that cleaning up Regional Rural Banks' balance sheets could cost about Rs. 2,000 crore. Options for restructuring of these banks are under active consideration of Government in consultation with the Reserve Bank of India and NABARD.

Chapter II examines the forces which have led to the financial and managerial weakening of banks and quantifies their financial position as revealed by the new accounting norms. Chapter III describes the approach to be followed in dealing with the financial weakness revealed in the existing portfolio, and discusses measures needed to prevent similar problems from recurring. Chaptrs IV and V deal with the managerial and institutional challenges confronting the banks and the changes in the competitive, legal and regulatory environment within which they will henceforth operate.

II. The Financial Condition of the Banks

The starting point for reform of the public sector banks must be the recognition that a financially sound bank needs both to be profitable and to have a strong balance-sheet and this is as true of public sector banks as of private sector banks. An adequate level of profits implies that the banks's interest and other earnings are sufficient to cover its financial and administrative expenses; that provisions exist for various items such as bad debts, tax liabilities and depreciation of financial assets; and that it retains sufficient surplus to pay dividends to its shareholders and to augment its reserves. From an economic point of view, profitability is also an important indicator of borrowers' health and of sound credit appraisal by the bank. A strong balance-sheet means that the bank has sufficient capital and reserves to protect its depositors and other creditors from the risks it bears on its assets. A loss-making bank will eat into its capital and reserves; when capital and reserves are exhausted, losses will begin to erode deposits. Sufficiency of capital ensures that a bank can bear occasional operating losses without threatening the safety of depositors' funds.

For public sector banks (at least in India), concerns of profitability and capital adequacy have received less attention and emphasis. The implicit assumption was that if banks owned by Government ran into problems, the Government would always find the resources needed to bail them out. This is an unacceptable basis for running public sector banks. It not only implies poor resource allocation for the economy but also that the Government's budget underwrites the banks' solvency. Such burdens are simply not sustainable in the long run. Public sector banks must, therefore, also aim for reasonable profitability and capital adequacy. They must be well-capitalised and generate profit, after making realistic loan-loss provisions, so as to build up reserves to support further business expansion. As banks begin to raise capital from the capital markets, their profits will need to be sufficient to attract shareholders through the promise of a reasonable and regular dividend and possible share-price appreciation.

Judged by these criteria of profitability and capital adequacy the financial position of our public sector banks has fallen well below international standards. Some problems have arisen because of factors external to the banks while others primarily reflect organisational and management shortcomings. It is also evident that there is interaction between the two, in that the external environment may have condoned, if not actively encouraged, poor management. Among the factors which have exerted financial pressure on all banks are the following:

(i) A large volume of bank resources have been statutorily preempted for investment in Government and other securities. While these are safe assets, their yield has not been remunerative.

(ii) Banks have been required to lend to designated priority sectors at subsidised rates of interest. In addition, the administrative and default costs associated with such lending have been very high. Some of the branch expansion required of the banks was not economically sustainable.

(iii) Profitability ranked low in the goals set for bank managements. This prevented banks from building up adequate capital and reserves through internal accruals, while budgetary pressures prevented adequate capital subscription by Government.

(iv) Deterioration in the quality of the loan portfolio, resulting in accumulation of a large proportion of non-income earning assets.

The impact of each of these factors on the profitability and capital position of the banks is discussed below.

Pre-emption of Bank Resources

Commercial banks in India are subject to two separate reserve requirements: the Cash Reserve Ratio (CRR) and the Statutory Liquidity Ratio (SLR). The CRR requires banks to hold a portion of their deposits (net demand and time liabilities) (DTL) in the form of cash balances with the Reserve Bank of India (RBI). While in the past these balances, beyond the 3 per cent basic statutory reserve, were paid a high interest rate, the increase in such balances (over end March 1990 levels) does not any longer earn interest. The SLR requires banks to invest a portion of their net DTL in Central and State Government and other approved securities. Until recently the interest rate on these securities was considerably lower than other market rates, even after adjusting for the difference in risk.

Virtually all banking systems worldwide require banks to hold a certain fraction of their deposits as reserves, as an instrument for monetary management. It is less common to impose mandatory holdings in Government securities, although banks do voluntarily invest a sizeable portion of their assets in such securities as a prudent part of liquidity and yield management. In India, although the CRR and SLR were initially at reasonable levels, they were increased steadily over time largely because of the growing pressures on the Government's budget. As the fiscal deficits of the Central and State Governments increased, this necessitated an increase in Government's market borrowings as well as greater resort to borrowing from the RBI. Increased borrowing from the RBI, in turn, created pressures for monetary expansion which were countered by upward adjustments in the CRR. The need to borrow large amounts from non-RBI sources led to repeated upward adjustments in the SLR, forcing banks to invest an increasing proportion of their resources in low-yielding Government securities. The resulting increase in CRR and SLR is shown in Table 2. Taken together, the two requirements, implied that 40 per cent of any increase in deposits had to be deposited with RBI, or invested in Government securities in 1981. This figure rose to as much as 63.5 per cent in 1991, and only 36.5 per cent of deposits were available for lending for productive purposes. The level of pre-emption in other developing countries is typically much lower, and has been going down over time.

The pre-emption of bank resources at the margin (through the combined impact of CRR and SLR) and the size of the fiscal deficit as a percentage of GDP are shown in Figure 2. While increasing pre-emptions may have reduced the direct interest costs of the Government on its borrowing, they carried a considerable cost for banks, with additional adverse effects on the rest of the economy. Bank profits were reduced and in turn, banks responded by raising interest rates on those advances where they were able to do so. High levels of CRR and SLR were therefore directly responsible for high interest rates on commercial advances, which are a common complaint of borrowers especially in the small scale sector. These high interest rates also encourage "disintermediation" from the banking sector, with the best borrowers opting out of the banking system and relying on non-bank sources which are bound to expand as the capital market develops.

Table 2
Fiscal Deficit and Pre-emption of Resources

Fiscal Deficit (Central Government)		*Marginal Pre-emption (as on March 31, in per cent)*		
		CRR	*SLR*	*Total*
1980-81	6.2	6	34@	40
1981-82	5.4	7.75	35@	42.75
1982-83	6.0	7	35@	42
1983-84	6.3	19	35@	54
1984-85	7.5	19*	36	55*
1985-86	8.3	19*	37	56*
1986-87	9.0	19.5*	37	56.5*
1987-88	8.1	20	38	58
1988-89	7.8	21*	38	59*
1989-90	7.8	15	38	53
1990-91	8.4	15	38.5	53.5
1991-92	6.0	25	38.5	63.5
1992-93	5.7	15*	30	45.0*
1993-94	4.7 #	14	25 @ @	39.0

Source: Economic Survey, 1992-93 and RBI

*   In these years, the release of previously impounded balances implies a slightly
     lower marginal pre-emption than the face value shown here.

@   On gross Demand and Time Liabilities

@ @   Effective from fortnight beginning October 16, 1993.

\#   Budget Estimate

Figure 2
Fiscal Deficit and Credit Pre-emption

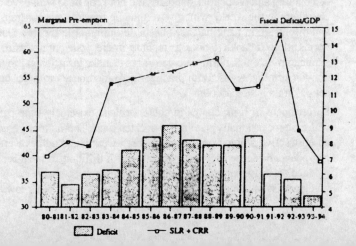

Priority Sector Lending

In addition to the CRR and SLR, banks were also required to allocate a substantial portion of their total advances to designated priority sectors (initially 33-1/3 per cent, later raised to 40 per cent). Until September 1990 virtually all priority sector lending was at below-market interest rates. Recovery of both principal and interest on portions of such lending was often poor, further adding to the burden borne by the banks. Instead of the subsidy coming from the budget, banks were called upon to cross-subsidise the priority sectors from their other operations. While the goal of expanding the credit coverage of the banking system was a laudable one, such lending had costs associated with it which banks were not allowed to recover. Since bank performance was judged by the volume of disbursements (and not recoveries), the specification of a quantitative target led to dilution of credit quality.

Decline in Credit Quality

Banks have also suffered because the quality of their loan portfolio has deteriorated over time. Even though accrued interest was booked as income, interest was not always received in cash. Such non-recovery of interest affected the true profitability of banks and greatly reduced recycling of funds to new borrowers.

Deterioration in the quality of the banks' loan portfolio was due to several factors:

* There was excessive focus on quantitative indicators: growth of total lending, sectoral deployment of credit and the outreach of banks were the main indicators of dynamism and strength in banking. There was inadequate concern with issues of credit quality and the capacity of borrowers to service loans granted to them. In such a climate, poor lending decisions were taken and the bank managements became more susceptible to outside pressures to make loans.

* Influential borrowers brought external pressure to bear on banks to tolerate defaults and this was tolerated because prudential norms were lax. In the case of smaller borrowers, the culture of repayment suffered because of periodic loan waiver schemes.

* Accounting and prudential standards did not keep pace with developments elsewhere in the world, which were moving towards greater transparency and disclosure in bank balance sheets. In India, loose income recognition norms allowed banks to book as income, interest due but not paid. Lack of explicit privisioning norms allowed banks to make insufficient provision for non-performing assets. Both practices permitted banks to defer corrective action on their sick accounts.

* Enforcement of bank claims in courts became extremely time-consuming with cases occasionally pending for over ten years. This naturally encouraged an obstructive attitude on the part of borrowers. Such delays were further compounded by the fact that banks found it difficult to have recourse to pledged security, particularly land. State Governments were not willing to give permission under the Urban Land Ceiling Act and other laws.

Concern for deteriorating credit quality led the RBI in 1985 to introduce a new Health Code System under which the advances portfolio of banks was classified into eight Health Codes ranging from 1 (best) to 8 (worst). This system indicated that by the early 1990s, about 14 per cent of domestic advances of public sector banks were non-performing (i.e., belonging to Health Codes 4-8). This was the average for all public sector banks with the percentage for some weaker banks being much higher. There was, however, a great deal of subjectivity involved in the Health Code System. Also income was recognised on an accrual basis and not on actual recovery of cash.

In recognition of these deficiencies, and based on the recommendations of the Narasimham Committee, the RBI in April 1992 announced a new set of norms (see Appendix) for income recognition, asset classification and provisioning for non-performing assets, initially applicable for the preparation of accounts as at 31st March 1993. The norms are to be progressively tightened to approach international standards over the next two years. Further adjustments may be made in the light of experience.

Under-capitalisation

A further problem afflicting all public sector banks was inadequacy of capital compared to the scale of risk exposure. The importance of capital adequacy was internationally acknowledged in the work of the Basle Committee in 1988. The Committee established the norm that commercial banks of developed countries engaged in international transactions should maintain unimpaired capital at least equal to 8 per cent of risk-weighted assets. This norm is now well establishd in international practice and has been widely accepted in most developing countries as well. Indeed, the tendency of privately-owned banks in many countries, after the financial turbulence of the 1980s, is to maintain even higher levels of capital.

The Reserve Bank of India, also in April 1992, prescribed new capital adequacy norms in line with the Basle Committee's recommendations. The norms are to be complied with over a three year period. As a first step all Indian banks were expected to reach a 4 per cent capital to risk-assets ratio (CRAR) by 31st March 1993 and 8 per cent by 31st March 1996. Since major Indian banks have branches in important money centers of the world, it is especially necessary for those banks to be well-capitalised. Banks with branches overseas[1] are, therefore, required to reach the 8 per cent norm by 31 st March 1994.

Attainment of these minimum capital levels will be affected by the simultaneous adoption of new norms of income recognition, asset classification and provisioning. The income recognition norms will tend to lower the reported profits of banks as will the provisioning norms, which require banks to make large additional provisions on the existing portfolio. It is important to note that it is not the norms that lower actual income and gross profits. Rather, the application of the norms require necessary adjustments to the accounts to reflect more accurately the quality of the loan portfolios and to obtain a true picture of the actual financial situation of each bank. This improvement in transparency and accuracy in the profit and loss statements and balance sheets of banks will permit more timely remedial action and great managerial accountability.

Financial Position Revealed By New Norms

The accounts of public sector banks for the financial year 1992-93 reflect the application of the new norms and therefore provide a realistic picture of the financial position of banks. The picture reveals significant weaknesses which call for urgent corrective action. However, there is considerable diversity across the banks and fortunately, a large share of advances and deposits is accounted for by the stronger banks.

The new asset classification norms reveal a much worse picture of portfolio quality than did the earlier Health Code System. Under the new norms, for advance limits above Rs. 25,000 the share of non-performing advances in total advances ranges from 8-10 per cent in the best banks to 35-45 per cent in the worst ones. For the public sector banks as a whole, non-performing advances are estimated at around 21 per cent of the advances portfolio (both domestic and foreign). This is an extremely high ratio by international standards, especially as the definition of non-performing advances does not as yet reflect the full stringency of the income-recognition norms that will ultimately apply when the norms are fully phased in. Also, the share of non-performing advances in advances below Rs. 25,000, which are not included in the above percentages could well be higher than for the larger advances. On the other hand it should be noted that since reserve requirements (CRR and SLR) have been high, the share of non-performing in total assets is substantially lower.

In terms of absolute size, based on the standards applied for the year ending March 31, 1993, the total non-performing advances of the public sector banks for limits above Rs. 25,000 are estimated at about Rs. 37,000 crore. Banks have, through their past earnings, provided part of the needed provisioning against the identified non-performing advances. However, additional provisions for 1992-93 amounting to Rs. 9,800 crore are required. In order to mitigate the impact on banks, the RBI has allowed them to meet the overall provisioning requirements in two stages, not less than 30 per cent in 1992-93 and the remainder in 1993-94. In the case of advances which are considered loss assets, full provisioning has been immediately effected.

Under earlier accounting practices, the aggregate operating profits of the 28 public sector banks amounted to Rs. 5,541 crore in 1991-92. This has been reduced by almost 45 per cent, to Rs. 3,068 crore in 1992-93, in part reflecting the tightening of income recognition standards. Concurrently there has been a sharp rise in provisions made by banks from Rs. 4,695 crore in 1991-92 to Rs. 6,437 crore in 1992-93. Thus aggregate published profits (i.e. profits after provisions and contingencies) declined from Rs. 804 crore in 1991-92 to a deficit of Rs. 3,369 crore in 1992-93. Of the 28 banks, 26 declared net profits in 1991-92 whereas only 15 were able to do so in 1992-93.

The net result of the application of the new norms is that the public sector banks are much less profitable than was earlier supposed and the need to make large provisions from their operating profits to cover the large volume of non-performing advances is now revealed. These provisions, even though they are being made in a phased manner, have created a deficit in terms of net profits which eats into the capital of the banks thus exacerbating the already existing under-capitalisation.

III. Financial Strengthening of the Banks

The scale of the financial problems facing the public sector banks, as quantified in the previous section calls for corrective action on several fronts. First, Government must change the financial and monetary policies that have weakened the banks in the past. Second, it is necessary to inject fresh capital into the banks to repair the damage of the past. Third, it is necessary to ensure that in future the recapitalised banks can and do operate in a manner that ensures sound financial operations and quality of lending. There is little to be gained by injecting fresh capital if the problems of the past are to recut. A meaningful and a sustainable financial restructuring programme must form part of a wider programme, including changes in the competitive environment, in the autonomy given to the banks, as well as in the management and internal systems of each bank, to enable the banks to function more effectively.

Changes in Financial Policies

The root cause of the progressive increase in pre-emption of bank resources via the CRR and SLR was the rise in the Centre's Fiscal deficit and a reversal of this process is an essential precondition for reducing the CRR and SLR. The reduction in the fiscal deficit in the past two years has already permitted a reduction in the CRR on incremental deposits from 25 per cent in 1991 to 14 per cent today and in the incremental SLR from 38.5 per cent to 25 per cent. The process of fiscal consolidation must continue and as the fiscal deficit is reduced further, it will be possible to reduce the average CRR to 10 per cent and the average SLR to 25 per cent. In incremental terms the reduction in these ratios will be much sharper. Reductions in SLR beyond these levels will depend on new systems for State Government borrowing being devised.

Lower levels of pre-emption are being accompanied by a shift of Government borrowing to market related rates. Central Government dated securities are now being placed on the market entirely by auction. Yields on these securities have increased while maturities have been reduced. In the case of Treasury Bills, in april 1992 the RBI introduced fortnightly auctions of 364-day Treasury Bills and in January 1993 commenced auction of 91-day Treasury Bills. Such auctions, which are open to all commercial banks and large institutional investors like the Unit Trust of India, the insurance companies and registered provident funds, have been well received. Both these developments - the reduction in the extent of pre-emption and the improvement in the yield on Government securities should improve the earnings potential of banks in the future.

The Narasimham Committee had recommended a reduction in the percentage of priority sector credit together with a narrowing of eligibility criteria. In Government's view, what is more important than particular targets, is to ensure availability of credit, quality of service, and quality of lending to these sectors. While the present degree of direction of bank resources to designated priority sectors is expected to continue for the time being, the element of cross-subsidy has been reduced and the complex interest rate structure vastly simplified. In 1989 there were over 50 lending categories with interest rate depending on loan size, usage and type of borrower. These were subsequently brought down to six, and today there are only three rates distinguishing borrowers only by size of loans: loans up to Rs. 25,000 carry an interest rate of 12 per cent, loans from Rs. 25,000 to Rs. 2 lakh carry a fixed interest rate of 15 per cent, and loans in excess of Rs. 2 lakh are subject to a minimum interest rate of 15 per cent. The objective of policy is to move from a three-tier to a simpler two-tier structure with a single concessional rate set no more than 3 percentage points below the normal rate. This structure would still imply a limited cross-subsidy in favour of small borrowers. Such a subsidy can only be justified and sustained if there is significant improvement in loan appraisal and recovery. Since the new prudential norms apply with full force to priority sector lending, significant improvements in portfolio quality are expected as a result of the new norms and the greater stress on recovery. Specific attention will also be given to improving recovery under government sponsored schemes such as the IRDP, where performance has been particularly poor. All bank lending, including loans to the priority sector, must conform to basic requirements of good banking. A major task ahead is to ensure that our banking system has an adequate incentive to meet legitimate credit needs of agriculture and other priority sector borrowers even in the absence of any compulsion in this regard.

Recapitalisation

Public sector banks have progressively to reach a minimum capital to risk assets ratio (CRAR) of 8 per cent by March 1996, starting from a 4 per cent minimum from March 1993 (banks with foreign branches have to attain the 8 per cent minimum by March 1994). Adequacy of capital can be measured only after required provisions have been made, since provisions not covered by operating profits are a charge against capital and reserves. To the extent that banks had overstated past income and profits and underprovided for bad debts, their capital position was also overstated.

Based on balance sheets for 1992-93, a capital shortfall of Rs. 2,500 crore was estimated for the nationalised banks to attain the 4 per cent minimum CRAR; banks in the State Bank Group have all reached the minimum. It can be expected that provisioning and capital requirements will continue to be heavy for the next year or two for several reasons:

* The lending capacity of banks will grow rapidly with the reduction in government pre-emptions.

* The loan classification and income accrual standards will become progressively tighter.

* The provisioning requirements will increase as existing non-performing loans continue to age.

* Most banks have provided only the minimum 30 per cent of required provisions in their 1992-93 account; the balance has to be met in 1993-94 financial statements.

* Additional provisions will be needed to reflect the fact that with rising interest rates, the market value of older, lower yielding government bonds has declined.

Current estimates are that over the three-year period to 1996, the aggregate requirements for additional capital by the nationalised banks would be of the order of Rs. 12,000 crore, while for the State Bank Group the figure could be of the order of Rs. 5,000 crore. These large sums do not include the capital requirements of Regional Rural Banks and certain other financial institutions.

While the 1993-94 Budget contains an allocation of Rs. 5,700 crore towards recapitalisation of the nationalised banks, the Government has already announced that its contribution must be supplemented by efforts of banks to mobilise capital (both equity and debt) from the market. State Bank of India and some financially stronger nationalised banks are preparing to do so. In the case of the State Bank of India, there is already a private sector holding. Under the State Bank of India Act, this can be further increased subject to the requirement that the holding of the RBI does not fall below 55 per cent. Accordingly, State Bank of India has announced plans to access the capital market for both debt and equity. In the case of nationalised banks, equity sales to the private sector require legislative changes in the Banking Companies (Acquisition and transfer of Undertaking) Acts 1970 and 1980; the necessary legislation is to be presented to Parliament in the winter session. Approaches to the markets for equity would follow; however, debt flotations could proceed earlier.

Even after legislative approval is obtained to raise private equity, there will remain practical and market constraints limiting the number of nationalised banks able to follow this route. The markets will rightly insist that past bad debts be provided for from public funds and that the bank in question be capable of declaring a profit. Certain potentially viable banks will face the problem of accumulated loss balances: these have to be covered by future profits before the bank is permitted to declare a dividend. There is also the potential problem of banks' having too much equity as a result of Government infusions of capital; a large equity base implies low earnings per share. Both these problems could be solved by the write-down of Government equity against accumulated losses, but this is not permitted under current law. A rather different set of issues arises with respect to the very weak banks. Here, the high proportion of non-performing assets coupled with high overhead costs (largely excess personnel) make any early return to profitability unlikely. Thus, for both these categories of banks, meeting minimum capital requirements will entail continuing budgetary support for at least two more years, over and above the allocation in the 1993-94 budget. The requirement for 1994-95 is likely to be at least of the same order as in 1993-94. Although the capital amount contributed is reinvested in Government bonds and to that extent, does not entail an immediate cash outflow, the Budget has to bear the interest burden of servicing these bonds, which will be very heavy.

The allocation of the Government's contribution of Rs. 5,700 crore to the nationalised banks is conditional upon each bank drawing up a corporate restructuring plan aimed at bringing the bank to a viable position over the next two to three years. (These corporate plans are discussed more fully in the next Chapter). Banks have provided specific time-bound commitments relating to earnings and profit ratios, funds management, use of technology, improvement in managerial standards etc., so as to ensure that the recapitalisation will endure. Agreements are being concluded between the RBI and the management of each bank. Based on specified parameters, performance indicators are being finalised after detailed discussions between the RBI and the top management of each bank. Amongst the most important indicators are recovery targets by half year, forecasts of profitability over the next two years and goals for technology adoption and branch rationalisation. To ensure accountability, the monitoring of the implementation of these commitments by each bank will be done at the level of the Chairman and Managing Director (CMD) and Executive Director (ED). On behalf of Government, the RBI will intensively review compliance on an on-going basis and ensure that banks fulfil their obligations on targeted dates. Non-fulfilment of the commitments will invite sanctions against banks, including action against bank management, the debarring of banks from any further capital support from government and restrictions on asset growth and acceptance of further deposits, etc. Banks which satisfactorily fulfil the commitments will be allowed greater operational flexibility, in terms of undertaking new business and expansion.

With respect to the very weak banks, the Government and RBI have already dealt with one case, the New Bank of India, which has been merged with a much stronger institution, the Punjab National Bank. Since weak banks vary significantly in terms of size, location and nature of underlying problems, solutions have to be tailor-made for each specific case. Bank-specific action plans are being devised by the RBI in consultation with the banks, including rationalization of branch net works and deployment of staff. As a precautionary measure, weak banks have been subjected to close operating restrictions, including tight limitations on their advances-deposits ratio and close surveillance by the RBI's Department of Banking Operations and Development.

Improving Loan Recovery

Non-performing advances lie at the core of the financial problems of the banks. Hence, efforts to improve recovery rates (i.e., cash realisation of amounts due from borrowers) must have high priority. There are two aspects to be considered. The first, on which there may be relatively limited room for maneouvre, relates to realisations on existing bad advances. The second, on which here is much greater scope for improvement, relates to improved recovery performance on new lending. In both cases, an important determinant of improved recovery will be the effectiveness of the legal system in allowing banks to exercise the remedies available to them in cases of default, and to realise the value of the collateral pledged to them.

There is no easy solution to the problem of enhancing recovery on existing bad advances. It is sometimes argued that it is counter-productive for a restructured bank to dwell excessively on the problems of recovery of past dues, as this diverts the energies of the bank management from the more important task of building for the future. This was the view taken by the Narasimham Committee when it recommended the establishment of a nation-wide Assets Reconstruction Fund (ARF). The Committee proposed that such a fund, capitalised by the Government of India, RBI and public financial institutions, should be set up to purchase poor quality assets from commercial banks (at fair market value). The Fund would then take on the responsibility of loan collection, with the net worth of the Fund benefiting from any excess of realisations over initial valuation. Such institutions have been set up in other countries: a well known example is the Resolution Trust Corporation (RTC) of the United States set up to acquire and dispose of property holdings of failed Savings and Loan institutions.

After careful consideration, the Government and the RBI have concluded that a generalised nation-wide ARF, taking over contaminated assets from all public sector banks, would not be advisable under Indian circumstances. This judgement is based on several considerations:

- the large geographic expanse of the country and the difficulty in setting up a new institution quickly.

- the difficulties of capitalising the ARF, over and above the huge existing capital needs of the banks.

- the relatively poor recovery experience of some countries that have set up ARFs.

It is felt that the degree of recovery will be greater if the originating banks retain the responsibility for such recovery. There is also the concern that absolving banks from responsibility for collection could weaken their own credit discipline in the future, and may even adversely affect the behaviour of borrowers in good standing.

Accordingly, improvement in recovery performance has been accorded a very high weightage in the corporate plans being developed by banks and in the agreements between government and bank managements. In particular, efforts are being made to ensure that assets in the sub-standard category, which account for about one-third of the total non-performing assets, can be restored to full performance. A number of banks have designated senior officials and special teams with exclusive responsibility for improving loan recovery, and initial results are encouraging. Banks are also aggressively pursuing compromise agreements with borrowers, with suitable safe-guards to ensure the integrity of the process. The establishment of the Special Tribunals has already motivated borrowers to arrive at out-of-court settlements with banks.

The maintenance of payments discipline requires that banks vigorously pursue recovery even for advances that have been provisioned against. At the same time, banks may wish to explore other financial and organizational devices to segregate the bad portfolios so as to clear the balance sheet of the main bank while providing intensive attention to the sick portfolio. A number of financial engineering innovations have been pioneered by banks in other countries that should be examined with the appropriate professional help.

Quite apart from recovery on past loans, what will be truly crucial is the recovery experience on new advances. Here, the incentives embodied in the new accounting norms are already making banks more alert to credit quality while making new loans, including loans to priority sector borrowers, while the enhanced provisioning norms will reduce the tendency to 'evergreening' of accumulated dues on past bad loans. The RBI should also intensify its efforts to inform banks of the outstanding exposure and past credit record of major borrowers, subject to suitable safeguards on confidentiality. However, banks cannot expect to be immune from the greater level of commercial risk that will confront their commercial borrowers in a freer economic environment. Managing these risks will require renewed attention to the development of credit evaluation skills and systems, as discussed in Chapter IV.

The Government has acted on the proposal of both Narasimham and Tiwari Committees that special recovery tribunals be established for quick disposal of banking disputes and realisation of collateral. The Recovery of Debt Due to Banks and Financial Institutions Bill, 1993 was passed by Parliament in August 1993, and these tribunals are expected to start functioning in the four metropolitan cities (Bombay, Calcutta, Madras and New Delhi) before the end of this year. It is expected that the existence of such tribunals will sharply reduce the average time needed to adjudge a case. The existence of such tribunals should improve the payments discipline among all borrowers.

Improving Profitability

Improvements in operating and net profits (i.e., profits after provisioning) are crucial for the future financial viability of public sector commercial banks. Strong operating profits allow for full prudential provisioning, while allocations from net profits are an important source of capital enhancement, essential for any bank to expand its lending activity. Capital raised in the markets is another source for capitalisation but this will only be possible on the basis of a good profit performance and the prospect of attractive dividend yields.

The major components of bank profitability are net interest margin, establishment costs, and provisioning and these are shown in Table 3. The best route to higher earnings is through improvement in the net interest margin which is the difference between interest earnings and interest expenses, expressed as a percentage of working funds. A good margin reflects effective deployment of high quality earning assets, a judicious mix of liabilities and good yields. The net interest margin of public sector banks for 1992-93 was 2.38 per cent of average working funds, while the corresponding figure for all scheduled commercial banks (including foreign banks) was 2.49 per cent. These margins are almost a percentage point lower than in 1991-92, reflecting primarily new income recognition norms, and also the slower adjustment of interest expenditure than interest income in a period of declining interest rates. Establishment and other costs were exceptionally high, exceeding the interest margin; employee compensation and other operating costs for public sector banks worked out to 1.87 per cent and 0.78 per cent of average working funds, respectively. These figures are comparable to those for the previous year. As a result, the surplus from the interest income was negative for public sector banks, at 0.27 per cent of average working funds. After taking into account income other than interest and allowing for provisions and contingencies, the net profit works out to a deficit of 1 per cent of working funds. Profitability performance at a deficit of 1 per cent of working funds needs to be compared with a target return on assets of 1 per cent in many private banking systems. If the public sector banks were able to achieve a 1 per cent return on working funds, the additional resources generated would be about Rs. 3400 crore in a year. The public sector banks as a whole thus need a big increase in profitability, which must come from all quarters: reduced overheads, improved margins, improved asset quality and increased non-fund business.

While overall profitability is low, it is important to recognise that there is considerable diversity in performance across the public sector banks which is indicative of the scope for improvement in the poor performers. The reasons for variations lie in the quality of liability and funds management and the varying quality of major assets, particularly advances. The level of non-performing assets and incidence of bad debts vary significantly among different banks. Low employee productivity levels and rising operating costs compound the problem further. Significantly, variations in performance are not related to the size of the branch network or to the size of business of a bank. Variations are clearly noticeable between banks of comparable size, whether small or large, suggesting that organisational culture and quality of management have played a crucial role in determining bank performance, even in a common policy setting.

While it is difficult to make generalisations, the more successful of the public sector banks appear to be those which have preserved a sense of institutional identity and *esprit de corps* over time. Partly this derives from the culture and systems that existed prior to nationalisation. There also appears to be a link with the appointments of Chief Executives. Banks with a tradition of promotion from within have typically been better managed and more resistant to undesirable external pressure in their lending and staffing decisions. This, in turn, has been reflected in the quality of their advances portfolio. The managerial and institutional agenda is a large one for all the banks and is vital to their recovery and modernisation, as is extensively discussed in the next Chapter.

Table 3
Profitability of Public Sector and all Scheduled Commercial Banks, 1992-93
(as percentages of average working funds)

		Public Sector Banks	All Scheduled Commercial Banks
1.	Interest Income	9.55	9.72
2.	Interest Expenditure	7.17	7.23
3.	**Net Interest Margin (1-2)**	**2.38**	**2.49**
4.	Employee Compensation	1.87	1.77
5.	Other Operating Costs	0.78	0.89
6.	**Total Non-interest Expenditure (4+5)**	**2.65**	**2.66**
7.	Surplus from Interest Income (3-6)	(-) 0.27	(-) 0.17
8.	Other income	1.18	1.17
9.	**Gross surplus (7+8)**	**0.91**	**1.00**
10.	Provisions and Contingencies	1.91	2.08
11.	**Profitability (9-10)**	**(-) 1.00**	**(-) 1.08**

Source: Accounts of Banks, 1992-93.

IV. Managerial and Institutional Strengthening

Public sector banks are entering a far more challenging environment in the future when they will face greater competition in the financial markets, greater demands from customers for a high quality service, and at the some time they will have to achieve internal financial strength if they are to survive. In order to respond to these and other challenges, public sector banks need to transform themselves into technologically sophisticated, commercially responsive, managerially innovative business units. It is sometimes argued that such responsiveness is impossible in institutions under majority public ownership. This was not however the view taken by the Narasimham Committee, nor is it the view of the Government. However, there is an urgent need to redefine the purposes of public ownership of the banks, reflect these in explicit corporate objectives, and correspondingly clarify and limit the acceptable forms of public intervention. The commercial orientation of public sector banks must be significantly enhanced and operational interference by the Government and RBI eliminated.

If public ownership is not to be discredited by a repeat of the huge losses and poor quality loan portfolios of the past, fundamental changes in the governance and management of the banks are essential. Banks will need to be given far greater autonomy and flexibility in their business and staffing decisions. While the agenda is large and priorities will differ for each bank, certain general considerations apply:

* The most urgent attention needs to be given to evolving well-grounded business strategies, and to developing the decision-support structures (management information systems, clear policy goals and written guidelines, asset and liability committees) needed for implementation.

* Concurrently, the banks need to be given greater control over a whole range of human resource issues.

* The weaker banks, in particular, will require intensive assistance in developing and implementing their recovery programmes. In addition to consulting assistance, this may require the infusion of experienced staff from outside the banks.

While there is much ground to be made up there is good reason for optimism. The competitive advantages of the nationalised banks are not inconsiderable. They have an unparalleled branch network, which will be near-impossible for new entrants to replicate. With appropriate management and some reshaping, this network provides a platform for distribution of a wide range of financial services (such as insurance and equity related services), in addition to its existing functions of deposit mobilisation and credit delivery. The banks' relationships with their existing customer base represent an unmatched stock of 'information capital' regarding the country's prime corporate and agricultural borrowers. When complemented by better information technology and a stronger legal enforcement infrastructure, these customer relationships will constitute a vital resource.

Corporate Recovery Strategies

The capacity for planning varies greatly among the public sector bank. While several of the larger banks have well-developed systems of corporate planning, even these systems need fundamental reorientation. Some of the weaker banks lack the human and information resources to diagnose their financial and organisational problems, and to fashion appropriate strategic responses. Paradoxically, it is the stronger banks that are seeking outside consulting assistance; this is a healthy trend which the weaker banks should emulate.

As part of the recapitalisation exercise, banks have prepared corporate plans of varying degrees of sophistication. Most of the business decisions needed to implement such plans lie within the competence of each bank. Banks already enjoy formal operational autonomy in relation to investments and loans (subject to the guidelines of the RBI). Such autonomy has been considerably expanded in the recent Credit Policy statement of the RBI. With the raising of consortium limits, banks will be allowed to compete for the business of all but the very largest borrowers. They also have greater freedom to assess the extent of financing that should be provided, rather than constained by norms provided by the RBI. Banks are increasingly free to decide the range of services to be offered by each branch and to concentrate on specific markets. Banks will need to cost business lines (such as payment of pensions, acceptance of income-tax payments and various special schemes where public sector banks are used as delivery vehicles) that are currently provided, to assess whether cost recovery is taking place.

Individual banks will have to determine the internal organisational structure which is most appropriate for their needs and business goals. Banks are already undertaking branch and functional reorganisation by concentrating on certain activities or market segments. They are now permitted to close down their loss-making branches (except in rural areas), and several are chosing to do so. Equally, banks which have met the specified capital adequacy standards are permitted to open new branches without reference to RBI. Strategic business alliances across public sector banks, or with private banks, should be explored, with or without equity cross-holdings, as ways of upgrading technological and professional sophistication. As a general principle, commercial banks should have the same freedom for entering into domestic and foreign partnerships as is currently available to the financial institutions.

Policies for Improved Risk Management

An important aspect of managerial strengthening is the development of better processes for managing the credit portfolio, and for asset and liability management more broadly. In order to avoid risk concentration and for maintenance of proper credit quality, banks have been developing a set of written loan policies as part of their recapitalisation commitments. The loan policy framework will cover the entire gamut of the credit operations of the banks and will serve as a comprehensive, transparent statement of the management objectives of the bank in regard to loan transactions. Such a loan policy will inter alia specify:

*   explicit individual customer and group exposure   limits;
*   standards for documentation;
*   sectoral exposure limits; and

    *   delegation of powers.

It will also formalise factors to be examined in pricing credit (above the floor rate) and the norms for recovery and write-offs. Similar policy codification is needed in the areas of investments and liquidity management, to promote clarity, accountability and delegation.

Banks will also have to systematise their asset and liability management process: define policies, develop information systems, and set up a decision-making structure (usually an asset and liability management committee), drawing upon senior officers from the range of functions that shapes the balance sheet (funding, credit, treasury, foreign exchange) to take a consolidated view of the balance sheet position and risk on a continuous basis.

Internal Control Systems

To revitalise and tone up the deficiencies in internal control systems banks are examining their existing internal inspection/audit arrangements and are taking various steps to strengthen these systems:

    *   Regular and surprise inspections are being carried out at sensitive functional and operational spots.

    *   A regular system of revenue audit has been introduced. Also a system of exclusive scrutiny of the credit portfolio focusing on larger advances and group exposures has been evolved.

    *   Preventive warning systems are being designed to pick up signals of deviation from the prescribed internal control norms.

    *   Concurrent audit has been instituted at all large branches

    *   A comprehensive, streamlined system of control returns is being formulated to support efficient financial transacting, while providing suitable checks and safeguards.

    *   The Long Form Audit Report submitted by statutory auditors, has been revised and a new narrative format has been introduced from 1992-93 which covers advances, funds management, internal control, profitability, etc. The findings will be placed before the bank boards clearly indicating the actions taken and proposed to be taken in regard to the observations made.

The arrangements for appointing statutory auditors for the banks needs review and improvement. The current system gives auditors inadequate time and incentive to develop a thorough understanding of each bank, and the tenures are too brief. While improvements in control systems can help reduce risk, they can only perform if they are implemented and acted upon; lack of compliance has more often been the true source of weakness. Equally, excessive controls can act to dampen delegation and initiative. A case in point is the impact of external surveillance and vigilance procedures. These have reached the point where they inhibit sensible commercial decision-making and downward delegation in the banks, and must be reviewed. Strengthening of bank-specific ombudsman systems may, over time, reduce the need and role for an external vigilance system.

Technology

Crucial to the success of many of the above initiatives is the need to modernise information technology. The new economic environment facing the banks and their customers necessitates a qualitative change in the range of services available from the banks, and much greater emphasis on the speed of transactions. Simultaneously, technological support for management information systems and processing of information relevant for credit appraisal have to become an integral part of managerial and organisational reform.

So far only thirteen public sector banks have installed mainframe computers in Head Offices. 307 minicomputers have been installed in regional/zonal offices and 28 branches have been taken up for full computerisation. Clearly, a great deal more needs to be done. The level of technology in public sector banks prevailing today is by any standards obsolete. Both management failures and trade union pressures are responsible for this deplorable situation. The modernisation programme long suggested by RBI has repeatedly suffered in the negotiated settlements reached with the employees' unions for computerisation of branches, zonal offices and headquarters. Fortunately, the most recent agreement (of October 1993) paves the way for much faster induction of computerisation. The foreign banks operating in India and non-bank financial services firms meanwhile have gone ahead to implement total modernisation and have introduced various technology-based services for customers. Public sector banks cannot afford to be left behind.

Technology use has to be aggressively pushed through to strengthen internal control, improve accuracy of transactions and records management, support decision-making and facilitate new services and a higher level of customer satisfaction. Banks therefore are being urged to draw up a well-defined, time-bound programme of computerisation. This will establish:

* The role to be played by computers and computer technology in each bank.
* The appropriate organisational scheme for improved technology absorption.
* An assessment of what is required at branch, regional and head office levels.
* How best to develop in-house capacity.
* Strategies for management relations with staff on technology issues, appropriate to local conditions.

Banks must lay stress on branch level computerisation. In all large branches above a daily voucher load of 750, all items of work should be immediately computerised. This would cover around 2500 branches located in 30 identified metropolitan/urban centres covering 51 per cent of the total banking transactions in India. On-line systems must be put in place combining real-time transaction processing with a networking of all machines and terminals. Selected city branches should be connected to one another to aid customer convenience.

Customer Service

While there are always individual exceptions, in general public sector banks tend to receive poor marks from customers for the quality of service provided, even though banking is fundamentally a service industry. Poor service, in turn, reflects a variety of factors: insufficient managerial attention to service issues, archaic procedures, a bureaucratic and monopolistic mindset, restrictive practices, poor motivation, over-staffing and inadequate technology. Indeed, a high and consistent level of customer service is the prime indicator of quality for a bank, and in that sense is a powerful indicator of its overall managerial health.

There is immense experience and understanding now available from all parts of the world on what is involved in ensuring the delivery of a quality service product in a large-scale, widely dispersed enterprise. There is no reason why these insights and techniques would not be effective in the public sector banks if they were applied consistently and conscientiously. As first steps, banks are being asked to establish systems to monitor the level of customer satisfaction, and to supplement their own reviews with periodic reviews by external agencies. Arrangements are being estab-lished, such as Ombudsmen, for investigating complaints relating to non-credit services, and resolving disputes expeditiously and fairly. A comprehensive Code of Banking Practice must be drawn up, outlining standards for disclosure of information about the banks' services and available products and the rights and obligations of its customers.

Human Resource Issues

The changes in organisational culture needed for successful recovery of the banks are inextricably linked to the management of their human resources. Some of the major issues requiring attention are:

* Board-level appointments

- Decision-making by Government has been slow, depriving banks of leader-ship at critical times.
- The tenure of senior management is frequently too brief for difficult issues to be tackled and change to be implemented.

* Promotion and placement policies

- Promotion is almost exclusively by seniority, making it difficult to recognise exceptional performers.
- There has been little lateral entry as a way of introducing fresh skills and thinking.
- More broadly, it has been difficult to attract persons of the necessary calibre to senior-level positions, commensurate with the scale, complexity and importance of these organisations.

* Staffing Levels, Deployment and Industrial Relations

- There is clear evidence of excess staffing in the public sector banks as a group. Such overstaffing affects efficency, profitability and morale.

- Banks have not developed a culture of self-regulation in staff numbers. Instead, the RBI has been forced to lay down certain aggregate parameters and ceilings, which carry their own inefficiencies.

- Inflexibility in work assignments and geographic preferences means that staff surpluses in certain areas co-exist with deficits in other areas, to the detriment of overall productivity.

- There has been a general disinclination to serve in the semi-urban and rural areas, which has affected the quality of banking operations in these areas.

- Many of the above rigidities are the product of the industrial relations structure and collective bargaining procedures prevalent in the public sector banks, which have not always served the best interests of the organisations or their employees.

* Recruitment and Compensation

- Centralised entry-level recruitment through the Banking Services Recruitment Board (BSRB) means that the nationalised banks do not have adequate flexibility to attract the best talent.

- Rigid pay structures and practices do not permit performance-related bonuses, or the offer of customised compensation packages to individuals with special skills.

* Training and upgrading of skills

- The mammoth training establishment that exists needs to be refocussed in support of the new business strategies and goals. Increased use of information technology will carry its own enormous training agenda.

There are no quick or easy solutions to these problems. However, a number of initiatives are currently underway:

* A review is being undertaken by a Committee headed by a RBI Deputy Governor, of the recruitment procedures and practices in public sector banks, so as to build up requisite professional cadres at various levels of management. Leading management experts from the field of personnel and recruitment have also beeen associated with the committee and the recommendations are expected in December 1993.

* A scheme has been formulated for lateral mobility of all senior officials in Scale V and above among nationalised banks, and is currently being examined.

* A Standing Coordination Committee has been constituted with representatives from RBI, Government, NABARD, banks, training institutions and Management Institutes to coordinate, monitor and guide training arrangements in banks. The quality and scale of training requires considerable strengthening, especially in the areas of asset management, detection of incipient sickness, marketing of banking products and services, risk and

exposure management.

* Clear-cut policies for human resource development are being evolved, which, *inter alia*, will include preparation of career charts for all categories of employees and officers, development of performance appraisal systems, training programes and periodic skill upgrading exercises. Greater account-ability is being introduced and strengthened by simplifying organisational structures, clearly defining roles and responsibilities and making use of independent profit and cost centres.

With regard to appointments of board level personnel such as Chairmen and Executive Directors, the Government is intensifying its efforts to locate individuals with the appropriate background and professional competence and expertise. In this process seniority should have some weight but it should not compromise the search for excellence. In order to ensure that chief executives have a reasonable time period in office the Government will not appoint persons to the position of Chairman if they have less than 3 years of tenure left or 2 years in the case of an internal candidates.

Individual banks are being encouraged to ensure that within the organisation there is a fast track for promoting individuals of outstanding merit. Only if this is done can merit-based succession planning be undertaken in an orderly fashion.

Currently, remuneration in public sector banks is linked to the general level of government and public sector salaries. It is unrealistic to think that public sector banks will be able to match the levels of pay offered in the private sector; instead, public sector banks will need to compete on the basis of an overall package combining experience, responsibility, training and diversity, which together could help in drawing and retaining good quality personnel. Over the years the system might evolve away from uniform pay scales for all public sector banks to one where managerial pay is set by individual bank boards. The desirability of performance related bonuses or other forms of incentive pay could be explored. Similarly, as suggested by the Narasimham Committee, the continuing usefulness of centralised recruitment through the Banking Services Recruitment Board (BSRB) should be reviewed, and assessed against bank-specific recruitment schemes. In the latter case, banks themselves could evolve policies to ensure that certain broad social concerns on equality of access and special reservations were honoured; compliance would be assessed on the basis of actual performance.

In the decade 1982-92, total staff strength rose at an annual rate of 3 per cent from 6.5 lakh to 8.8 lakh employees. There are large differences across banks in the ratio of staff to various indicators of business activity. Excess staff is particularly pronounced in the controlling office of banks such as head offices, and in metropolitan branches. Rural branches on the other hand remain under-staffed. Staff deployment will be an essential part of the adjustment process in the banks, but will need to occur in an orderly, negotiated fashion. Overall employment will be best protected if banks negotiate greater freedom for redeployment of staff. While some reduction in numbers will occur through attrition, properly conceived voluntary retirement schemes can be largely self-financing and should be explored.

Organisational Culture and Decision-making

Although the public sector banks operate in diverse parts of the country and are after large organisation, there has been a tendency towards extreme centralisation of decision-making, centred on the office of the Chairman and Managing Director. At senior levels (between the CMD and the ED or between the CMD and the Board) communications have often been poor. The top-heavy control structure of Zonal and Regional offices weakens decision-making power at the level of the branch where contact with the customer occurs. Managerial morale has been additionally undermined by the factors mentioned earlier: an over-developed vigilance apparatus which can be activated without reference to bank management and by restrictive practices that deny flexibility in even routine managerial functions.

Despite these problems, it is also true that enlightened management in the better banks has succeeded in infusing a sense of team-work and disciplined risk-taking into their organisations. This needs to be made the norm rather than the exception and for this the decision-making culture in banks will need to change. A strong, shared sense of corporate purpose must start with professionalism at the Board level. One proposal sometimes made is to split the functions of Chairman and Managing Director, with the Chairman serving in a part-time non-executive capacity. It has been argued that this would ensure that strategic and policy issues are not neglected under the weight of operational pressure. The Board, in turn, would be instrumental in ensuring that top management operates as a cohesive team in the best interests of the bank. The Central Government could restrict its role to specifying a limited number of corporate objectives over a multi-year period, with the performance of the Board and Chief Executive being assessed only at the end of a planning cycle.

V. Supervision and Competition

Two additional factors that will have a major impact on the public sector banks are a changed system of supervision and increased competition from both new private sector banks and foreign banks.

Supervision of Banks

As demonstrated by the securities irregularities, there has to be better monitoring to ensure that banks behave in a responsible fashion and comply with the prudential guidelines and directives of the RBI. However, supervision can at best be a second line of defence; the main mechanisms of compliance and control must operate within each financial institution. In line with modern international practice, supervision must increasingly concern itself with assessing the effectiveness of internal control and risk assessment systems within different constitutents of the financial system: banks, financial institutions and non-banking financial intermediaries.

Accordingly, the system of external supervision is being completely revamped with the setting up of an autonomous Board for Financial Supervision (BFS) within the RBI. The Board is expected to become operational by the end of this year. The functions of credit policy and bank supervision will be separated: the BFS will concentrate exclusively on supervisory issues and will ensure compliance with regulations and guidelines in the areas of credit management, asset classification, income recognition, capital adequacy, provisioning and treasury operations. As with the system followed by the Federal Deposit Insurance Corporation in the U.S. which assesses banks on a range of factors (Capital, Asset Quality, Management, Earnings and Liquidity the so-called CAMEL system), the aim will be to arrive at a rounded evaluation of the strength, soundness and performance of banks, possibly with numerical points being assigned. The scope of supervision over financial institutions and non-bank financial intermediaries, which is limited at present, will be expanded. The Board shall also deal with financial sector frauds, confining itself to the establishment of *prima facie* incidence of irregularities.

The Board will have an Advisory Committee consisting of persons of eminence, drawn from different walks of public life and with knowledge and experience of the economic and financial system. Operational support to the Board will come from a new Department of Supervision, being up within the RBI. The Department will report directly to the Board and will consist of personnel both from within and outside RBI. The wider powers vested in the Board will enhance the effectiveness of the supervisory mechanism. Supervisory intervention shall be in the form of removal of managerial and other persons; recommending suspension of business, amalgamation, merger or winding up; issuance of directives; and imposition of penalties for non-compliance. While supervision shall be in the exclusive purview of the Board, RBI will continue to attend to all credit, monetary, regulatory and developmental matters pertaining to the financial system.

Competition from Private and Foreign Banks

Along with strengthening the public sector banks, private sector banks, are being allowed to expand their operation, including the entry of new private sector banks. With regard to existing private banks, Government has declared that there should be no fear of further nationalisation. Accordingly, the growth of these banks can occur unhindered, provided the applicable prudential norms are met. Guidelines for granting licences to new private sector banks were announced by the Reserve Bank in January 1993. The guidelines aimed at ensuring that the new entrants are professionally managed, financially viable and technologically strong and that there would be no adverse consequence such as concentration of credit, cross-holding with industrial groups, etc.

A number of proposals have been received for establishment of new banks in the private sector following the announcement of the guidelines. 'In principle' approval has been given to seven institutions - ICICI, UTI, HDFC, one professional group, one finance company and two for starting new banking companies. As these banks get established, they are expected to have substantial widely held private sector equity. The new banks will set up branches in rural, semi-urban and urban areas, fulfil the requirements for priority sector and meet the capital adequacy norm of 8 per cent of risk weighted assets from inception. A minimum capital base of Rs. 100 crore has been specified. Recently, foreign participation in new banks has been permitted up to 20 per cent by foreign companies (including banks) and to 40 per cent by NRIs. The latter brings the investment rules for NRI's in banking on par with the rules for NRI's entry into Industry.

The guidelines for new private sector banks included certain existing provisions of the Banking Regulation Act 1949. Certain of these, particularly the restriction of voting rights by individual shareholders to no more than one per cent (regardless of the size of equity holding) and the outside interests of the Chairman and Directors require review. While individual exceptions have been granted, Government is intending a broader revision of the Banking Regulation Act, which is expected to be presented to Parliament in the next session. Other amendments being proposed include provisions for auditors to report directly to RBI with regard to contravertion of banking regulations and increase in penalty limits to make them more effective. While attention has so far been devoted to the setting up of completely new banks, a further possibility that could be considered is for private investors to have minority equity holdings (with Board representation) in public sector banks. This could assist such banks in their capitalisation, introduce new management techniques, controls and technology quickly, and help maximise value from the branch network.

Foreign banks have had a long-standing presence in India and have an important role to play in the emerging environment. While primarily represented in the metropolitan and port areas, the foreign banks have provided competition to the public sector banks in terms of customer service and efficiency. Given their global affiliations and international experience, including operations in other developing countries, these banks have been rendering specialised services to India's export-import trade, in arranging foreign currency loans for Indian corporates, providing a meeting ground for Indian and foreign businesses and facilitating joint ventures and collaboration. Currently, there are 24 foreign banks operating in India, with 141 branches and four representative offices. Besides, 20 other foreign banks have a representative office each and 12 others have tie-up/agency agreement with six Indian merchant banking firms. Thus, 56 foreign banks from 21 countries have presence in one form or the other in the country. In 1991, the decision was taken to approve the requests received from foreign banks for opening maiden branches and permit branch expansion by the existing foreign banks on a case by case basis. Since Novermber 1991, "in principle' approval has been given to three new foreign banks to set up operations in India. In addition, approval has also been granted for opening 16 additional branches.

Foreign banks have also shown interest in participating in the equity of new private banks. Until recently, the only operational vehicle available to foreign banks to enter the Indian banking system was through a branch. With the recent decision permitting foreign institutions to have equity participation up to 20 per cent in new banks, technical and financial collaboration by foreign banks will be further promoted.

The priority sector lending obligations of foreign banks have recently been reformulated, taking account of the difficulties that they face in lending to the agricultural sector. Foreign banks are now required to place 32 per cent of their advances in the priority sector, but, unlike Indian banks, are permitted to include export credit in this total. They may also satisfy their priority sector obligations through investment in bonds of the Small-scale Industries Development Bank of India (SIDBI).

The Role of Government and the Reserve Bank of India

The Government, as the owner, must continue to exercise proprietary control. However, Government has to ensure full operational autonomy to the managements, as is the case in countries like France. There is already a substantial delegation of authority in operational matters, such as raising of funds, investments and making of advances. There are only a few matters relating to overall staff strength and creation of posts, where either the general guidelines lay down maximum limits of expansion, or where specific approval of Government is required. These guidelines and limits have been placed so as to control the excess proliferation of staff as there is a general perception that banks are over-staffed. Additional measures, such as easing foreign travel curbs and allowing staff expansion in the well-run banks are under active consideration. In the context of assuring autonomy to banks, it has also been suggested that bank managements, including their Boards, should be held fully accountable for the performance of their institutions in all respects and in order to make this accountability effective and transparent, the Government should not appoint its officers on the Boards of the banks.

All matters relating to bank licensing and supervision fall squarely within the role and responsibility of the RBI and its Board of Financial Supervision. With the entry of additional private domestic and foreign banks, RBI will need to behave in a scrupulously even-handed fashion with all banks. In this regard the suggestion of the Narasimham Committee, that RBI withdraw from the Boards of Banks, could be examined.

VI. Summing Up

India's public sector banks have a vital role to play in the new economic environment. They were able to respond to the mandate given to them at the time of nationalisation: the spread of their branches, the expansion of their deposits and diversification of their borrowers all bear testimony to that success. This quantitative success was, however, achieved at the expense of deterioration in qualitative factors such as profitability, efficiency, and the most important, the quality of the loan portfolio, which now need to take the centre stage.

This paper has articulated a recovery programme that the Government, the Reserve Bank of India and banks themselves have formulated to address this agenda of qualitative reform. The programme is designed to provide full protection to all depositors of every public sector bank while banks go through a necessary transition.

To reiterate, the elements of the recovery programme are as follows:

(i) Reduce preemption of lending capacity through staged reductions in SLR and CRR, while moving the yield on government debt to market-related levels.

(ii) Stress availability rather than subsidy in provision of credit to the priority sector, and restrict cross-subsidy only to the smaller borrowers. The goal should be to establish incentives that induce adequate flows of credit to priority uses especially agriculture without compromising on prudential and commercial considerations.

(iii) Move to objective, internationally recognised accounting standards, with suitable transitional provisions to give banks time to adjust. These accounting norms will clarify and strengthen the incentives for bank managements to exercise greater care in credit assessment and recovery.

(iv) Make additional capital available from the government and the capital markets to strengthen banks' financial position and provide a basis for future growth. Provision of capital by the government will be conditional on monitorable improvements in the management and recovery performance of each bank. Access to the markets will impose the additional discipline of prospectus registration or assessment by credit-rating agencies and accountability to non-governmental shareholders.

(v) Improve prospects for recovery by setting up special recovery tribunals in major metropolitan areas.

(vi) Set up a credit information database for exchange of information on credit history of large borrowers, subject to confidentiality.

(vii) Upgrade the calibre of appointees to Board level posts stressing longevity and security of tenure.

(viii) Enhance managerial accountability and autonomy; stress performance-related promotion.

(ix) Encourage technological modernisation in banks through Computerisation and greater labour flexibility.

(x) Encourage greater competition for public sector banks through controlled entry of modern, professional private sector banks including foreign banks.

(xi) Create a new Board for Financial Supervision to devote exclusive attention to issues of compliance and supervision; review the Banking Regulation Act.

(xii) Ensure viable mechanisms for supply of credit to rural sector, small scale industry and weaker sections.

The steadfast pursuit of this agenda promises to transform Indian banking-and the public sector banks in particular - over the next three years. By June 1996, all public sector banks will have attained an 8 per cent Capital-to-Risk-Assets ratio; half the public sector banks (weighted by deposits) should be quoted on the stock market, with appropriate representation of the shareholders on bank boards; there would have been significant entry of new private sector banks; SLR and CRR would be appreciably reduced; interest rates would be deregulated, save for one concessional rate; at least 500 branches of public sector banks would be fully computerised, and the share of non-performing assets in total loan assets would have appreciably declined. These are ambitious objectives for institutional change in the banking sector, but they can be achieved. The needs of India deserve no less.

Appendix

Norms for income recognition, asset classification and provisioning for assets

Income recognition

Banks are not allowed to book interest income on non-performing assets.

A non-performing asset has been defined as a credit facility in respect of which interest has remained unpaid:

- For a period of 4 quarters from the date it has become 'past due' during the year ended 31 March 1993.

- For a period of 3 quarters from the date it has become 'past due' in the financial year ending March 1994.

- For a period of 2 quarters (180 days) from the date it has become 'past due' in the year ending March 1995.

A credit facility is treated as 'past due' when interest has not been paid for 30 days from due date.

Asset classification and provisioning for assets*

Reserve Bank of India minimum norms for asset classification and provisioning are as follows:

Classification of Asset	Provisioning Requirements
1) Standard Assets	NIL
2) Sub-standard Assets -	10%

An asset which has been classified as non-performing asset for a period not exceeding 2 years. (an asset becomes non-performing if interest has remained unpaid for a period of 4 quarters and 'past due' for 30 days during the year ended 31.3.93;3 quarters and 'past due' for 30 days during the period ending 31.3.94;2 quarters and 'past due' for 30 days during the year 31.3.95 and onwards. Even on reschedulement the asset can be upgraded to standard category only after it has performed satisfactorily for at least 2 years).

3) Doubtful Assets -

An asset which has remained non-performing for a period exceeding 2 years.

100% of the unsecured portion.
For the secured portion:

Status as Doubtful Asset	Provision
Upto 1 year	20%
1 to 3 years	30%
More than 3 years	50%
	100%

4) Loss Assets -

An asset is considered a loss asset when it is so
identified by the bank or its internal/external
auditors or the RBI inspectors.

**Phasing for provisioning requirements identi-
fied as on 31.3.93 :**

Loss Assets	100% provisions in the year ended 31.3.93
Doubtful Assets	30% of the provisions in
Sub-standard Assets	the accounts for the year
Advances below Rs. 25,000	ended 31.3.93.
70% of the provisions in	the accounts for the year ending 31.3.94.

* N.B. : *Advances with outstanding balance of Rs. 25,000 and less, were not
required to be classified for the balance sheet ended 31.3.1993. An
aggregate provision to the extent of 2.5% of total outstanding (below Rs.
25,000) to this category was, however, required to be made.*

Government of India, Ministry of Finance, Department of Economic Affairs, Discussion
Paper, December, 1993.

14

Tax Reforms Committee Final Report (Part II)

C helliah Committee report on Tax Reforms Part II gives the committee's final recommendations on the changes to be effected in the duty structure relating to specific group of industries and the time period within which changes should be brought about. The report also deals with the restructuring of excise duties and review of exemption notifications in the import tariff. The basic recommendations relating to import duty reduction and the concluding remarks of the report are reproduced below.

Basic Considerations Relating to Import Duty Reduction

The Objectives

In our Interim Report, we had given a fairly detailed description of the very complex and economically irrational import tariff system prevalent in India. The very high or high rates applicable to most commodities, the multiplicity of statutory rates, the wide spread of rates and the continued issue of a large number of exemption or concessional rate notifications not only made the administration of the system extremely complicated, but led to unintended and undesirable effects on the allocation of resources in the economy. All of this was documented in the Interim Report (Paragraphs 4.28 to 4.30 and Paragraphs 8.2 to 8.5). Further, there is general agreement now that the import tariff system should be drastically simplified, the levels and spread of the rates of duty must be reduced significantly, and as early as possible with the re-structuring of the duties, most of the notifications must be eliminated. We will, in this Chapter, discuss some broad aspects that should weigh in shaping the Tariff struture in the next three or four years. The questions that need to be answered are:

    a.   What should be the guiding principles for initiating and bringing about duty reductions?

    b.   What should be the structure of rates at the end of the reform period and what economic principles should determine this structure? and,

    c.   What should be the time period by which the reform should be completed?

In what follows, we attempt to provide answers to these questions. Before we take up these and related matters, we would like to urge that, in accordance with our recommendation in the Interim Report (Para 8.16), basic and auxiliary duties should be combined into one protective duty for a given commodity. It could have been argued earlier that the arrangement for preferential rates of duty with some developing countries stood in the way of such a merger. However, according to the decision already taken by the Government, the preferential rates of duty under the GATT Protocol and the Tripartite Agreement will cease to be applicable after March, 1993. In the case of the remaining preferential trading arrangements, the rate applicable should be the single rate emerging on combining the basic and auxiliary duties.

Degree of Protection in 1992-93 as Compared to that in 1986-87

In the Interim Report (Para 8.5), we had pointed out that between 1980-81 and 1989-90, the trade-weighted real effective exchange rate of the rupee depreciated by about 28 per cent and that the import-weighted average rate of import duty increased from 38 per cent to 87 per cent during the same period. This meant that the level of protection, quite clearly the nominal rate of protection, enjoyed by Indian industries went up substantially. The increase in the same average duty for manufactured products during this period was from 38 per cent to 98 per cent. "Thus, compared to the average level of nominal protection enjoyed by Indian manufacturing in 1980-81 (which was already high), the average level of nominal protection of Indian manufacturing in 1989-90 was higher by about 88 percentage points" (Interim Report, p. 95).[1]

We note that the real effective exchange rate depreciation in the 7-year period between 1985-86 and 1992-93 has been much greater than during the earlier period considered. This means that Indian industry in general is getting, as of 1992-93, a much higher nominal rate of protection than in the early 1980's. We have, for our purposes, gone only as far back as 1985-86. As Table 2.1 shows, the import-weighted real exchange rate appreciation of the basket of four major currencies has been of the order of 135 per cent between 1985-86 and 1992-93. In other words, the real exchange rate of the rupee has depreciated by 57.45 per cent during the period. Hence, the nominal rate of protection, other things remaining the same, would have increased to an undesirably large extent. Even if we take 1986-87 as the base, the appreciation is seen to be to the extent of 105 per cent. However, duty reductions and fall in international prices in respect of particular commodities, increases in input costs higher than the general rate of domestic inflation and any increases in the duty rates on imported inputs of the concerned commodities, would have partially neutralised the increase in the nominal rate of protection. Nevertheless, the increase in the nominal rate of protection due to the depreciation in the external value of the rupee has been so great that the net increase in the nominal rate of protection is bound to be substantial in most cases. And wherever the proportion of the cost of imported inputs to total costs is small, the effective rate of protection would also have risen substantially.

Table 2.2 gives the nominal tariff rates applied to 50 imported items in six different groups of commodities in the years 1986-87[2] and 1992-93. It will be seen that there have been substantial percentage point reductions in rates of duty between the two years in the case of a number of items. However, as the figures under the heading (4) in the table show, because of the depreciation in the external value of the rupee, the nominal rate of protection given, other things remaining the same, has increased in all cases. Thus, for example, in the case of item 3, DMT, the degree of protection has increased by 48 per cent in 1992-93 as compared to 1986-87, if only the depreciation in the external value of the rupee and the change in the import duty rate are taken into account. Thus although the duty has been reduced from 190 per cent to 110 per cent, it is as though the duty is now 330.5 per cent with unchanged exchange rate.[3] Hence even a duty reduction by 50 percentage points would still leave the commodity well "protected", since the international price of the commodity has not fallen in relation to the price level in 1986-87.[4] If duty reductions are applied to most commodities, then the effective rate of protection will also be maintained at the higher level.

The tables and the inferences drawn from them are merely intended to demonstrate that an across the board duty reduction by a fairly substantial margin would not in general hurt Indian industry. This is more true now than when the Interim Report was written and submitted (December, 1991). Having said this, it must be pointed out that in working out the desirable and feasible extent of import duty reduction in respect of different commodities, we have taken into account the international prices in rupees and have worked out the cif prices or taken the cif prices as furnished to us by the industry. Wherever possible, we have obtained domestic costs and in some cases studied the extent to which these costs are affected by high import duties on imported inputs. We have then worked out "the implicit tariff rate" which would equate the international price and the estimated, or in some cases, prevailing domestic prices.

In arriving at the extent of reduction in the import duty rates, we have taken into account as many relevant factors as possible. As far as domestic industries are concerned, we have tried to ensure that they would not be hurt and would be given adequate time for adjustment. For this purpose we have kept in mind the inherent disadvantages from which varying types of Indian industrial units suffer because of the general inefficiencies in the economy such as higher interest costs, power cuts, lack of efficient infrastructure and cascading types of State and local taxes. All these disadvantages cannot be precisely quantified in monetary terms. Nevertheless, we have attempted to form a broad idea of the extent of cost disadvantage that could be said to arise at the present time. Of course, as the reform process proceeds, these disadvantages would be gradually reduced.

The Structure of Duties

Many economists would argue that it would be best to have only one (ad valorem) rate of import duty. Apart from achieving administrative ease, this would least hinder the allocation of resources for domestic production by the market forces. In addition to the single rate, a surcharge or additional duty could be imposed on the products of a new or infant industry, which might not be able to withstand competition from established foreign producers, until it achieves scale economies and establishes itself firmly with a proper marketing framework, etc. Such a surcharge or additional duty would have to be subject to a "sunset" provision whereby the extra protection will be removed within a period of, say, 5-7 years.

The prescription of a single import duty rate is given on the premise that national economic policy need not really concern itself with the pattern of industrialisation and need not, or should not, discriminate as between final products, capital goods, raw materials and intermediates. But tariff policy should have some relation to the stage of development and in a developing country, while the market should have a large role to play, the structure of import duties should be used to achieve the longer term goals of industrialisation and to further the strategy of dealing with the world market. We note that except for one developing country, namely, Chile, at least a few import duty rates prevail in all other developing countries that we have looked at.

We take as datum the fact that petroleum products and agricultural products are subject to quantitative restrictions and that the imports of non-essential goods are banned except when they come as part of baggage. We shall have to deal with these three classes of goods separately. As for the others, as indicated in the Interim Report (Para 8.22), the basic duty rate structure suggested in the Long Term Fiscal Policy Document (1985) could be taken as providing the guiding principles. Accordingly, we are recommending that essential goods such as inputs for fertiliser and newsprint should be subject to very low rate of 5 per cent, a low rate of 10 to 15 per cent should apply to basic raw materials such as metals, the next higher rung of rates to capital goods and parts and slightly higher rates to chemical intermediates. Final products will attract the highest rate of duty of 30 per cent.

In the Interim Report we had envisaged that the task of re-structuring the import duties could be completed by the year 1998-99, when the average rate of duty could be brought down to around 25 per cent (Para 8.47). We had not then anticipated the shift to partial convertibility and the consequent further depreciation in the value of the rupee and the corresponding increase in the cost of most imports. We had, therefore, envisaged a somewhat longer period within which restructuring of import duties should be achieved than what seems called for now. We now feel that the basic reform of the tariff structure could be completed by 1996-97 or latest by 1997-98. By that time the import weighted average rate of duties should have come down to around 25 per cent (excluding any zero rated commodities, but including consumer goods).

While we have ruled out a single duty rate regime, we are clearly in favour of having only a very limited number of rates and of abolishing the zero rate in course of time. A large number of rates not only create administrative problems, but leads to non-transparency in the degrees of effective protection given to different products as well as to distortions in the allocation of resources. By keeping only a limited number of rates, we shall render administration of the tariff a fairly easy task, and by limiting the spread, we shall minimise distortions. The structure of duties will be such as to encourage value addition activities and to ensure that products at later stages are not subjected to negative effective rate of protection. In the Chapters that follow, which deal with different groups of products, we are applying the above-mentioned principles to determine the appropriate rates. We are recommending that by 1997 or 1998 March end, the structure of ad valorem rates of duties in place should be: 5, 10, 15, 20,

25 and 30. In addition, when non-essential consumer goods are allowed to be imported, there should be another "slot" for them, namely, 50 per cent.

In the Interim Report, we had suggested that all goods should be subject at least to a minimum tariff. Even if the goods are essential and/or their imports are restricted, there is no reason why the domestic producers of those goods should not be entitled to any protection. We suggest that the minimum of rate of 5 per cent should be applied to those that are now exempt. It may not be possible, for some reasons, to apply immediately this rate to fertiliser and ammonia and phosphoric acid used in the manufacture of fertilizer. Even these commodities should be made subject to duty at the earliest possible opportunity.

We may, at this stage, point out the necessary consequences of exempting the capital goods and inputs for the fertiliser industry from all import duty. This means that while substantial protection is being extended to most industries, industries producing machinery, parts of machinery and inputs for the fertiliser industry will receive no protection at all. A necessary consequence of this is that domestic production of these goods would be discouraged; and a probable long-term consequence will be that we shall become largely dependent on imports in respect of machinery and inputs for the fertiliser industry. These are not desirable consequences.

Anti-dumping

A number of complaints have been received in recent years from the domestic producers alleging the adoption of the unfair trade practice of dumping by some foreign exporters. In a low tariff regime that we are recommending, it is essential that provision is made to see that the domestic industry does not fall a victim to such unfair practices.

The Indian law relating to anti-dumping has adopted GATT guidelines and would appear to be an adequately powerful weapon. The effectiveness of this weapon, however, is considerably lessened because of the lengthy procedure involved in initiating the proceedings and completing the investigation to arrive at the final findings. No doubt, the Customs Tariff (Identification, Assessment and Collection of Duty or Additional Duty on Dumped Articles and for Determination of Injury) Rules, 1985 provide a time-limit of one year from the date of initiating of an investigation (or within an extended period in exceptional cases) to give the final findings and a time-limit of six months of the publication of final findings for imposition of duty. We are of the view that these time-limits are too long and could be curtailed, though we do appreciate that by their very nature, such investigations are time-consuming. We would suggest that the time-limit for giving the final findings could be reduced to six months and the time-limit for imposition of duty to three months.

The Rules provide for the imposition of provisional duty at any time, after a preliminary finding that there is dumping in respect of articles which are the subject matter of investigation. This provision should be invariably made use of where the final findings are not likely to be arrived at within a month or two of the preliminary finding.

We also feel that the machinery for dealing with anti-dumping matters needs to be strengthened.

Table 2.1

Effective Exchange Rate Depreciation of the Rupee by 1992-93 in Terms of Appreciation of a Basket of Four Major Foreign Currencies

Base year	UK Pound	US Dollar	Deutsche (German) Mark	Japanese Yen	4-Country REER depreciation		
						Weighted by	
					Imports	Exports	Trade
A. Real Exchange Rate Depreciation							
1985-86	2.77	1.63	3.03	2.64	2.35	2.23	2.29
1986-87	2.36	1.72	2.35	1.99	2.05	1.98	2.02
1987-88	2.31	1.80	2.12	1.95	2.01	1.96	1.99
1988-89	2.01	1.67	2.00	1.71	1.82	1.78	1.80
1989-90	1.94	1.49	1.95	1.66	1.72	1.67	1.70
1990-91	1.75	1.53	1.73	1.86	1.69	1.68	1.69
1991-92	1.70	1.45	1.73	1.60	1.60	1.57	1.58
1992-93	1.00	1.00	1.00	1.00	1.00	1.00	1.00
B. Nominal Exchange Rate Depreciation							
1985-86	3.63	2.47	4.98	4.93	3.69	3.53	3.62
1986-87	3.07	2.45	3.59	3.26	2.99	2.91	2.96
1987-88	2.82	2.38	2.87	2.80	2.67	2.63	2.65
1988-89	2.42	2.17	2.62	2.32	2.35	2.32	2.34
1989-90	2.27	1.86	2.41	2.12	2.12	2.07	2.10
1990-91	1.92	1.76	1.94	2.15	1.92	1.91	1.91
1991-92	1.70	1.46	1.73	1.61	1.60	1.58	1.59
1992-93	1.00	1.00	1.00	1.00	1.00	1.00	1.00

Note : 1   The following examples illustrate how the table is to be read:

Ex. 1.   Entry of 2.35 in the second row fourth column of Part A:

"It takes 2.35 times as many rupees in 1992-93 to obtain one DM as it took in 1986-87 after correcting for inflation in India and Germany".

Ex. 2.   Entry of 1.91 in the sixth row seventh column of Part B:

"It takes, on average, 1.91 times as many rupees in 1992-93 to obtain one foreign currency unit as it took in 1990-91".

Note: 2.   Computation of real Effective Exchange Rate Depreciation: Methodology

Levy of Surcharge

Where international prices dip steeply (not due to dumping), say, by as much as 25 per cent or so, a regulatory duty may be imposed for a specified period of time so that the domestic industry is given an opportunity to adjust itself. The regulatory duty may be expressed in specific terms and may be withdrawn, once the prices reach the "normal" level. The period in any case should not be more than a year; in other words, if the lower level has come to prevail, Indian industry should adjust itself to it, and the consumer should be allowed to benefit from it.

Additional or special protection can be given for a specified period to a new industry to be established or a new product to be launched through a new technology in strategic area. Such protection could be through an additional duty, say, not exceeding 25 per cent of the basic duty to be in force for a period of 5 to 7 years, as may be determined.

Advance Licensing for Exporters

Because of the inherent disadvantages suffered by Indian industry due to the inefficiencies present in the economy, including those attributable to irrationalities in the tax system, it is not possible to reduce import duty rates to very low levels as in some other developing countries. Hence, the system of advance licensing for exporters should continue. Furthermore, since there is no remission of duty on capital goods for exports, it is necessary that the import duty on capital goods should be brought down according to our recommendations.

As the structural reform process continues, the inefficiencies and cost disadvantages would gradually diminish. We would urge that Government should take steps to remove infrastructural deficiencies quickly. Equally important is the improvement in the movement of goods which are now subject to delays caused by some of the policies of the State Government and local authorities. It is also extremely important that State and local indirect taxes must be reformed so that they do not add to the cost of production, thereby hindering export effort and preventing the lowering of import tariff.

The Nominal Exchange Rate (NER) against any foreign currency is the number of Indian rupees needed to obtain a unit of that foreign currency. In a dual exchange rate system, as prevails in India at present, more than one nominal exchange rate may co-exist. In computations made, market exchange rates have been used as these are the rates relevant to the majority of imports, the focus of this exercise.

The Real Exchange Rate (RER) against any foreign currency is the number of Indian rupees needed to obtain a unit of that foreign currency after correcting for erosion in the value of both currencies due to inflation. If I_i and I_f are, respectively, the (cumulative) Indian and foreign inflation relative to a chosen base year, then RER = NER x $(1+I_f)/(1+I_i)$. The price indices used should ideally be for tradeable goods relevant to the group being studied (in this case importers). Due to data limitations, wholesale or producer price indices have been used.[5]

When the RER (or NER) of any year is divided by the RER of the chosen base year, the *real depreciation of the Indian rupee against the foreign currency*, that has occurred since the chosen base year, is obtained. Similarly, if relative inflation rates are not taken into account, *nominal exchange rate depreciation* is obtained. Table 1 A and 1B provide estimates of real and nominal exchange rate depreciation in the value of the Indian rupee against the Pound Sterling, the US Dollar, the Deutsche (German) Mark and the Japanese Yen. Figures show the depreciation that has occurred by 1992-93 since each of the (base) years indicated in the first column.[6]

The weighted average of the RER or the NER across countries gives the *Real Effective Exchange Rate (REER)* and the *Nominal Effective Exchange Rate (NEER)* of the rupee. The weights chosen should be relevant to the group being studied. Clearly, import weights (that is the bilateral import shares of import originating countries) should be taken in this exercise. The weights used are the average import shares (among the four countries considered) for the three year period 1988-89 to 1990-91.[7] Export and trade Weighted indices are also reported in Table 1 for comparison. The percentage weights are given below along with the share of the four countries (the UK, the US, Germany and Japan) in total imports, exports or trade.

Weights	Pound Sterling	US Dollar	Deutsche Mark	Japanese Yen	4-country share in total
Import	21.69	32.93	22.59	22.80	36.18
Export	15.36	41.90	17.37	25.37	39.18
Trade	18.87	36.91	20.27	23.94	37.47

Concluding Remarks

Table 12.1, brings together our recommendations on the structure of tariff rates to be brought into existence by 1997-98, or if possible, by 1996-97, for the major commodities in the various groups considered in this report. The duty rates on other items which we have not considered specifically in the preceding chapters could be dovetailed with the general pattern of rates indicated in the aforesaid Table. It will be seen that the structure implements the guiding principles with which we started. The rates on finished products are kept distinctly higher than on the basic raw materials, and the rates of duty on components and machinery come in between. This structure is intended to encourage value addition activites at home, while the fairly low rates on the metals and the other basic raw materials will serve to keep the costs of production low throughout the economy. At the same time, we have endeavoured to ensure that the industries producing all the raw materials and components and machinery would be reasonably protected so that backward integration will not be hindered and that India will continue to have a diversified industrial economy.

Table 2.2

Effect of Import Duty and Real Effective Exchange Rate Changes on the Real Landed Cost of Import of Selected Items

Description of Product/Product Category	Nominal tariff rate as a percentage of cif price*		Tariff mark-up in 1992-93 as a %age tariff mark-up in 1986-87	Real landed cost of imports in 1992-93 as a %age of real landed cost of imports in 1986-87	Tariff rate for 1992-93 giving the same real landed cost of imports in 1986-87
	1986-87	1992-93			
	(1)	(2)	(3)	(4)	(5)
Chemicals and Minerals					
1. Naphtha	0	0	100	205	- 51
2. Propylene	110	80	86	176	2
3. Dimethyl Teraphthalate (DMT)	190	110	72	148	41
4. Monoethyl glycol (MEG)	110	110	100	205	2
5. Caprolactum	90	50	79	162	- 7
Polymers and Plastics					
6. Low Density Polyethylene (LDPE)	120	63	74	152	7
7. High Density Polyethylene (HDPE)	100	64	82	168	-2
8. Polypropylene	100	80	90	184	-2
9. Polyvinyl chloride (PVC)	75	41	81	165	-15
Iron and Steel					
10. Pig Iron	65	35	82	168	-20
11. Iron Bars & Rods	100	105	102	210	-2
12. Iron and Steel Structurals	100	105	102	210	-2
13. Hot Rolled Iron Coils	100	57	78	161	-2

	(1)	(2)	(3)	(4)	(5)
14. Cold Rolled Iron Coils	140	95	81	167	17
15. Galvanised Plain (GP) Sheets	140	110	88	179	17
16. Tinplate	95	85	95	194	-5
17. Tin Mill Black Plate (TMBP) Coils	100	50	75	154	-2
18. Steel Billets	55	45	94	192	-24
19. Steel Melting Scrap	25	10	88	180	-39
20. Specified Alloy Steels	80	90	106	216	-12
Non-Ferrous Metals					
21. Copper Wire Rods and Bars	75	54	88	180	-15
22. Unwrought Nickel	80	60	89	182	-12
23. Unwrought Aluminium Ingots	50	35	90	184	-27
24. Other Unwrought Aluminium	90	105	108	221	-7
25. Unwrought Tin	80	85	103	211	-12
26. Unwrought Zinc	125	53	68	139	10
27. Unwrought Lead	125	85	82	169	10
Machinery and Equipment					
28. Super Heated Water Boilers	75	55	89	182	-15
29. Machine Tools: Peak Rated Items	110	110	100	205	2
30. Machine Tools: General Rate	75	80	103	211	-15
31. Machine Tools: Specified Milling Machines	35	60	119	243	-34
32. Machine Tools: Parts & Accessories	35	35	100	205	-34
33. Moulds and Dies for Plastic Articles	25	50	120	246	-39
34. Tower Cranes	75	55	89	182	-15
35. Self-Propelled Fork Lift Trucks	100	95	97	200	-2

	(1)	(2)	(3)	(4)	(5)
36. Domestic Refrigerators	150	110	84	172	22
37. Generators with Output over 750 Watts	75	55	89	182	-15
38. Transformers with above 1 KVA capacity	75	55	89	182	-15
39. DC Micromotors (upto 13.5 Volts and 20 Watts)	75	75	100	205	-15
40. Electrical Resistors	75	80	103	211	-15
41. Black and White Television Picture Tubes	75	80	103	211	-15
42. Radio Transmitters	140	95	81	167	17
43. Oscilloscopes	100	95	97	200	-2
44. Specified Medical Equipment	40	40	100	205	-32
45. Specified Machinery for the Leather Industry	35	35	100	205	-34
46. Specific Machinery for the Garment Industry	35	40	104	213	-34
47. Specified Food Processing Machinery	50	40	93	191	-27
Other Items					
48. Mechanical Wrist Watches	140	110	88	179	17
49. Parts of Mechanical Wrist Watches	50	70	113	232	-27
50. Project Imports	55	55	100	205	-24
Unweighted Average of 50 Items	86	70	93	190	-10

Notes: (*) Nominal Tariff Rates: Basic Duty plus Auxiliary Duty less the effect of applicable exemption notifications. Unless otherwise indicated end-use based exemption notifications are not taken into account.

We have assumed that even by the end of our reference period imports and exports of agricultural products would be subject to restrictions as of now and such products would in general be allowed to be imported only when domestic supplies are felt to be insufficient. We are of the view that agricultural imports when permitted also should be subject to some "protective" import duty. However, in respect of cereals like wheat and rice, the duty free tariff may continue. Other essential agricultural goods such as oil seeds and pulses could be subjected to a duty rate of 10 per cent. Non-essential agricultural products like almonds and cashew nuts are now subject to a very high rate of duty. Duty rates on them should be brought down to 50 per cent.

The domestic prices of petroleum products are under the regime of administered prices. Since we have not considered the question of rationalisation of these prices, we have refrained from making any recommendations on excises and customs on petroleum products. Nevertheless we feel that with the opening up of the petroleum sector to private enterprise and given the wide ramification of any duties on a petroleum product, the customs duty on crude oil, etc., should be such as to fit into the broad structure of the tariff.

In the Interim Report, we had suggested that as and when the non-essential consumer goods (mainly durable consumer goods) are removed from the negative list, they should be subjected to an import duty of 50 per cent. Since these goods will in addition be subject to CVD, the total tax burden on them will be sufficiently high to discourage imports; at the same time the unlimited protection enjoyed by the domestic manufacturers of these goods will be brought under limit. Of course, to the extent that there has been considerable smuggling of many of these goods, the degree of protection has been under some restraint. With the imports of these goods coming in legally, smuggling will go down and government revenue would gain without any additional drain on foreign exchange.

It is difficult to predict what the pattern of imports would be with the much reduced level of duties on many items, which are now highly taxed. If there is no radical change in the pattern and if consumer goods are also allowed to be imported, the import-weighted average rate of duties would be around 25 per cent. This is on the assumption that all imports will be subject to at least a minimum rate of duty.

The structure of duties that we have recommended, while taking care of the needs of industrialisation of the country, is such as to make administration vastly easier than totay. With the reduction in the general level of rates, most of the notifications would become redundant and can be rescinded and the resultant reduction in the number of effective rates of import duty would all but eliminate classification disputes. Moreover, the abolition of end-use exemptions and concessional rates of duty for particularised items will ease the administrative burden and cut out delays and abuse of provisions.

Government should rigidly adhere to one basic principle, namely, while consumers should not be asked to bear undue burnden through unwarrantedly high protection to particular groups of producers, domestic producers should not be exposed to unfair competition in the name of not adding anything to the cost of "essential goods". Hence we recommend that even the so-called essential goods like inputs for fertilisers and newsprint should be subjected to a minimum rate of duty, say 5 per cent, so that domestic manufacturers would get some protection. Similarly, we have suggested levy of import duty of 20 per cent in 1997-98 on medical equipments (electronic and non-electronic) for protecting the domestic manufacturers and encouraging indigenous production of medical equipments. Incidentally, if our recommendation is implemented, much of paper work and delay would be eliminated along with the abuse of existing provisions regarding exemption of equipment acquired by hospitals obtaining the required certificates.

We are aware that the duty rates that we have recommended for some groups of commodities, for example, machinery, are higher than in several other developing as well as developed countries. We feel that low rates would not be appropriate within the medium term context that we have in view. Some of the cost disadvantages from which Indian industry suffers will be removed or scaled down when the import duties on inputs are reduced. However, disadvantages due to the inefficiencies present in the economy will remain. In some cases, scale economies have yet to be fully reaped, and in some other cases adequate time for re-structuring and adjustment must be given. The situation can be reviewed during the next decade. Meanwhile, Government should take urgent action designed to remove all of the important factors creating inefficiencies and leading to higher costs.

It will be difficult to reform the import tariff without hurting the domestic industries if the irrational excise duty regime is allowed to continue. We are of the view that it should be possible to implement the proposed restructuring of excise duties and extend Modvat fully over the period of the next three to four years without losing any revenue.

We would also emphasise the need for strengthening the administrative machinery for collection of indirect taxes on the lines suggested by us in the Final Report, Part I. Needless to say, the thorough reform of the system of domestic indirect taxes should figure high in the agenda of policies for minimising distortions and costs in the Indian economy.

Table 12.1
Import Duty Structure Recommended for 1997-98

	Industry	Import Duty (excluding CVD) (in per cent ad valorem)
1.	Essential agricultural goods like wheat and rice	0
2.	Other agricultural goods like oilseeds and pulses	10
3.	Non-essential agricultural goods like almond and cashewnut	50
4.	Petrochemical building blocks*	15
5.	Organic and inorganic chemicals*	20
6.	Polymers*	25

contd...

7.	Textile fibres and yarn	25
8.	Iron and steel -	
	a. Pig iron	15
	b. Semi and finished steel including stainless steel and other alloy steel	20
9.	Copper	20
10.	Aluminium	15
11.	Nickel	15
12.	Lead and zinc	20
13.	Tin	15
14.	Wastes and scrap and concentrates of ferrous and non-ferrous metals	10
15.	Articles of iron and steel	30
16.	Articles of non-ferrous metals-	
	a. of copper, lead and zinc	30
	b. of aluminium, nickel and tin	25
17.	Machinery including machine tools	20**
18.	Electronics-	
	a. Raw materials	20
	b. Piece parts, components, sub-assembly and equipment	30
19.	Instruments	30
20.	Medical equipment	20

* Example of petrochemical building blocks are ethylene, propylene, butadiene, benzene, ethyl benzene and styrene. Organic chemicals will not include drugs in respect of which we are not making any recommendation but drug intermediates will be covered under this heading. Polymers include LDPE/LLDPE, HDPE, PP, PVC, PS, polyesters, synthetic and natural rubber and the whole range of plastics and synthetic resins.

** At present there is no CVD. We are suggesting 10 per cent CVD which is to be modvated over a period of four years.

Government of India, Ministry of Finance, Tax Reforms Committee Final Report (Part — II) chaired by Prof. Raja J. Chelliah, January, 1993. Extracts.

15

Insurance Sector Reforms

Government has taken a number of initiatives in the area of financial sector reforms covering the banking system and the capital markets aimed at creating a more efficient and competitive financial system suitable for the requirements of the economy keeping in mind structural changes currently underway. Insurance is an important part of the overall financial system and it is necessary to address the need for similar reforms in this sector. Therefore, under the chairmanship of the former governor of the Reserve Bank of India, Mr. R.N. Malhotra, the Government appointed a Committee on Reforms in the Insurance sector to go into these issues in depth and make recommendations. The Committee examined the issues relating to restructuring of insurance companies : (1) Life Insurance, (2) General Insurance and (3) Liberalisation of the Insurance Industry.

Restructuring of the Insurance Industry

I. Life Insurance

There has been rapid growth in the volume of LIC's business. The number of new policies issued every year is now of the order of one crore and the number of policies in force is 5.7 crore. There is a vast scope for further growth of business. In this context, the Committee examined the adequacy of the present structure of LIC to meet the future challenges. It would appear that handling of this business at the branch level is already confronting some difficulties. Even though delegation of policy servicing responsibilities to the branch level has been of considerable help, there is still substantial customer dissatisfaction. Delegation of authority to zonal and divisional offices and the system of supervision and control are inadequate. Lines of communication within the organisation have lengthened greatly. Due to hierarchical functioning at the central office and the zonal offices, decision taking has slowed down, and responsiveness to customer needs and market situations leaves much to be desired. In this context, there is a strong view that the presesnt structure of LIC and the way it is functioning does not provide sufficient assurance that the organisation can handle efficiently the vast potential growth of business. It has been suggested that quite a few of its problems flow from its gigantic size and, therefore, breaking up LIC into smaller organisations would help as these would be more efficient and effective in addressing changing conditions. It is also acknowledged, however, that breaking up LIC would involve some complex technical and other problems. These include issues relating to bonus on existing 'with profit' policies, which now constitute over 90% of the total portfolio, distribution of assets and liabilities, and allocation of personnel. While these problems are not insurmountable, they can prove to be particularly difficult if the insurance sector were to be opened up to competition. It has, on the other hand, been argued that the large size and spread of LIC is not a weakness but a strength which can be exploited fully by an appropriate internal restructuring of the organisation. The key to such restructuring would be to make the zonal offices into *de facto* head offices for all operational purposes and limiting the functions of the central office to policy formulation, review and evaluation; product development, pricing and actuarial valuation; investments; personnel policies; systems development and accounts of the corporation. The other inescapable element of reform would be to go in for comprehensive computerisation for handling business at all levels and for developing effective management information systems. The divisional offices have to effectively discharge their primary function of supervising branch offices. At present, they exercise this function mainly through on-site inspections. This needs to be upgraded and supplemented by development of better structured and more informative reporting systems. The divisional offices should improve their role in guiding officials at the branch level. At the same time, to enable branches to handle future growth of business, these should be suitably strengthened. Another crucial area to be addressed is the elimination of restrictive practices with a view to improving productivity and work culture.

With regard to the Life Insurance Corporation of India, the Committee has recommended that :

i) Central office should basically concentrate on: (a) policy formulation, review and evaluation, (b) product development, pricing and actuarial valuation, (c) investments, (d) personnel policies, (e) systems development and (f) accounts of the corporation. Reflecting the nature of its functions, the central office should be a compact and highly professionalised establishment. The central office is at present highly over-staffed and should shed its surplus.

ii) Subject to the above, the zonal offices should, for all intents and purposes, be the head offices for insurance business and related matters in their jurisdiction. To this end, delegation of financial, administrative and operational authority to the zonal offices should be effected immediately.

iii) The process of reorganisation of the central office and zonal offices should be completed within a period of six months.

iv) At present, there are zonal advisory boards which should be substituted by duly empowered zonal boards headed by the zonal managers.

v) To reflect their new position and role, zonal managers should be made members of LIC Board.

vi) Zonal offices are also heavily over-staffed. Devolution of functions from central office to zonal offices as recommended above should not be construed as providing justification for retention of excess staff. In fact, there would still be scope for substantial reduction. Excess staff should be suitably re-deployed, preferably to the branches where the impact of growth of business is immediately felt.

vii) At present, on the average, a divisional office supervises about 20 branches. The span of control of divisional offices could be considerably larger, say 30 branches. However, the span of control could be suitably reduced where branches are spread over a large area.

viii) The present number of zones and divisions are more than sufficient for the near future. Zonal and divisional offices are cost centres and their augmentation is not warranted.

ix) The divisional offices have to effectively discharge their primary function of supervising branch offices. At present they exercise this function mainly through on-site inspections. This needs to be upgraded and supplemented by development of better structured and more informative reporting systems. The divisional offices should improve their role for guiding officials at the branch level.

x) The image of the organisation depends primarily on the quality and efficiency of service rendered at the point of delivery. It is important to strengthen the role of branches further as the single point of service and contact for customers. For very large branches the appointment of senior officers as branch managers should be considered.

xi) Over the years, while staff unions have performed a role in improving the terms and conditions of service of their members, a number of restrictive practices have grown which constrain efficient and economical functioning of the organisation at various levels. As a result, there has been some deterioration in the organisation's productivity and work culture. It is essential to work towards elimination of restrictive practices.

xii) The Committee is of the firm view that comprehensive computerisation in LIC for handling business at all levels and the development of an effective management information system, are inescapable and should be undertaken and completed within 12 to 18 months. The Committee's recommendation that LIC continue as a single entity is on the assumption that its work would be reorganised as indicated above and its operations would be comprehensively computerised. If these conditions are not met, LIC would be unable to handle growth of business or to face the challenge of competition.

xiii) As a wholly state-owned organisation LIC's operational flexibility and its ability to respond to changing conditions is constrained. Some of these constraints are related to the fact that it falls under the definition of 'State'. It is the considered view of the Committee that LIC's ownership pattern should be so changed as to take it out of the definition of 'State'. This would be possible if the share holding of government is reduced to 50%. The Committee notes that there is already a decision to reduce government's equity in selected public sector under-takings by 49%. If a similar prescription is applied to LIC, it may help, to some extent, by broad-basing its share-holding and the composition of its board, but the substantive problems which inhibit its commercial functioning would remain. The recommendation made above in this paragraph is intended to overcome these genuine problems and to make LIC a board-run undertaking while maintaining government's dominant share-holding. To give effect to this recommendation, it will be necessary to convert LIC into a company which will be registered under the Companies Act and would carry on the business of LIC. For this purpose, the government may take such necessary legislative and other measures as may be considered appropriate, including possible repeal of LIC Act.

xiv) At present, LIC has a capital of Rs 5 crore, contributed entirely by the Central Government. This amount is not adequate for a life insurer of the size of LIC. The present capital of Rs 5 crore may, therefore, be raised to Rs 200 crore, with the government holding 50% thereof and the remainder being held by the public at large, including company employees for whom a suitable proportion may be reserved. As has been suggested elsewhere, no share-holder other than the promoters should hold more than 1% of the share capital. It is noticed that at present LIC has no free reserves outside its Life Fund. It is important for LIC to build its net worth by annually appropriating to free reserves a suitable portion of the valuation surplus allocated to its share-holders.

xv) All provisions of the Insurance Act, 1938 should apply to LIC and special dispensations in its favour regarding the non-applicability or modified applica-tion of several provisions of the Insurance Act should cease.

II-General Insurance

The set-up adopted by Government at the time of nationalisation of general insurance business was that of a holding company and four subsidiaries. At that time, there were 107 companies of varying sizes with widely different levels of professionalism, business ethics and work cultures. It was, therefore, considered necessary to have a holding company which would aid, assist, advise and direct the subsidiary companies in their formative years and to set-up standards of conduct of business and sound practices. At the same time, GIC was to keep in view the objective of encouraging competition among the subsidiaries. Over the last two decades, general insurance industry has come a long way. The subsidiary companies have acquired considerable experience, expertise and financial strength and have also established reasonable standards of conduct of business. However, the expectation that the subsidiary companies would provide effective competi-tion to each other has been largely belied. This is partly because of tariffs, market agreements on some non-tariff business and arrangements for market sharing of business. The other important reasons appear to be GIC's preoccupation with establishing uniformity in most of the operational areas and far too detailed guidance and control by it. Functioning under the shadow of GIC the subsidiaries have been inhibited from developing themselves into effective competitive com-panies and from building strong identities of their own.

The Committee considers it important that the subsidiaries should now stand on their own and begin functioning as independent companies. Without this it would not be possible for them to provide genuine competition to each other, or to acquire a new dynamism which would be called for in a more competitive environment.

It follows that GIC should cease to be a holding company. It should, however, continue to function exclusively as a reinsurance company and as the Indian reinsurer under section 101A of the Insurance Act. It should also shed its limited direct insurance business which it undertakes at present.

Since the total share capital of GIC and its subsidiaries is directly or indirectly held by the Government of India they come within the definition of 'State'. While government ownership has provided monopoly status and financial strength to these companies, the fact that they are regarded as 'State' has also entailed several drawbacks which handicap their functioning as service-oriented commercial institutions. In the Committee's view while the removal of such handicaps is needed even under the present set-up, this would be essential if these companies have to operate in a more competitive environment. Measures would, therefore, have to be taken by way of broad-basing their share-holding so that they are enabled to function as board-run companies. This would require that the share-holding of government should not exceed 50% of the total. The proposed course of action would greatly enhance their autonomy as well as their capacity to respond to changing market conditions.

The Committee has noticed that the four subsidiary companies are over-staffed, particularly in their head offices, regional offices and even divisional offices. While many metropolitan and urban branches tend to be over-staffed, rural and semi-urban branches are often under-manned. It is necessary to rationalise the staff structures and hierarchies in various offices and go in for greater delegation of powers. The excess staff at the higher echelons in the companies should as far as possible be utilised for strengthening the branches with the objective of ensuring that most of the business is transacted at this crucial point of service. It is understood that there are numerous restrictive practices which need to be eliminated in order to improve productivity and work culture.

Though general insurance requires a host of statistics for efficient rate-setting and supervision of business, such information and its processing is at present insufficient. Integrated and adequate management information systems are not in place.

In the light of the foregoing, the Committee makes the following recommendations:

i) GIC should cease to be the holding company of the four subsidiary companies and these should thereafter function as independent companies on their own. GIC should, in future, function exclusively as a reinsurance company and as the Indian reinsurer under the Insurance Act.

ii) Though GIC's net worth is sufficiently large its share capital at present stands only at Rs 107.5 crore. This should be raised to Rs 200 crore, 50%

which should be held by Government, the remainder being held by the public at large including employees of GIC for whom a suitable proportion may be reserved. This should have the effect of making GIC a board-run company.

iii) At present GIC holds 100% of the capital of the subsidiary companies with each company having a share capital of Rs 40 crore. To fully de-link the subsidiary companies from GIC, Government should acquire the latter's total holding in each of them. The capital of each such comapany should be raised to Rs 100 crore, with government holding 50% thereof the remainder being held by the public at large including employees of the respective companies.

iv) The organisation of the head offices of the four companies and that of their regional offices needs to be reviewed in order to reduce excessive staff and the number of levels within their hierarchies.

v) The four subsidiary companies are over-staffed and need to reorganise their work in order to use the available manpower in an optimal manner. In a competitive environment, economy in costs would be crucial to their success. There are at present 1124 divisional offices in the four subsidiaries, which supervise 3151 branches, that is, there is one divisional office for about three branches on the average. Divisional offices, apart from their supervisory functions, also underwrite certain classes of business, process claims and look after other technical aspects. The span of control of divisional offices should be considerably expanded thus substantially reducing their number.

vi) The extra staff which would become available as a result of the suggested rationalisation of the head offices, regional offices and divisional offices, should be posted to branch offices with a view to strengthen branches where most of the business is transacted. For this purpose, officers of senior rank should head large branches with substantial workloads and should be provided appropriate technical personnel back-up. Simultaneously, the financial authority of various branches should be reviewed in the light of the functions assigned to them.

vii) Certain lines of business have not been adequately addressed by the general insurance industry. The companies should examine how branch offices can develop such neglected lines of business.

viii) Computerisation is all the more important for general insurance companies because of the large data which they must generate and handle for product development and pricing, apart from the need for prompt and effective customer service. All the four companies must go in for comprehensive computerisation for handling their business at all levels and for developing effective management information systems. This brooks no delay and should be undertaken and completed within the next 12 to 18 months.

xi) Restrictive practices have proliferated in these companies and it is important for their managements to eliminate the same as soon as possible with a view to improving productivity and work culture.

x) The above recommendations for making the present general insurance companies board-run enterprises would call for legislative measures, including the possible repeal of the General Insurance Business (Nationalisation) Act.

xi) The provisions of the Insurance Act, 1938 should apply to GIC and the four companies, and special dispensations with regard to the non-applicability or modified application of several provisions of the Insurance Act should be withdrawn.

III-Liberalisation of the Insurance Industry

The Committee has given careful thought to the question whether the insurance sector, which has for long been a State monopoly, should be opened up to competition and has concluded that this would be desirable for the following reasons:

(a) While nationalised insurance companies have done a commendable job in extending their presence and services throughout the country and are handling large volumes of business, the choice available to the insuring public is inadequate in terms of service, products and prices. Introduction of competition should result in better customer service and help improve the variety and price of insurance products.

(b) The employees' unions and representatives of agents have expressed opposition to the idea of introducing competition. There is, however, a strong view among corporate respondents covered by the MARG survey as well as among many of those who appeared before the Committee that the private sector should be allowed to enter general insurance business. As for life insurance, individual policyholders covered by the MARG survey were equally divided on the issue. Almost half of such respondents were opposed to the idea on the ground that their savings may not be safe with private companies. At the same time, when asked to indicate what they thought would be the advantages of a reputed private organisation offering life insurance, identified these as better service, prompt settlement of claims and better return on their polcies. A large majority of respondents who are corporate clients of LIC favoured the entry of the private sector in life insurance business.

c) Even though the nationalised insurance industry has, over the decades, built up extensive business, there is still a vast untapped potential and many lines of business have remained under-developed. Arrival of new players should speed up the spread of both life and general insurance.

d) The nationalised insurance companies are financially strong and have built up a large infrastructure in terms of professional talent, and marketing and servicing networks. They are in a position to face competition.

e) There is growing competition within the banking sector which already includes nationalised banks, co-operative banks and private banks, both Indian and foreign. The private sector has also been allowed to float mutual funds and is quite active in merchant banking, leasing and non-banking financial areas. There is little reason for keeping insurance as a monopoly. The private sector should therefore be allowed to enter insurance business.

The Committee has noted the apprehensions expressed in some quarters regarding the safety of their money in case private insurance companies are allowed to